Rutherford Studies i

Edi

DAVID F. WRIGHT
Senior Lecturer in Ecclesiastical History,
New College, University of Edinburgh

DONALD MACLEOD
Professor of Systematic Theology,
Free Church College, Edinburgh

RELIGIOUS RADICALISM
IN
ENGLAND 1535–1565

Rutherford Studies – Titles Available

Rutherford Studies in Contemporary Theology

R.T. Allen
Transcendence and Immanence in the Philosophy of Michael Polanyi and Christian Theism

Timothy Bradshaw
Trinity and Ontology—A Comparative Study of the Theologies of Karl Barth and Wolfhart Pannenberg

Charles Cameron
The Problem of Polarization: An approach based on the writings of G.C. Berkouwer

John Colwell
Actuality and Provisionality: Eternity and Election in the Theology of Karl Barth

Robert Dickinson
God Does Heal Today: Pastoral Principles and Practice of Faith Healing

Loránt Hegedüs
A Study of the Concept of Transcendence in Contemporary Theology

Charles Sherlock
The God Who Fights: The War Tradition in Holy Scripture

Rutherford Studies in Historical Theology

C.J. Clement
Religious Radicalism in England 1535–1565

Ian Hamilton
Erosion of Calvinist Orthodoxy: Seceders and Subscription in Scottish Presbyterianism

A.T.B. McGowan
The Federal Theology of Thomas Boston

W.D.J. McKay
An Ecclesiastical Republic: Church Government in the writings of George Gillespie

Nicholas Needham
Thomas Erskine of Linlathen: His Life and Theology 1788–1837

Kenneth Ross
Church and Creed in Scotland: The Free Church Case 1900–1904 and its Origins

Forthcoming:

Roy Kearsley
Tertullian's Theology of Divine Power

John Roxborogh
Thomas Chalmers: Enthusiast for Mission

Philip G Ryken
Thomas Boston as Preacher of the Fourfold State

RELIGIOUS RADICALISM
IN
ENGLAND 1535–1565

C.J. Clement

Published for Rutherford House

by

paternoster press

First Published 1996
by The Paternoster Press, P.O. Box 300, Carlisle, Cumbria
CA3 0QS U.K., and Rutherford House, 17 Claremont Park
Edinburgh EH6 7PJ, Scotland

01 00 99 98 97 96 95   7 6 5 4 3 2 1

British Library Cataloguing in Publication Data

Clement, C.J.
  Religious radicalism in England 1535–1565

ISBN 0-946068-44-5

Typeset by Rutherford House, Edinburgh

Dedication

For Maureen, my dear wife
and Lydia, Jonathan, Dora—our beloved children
Psalm 128:3–4

Note

Rutherford House wishes to apologise to the author for the late publication of this book, and to thank him for his patience and cooperation throughout the unavoidable delays in its production.

FOREWORD

The radical nature of Christianity can readily be discerned in the history of sects and sectaries, and reformation of the Church in sixteenth-century Europe affords rich terrain for such study. Mining operations have long been in progress, and many a deep shaft has yielded nuggets of real worth. If the principal areas of production have hitherto been found on the Continent, Dr Clement has chosen to prospect in England, and this book records his progress and achievement.

The analysis of anabaptism the author offers here is especially stimulating because, with findings that stress both similarities and dissimilarities, early and mid-Tudor sectaries are at once recognised to be not merely anabaptist disciples but radicals in their own right. The colourful cast of characters playing before the reader certainly offers some fine lines, and a full range of quotations – inset and from the the primary-sources – affords rich insights of doctrinal diversity. Those who seek new names espousing old heresies can move from Assheton to Wilkinson and from Barre to Upcharde; while those long intrigued by Bocher, Harte and Vittels will find their reward in particularly fruitful pages of late-night final research. Among the great strengths of the book too is the author's evident and steadfast refusal to apply those traditional but *simpliste* labels to his sectaries. For to do so, much in the manner of those selecting doves for a holy dove show caging their birds by precise categories, provides the kind of tidy approach that bears little or no resemblance to the period incidence of heresies remarkable for their very lack of uniformity. *Ende gut alles gut* in fact, for in an impressive *grande finale* Dr Clement skilfully relates the theology of a whole range of largely anti-trinitarian radicals to a trinity that, thanks to the work of both Professor A.G. Dickens and his detractors is now as well known to the general reader as it is to Church historians – Lollardy, Anabaptism and Anglicanism.

Peter Newman Brooks, The Divinity School, Cambridge

Contents

Abbreviations

AM	*The Acts and Monuments of the Martyrs* (by John Foxe)
APC	*Acts of the Privy Council of England*
BL	British Library
DNB	*Dictionary of National Biography*
EM	*Ecclesiastical Memorials* (by John Strype)
Hist. MSS. Com. Rep.	*Historical Manuscripts Commission Report*
JEH	*Journal of Ecclesiastical History*
LP	*Letters and Papers, Foreign and Domestic, of the Reign of Henry VIII*
ME	*The Mennonite Encyclopedia*
MQR	*The Mennonite Quarterly Review*
PRO	Public Record Office
PS	Parker Society
STC;RSTC	*A Short-Title Catalogue of Books Printed in England, Scotland, & Ireland, and of English Books Printed Abroad 1475-1640*, volume I; RSTC = volume II (revised edition, 1976)
TRP	*Tudor Royal Proclamations*
VCH	*Victoria County History*
Wing STC	*Short-Title Catalogue of Books Printed in England, Scotland, Ireland, Wales, and British America and of English Books Printed in Other Countries, 1641-1700*

The original spelling, punctuation, capitalisation and abbreviation has been retained in quotations. Archaisms are explained in accordance with the definitions in *The Oxford English Dictionary* (1933 edition).

Acknowledgements

My indebtedness to my Cambridge supervisor – the late Professor E. G. Rupp – is not readily apparent from the references and quotations found in this work. Nonetheless it was Professor Rupp's judicious counsel based on his encyclopaedic knowledge of the Reformation era that guided my original research to its successful outcome. More obvious from references cited in the ensuing pages is my debt to Professor Irvin B. Horst – to Dr S.J. Davies – and to Mr N. A. Penrhys-Evans which is here gratefully acknowledged. I also wish to record my thanks to Mr Gervase Duffield for his expert advice on the format of my work, assistance with the first chapter and guidance in preparing the appendix. For many years the assistants in the Rare Books Room of Cambridge University Library have been unfailingly patient and helpful, and I thank them – and the Librarians of Emmanuel College, Cambridge, the Bodleian, Oxford and the Folger Shakespeare Library, Washington D.C. for the use of manuscripts held by their respective libraries. Dr P.N. Brooks of Robinson College, Cambridge and Professor P. Collinson of the University of Cambridge provided the initial impetus to publish my research and subsequently encouraged me to persevere with that quest. My Edinburgh supervisor, Mr D.F. Wright – has also given me considerable help and encouragement during the years since I graduated from New College.

Several institutions have generously granted financial assistance along the way. The fellows of my former college – Downing – supplied the funds which enabled my original dissertation to be re-typed in expanded form. The trustees of the Bethune-Baker Fund, Cambridge and the Hope Trust, Edinburgh, have made substantial grants towards the cost of placing the manuscript on disk. In conclusion I wish to place on record my thanks to Dr N. M. de S. Cameron and to Vivienne Goddard of the staff of Rutherford House who unearthed my work after its long interment – and finally ushered it into the light of publication.

INTRODUCTION

This monograph had its origins in a thesis on religious radicalism in England in the mid-sixteenth century which was researched largely in Cambridge during the years 1976-79 and which culminated in the award of a PhD (Cantab.) in 1980. During the following decade scholarly interest in the left wing of the Reformation barely slackened. Anabaptism has now been a focus of attention for Reformation scholarship for half a century. Thorough investigation has revealed the inadequacy of the traditional term anabaptist to describe, define and comprehend all those individuals and ideologies that cannot be classified as either Roman Catholic or Lutheran or Reformed.[1] Among consequent attempts to construct an adequate classification of this fourth movement within the religious spectrum of sixteenth century Europe, that of George H. Williams is probably the most widely recognised.[2] Williams contrasts the Radical Reformation (a term which he suggests in place of the Left Wing) with the Magisterial Reformation. Within the Radical Reformation he distinguishes the Rationalists, the Anabaptists and the Spiritualists. In this study Williams' basic three-fold classification has been adopted because, as Keeney states, [his] nomenclature as a whole is the best yet suggested.[3]

Although the source-material for English religious radicalism in the mid-sixteenth century is diverse and fragmentary, it is by no means as slender as might be supposed. Furthermore, not all of the information is derived second-hand from hostile contemporary witnesses. Two publications of Henry Harte, and one each from John Champneys and John Trewe are extant. Two of Christopher Vitells' writings survive, as does a very early and detailed Familist confession. Other works produced by Harte and Robert Cooche are cited at great length by their opponents. Thomas Cole's printed sermon of 1553 is replete with information on the doctrine and practice of the Kentish radicals. Some of the correspondence between the free-willers and their predestinarian opponents during the controversies of the 1550s and early 60s has been preserved in manuscript transcriptions. Finally there are the surviving records of interrogations conducted by the civil and ecclesiastical authorities.

---

[1]   W.E.Keeney, *The Development of Dutch Anabaptist Thought and Practice from 1539-1564* (Nieuwkoop, 1968), 13-15.
[2]   *Spiritual and Anabaptist Writers*, eds. Williams and Mergal, Library of Christian Classics XXV (Philadelphia, 1957), 19-38.
[3]   Keeney, 14.

Several new pieces of evidence were uncovered during the course of my original investigation. Henry Harte's *A Consultorie for all Christians* (probably his first and most important manifesto) had never been examined or even positively ascribed. His letter to the prisoners in Newgate has been transcribed from the collection of transcripts known as Letters of the Martyrs (Emmanuel College, Cambridge, ms.260) and analysed. At the time my research was completed no detailed examination of either John Champneys' *The Harvest is at Hand* or Thomas Cole's *A Godly and Frutefull Sermon* had been published. Likewise, Robert Cooche's tract against infant baptism - preserved within William Turner's *A Preservative or triacle* - had never been reconstructed. The correspondence of Augustine Bernhere, lodged among the contents of Bodleian ms 53, had never been thoroughly examined. With the help of John Trewe's account of the controversy in the King's Bench a blow by blow commentary on that influential dispute is recorded for the first time. In addition, several surprising features in the subsequent careers of these English radicals whom the Edwardine Reformers labelled as 'anabaptists' have come to light.

This study was by no means the first investigation of heresy and religious dissent in sixteenth century England. In 1968 J.F. Davis completed a thesis entitled 'Heresy in South-East England, 1520-1659', N.A. Penrhys-Evans completed a dissertation on 'The Family of Love in England, 1550-1650' in 1971, and I.B. Horst published a pioneer scholarly treatment, *The Radical Brethren - Anabaptism and the English Reformation to 1558*[4] in 1972. Subsequent research, including my own, has substantiated Horst's fundamental thesis - that the English radicals (like the English magisterial Reformers) were influenced and inspired by their Continental brethren.

Among the publications of the past decade two general studies must be singled out as of prime importance. First, Anne Hudson's magnum opus *The Premature Reformation: Wycliffite texts and Lollard history*[5] which one reviewer describes as 'a milestone in research on Wycliffism' which 'closes an epoch in the study of pre-Reformation trends.'[6] It provides convincing evidence that 'Lollardy held, at least in embryo, almost all of the essential reformation concepts'.[7] The following year (1989) brought the long-awaited second revised edition of A.G. Dickens' classic *The English Reformation*,[8] which represents the fruits of twenty-five years'

---

[4]   Nieuwkoop, 1972.
[5]   Oxford, 1988.
[6]   Jiri Kejr, *JEH* 40 (1989), 599-602.
[7]   D. D. Smeeton, *Sixteenth Century Journal* 20 (1989), 507.
[8]   London, 1989.

further research by Professor Dickens and his pupils. Two monographs dealing specifically with English religious radicalism have been published since 1980: J.F.Davis, *Heresy and Reformation in the South East of England, 1520-1559*[9] and J.W. Martin, *Religious Radicals in Tudor England*.[10] The former work is a severely edited and abbreviated version of Davis' thesis, while the latter is largely a collection of previously published articles. Martin supplies a comprehensive survey of the subject and a very useful biographical register of the 'free-willers'.[11] Finally, two studies of The Family of Love should be mentioned: Alastair Hamilton's *The Family of Love*[12] and Jean D. Moss, *'Godded with God': Hendrik Niclaes and His Family of Love*.[13] In an appendix Moss prints the 1561 Familist depositions from the original manuscript which is now in the Folger Library.[14] However, Moss's work is not readily accessible in this country and so my transcription of the depositions has been retained.[15]

The chronological limits selected for this investigation are not entirely satisfactory. Ideally one would wish to begin with the re-emergence of Lollardy and its literature *circa* 1510 and conclude with the edict which proscribed the English Familists in 1580.[16] However such a lengthy period could not be comprehended without sacrificing much detailed analysis of important source material. Therefore, 1535 has been selected as the *terminus a quo* for this study because the earliest record of 'anabaptists' in England dates from about that year. It concludes in 1565 because by that date English religious radicalism had crystallised into Familism. Moreover, within that span of thirty years - a single generation - the ecclesiastical history of England passed through the closing of the Middle Ages into the dawn of the Early Modern period.

In the opening chapter evidence of the influence of radical refugees from the Continent during the latter years of the reign of Henry VIII (1535-47) is examined. The determinative years for the English radicals were 1547-58. During those years they were faced with two great challenges: the Edwardine reforms and the Marian persecution. Chapters Two and

---

9   Studies in History 34 (London, 1983).
10   London and Ronceverte, 1989.
11   *Ibid.*, 63-70.
12   Cambridge, 1981.
13   Transactions of the American Philosophical Society N. S. 71 (Philadelphia, 1981).
14   *Ibid.*, 70-74.
15   Appendix IV.
16   *Tudor Royal Proclamations*, eds. Hughes and Larkin (New Haven and London, 1964, 1969) II, 474-5.

Three deal with that period, and therefore they contain the bulk of the material. In the fourth chapter the progress, and more clearly defined nature, of English radicalism during the initial years of the reign of Elizabeth I (1558-65) are described. The final chapter is an attempt to summarise the features of English radicalism, and to indicate both its origins in later Lollardy and its debt to Continental luminaries.

Chapter 1

The English Radicals under Henry VIII, 1535-47

> For because that of late many strangers, born out
> of the King's obedience, are arrived and come into
> this realm, which, albeit that they were baptised in
> their infancy and childhood according to the ordinance
> of the universal Church of Christ, yet that notwithstanding,
> in contempt of the holy sacrament of baptism so given
> and received, they have of their own presumption and
> authority lately rebaptised themselves....
> ...The King's most royal majesty...commandeth
> that all and singular strangers now being in this
> his realm...that have or do hold or teach those
> or any other erroneous opinions or heresies against
> God and his Holy Scriptures shall within twelve
> days next after this present proclamation depart
> out of this his realm and of all other his dominions
> on pain to suffer death.... [1]

Issued in March 1535, this proclamation represents the earliest official acknowledgement that anabaptist doctrines formulated on the Continent had reached the shores of England.[2] Evidently the Henrician authorities, learning of the recent arrival in the country of a number of foreign anabaptists, promptly attempted to remove them. Were these heretical strangers merely the first to be detected? To what extent were

---

[1]   *TRP.*, I, 227-8.
[2]   W. K. Jordan, *The Development of Religious Toleration in England* (London, 1932), 57-8 and D. B. Heriot, 'Anabaptism in England during the 16th and 17th centuries', *Transactions of the Congregational Historical Society*, XII (1933-6), 258-9, were surely mistaken in regarding any of the imported books condemned by Archbishop Warham in May 1530 as anabaptist publications (D. Wilkins, *Concilia Magnae Britanniae et Hiberniae*, III (London, 1737), 727-37). Apart from Tyndale's New Testament and *Obedience of a Christian Man* they included several new editions of Lollard tracts. Tyndale edited and republished *The Examination of Wm. Thorpe and Oldcastle* and *The Prayer and Complaint of the plowman* in circa 1528. Printed about 1539 were, *The Lantern of Light, A Compendious old treatise shewing how we ought to have the scripture in English,* and *A proper dialogue between a gentleman and a husbandman.* In 1536 John Gough published *The door of Holy Scripture* which was John Purvey's prologue to his revision of Wycliffe's Bible.

native Englishmen involved with them? These are questions to which answers are sought in this chapter.

(a) Before 1535
Scholars differ on the extent to which Lollardy contributed to the English Reformer's doctrine.[3] Nevertheless it is clear that Lollards were active in England at the dawn of the Reformation because interrogations, abjurations and executions continued into the 1530s.[4] Davis cites the abjuration of Thomas Batman, prior of the Hospital of S. Bartholomew, Rochester, before Bishop Fisher in 1528 as an example of the abjuration of articles 'predominantly Lollard in character'. He continues,

Lollardy was a broad conditioning factor in the opening stages of the English Reformation. It was a spring board for early reforming ideas, providing the academic preachers with an audience and the Biblical translators with readers.[5]

Mutual love of the Bible formed the link between unsophisticated Lollards and the educated pioneers of reform, and there are several examples of Lollards who, upon coming into contact with 'Lutheranism', accepted its teaching.[6] However our concern is not with those who embraced 'Lutheranism', but with their more recalcitrant brethren who remained apart from the main stream of the English Reformation and who were frequently accused of 'anabaptism'.

The first item on Thomas Cromwell's list of 'remembrances' for the month of March 1535 reads, 'What the King will do with the

---

[3] See for example M. Aston, 'Lollardy and the Reformation: Survival or Revival?', *History* NS 49 (1964), 149-70 who is answered by J. F. Davis, 'John Wyclif's Reformation Reputation', *The Churchman*, 83 (1969), 97-102. More recently Anne Hudson has supplied a fairly conclusive answer to this question, she prefers the term 're-emergence' to either 'survival' or 'revival'. Anne Hudson, *Lollards and their books* (London and Ronceverte, 1985) especially pp. 227-48 and *The Premature Reformation. Wycliffite texts and Lollard history* (Oxford, 1988).

[4] John Foxe, *The Acts and Monuments of the Martyrs*, eds. Townshend and Cattley (London, 1837-41), IV, 580-2, 619, 706-7.

[5] J. F. Davis, 'Heresy in south-east England, 1520-59' (Oxford D. Phil. thesis, 1968), 101.

[6] Foxe, *AM*, IV, 178-9, 583-4; Strype, *EM*, I (ii), 55.

Anabaptists'.[7] This suggests that some anabaptists had been taken into custody, and that the authorities were awaiting the King's pleasure before taking any further action against them. The proclamation against foreign anabaptists doubtless represents the King's response to Cromwell's enquiry. The proclamation itself refers to 'strangers' who have 'recanted and revoked their said heresies',[8] which again indicates that some foreigners had been arrested and examined, and that confessions of heresy had been secured. It appears, therefore, that early in 1535 some foreigners who practised anabaptism were arrested in England. When this was brought to the King's attention the proclamation of March 1535 was issued.

There is, however, some evidence which suggests the presence of foreign anabaptists in England before 1535. At her trial on 23 January 1535, the repentant Amsterdam anabaptist Jannetje Thijsdochter confessed that ministers had recently come from England and lodged in the house of an anabaptist in Amsterdam. Furthermore, she stated that during that winter thirty-two ministers had met at Spaarndam – an isolated marshland hamlet near Haarlem frequently used by anabaptists as a place of refuge. This meeting was probably held in December 1534, the main subject under discussion being the proposals of a revolutionary minority to seize Amsterdam. If Thijsdochter's evidence is taken at its face value, it indicates that Dutch anabaptists in England were sufficiently well settled and organised in 1534 to send recognised leaders back to Spaarndam to represent them at the conference.[9]

More concrete evidence of the spread of radical religious doctrines from the Continent in the early 1530s is supplied by an undated deposition among the state papers in the Public Records Office.[10] The document is headed 'The names of those that be apprehended for the bokes of Anabaptistes Confession.' It reports the arrest of five Londoners who

---

[7] *Letters and Papers, Foreign and Domestic, of the Reign of Henry VIII* arr. Gairdner, vol. VIII, (London, 1885), 183.

[8] *TRP*, I, 228.

[9] *The Mennonite Encyclopedia* ed. Bender *et al.*, vol. III (Scottdale, 1957), 90; IV (Scottdale, 1959), 591; Irvin B. Horst, *The Radical Brethren*, 54-5.

[10] P. R. O. State Papers 1/237, No. 290, printed in *LP. Addenda* I (i), 281-2. A complete description of this document, together with the full text, is to be found in Horst, Appendix A, pp. 183-4.

had been responsible for the importation and distribution of large quantities of this heretical book, and it names four others who escaped arrest. Six of those named were English, one was a Scot, and the remaining two Flemish. Among those arrested were,

John Raulinges, dwelling in Bassynges Hall which had 40 of the said bokes, & hath sparpled and delyuered them he can not tell to whom. And farther, at his house many of the sayd faction dyuers tymes assembled...

Paul Baughton... whiche had of the forsayd bokes, & is styffe in this opinion, that he will beleue nothyng but the scripture, & that with out exposition. And touchyng the humanitie of Christe, he hath strange opinions.

Andrew Pierson a scottische man, an organmaker... hath had of the same bokes...

John Clarke, Taylor, dwellyng in berebynder lane. Of hym we had 44 of the same bokes, and wold acknowledge no more but as we coniecture, he hath resceyued about 300. This man also we vehemently suspecte to be an anabaptiste.[11]

Among those who evaded the searchers were,

George Jonson botchard, a flemmynge borne... this man is an ernest Anabaptiste, & also the holder of ther damnable opinions concernynge the humanitie of Christe.

Nicholas Whilar, whiche brought in the bokes of the anabaptistes confession, & is a great farderer of that secte.

one Bastiane, a flemmyng, which is sayd to be the byshop and reder to the Anabaptistes....[12]

It is significant that the initiative in this activity apparently came from the English members of the group. Although Bastian the Fleming was their instructor, it was Nicholas Whilar who was responsible for importing the books, Englishmen distributed them, and they regularly assembled at the house of John Raulinges in 'Bassynges Hall'. This was a cloth market in the parish of S. Michael Bassishaw which was frequented by foreign merchants.

---

[11]   Horst, 183.
[12]   *Ibid.*, 183-4.

Although no details are given regarding the content of the heretical book, two statements in this deposition strongly suggest that the members of this conventicle were being influenced by radical 'anabaptist' ideas emanating from the Continent. At least two of them held 'strange' and 'damnable' opinions 'touchyng the humanitie of Christe'. One of the distinctive doctrines maintained by early generations of anabaptists in the Netherlands was the so-called Melchiorite doctrine of the celestial flesh of Christ. That is, that Christ at his incarnation did not receive his body from Mary because of her sinful nature. Instead, he received his fully human body as a divine act. This view was strongly held by Melchior Hofmann, the founder of anabaptism in the Netherlands, and his teaching had a profound influence upon all the early leaders of the movement in North Germany, Holland and Flanders. This doctrine was not a product of the sixteenth century radical reformation. It had many adherents throughout the history of the Church.[13] Nevertheless, there is no evidence that this unorthodox christology was maintained by any English heretics or sectaries before the 1530s.[14]

The second feature indicating Continental influence upon this London conventicle is the description of Bastiane as the sect's 'byshop & reder'. In North Germany and the Netherlands, 'bishop' was the usual title accorded to the ordained leaders of the various manifestations of the radical reformation. Horst comments,

This may be one of the most helpful clues in the document. It indicates not only a co-operation among English and Flemish members but also an amalgamation of Lollard and anabaptist traditions. 'Reader' is typically Lollard, while 'byshop' is the common designation of the office held by leaders among the Dutch and Flemish anabaptists.[15]

If Horst's identification of Bastiane with Herman Bastian, the printer who was associated with Peter Tasch,[16] is correct, then this document

---

[13] See Hans Joachim Schoeps, *Von himmlischen Fleisch Christi*, (Tübingen, 1951).

[14] Crude anti-Marian sentiments expressed by some extreme Lollards reacting against 'Mother of God' mariolatry cannot be equated with a positive doctrine of the celestial flesh of Christ.

[15] Horst, 51.

[16] Below, 17-18.

supplies conclusive proof than an association existed between English religious radicals and Continental anabaptists.

There is, moreover, further evidence that this deposition depicts a coalescence of the native English Lollard tradition with the Continental anabaptist movement. The firm refusal of two of the English prisoners, John Raulinges and Paule Baughton, to 'beleue nothyng but the scripture', together with their suspicion of learned expositions of the Bible, has a distinct Lollard tone. In addition, Paule Baughton may have been heir to a strong family tradition of Lollardy. On 28 April 1494 Joan Boughton of London, who was more than eighty years old, was burnt at Smithfield. Her daughter, Lady Yonge, widow of a former mayor, Sir John Yonge, was also suspected of heresy and may have died a martyr's death.[17] These ladies were members of the London aristocracy and not from the artisan class. It may be significant that Paule Baughton is not listed as a tradesman.[18]

The book which brought about the detection and dispersal of the conventicle is described as 'the anabaptistes confession'. It was evidently printed in English, probably in Antwerp since at least two Flemings were members of the group and most of Tyndale's work was being printed there at this time. The work is no longer extant, or perhaps it remains unrecorded because this edition ran to about five hundred copies. Horst suggests that it was an English translation of the seven articles of faith which were drawn up by Swiss brethren at Schleitheim in February 1527.[19] This was the first anabaptist confession of faith and became widely accepted among Swiss and South German anabaptists.

---

[17] John Foxe, *The Acts and Monuments of the Martyrs*, eds. Townsend and Cattley (London, 1837-41), III, 704n, 706; IV, 7, 175, 710; J.A.F. Thomson, *The Later Lollards 1414-1520*, (Oxford, 1965), 156.

[18] John Raulinges was almost certainly a cloth or wool merchant. George Jonson 'a flemmynge borne' may perhaps be the John Hig, *alias* Noke, *alias* Jonson of Cheshunt who read German books and possessed 'a boke of the Gospels in the Doche tongue', and who abjured before Bishop Tunstall's vicar-general on 8 March 1528 (*LP.*, IV (ii), 1793-4). According to Foxe, this man had been in trouble with Tunstall and his vicar-general in 1523 for favouring 'the doctrines and opinions of Martin Luther' (*AM*, IV, 174, 178-9). If George and John Jonson were one and the same person then the connection between this 'anabaptist' conventicle and earlier conventicles of Lollards in London and Buckinghamshire is proven.

[19] Horst, 50-1.

However, while the earliest printed edition extant dates from 1533, the first known Dutch edition did not appear until 1560. Furthermore, the Swiss Brethren did not accept Melchior Hofmann's christological teaching; the articles do not mention christology.[20] Nevertheless, the Schleitheim Articles were widely distributed (Calvin possessed a copy in French in 1544) and no other anabaptist confession is known to have been printed as early as 1533. In the absence of a copy of the book Horst's suggestion must be taken seriously, but with reservations.[21]

An even stronger element of doubt must be accorded to Horst's dating of the deposition. Here he follows the editor of the *Letters and Papers Addenda* in placing it under the year 1532. However Horst admits that this may be too early.[22] The fifth Englishman to be arrested was, 'John Gough for printyng of the Confession of the citie of Geneua'.[23] In 1532 John Nicholson (*alias* Lambert) was brought to London from Cambridge by Sir Thomas More and accused of translating a heretical work entitled *The Articles of Geneva*.[24] Doubtless this is to be identified with the 'Confession of the citie of Geneua'. However, while manuscript copies of Lambert's translation may have been circulating in 1532, it may not have been printed until much later when Cromwell's influence was at its height and circumstances appeared to be favouring more radical reforms. Evidently Gough was arrested at the same time as the importers of the 'anabaptistes confession', that is, during a search for heretical literature, but there is nothing in the deposition to suggest that he was associated with them. In fact, Gough had been in trouble with the authorities as early as 1528, and he was imprisoned again in 1541.[25]

If Horst is correct in identifying the 'byshop & reder' Bastiane with Herman Bastian, the anabaptist printer, then the *terminus ad quem* for

---

[20] ME., I, 447-8; 'The Schleitheim Confession of Faith', trans. Wenger, *Mennonite Quarterly Review* 19 (1945), 243-53; Beatrice Jenny, *Das Schleitheimer Täuferbekenntnis 1527*, (Thayngen, 1951), 7-10.

[21] Arnold Snyder, 'The influence of the Schleitheim Articles on the Anabaptist Movement: An Historical Evaluation', *MQR* 63 (1989), 323-44, concludes that 'there is reason for serious doubt... that any connection or influence of Schleitheim will ever be established for the Dutch tradition' (344). Horst further suggests that John Calvin may have written his *Briève instruction pour armer tous bons fideles contre les erreurs de la secte des Anabaptistes* in 1544 (translated into English in 1548) in response to a request that he should combat the anabaptist confession circulated in England (Horst, 50 and Appendix B). David A. Haury rejects Horst's suggestion arguing that Calvin was not responding to a request from England (*MQR* 57, 1983, 145-51).

[22] Horst, 50, 53.

[23] *loc. cit.*

[24] *Dictionary of National Biography* ed. Lee (London, 1892), XXXII.

[25] *DNB.*, XXII.

this document must be early 1536. In the spring of 1536 Herman Bastian was arrested at Gmünden an der Wohra in the Cassel district of Hesse along with George Schnabel and some thirty other anabaptists. Ten of them, including Bastian and Schnabel, were imprisoned at Wolkersdorf. Two years later Peter Tasch wrote to these prisoners giving them news of the progress of the movement in England.[26]

Undoubtedly this document is of the utmost importance because of the light it throws on the early history of anabaptism in England. It suggests that a conventicle of English religious radicals, who would doubtless have been described as Lollards a decade earlier, had appointed a Flemish anabaptist bishop to be their reader, that they had embraced at least one characteristic doctrine of the Melchiorite version of anabaptism, and that they were actively engaged in the importation and dissemination of an anabaptist confession of faith among their English contacts. It reveals a high degree of communion and co-operation between English Lollards and Melchiorite anabaptists from the Netherlands. However, the depth of involvement by native Englishmen and the strength of organisation to which this deposition testifies suggest a date closer to 1535 than 1532. If this search for heretical literature followed the proclamation of March 1535, Bastian could have fled to the Continent and been arrested in Hesse the following year.

(b) Evidence dating from 1535
Reference has already been made to the royal proclamation of March 1535.[27] This apparently arose from the arrest and examination of a number of foreign anabaptists who are described as having 'of their own presumption and authority lately rebaptised themselves'.[28] The

---

26   G. H. Williams, *The Radical Reformation* (Philadelphia, 1962), 444.
27   Above, 1.
28   *loc. cit.*

authorities show no awareness of an anabaptist confession that had been printed in English and brought into the country. Indeed, unlike the later anti-anabaptist proclamation of November 1538, this proclamation makes no mention of anabaptist literature. Moreover, the authorities do not seem to have known of the involvement of native Englishmen in the movement. Rather, the proclamation reveals the King's concern that his own subjects should not be 'infected' with anabaptist doctrine –

> The King's most royal majesty ... minding above all things to save his loving subjects... from falling into any erroneous opinions and damnable heresies, into which they might happen to fall, and be infected by the communion and conversation of such corrupt, seditious and erroneous persons: ordaineth and straightly chargeth and commandeth that all and singular strangers now being in his realm... that have or do hold or teach those or any other erroneous opinions or heresies against God and his Holy Scriptures shall within twelve days next after this present proclamation depart out of this his realm and of all other his dominions on pain to suffer death....[29]

No doubt this proclamation focused attention upon foreign religious radicals, revealing a greater degree of native involvement than the authorities had suspected. Thus, it was decided to make an example of those anabaptists already in custody in order to prevent the infection from spreading.

The official records concerning the arrest, trial and sentencing of these foreigners are no longer extant. However several contemporary writers refer to the executions, but their accounts are fragmentary and they disagree over the numbers involved. Foxe, using 'the registers of London', states that ten were executed at various places in 1535, while ten others recanted and were spared. He records the names of those who were put to death.[30] In a letter to Charles V written from London dated 5 June 1535, Eustace Chapuys, the imperial ambassador, reported –

> About a score of Dutch Anabaptists have been taken here, of whom 13 have been condemned to the fire, and will be burnt in different parts of the Kingdom, as the King and Cromwell have informed me. The others, who have been reconciled to the Church, will be sent into

---

[29]   *loc. cit.*
[30]   John Foxe, *The Acts and Monuments of the Martyrs*, V, 44.

Flanders to the Queen to be dealt with as seems right.[31]
A report sent to Rome by the papal nuncio in France dated Amiens, 8
June 1535 includes the following information on the persecution of
anabaptists in England –

They have also taken in England about 25 Anabaptists, with whom
Cranmer, and others of the Court disputed; and not knowing how to
defend themselves, they said that the Holy Spirit inclined them to it.
For this several of them have already been executed, and it appears that
the King intends to persecute this sect as much as he can, as it already
has firm footing in England.[32]

Charles Wriothesley recorded under 1535,

This yeare, the 4th day of June, were diuerse Dutch men and weomen
convicted for heresie to the number of 22, of the which 14 were
condemned, and two of them, that is to say a man and a woman, were
brent in Smythfeild this day at three of the clocke in the afternoone,
and the other 12 were sent to diuerse good townes in England, there to
be brent; and the residue were converted and commaunded to departe
out of this realme within 14 dayes into their countries, on payne of
death at the Kings pleasure.[33]

Although John Stow compiled his *Annales* during the reign of Elizabeth,
he seems to have had access to the London registers used by Foxe. He
preserves valuable additional information on the religious views of the
condemned heretics. Stow writes,

The five and twentith daie of May, was in S Paules church at London
examined nineteene men and sixe women borne in Holland, whose
opinions were: first, that in Christ is not two natures, God and man:
secondly: that Christ tooke neither flesh nor bloud of the virgine
Marie: thirdly, that children borne of infidels shall be saued: fourthly,
that baptisme of children is to none effect: fiftly, that the sacrament of
Christs bodie is but bread onely: sixtly, that he who after his baptisme
sinneth wittingly, sinneth deadly, and cannot be saued. Foureteene of
them were condemned, a man and a woman of them were burned in

---

[31] *LP.*, VIII, 317.
[32] *Ibid.*, 323.
[33] Charles Wriothesley, *A Chronicle of England During the Reigns of the Tudors*,
ed. Hamilton, Camden Society, N. S. XI, XX (London, 1875, 1877), I, 28.

Smithfield, the other twelue were sent to other townes there to be brent.[34]

Thus, between twenty and twenty-five Dutch anabaptists had been taken into custody since the beginning of the year.[35] They were finally tried in S. Paul's on 25 May where Archbishop Cranmer and others debated with them. They were found guilty of heresy. Thirteen or fourteen refused to recant and were condemned to death, the remainder renounced their beliefs. On 4 June the King personally confirmed the sentences, but according to Foxe he reprieved two more who had subsequently recanted. He further ordered the expulsion from the country of all those who had recanted. That same afternoon a man and a woman were burned at Smithfield, the remainder (about ten) were sent to various provincial towns for execution. These actions were entirely in accord with the King's March proclamation, his intention being to deter potential English recruits to the movement. However, according to the Vatican report, the authorities had since discovered that anabaptism was already firmly established in England.

An analysis of the articles of faith for which these foreigners suffered reveals that they were Melchiorite anabaptists. Points one and two relate to the characteristic celestial flesh christology of Melchior Hofmaan. Although the first is either a mistaken deduction or a deliberate misinterpretation of their emphasis upon the sinless human nature of Christ. Points three and four concern the ordinance of baptism. Anabaptists maintained that all children were saved until they reached the years of accountability.[36] Point five is the sacramentarian doctrine maintained by anabaptists and Lollards alike. The final point regarding post-baptismal (or post-regeneration) sin was also held by many of those anabaptists and spiritualists in the Netherlands who had come under the influence of Melchior Hofmann.[37] Additionally, according to

---

[34]   John Stow, *The Annales of England* (London, 1605) RSTC 23337, 963.

[35]   Williams' suggestion (p. 402) that they had fled to England after the failure of the Amsterdam uprising is unlikely. The rising did not occur until 10 May 1535 and there is clear evidence that a number of foreign anabaptists had been held in custody since March. Nevertheless, news of the revolt may have spurred the English authorities to take immediate action against the prisoners, and mount a search for anabaptist literature.

[36]   Horst, 62.

[37]   Williams, *The Radical Reformation*, 799; Horst, 171ff.; *Spiritual and Anabaptist Writers*, 183f., C. Krahn, *Dutch Anabaptism* (Den Haag, 1968), 112-17.

the papal nuncio's report, the defendants appealed beyond Scripture to the authority of the Holy Spirit. His explanation is that they did not know how to defend themselves; and yet the articles for which they were condemned were very clearly formulated. As Horst points out, among anabaptists with spiritualist tendencies 'the appeal to the Holy Spirit was not a last resort in argument'.[38]

On 25 June 1535 the city of Münster was captured after a long siege by the army of its bishop. In a letter written from Antwerp on 4 July 1535 Cromwell's agent, Walter Mersche, reported –

The bearer, Thos. Johnson, is an Englishman living at Amsterdam, and can show you how Mynster was taken, and the behaviour of the people.... It is reported that they are fleeing from the country, and many of them to England.[39]

There is no evidence to confirm that any of the refugees from Münster actually reached England. However, there is evidence that refugees fleeing from the earlier abortive coup at Amsterdam (10 May) arrived safely in England. In his *Tumultuum Anabaptistarum liber vnus* (Basel, 1548) the contemporary Dutch chronicler, Lambertus Hortensius, recorded that a band of anabaptists had fled to England. They had travelled by boat to assist Jan van Geelen, the leader of the Amsterdam uprising, but they arrived too late. Hearing that the cause was lost and van Geelen dead, they immediately put back to sea and sailed directly to England. Hortensius adds that they had remained in England ever since.[40] A Dutch translation of the work (Enchuysen, 1614) contains a marginal note that three hundred anabaptists sailed to England in two ships.[41]

One of the most influential of the anabaptist bishops in Amsterdam, Jan Mathijs van Middleburg also succeeded in escaping to England at this time. Evidently his leadership continued to be recognised in England because he was one of the 'English' representatives at Bocholt in

---

38   Horst, 63; Williams, 477ff. and especially 823-6.
39   *LP.*, VIII, 388.
40   Quoted in Horst, 73-4.
41   This figure is probably far too large. See Horst, 74. n.46.

1536.[42] Anneken Jansz, at her trial in Rotterdam in January 1539, spoke of her arrival in England in 1536 and how she and her husband had met another anabaptist couple already living there. Mathijs van den Donck, a physician, and his wife, Christiana, had fled from Louvain. At her own trial Christiana van den Donck referred to another anabaptist from Louvain, named Lijnken, who had also fled to England and died of the plague while there.[43]

Another anabaptist who was to play a leading role both at Bocholt and in the subsequent history of the Dutch anabaptist movement was David Joris of Delft. He also attempted to seek refuge in England after the failure of the Amsterdam insurrection. As a young man Joris had spent two years in England (*circa* 1520) and probably had several English contacts besides Dutch refugee friends.[44] He arrived at Flushing shortly after Whitsunday 1535 (*i.e.* after 18 May) with his wife and child. They actually set sail for England but their ship was turned back by a storm. While they waited in lodgings for milder weather three men arrived from England.[45] They told Joris about 'the great persecution there, how hotly suspects were pursued; one could not enter the country, they said, without being investigated.... When David Joris heard this about England.... He and his family turned back and went into hiding at Dordrecht'.[46] This report provides a further glimpse into the situation confronting anabaptists in England after the Amsterdam uprising of May 1535.

(c) Evidence dating from 1536
In the spring of this year (March or April) the English bishops met and drafted a series of articles, ten of which were promulgated the following July. One of the draft articles that were unused is of interest since it represents the first known attempt by English prelates to formulate a

---

42   Horst, 74-5.

43   T. J. van Braght, *Het Bloedig Tooneel, of Martelaers Spiegel der Doops –
gesinde* (Amsterdam, 1685), vol. II, 144-5, quoted in Horst, 54.

44   Roland Bainton, *David Joris, Wiedertaüfer und Kämpfer für Toleranz im 16.
Jahrhundert*, (Leipzig, 1937), 3; below, 186-7.

45   One is tempted to call them Jonson, Whilar and Bastiane! See above, 4ff.

46   Gottfried Arnold, *Kirchen und Ketzer-Historie*, (Franckfurt am Mayn, 1729), II,
708, quoted in Horst, 76.

statement against the anabaptists. It is entitled 'Saluacion of children, infantes, & innocentes' and reads,

Chyldren, infantes, & innocentes, so dyynge, be saued by the vertue & grace of the sacramente of baptisme, in the faythe of the Churche & theyr parentes.... And all the Anabaptistes opynions contrary to hit, or any other manes opinione in oney thynge to the Anabaptistes agreable therein or aney parte thereof, to be reputed amonge vs hereses erroneous & detestable.[47]

It is significant that this particular article was not used. It suggests that the authorities believed that the threat to England following the anabaptist failures at Amsterdam and Münster had abated, that the firm measures they had taken during the spring and summer of the previous year had been successful in deterring English recruits to anabaptism. Certainly the movement now enjoyed nearly three years' respite from persecution. During the years 1536 and 1537 England was one of the safest havens in Europe for anabaptists.

Gathered churches tend to gather around recognised leaders, and this was certainly the case among the various groups of first generation anabaptists. The Münster débacle only served to increase the disunity among the anabaptists in North Germany, the Netherlands and Flanders, particularly between those who were prepared to resort to violence to achieve their ends and those who were not. The respite in England enabled anabaptists there to take an initiative to unify the movement. Thus, 'an Englishman named Henry' proposed that the leaders of the contending parties should meet and confer at his expense.[48] This Englishman cannot be positively identified, but as Horst observes, 'he must have been a person of some means with influence in both England and abroad'.[49]

The conference duly took place in August 1536 at Bocholt, about four miles from Wesel in Westphalia. Between twenty and twenty-five anabaptist leaders attended the meeting. At least three main groupings were represented:– the erstwhile followers of Melchior Hofmann who now looked to Obbe Philips for leadership and who were committed pacifists, the Batenburgers who followed John of Batenburg and who

47   Alan Kreider, 'An English Episcopal Draft Article Against the Anabaptists, 1536', *MQR*, 49 (1975), 38-42, 40.
48   Arnold, II, 711.
49   Horst, 79; below, 186-7.

were militant extremists, and the surviving chiliastic Münsterites. Two representatives came from England, Jan Mathijs van Middleburg and Johan van Utrecht. In Blesdijk's account of the conference Jan Mathijs is initially referred to as from Middelburg but subsequently as from London in England. He also states that Mathijs and his colleague were followers of the doctrines of Melchior Hofmann and strongly opposed the Münsterite position.[50] Significantly, it was Jan Mathijs who specifically invited David Joris to come from Strasbourg and join the conference. Was this a deliberate attempt on the part of the anabaptists in England to secure David Joris as leader of a united Melchiorite movement? Did the Englishmen 'Henry' have anything to do with it?

David Joris was not a member of any of the main parties, and thus he was able to adopt the role of mediator. As such he became the dominant figure at the conference. By spiritualising and allegorising the beliefs and programmes of the contending parties Joris was able to secure superficial agreement between them. Rebaptism was to be abandoned, the use of the sword was declared justifiable but inexpedient since the millenium was clearly not yet at hand, polygamy was rejected but Adamic nakedness permitted if compelled by the Spirit.[51] While the conference at Bocholt failed to secure a permanent unity (neither Menno Simons, nor Obbe nor Dirk Philips attended it) and must have been a disappointment to anabaptists in England, yet it served as the platform on which David Joris was brought to prominence.

David Joris was probably born in Flanders in 1501,[52] his baptismal name was John. His father was an actor, and Joris evidently inherited his flamboyant character and artistic talents. These gifts, together with his striking appearance, made him an obvious leader. He became a skilled glass-painter, working in Flanders, France and England, before settling in Delft in 1524.[53] There he married Dirkgen Willem, and there

---

[50] Nicolaus Blesdikius, *Historia vitae, doctrinae ac rerum gestarum Davidis Georgii Haeresiarchae*, (Daventriae, 1642), 14. Blesdijk was the son-in-law of David Joris, and his biography may be accepted as authoritative. See Williams, 483-4.
[51] Williams, 382-3.
[52] Bainton, 1.
[53] *Ibid.*, 2-3.

he became a Sacramentarian. For four years he boldly proclaimed sacramentarianism, becoming leader of the Delft conventicle. In 1528 he led a group of iconoclasts in an attack on the Assumption Day procession. He was sentenced to be scourged, his tongue was bored, and he was banished from the city for three years.[54] In 1530 he witnessed the execution of a group of anabaptists in The Hague and was deeply moved by their spirit of martyrdom.[55] When he returned to Delft he joined the Melchiorite conventicle, and was baptised by Obbe Philips in September 1534. As an outward sign of his rebirth he reassumed the name which his father had originally bestowed upon him – David.[56] Sometime after his abortive attempt to return to England in May 1535 Joris and his family reached the comparative safety of Strasbourg. There in the spring of 1536 Obbe Philips ordained him as an elder (or bishop) of the movement,[57] and there a few weeks later he received Mathijs' invitation to join the other leaders at Bocholt.

Shortly after the conference at Bocholt, Joris received an adulatory letter from Anneken Jansz of Rotterdam – a woman of considerable wealth, talents and influence. Her husband, Arent Jansz, was a physician. Evidently she was closely acquainted with Joris' management of the proceedings at Bocholt, and now she acclaimed him as 'the fan in the hand of the Lord to winnow and prepare for him an acceptable people that he may speedily come to his temple'. She urged Joris to 'complete what thou hast begun in the house of the Lord'.[58] Since 1529 Joris had been composing hymns whose sentiments reveal the increasing influence of Melchiorite doctrine and spirituality.[59] Anneken Jansz' letter galvanised him. From that moment he began to dream dreams, see visions, and write furiously. In his first tract, Joris made use of the three ages *schema* of Bernard Rothmann.[60] The three epochs of human history are centred upon three 'Davids'. The first was David

---

[54] Williams, 346.
[55] Bainton, 5.
[56] Williams, 381.
[57] Bainton, 17-18; Williams, 359.
[58] Williams, 383.
[59] Bainton, 18.
[60] For the background to anabaptist apocalyptic see M. Reeves, *The Influence of Prophecy in the Later Middle Ages: A Study in Joachimism* (Oxford, 1969) and R. Bauckham, *Tudor Apocalypse* (Appleford, 1978) especially pp. 38-53.

the King, who was a type of the second (and greatest) – Christ the son of David. The third is an ambassador and servant to the second. Three Davids are to be expected since almighty God is three in one.[61] Joris now claimed to be that 'third David' – a new anabaptist prophet had emerged.

Under the sponsorship of Anneken Jansz, David Joris returned to Delft where an increasing number of peaceful Melchiorites rallied around his charismatic leadership. However, within a few weeks Anneken and her husband were forced to leave Den Briel in Holland. They fled to England, where they remained for over two years and where Arent Jansz died.[62] Thus, during these two crucial years of peace and quiet consolidation (1536-8), anabaptism in England was under the influence of the pacifist Melchiorite bishop Jan Mathijs van Middleburg and the mystical disciple of David Joris, Anneken Jansz. Although the sources are slender, they continue to indicate that the impetus for the movement derived from foreign refugees who continued to take an active interest in affairs on the Continent. A few native Englishmen were involved, but they remained on the periphery of the movement.

(d) Evidence dating from 1538

The Hessian anabaptists whom the Landgrave Philip had imprisoned, first at Marburg in 1536 and then at Wolkersdorf,[63] had considerable freedom of movement. Sometime in 1538 an undated letter from Peter Tasch – leader of the movement in Jülich – was found in their possession. It was addressed to George Schnabel and written while Tasch was on a journey to Strasbourg. In the course of the letter Tasch mentions anabaptist leaders in other countries and first he gives news of the movement in England, which suggests that it was of particular interest to the recipients. Tasch reports,

> In Engelland gait die wairheit Kretich in stille fort, der herr weist, wie long. Die bruder haben ein buch offentlich in druck ausgegeben van der minschwerdung Christi. Ich habs wol gelesen. Ich freuwe mich der gaben. Dan ich fulet wail, das der her mit im ist, und ich hette auch in Engelland gereiset, wo ich neit in meinen gewissen genotiget

---

61   *Ibid.*, 30-1.
62   *ME*, I, 126-7; Williams, 402, above 13.
63   Above, 5, 8.

were gewest, bis hieher zu reisen. Der her kans noch wol schicken....[64] Thus from the anabaptist viewpoint, the situation in England was highly satisfactory. The movement was growing steadily, a book had been published, and the blessing of God was apparent. Unfortunately, the book that brought Tasch such satisfaction is no longer extant. Evidently it was either a defence or an explanation of the characteristic Melchiorite christology. It was printed in English, and this suggests that the refugees were actively seeking to proselytise among their English acquaintances.

Early in 1538 the German Protestant princes had sent a delegation to England to secure Henry VIII's support for the Schmalkaldic alliance. To further their cause Philip of Hesse sent a copy of Tasch's letter to John Frederick, the Elector of Saxony, with the suggestion that they should warn Henry VIII. Melanchthon was commissioned to translate Tasch's letter into Latin and write a covering letter to the King of England. A draft was sent to Philip, who made a number of alterations. It was, however, the Wittenburg authorities who produced the final text, and they rejected many of Philip's moderating emendations. This letter was sent to Henry VIII in the name of both princes under the date 25 September 1538.[65] Although he did not reply until 20 January 1539, it is evident that the King acted with alacrity upon receipt of this intelligence from Germany. On 1 October 1538 an ecclesiastical commission, which included Thomas Cranmer, John Stokesley and Robert Barnes, was appointed to 'search for and examine Anabaptists, receive back into the Church such as renounce their error, hand over those who persist... and destroy all books of that detestable sect'.[66] Unfortunately the records of this commission have not survived.

---

[64] 'Wiedertaüferakten 1527-1626', *Urkundliche Quellen zur hessischen Reformationsgeschichte*, eds. Franz *et al.*, IV (Marburg, 1951), no. 62, pp. 160-1. 'In England the truth grows quietly and is spreading steadily, the Lord knows how long. The brethren have brought out a printed book on the incarnation of Christ. I have read it, and I rejoice for such gifts to us. I feel that the Lord is indeed with them, and I would have travelled to England had I not been compelled by my conscience to journey here. God may still give me the opportunity to go there'. (trans. Horst).

[65] *LP.*, XIII (ii), 105, 163; Horst, 83.

[66] *LP.*, XIII (ii), 195.

On 16 November the King issued a royal proclamation dealing with various matters concerning religion.[67] Major sections dealt with anabaptists, sacramentarians, and the publishers or importers of heretical books. The preamble appears to reflect the current situation as reported by the royal commissioners –

> The King's most royal majesty, being informed that sundry contentions and sinister opinions have, by wrong teaching and naughty printed books, increased and grown within this his realm of England... among his loving subjects... by occasion of sundry printed books in the English tongue that be brought from outward parts, and by such like books as have been printed within this his realm... by sundry strange persons called Anabaptists and Sacramentaries, which be lately come into this realm, where some of them do remain privily unknown, and by some his highness' subjects... whereby divers and many of his loving simple subjects have been induced and encouraged... to argue and dispute in open places, taverns and alehouses, not only upon the Holy Sacrament of baptism, but also upon the most Blessed Sacrament of the altar....[68]

The book on the incarnation of Christ mentioned in Tasch's letter was doubtless included among these 'naughty printed books'. In contrast with the 1535 proclamation the authorities were now aware that heretical literature was being printed at home as well as being imported from overseas. Another development from the earlier proclamation is the admission that these abominable doctrines had spread among the King's 'loving subjects'. Furthermore, 'some of his highness' subjects' – not only recently arrived foreign refugees – were actively engaged in promoting these books and doctrines among ordinary English people. Certainly English sacramentarian books and beliefs are included here with anabaptism, but anabaptists were sacramentarians and there is no valid reason for drawing a rigid distinction between native sacramentarians and foreign anabaptists. In 1538, both ordinances were under vigorous reappraisal in the taverns of south-east England.

Several injunctions are then listed in the proclamation. The first three deal with the printing, importation and distribution of books. First, no books printed in English were to be imported into England without

---

[67]   *TRP.*, I, 270-6.
[68]   *Ibid.*, 270-1.

special royal license. Secondly, no books were to be printed in England in English without being examined and licensed by the Privy Council. Thirdly no 'books of Scripture' in English were to be published without examination and approval by the authorities. The fourth injunction deals specifically with sacramentarians and anabaptists. Once again the contemporary situation is revealed in the opening statement –

> Forasmuch as diuers and sundry strangers of the sect and false opinion of the Anabaptists and Sacramentaries been lately come into this realm, where they lurk secretly in diuers corners and places, minding craftily and subtly to provoke and stir the King's loving subjects to their errors and opinions, whereof part of them by the great travail and diligence of the King's highness and his council be apprehended and taken....[69]

Again this is evidence of vigorous proselytisation of the natives by foreign refugees, who are here described as both anabaptists and 'Sacramentaries'.[70]

As in the 1535 proclamation, the King's purpose was to deter his subjects from becoming involved with religious radicalism. To this end he again intended to make an example of those whom his commissioners had detected and apprehended –

> ...the King... abhorreth and detesteth the same sects... and intendeth to proceed against such of them as already be apprehended... to the intent his subjects shall take example by their punishments not to adhere to their false and detestable opinions, but utterly forsake and relinquish the same, which his highness straightly commandeth them to do, upon pain of like punishment. [71]

It is significant, however, that by 1538 the King was commanding his subjects 'to forsake and relinquish' these heresies. Despite the 1535 proclamation Englishmen had become involved.

Finally, the fourth injunction deals with those foreign radicals who had avoided either arrest or detection. The text reads,

---

[69]   *Ibid.*, 272.
[70]   For over ten years English Reformers in exile such as Tyndale and Frith had been described as 'sacramentaries', but here the term is associated with those who held more extreme opinions.
[71]   *Ibid.*

... his majesty straightly chargeth and commandeth all other strangers of the same Anabaptists' and Sacramentaries' erroneous sects, not being apprehended or known, that they within eight or ten days after this present proclamation, with all celerity shall depart out of this realm and all other his dominions, upon pain of loss of their lives and forfeiture of all their goods....[72]

Evidently the commissioners were aware that some foreign anabaptists had gone into hiding.

On 22 November 1538 a new proclamation was directed against foreign anabaptists.[73] It ordered all strangers 'who have lately rebaptised themselves and who deny that the Sacrament of the Altar is the very body of our Lord' to leave the country within twelve days, whether they have recanted or not, on pain of death. Furthermore persons belonging to these sects were forbidden to enter the Kingdom. Once again the King's subjects were forbidden to hold such heresies, and finally all persons were ordered to assist in arresting the guilty.[74]

Horst notes that the royal commission which was authorised on 1 October mentioned only anabaptists and their books, whereas in the proclamation of 16 November sacramentarians were linked with anabaptists and equally condemned.[75] Certainly these sects were clearly distinguished in the subsequent proclamations of 1539-40. The October commission was authorised above the signature of Thomas Cromwell and represents an immediate reaction to the receipt of information from Hesse concerning the activities of anabaptists in England. Horst suggests that the King had 'a more direct hand' in the drafting of the proclamation than in the authorisation of the ecclesiastical commission.[76] In early November 1538 the King – under the influence of Stephen Gardiner – was preparing for a 'show trial' of the sacramentarian John Nicholson.[77] The date for the trial had been chosen

---

[72] *Ibid.*, 273.
[73] *LP.*, XIII (ii), 371. Possibly it was an amended reissue of the earlier proclamation, see Wriothesley, I, 89-90.
[74] *Ibid.*
[75] Horst, 87.
[76] *Ibid.* The draft proclamation appears to have been amended by the King himself with the insertion of 'sacramentarys' in the penal clauses. (B.L., MS. Cot. Cleo. Ev, f. 357^r).
[77] Foxe, *AM.*, V, 228-9.

well in advance. It was 16 November – the day on which the proclamation was issued. Since Henry was determined to make an example of Nicholson, it may well be that the injunctions against 'sacramentaries' were included on his personal direction in order to cover the case of Nicholson and legalise his condemnation. It is surely no coincidence that an amended proclamation, with the relevant clause now directed solely against anabaptists, was issued on the very day of Nicholson's execution – 22 November 1538 – the day on which the arrested anabaptists were tried and condemned.

In late November 1538 Anneken Jansz and Christiana Barents left England.[78] This suggests that, fearing detection by the authorities, they had gone into hiding, and then fled the country. On arrival in Rotterdam the two women re-embarked for Delft, their intention being to join David Joris and his followers. As they entered the ship they were arrested.

The proclamation of 16 November stated that some of the foreign anabaptists had been arrested. The evidence indicates that the number was not large. In a letter to Lord Lisle, dated from London 23 November, John Husee wrote,

Yesterday, the 22nd, Lambert, alias John Nycolson, was burnt in Smithfield, and the same day two Flemings, and one of their wives, were adjudged to death. A third man abjured. These were Anabaptists....[79]

Wriothesley records.

Also the 24th day of November, beinge Sonday... foure persons of the Anabaptistes heretykely bare fagottes the same daye at Paules Crosse, 3 men and 1 woman, all Duchemen borne.

Allso, on St. Andrewes even, was a man and a woman of the Anabaptistes burnt in Smithfield, Duch persons, for heresy against the sacrament of the aulter, allso, on St. Andrewes day, was burnt at Colchester a Duch man, which was husband to the sayd woman that was burnt in Smythfield, which was a goodly yong man, and about 22 yeres of age, for the same opinion.[80]

---

[78] Williams, 403; Horst, 54.
[79] *LP.*, XIII (ii), 373-4.
[80] Wriothesley, I, 90.

The *Chronicle of the Grey Friars of London* supplies the names of those burnt in London –
> And the XXIX of November was burnyd in Smythfelde John Mattessey a Docheman, Peter Franke and hys wyffe, for erryse.[81]

From these three sources it appears that four Dutch or Flemish anabaptists had been arrested. They were tried on 22 November, found guilty of sacramentarian heresy and condemned to be burnt, whereupon one of the men abjured. The following Sunday all four were compelled to stand as penitents at S. Paul's Cross. A week after their trial, on the evening of 29 November, Jan Mathijs and the wife of Peter Franke were burned at Smithfield. The following day Peter Franke was burned at Colchester. This is significant because it suggests that the authorities had discovered anabaptist sympathisers at Colchester. If they expected Franke's punishment to deter any religious radicals in Colchester then their plan misfired. Seven years later, John Bale wrote of those whom he had met at Colchester who had been converted from Catholicism through witnessing the fearless and patient demeanour of Peter Franke as he suffered martyrdom.[82]

Franke came from Bruges where he was known as Pieter de Bontwerker.[83] In his refutation of 'Ponce Pantolabus' (John Huntington), Bale quotes at length from his verse, and in so doing supplies further information about Franke. Huntington wrote,
> Next after him [John Lambert]
> Came in a lymme,
> Of Antichrist
> An Anabaptyst,
> One Peter Franke,
> Which sayd full rank,
> That Christ and God,

81 *Chronicle of the Grey Friars of London*, ed. Nichols, Camden Society Old Series, LIII (London, 1852), 42.
82 John Bale, *A mysterye of inyquyte contayned within the heretycall Genealogye of Ponce Pantolabus* (Geneva, 1545), STC. 1303, sig. H5ʳ-H8ʳ. Bishop Latimer's subsequent comments about popular sympathy for anabaptists being aroused through their exemplary demeanour during suffering, *The seconde Sermon of Master Hughe Latimer* (London, 1549) RSTC 15274, sig. L8ᵛ-M1ʳ, may not reflect the preacher's personal experience. Latimer had probably read Bale's work, and his comments here may represent a retort to Bale's sympathetic description of the reaction in Colchester to Franke's martyrdom.
83 Horst, 88.

Toke not manhode,
Of Marye the Virgine
Which was without synne.[84]
Evidently Franke maintained the Melchiorite version of christology, and so, presumably, did his wife and two associates.

On 23 December two Englishmen were burned at Smithfield – Richard Turner, weaver, and Peter Florence, butcher. Presumably they had been arrested during the current campaign against religious radicalism and convicted of heresy. However, their crimes are not recorded.[85]

Although only a few individuals suffered during the autumn 1538 persecution, their loss must have constituted a severe reverse for the movement in England. John Mathijs was an able and experienced anabaptist bishop, Peter Franke and his wife were evidently highly regarded, and Anneken Jansz was a woman of ability and influence.[86] When King Henry finally replied to the German princes on 20 January 1539 he was able to regard the anabaptist threat with equanimity. He merely instructed his ambassador to thank the Duke of Saxony and the Landgrave of Hesse for their letters and tell them that he had, 'condemned such leaders of that faction as could be apprehended and had banished the rest by proclamation.[87]The German princes would never have imagined from this sanguine reply what a fervour of investigation, edicts and examinations their letter had produced. Likewise, Peter Tasch, when he wrote from Strasbourg to Hesse in 1538, could never have imagined what trouble his letter was going to bring upon his brethren in England before the end of the year.

(e) Evidence dating from 1539
By February 1539 the King was able to moderate his repressive edicts. On 26 February a further proclamation was issued which mainly dealt with rites and ceremonies, but the concluding paragraphs concern the punishment of heresy.[88] It refers to 'many simple persons of the King's

---

[84]   Bale, *loc. cit.* quoted in Horst, 88.
[85]   *Chronicle of the Grey Friars of London*, 42.
[86]   Williams, 383ff.
[87]   *LP.*, XIV (i), 40.
[88]   *TRP.*, I, 278-80.

subjects' who had been 'seduced' by 'certain Anabaptists and Sacramentaries, coming out of outward parts into this realm'. The King trusted that they 'now be sorry for their offenses'. 'Like a most loving parent much moved to pity' and 'fearing also that great fear of extreme punishment might turn their simplicity to obstinacy', the king, –

> remitteth, pardoneth, and forgiveth to all and singular persons, as well his grace's subjects as other, all such faults as they have committed by falling into such wrong and perverse opinions.... So that for any such fault done or committed before 23rd day of February [1539] not already judged against them, they shall not be further troubled or vexed, but clearly acquitted from all worldly punishment therefor....[89]

Nevertheless, a final warning is added that if any of those pardoned, or any others, should subsequently embrace 'such detestable and damnable opinions' then, 'without further mercy his grace's laws shall be straightly executed against them that shall so offend'.[90]

Within six months (28 June 1539) the Act of Six Articles had become law. This 'Act for Abolishing of Diversity of Opinions' represented the King's final attempt to secure religious uniformity in England. It also represented the first fruits of the increased influence of Norfolk and Gardiner. They had taken advantage of the stand that the King had made against John Nicholson's sacramentarianism. The first article, which reaffirmed transubstantiation, is clearly the most important. It alone carried the death penalty and confiscation of property for a first offence.[91] The King and his councillors were well aware that sacramentarianism was the most prevalent 'heresy' in England in the 1530s – not anabaptism.

(f) Evidence dating from 1540

In the spring of 1540 more foreign anabaptists were detected in London and arrested. On 10 April 1540 Charles de Marillac, the French ambassador, reported that the King had imprisoned Robert Barnes and his associates in the Tower along with '15 or 20 strangers, mostly from

---

[89] *Ibid.*, 280.
[90] *Ibid.*
[91] *Stat.Realm* III, 812.

Flanders, and all Anabaptists'.[92] On 8 May he further reported,

> These days have been executed three persons of very low condition, two Flemings and an Englishman, for speaking irreverently of the Holy Sacrament, and refusing to revoke their errors....[93]

Wriothesley also recorded this event,

> Also the third daie of Maie were three persons brent without Sainct Georges Barre in Southwark in the high waie almost at Newington for heresie against the sacrament of the aulter; one was a groome to the Queene named Maundevild, a French man borne, another an paynter, an Italian, and an Englishman.[94]

Another account was given in a letter written from London by Richard Hilles to Heinrich Bullinger in Zurich,

> Before Whitsuntide three persons were burned in the suburbs of London, in that part of the city belonging to the diocese of Winchester, because they denied transubstantiation, and had not received the sacrament at Easter. And as these things took place in the diocese of Winchester, it was remarked by persons that those three men were brought to the stake by the procurement of the bishop, just as he burned, shortly after, a crazed man of the name of Collins.[95]

Stow supplies the date of their initial examination,

> The 29 of April one named Maundeveld, one other named Colens, and one other were examined in S. Margarets Church, and were condemned for anabaptists, and were on the third of May brent in the high way beyond Southwark towards Newenton.[96]

Wriothesley, however, states that Collins was not burned until 7 July –

> This yeare the 7th daie of Julie one Collins was brent without Sainct Georges Barres in Southwarke for heresie against the sacrament of the aulter, but at his death he confessed his error and died verie penitentlie.[97]

---

[92] *LP.*, XV, 206.
[93] *Ibid.*, 310.
[94] Wriothesley, I, 118.
[95] *Original Letters Relative to the English Reformation*, ed. Robinson, Parker Society (Cambridge, 1846), I, 200-201.
[96] Stow, 974.
[97] Wriothesley, I, 119.

From these references it cannot be determined whether one or two Englishmen were executed. Evidently three men were examined, found guilty of heresy, and sentenced in Southwark on 29 April, and three men were burned on the main road into Surrey on 3 May. Hilles' account confirms Wriothesley's record that an Englishman named Collins was burnt in the same neighbourhood on 7 July. Perhaps Stow wrongly assumed that the Englishman who was examined in S. Margaret Pattens on 29 April and subsequently burned on 3 May was named Collins – or perhaps he supplies the name of the otherwise anonymous Englishman (Colens).

Hilles' description of Collins as a 'crazed man' is corroborated by John Foxe. He records that an insane lawyer named William Collins was burnt in Smithfield in 1538, shortly after John Lambert, for blasphemous behaviour during mass.[98] Foxe, however, was mistaken concerning the time and place of Collins' execution. This man had been in trouble with the authorities in April 1536. On that occasion Collins had been accused before the London magistrates as a 'comen brawler, fyghter and comon scolde'. Apparently he had fired an arrow at the famous rood in S. Margaret Pattens Church, Southwark. He had then challenged it to defend itself and punish him if it were able.[99] Collins was imprisoned with Lambert, but despite the gravity of his offences he did not suffer with him. In fact it may have been Collins who advised Lambert to appeal directly to the King over the head of Bishop Gardiner.[100] Foxe states that Collins was 'a lawyer and a gentleman'. In March 1539 he also wrote to the King asking for release. He explained that the 'raging of his tongue against the Church' was due to youthful indiscretion, and he signed himself 'legislator'.[101] Brigden comments, 'Had [Collins] been a rude artisan he might perhaps have been treated with less leniency.'[102]

Both Hilles and Foxe agree that it was Gardiner who was responsible for bringing all of these men to the stake in 1540. On 22 May 1538 an iconoclastic mob had pulled down the rood in S. Margaret

---

[98]   Foxe, *AM.*, V, 251.
[99]   S.E.Brigden, 'The Early Reformation in London, 1520-1547: the conflict in the Parishes' (unpublished Cambridge Ph.D thesis, 1979), 193.
[100] *Original Letters*, I, 201.
[101] *LP.*, XIV (i), 647.
[102] Brigden, 193.

Pattens. Brigden makes the plausible suggestion that Maundevild, the Italian painter, and the unnamed Englishman may have been the serving men who had provoked a riot at Gardiner's sermon at Paul's Cross on 11 April 1540.[103] Equally they could have been responsible for the earlier iconoclasm at S. Margaret Pattens, and Gardiner was not able to punish them until after the fall of Cromwell. Certainly William Collins had committed an act of iconoclasm in that church, and it would have been thought fitting for such iconoclasts to be tried at the scene of their crime.

It is suggested, therefore, that those who were burnt in Southwark in May and July 1540 were not anabaptists *per se* but violent sacramentarians. William Collins was a young hot head. Like the others, he was an 'anabaptist' only in the sense that he was a social revolutionary and a disturber of the peace.[104]

Clearly native Englishmen as well as foreigners suffered during this persecution, but it is impossible to discern whether their heretical opinions extended beyond sacramentarianism to anabaptism. There was, perhaps, a tendency on the part of the authorities to regard all foreign-born religious radicals as anabaptists, and all native heretics as sacramentarians. Sacramentarianism was an indigenous heresy with a long pedigree. Furthermore, the Act of Six Articles (1539) tended to reduce all heretics to plain sacramentarians, whether their commitment lay with English Lollardy or Continental anabaptism.

Nevertheless, when the King's general pardon was proclaimed in July 1540 the doctrines of the sacramentarians and anabaptists were clearly differentiated. Both were excepted from the pardon, but the characteristic tenets of the latter were listed separately in the concluding paragraph.[105] These were as follows:–

That infants ought not to be baptised and if they be baptised they ought to be rebaptised when they com to laufull age; That it is not leaful for a Christen man to beare office or rule in the Comen Welth; That no mans lawes ought to be obeyed; That it is not leafull for a

---

[103] Wriothesley, I, 115; Brigden, 219 n.1.

[104] Indeed, Hilles suspected that the real cause of Collins' imprisonment was his vigorous denunciation of nobles who were exploiting their neighbours (*loc. cit.*).

[105] *The Statutes of the Realm*, eds. Luders *et al.*, (London, 1810), III 811, 812.

Christen Man to take an othe before any Judge; That Christe toke no
bodily substaunce of o^r blissid lady; That Synners aftre baptisme
cannot be restored by repentaunce; That every maner of Death, w^t the
tyme and houre thereof, is so certainely prescribed, appointed, and
determyned to evry man of God, that neither any prynce by his sworde
can altre it, ne any man by his owne wilfulnes prevent or chaunge it;
That all things be comon and nothing severall.[106]
Presumably these tenets had been gleaned from anabaptists who had
been examined during the previous two years, or from their literature.
Horst points out that these doctrines are formulated in the language of
opponents. He concludes,

The eight points... confirm the thesis that anabaptism in England was
Melchiorite in persuasion and that it had much in common with that
party in the Netherlands.....[107]

Horst also notes that a central feature of anabaptist doctrine – the
freedom of the will – is absent from this list.[108] In fact the seventh point
appears to maintain the very reverse. However, at this time the concept of
human autonomy was still generally accepted in England. Hence the
determinism reflected by the seventh point was accounted heretical, not
human freedom. It was not until the reign of Edward VI and the arrival of
Reformed theologians from the Continent that the doctrine was seriously
questioned and debated.[109] The authorities may well have derived the
seventh point from the fatalistic attitude of captive anabaptists to their
arrest and punishment.[110]

Foxe records a total of twenty-one persons who were burned for
violation of the Six Articles during the years 1540 to 1546,[111] but it is
unlikely that any of them had embraced anabaptist doctrines. Evidence
from the chronicles reveals that Foxe's account was not exhaustive. It
may be that he deliberately omitted those with anabaptist sympathies,
because he was embarrassed by English religious radicals like Joan

---

[106] *Ibid.*, 812.
[107] Horst, 92.
[108] *Ibid.*
[109] Charles D. Cremeans, 'The Reception of Calvinistic Thought in England',
        University of Illinois Bulletin XXXI (1949), 1-127, especially pp. 29-31.
[110] Such an attitude can be seen, for example, in the contents of Peter Tasch's
        letter, *loc. cit.*
[111] Foxe, *AM.*, V, 443ff.

Bocher and Henry Harte who did not share his theological opinions. In which case, the three men who were burned beyond Southwark on 3 May 1540, and whose sufferings were not recorded by Foxe, have added significance.

(g) Conclusions

Anabaptism in England began with the arrival of Dutch and Flemish refugees from persecution in the Netherlands *circa* 1534. After the failure of the Amsterdam uprising in May 1535 large numbers of their compatriots joined them. They settled in London (especially in Southwark), Colchester and possibly other eastern coastal towns possessing trading connections with the Netherlands. From the start they sought to proselytise among their native English neighbours, that is, among those who sympathised with Lollard sectarianism and perhaps still gathered in Bible-reading conventicles. This aggressive proselytisation began to make an impact, especially in London during the peaceful years 1536-38. However, the number of Englishmen who embraced anabaptist doctrines remained small. The movement was dominated by the refugees – men and women of high spiritual calibre who remained in close contact with anabaptist leaders on the Continent.

These Flemish and Dutch refugees were, in the full sense of the word, anabaptists. All the sources make it clear that they had recently undergone believer's baptism. However, they were all strongly influenced by the teaching of the founder of anabaptism in North Germany and the Netherlands, Melchior Hofmann. In December 1531 Hofmann had ordered a two year suspension in the administration of the baptismal ordinance. By the end of the two years Hofmann was in the Strasbourg prison where he was to remain for the rest of his life. Although some of his followers in the Netherlands resumed the practice, it is doubtful whether Hofmann himself ever advocated its resumption. By 1539 Hofmann himself had recanted his views on believer's baptism.[112] Meanwhile at Bocholt in 1536, the conference had, under David Joris's leadership, agreed to abandon rebaptism. From the outset anabaptism in England was influenced by the Melchiorite tendency to spiritualise and internalise the ordinances, after 1536 the influence of

---

[112] R.S.Armour, *Anabaptist Baptism: A Representative Study,* (Scottdale, 1966), 107, 109-110.

David Joris was paramount, and thus it is unlikely that believer's baptism was ever administered in England, even in the most peaceful period.[113]

If the practice of believer's baptism is regarded as the sole criterion by which anabaptists are to be distinguished, then there were probably no English anabaptists. For that reason, the designation 'radical' is perhaps more appropriate. Nevertheless, as the General Pardon of July 1540 testifies, there are other criteria by which the influence of anabaptism upon English men and women can be assessed. While neither anabaptist teaching on the magistracy nor their advocacy of the community of goods are readily apparent in England, (possibly due to the influence of Davidist 'Nicodemism'), the characteristic Melchiorite christology was embraced by some Englishmen. Melchiorite belief in impeccability after baptism was found in England in the refined view that the regenerate cannot sin. Finally the anabaptists' insistence upon the freedom of the will[114] was also vigorously maintained by some English sectarians long after the English Reformation had embraced Calvinist determinism.[115]

This, then, was the nursery that produced Joan Bocher, John Champneys, Henry Harte, Robert Cooche and Christopher Vitells. The initiative had come from the refugees, and for as long as Henry VIII reigned, foreigners dominated anabaptism in England. However, when the Henrician grip finally relaxed in January 1547, there were native Englishmen ready to promulgate the new doctrines.

---

[113] *Ibid.,* 101-2.

[114] *Ibid.,* 98-9.

[115] Luther and Calvin's teaching on predestination was a logical development from their understanding of justification by faith alone – and essential to it – as all the mainstream English Reformers clearly perceived. For that reason they strenuously opposed those 'sectaries', 'Pelagians' and 'anabaptists' who advocated free will doctrines in Marian and early Elizabethan England.

Chapter Two

The English Radicals under Edward VI, 1547-53

When Edward VI's first parliament met in November 1547, one of its first acts was to repeal the old laws against heresy, including the late King's Act of Six Articles. In practice, however, these laws had been in abeyance since the beginning of the year.[1]

According to Strype, Bishop Ridley of Rochester had already (June 1547) been instructed to deal with two anabaptists in Kent, whose extreme sacramentarianism was beginning to infect the locality.[2] A year later Archbishop Cranmer was examining an even more extreme case of religious radicalism. John Assheton, parson of Shiltelington in the diocese of Lincoln, was accused by two of his fellow priests of anti-trinitarian heresy. In a written deposition they accused Assheton of denying the doctrine of the Trinity as expressed in the Athanasian Creed. Assheton argued that the formula was wholly dependent upon a particular interpretation of a psalm. Furthermore, he denied the personality of the Holy Spirit, describing him as 'a certen power of the father'. He also maintained that, although Jesus Christ was a holy prophet sent to reveal the power of God, he was not part of the Godhead because 'he was seen and lyued, hungered and thirsted'.[3] In December 1548 Assheton confessed that he had taught these 'errors, heresies and damnable opinions'; he renounced them and did penance. Wilbur may be correct in regarding John Assheton as the first English anti-trinitarian of the Reformation era,[4] but this seems to have been an isolated case. Davis suggests that Assheton is to be identified with the John Assheton, vicar of Spandan and chaplain to the Lord Chancellor, who obtained a licence for non-residence and pluralism on 3 April 1535, and subsequently spent some years in the Rhineland.[5] If this is the case, then Assheton probably learned his radical theology on the Continent.

---

[1] The influence of the Six Articles began to decline in the autumn of 1543 with the failure of Gardiner's plot against Cranmer (Below pp. 45-9) and Henry's marriage to the devoutly Protestant Catherine Parr. Edward VI c. 12; (*Statutes of the Realm*, IV, 19).

[2] John Strype, *Ecclesiastical Memorials* (Oxford, 1816), II (i), 107-8. Doubtless, Strype is following Foxe (*AM.*, VII, 523) here. However J.G.Ridley, *Nicholas Ridley* (London, 1957), 139n. argues convincingly against the accuracy of this statement.

[3] Wilkins, *Concilia*, IV, 40-2.

[4] E. M. Wilbur, *A History of Unitarianism in Transylvania, England, and America* (Cambridge Massachusetts, 1952), 169-70.

[5] J. F. Davis, *Heresy in south-east England, 1520-59*, (Oxford D.Phil. thesis, 1968), 406-7.

The Duke of Somerset and his Council had rather naively imagined that, given freedom of discussion, all reasonable and devout men would arrive at the same general position.[6] By the close of the second year of Edward's reign it had become evident that unfettered reading of the Scriptures was not producing doctrinal unanimity. Throughout 1547 and 1548 crudely printed Protestant tracts had poured unhindered from the English presses. A growing band of vociferous radicals in and around London seemed determined to undermine the establishment of a reformed national church. In October 1548 John Calvin wrote to the Duke of Somerset from Geneva urging him to 'restrain by the sword' that party 'of fantastical people who, under colour of the Gospel, would throw everything into confusion'.[7] Hugh Latimer was particularly concerned by the disruptive nonconformity of these 'anabaptists'. In a sermon preached before the young King on 29 March 1549, Latimer denounced the anarchical teachings of the anabaptists. They were 'a sect of heretics', which 'will have no magistrates nor judges on the earth'. Then the preacher informed the King that he had recently learned from a reputable source, 'of a town in this realm of England, that hath above five hundred heretics of this erroneous opinion in it'. Later he asked,

And will you know where this town is?... Where is it? Where the bishop of the diocese is an unpreaching prelate.[8]

This strongly suggests that Latimer was referring to a town within the diocese of London where Bonner was still at the helm – possibly

---

6   Edward Seymour was influenced by Erasmian humanism. By the Royal Injunctions of 1547 he overturned the legal restraints on popular reading imposed by Henry VIII – but by relaxing the censorship of Protestant books Seymour opened the flood-gates for radical Protestant propaganda because the book trade was in the hands of Protestant sympathisers. For a detailed discussion of Seymour's policy towards the press see John N. King, 'Freedom of the Press, Protestant Propaganda and Protector Somerset', *Huntingdon Library Quarterly* 60 (1976), 9ff.

7   G. C. Gorham, *Gleanings of a few Scattered Ears*, (London, 1857), 55-71, especially 59-60.

8   Hugh Latimer, *Sermons*, ed. Corrie (PS. Cambridge, 1844), 151-2.

Colchester, or even London itself. Exactly a fortnight later (12 April 1549) an ecclesiastical commission, which included Archbishop Cranmer and six other bishops, was appointed to search out and examine those who 'are reviving the wicked errors of the Anabaptists'. It was given power to excommunicate and imprison such heretics, or to hand them over to the secular authorities for further punishment.[9]

A. THE HERESY COMMISSION OF 1549

The records of this commission are no longer extant. However several chroniclers noted its activities. Furthermore the findings and sentences pronounced against three of the accused – John Champneys, Joan Bocher and Michael Thombe – are recorded in Cranmer's register.[10] On 22 April the commission examined its first heretic in the Lady Chapel at S. Paul's – Joan Bocher *alias* Barnes *alias* Baron *alias* Joan of Kent. According to Jordan, Joan had been reported to the Privy Council by Kentish magistrates as a confirmed anabaptist.[11]

I JOAN BOCHER

Undoubtedly, Joan Bocher or Boucher or Butcher, *alias* Joan Baron, Barnes or Knell, and frequently referred to as Joan of Kent, was the most famous heretic of Edward's reign. Unfortunately, no detailed account of her doctrine has survived, and there is no evidence that she ever expressed her beliefs in writing. Nevertheless, her case is better documented than that of the other religious deviants who appeared before the heresy commission in 1549.

Jordan suggests that she may have been the wife of 'a London butcher named Thombe' who also appeared before the commissioners charged with anabaptist heresy.[12] On 2 May 1549 Thombe abjured similar Melchiorite christological beliefs to those maintained by Joan, but there is no evidence to support Jordan's suggestion that they were married to

---

9   *Foedera*, ed. Rymer, (London, 1713), XV, 181-3. The heresy commission's mandate was renewed in January 1551 (XV, 250-2).
10 folios 71ff. These three cases, together with those of John Assheton and George van Parris were printed by Wilkins in *Concilia*, IV, 39-45.
11 W. K. Jordan, *Edward VI: the Threshold of Power*, (London, 1970), 328.
12 *Ibid.*, 327-8.

each other. Horst's contrasting claim that Joan was 'a lady of considerable social standing, possibly of noble blood'[13] is equally unsubstantiated. The fact that she knew Anne Askew and some of the ladies at Court, and that Cranmer may have been acquainted with her, does not prove high social standing. Her demeanour under examination, her inability to express her opinions in writing, or to defend them orally with a similar facility to that shown by Anne Askew and above all, the evidence of her Lollard origins – all indicate that she came from humble stock.

The case of Joan Bocher is important – not only for the publicity her execution received and her posthumous fame – but because it is possible to trace the development of her theology.

(a) The Lollard

During the late 1520s Lollardy gained a new source of inspiration through the arrival in England of Tyndale's works, especially his translation of the New Testament. Bishop Tunstal of London was, however, determined to stop the distribution of this heretical literature in his diocese. On 24 October 1526 he ordered his archdeacons to warn all who possessed such books to surrender them within thirty days.[14]

In 1527 Geoffrey Wharton, Tunstal's vicar-general, began a rigorous visitation of the diocese. This uncovered widespread heresy, particularly in North Essex.[15] The heresy hunt continued into the following year, and on 28 April 1528 John Tybal of Steeple Bumpstead was examined before Tunstal. Besides the usual Lollard sacramentarian heresies, Tybal maintained that the priesthood was unnecessary, that laymen could administer the sacraments, that confession to a priest was unnecessary, and that the clergy should be married. Tybal abjured his heresies, did penance, and betrayed many of his fellow Lollards. As a result, on 11 May 1528, several members of the Steeple Bumpstead conventicle appeared before the Bishop of London.

---

13 Horst, 109.
14 Foxe, *AM.*, IV, 666-70.
15 BL., MS. Harl., 421, ff. 9-36.

Among those examined were Robert and Thomas Hemsted. Robert, who is described as an 'husbandman', was evidently illiterate because his abjuration of the belief that 'the sacrament of the altar is not the very body of Christ, and that pardons are of no effect' was 'Signed with a cross'.[16] The confession of Thomas Hemsted is particularly valuable:

> Thos. Hemsted confesses that his wife taught him the 'Paternoster', 'Ave Maria', and 'Credo' in English, which she learned of Gilbert Shipwright, deceased. Sometime after, he was chosen churchwarden of Bumstede, with John Tyball, and was often in his company and that of Sir Richard Fox, who, knowing what his wife had taught him, called him 'brother in Christ', and 'a known man'. [Hemstede] has heard their reading and teaching for a year without disclosing them. About Shrovetide last was taught by Thomas Hilles that pardons were not profitable; and about 'Fastyngham' last, was taught by Fox that the sacrament of the altar is not the very body of Christ, but done for a remembrance of Christ's Passion; and that pilgrimages were of no effect.

Thomas Hemsted then followed Tybal's example and betrayed the other members of the Steeple Bumpstead conventicle:

> The Following persons are of the same sect, and have been taught by Fox, Tyball and Friar Gardyner: Edmond Tyball and his wife, Joan Bocher, widow, the wife of George Preston, Joan Hempsted, the respondent's wife, John 'filius ejus naturalis', and Robert Faire, lay persons of Bumpstede; John Wyggen, Thomas Topley and William Gardyner, Austin Friars of Clare; John Chapman and Thomas Hilles of Wytham; William Browne and John Craneford of Bumstede.[17]

The confession and abjuration of William Bocher, ploughwright, of Steeple Bumpstead also occurred at the same date and location. The original document is no longer extant, but fortunately Strype made use of it, printing it *in extenso*.[18] William Bocher abjured typical Lollard heresies concerning the sacrament of the altar, pardons and pilgrimages, and like Robert Hemsted, he signed his confession with a cross. Underneath this abjuration a note in Latin has been added. It states that

---

[16]   *Ibid.*, f.27, printed in LP., IV (ii), 1875-6.
[17]   *Ibid.*
[18]   Strype, *EM.*, I (ii):59-61.

William Bocher came from tainted stock, for his father had been burnt for heresy.[19]

In October 1528, Thomas Hilles of Witham was examined. He confessed that, while at Steeple Bumpstead, he had worked with John Tybal who had read to him the Gospels and Paul's epistles in English, and taught him heresy. He had gone to [Gilbert] Shipwright's house with Tybal, Fox, Friar Topley and Friar Gardiner, where they had read the New Testament and talked heresy. They had also met at Bower Hall, at Mother Bocher's and Mother Charles's for New Testament reading. John Smyth had been present but expressed no opinions. He had read the New Testament he bought in London at the houses of Mother Bocher, Mother Charles and Roger, a tanner of Bowers Gifford, and then sold it to Fox.[20]

Among the testimonies against Archbishop Cranmer and his commissary, Christopher Nevinson, produced by the Canterbury prebendaries in 1543, several concern their lenient treatment of Joan Bocher. Two of these depositions refer to Joan's earlier career, John Milles stated:

Also, at that time came forth to the Court[21] the parson of Westbere with 2 honest men of the parish, that said that they heard her husband say that she was abjured at Colchester. Then said Mr Commissary 'Do you know it for truth that she was abjured?' 'No', said they, 'but thus said her husband....'[22]

Part of the deposition of Prebendary Robert Serles reads as follows:

...that one Joan Bocher, as it is said, abjured of heresy at Colchester for opinions sustained against the Sacrament of the Altar; which has since spoken and defended openly her erronious opinions in Canterbury before many, and yet she is quit by a pardon.[23]

---

[19] 'Nota, quod iste oritur de stirpe vitiata, quia avus patris sui erat ob haeresim concrematus, ut dicitur'. *Ibid.*, 61.

[20] Harleian MS. 421. Quoted by J. E. Oxley, *The Reformation in Essex* (Manchester, 1965), 13.

[21] *i.e.* before Nevinson at the Canterbury consistorial court in 1542.

[22] Corpus Christi College, Cambridge, MS. 128. Printed in *LP.*, XVIII (ii), 313-4.

[23] *LP.*, XVIII (ii), 331.

While 'Bocher' was a very common surname at that time, it is not unreasonable to suggest that the Joan Bocher of Kent who had once abjured sacramentarian heresy at Colchester is the Joan Bocher, widow, of Steeple Bumpstead mentioned in the Lollard confessions of 1528. Davis maintains,

> ... there is little doubt that the Joan Bocher, widow, mentioned in Thomas Hemsted's abjuration of 1528 as a disciple of Richard Fox, was the Essex Lollard of Steeple Bumpstead who later became 'Joan of Kent'.[24]

On the 15th, 16th and 17th of July 1528, Geoffrey Wharton examined the wives of those Essex Lollards from Steeple Bumpstead, Colchester, Witham and Bocking who had been detected, arrested and taken to London. They were examined in the monastery of S. John's at Colchester. Although Joan Bocher is not listed among those women who appeared before the vicar-general, her abjuration probably occurred at that time.[25]

Furthermore, it may well be that Joan Bocher was related by marriage to William Bocher, the Steeple Bumpstead ploughwright whose Lollard convictions and activities were considered sufficiently serious to warrant his conveyance to London to be examined before Bishop Tunstal. If so, then Joan had married into a family with a tradition of heresy and martyrdom.[26] Her subsequent retention of – or, at least, preference for – the surname 'Bocher' even after remarriage, together with the recalcitrance and vigour with which later she courted martyrdom, indicate that she took pride in her family pedigree and desired to live up to its traditions.

---

[24] Davis, *op. cit.*, 412.
[25] Strype, *EM.*, I (i), 132-3.
[26] Thomas Hilles referred to her as 'Mother Bocher' – she could have been the mother of William Bocher. In which case her first husband had been burnt for heresy. Thirty years later during the Marian persecution William Adam, *alias* Bocher or Butcher, smith of Steeple Bumpstead, was one of three prisoners pardoned for sacramentarianism. On 13th June 1556 William Bocher was condemned to be burned as a heretic but on 3rd July 1556 he was dispensed by Archbishop Pole (Foxe, *AM.*, VIII, 154, 154n., 763; Strype, *EM.*, VI, 467-8). This tends to confirm that William Bocher was Joan Bocher's son – or possibly her nephew. See also John Davis, 'Joan of Kent, Lollardy and the English Reformation', *JEH*, 33 (1982), 225-33.

Therefore, it would appear that, in 1528, Joan Bocher was an important member of the Lollard conventicle at Steeple Bumpstead. Clandestine meetings took place in her house where both the old Wycliffite manuscript versions of the Gospels and Pauline epistles and the recently published Tyndale New Testament were read, expounded and discussed. Members of this conventicle held the usual Lollard opinions regarding the profitlessness of pardons and pilgrimages. They were sacramentarians who not only denied the real presence but held a developed 'Zwinglian' commemorative view of the Lord's Supper. At some unknown date after her detection Joan Bocher was taken to Colchester where she followed usual Lollard practice by abjuring her sacramentarian opinions.

(b) The Protestant

At least ten years elapse before the next record of Joan Bocher. By the late 1530s she was a distributor of Tyndale's New Testament among the ladies at the court of Henry VIII.[27] How she gained an entrée into such society is a mystery; possibly it was a consequence of William Bocher's trip to London. Robert Parsons (born 1546) writing in 1599, states –

In King Henries tyme when Tindal had translated and printed the new Testament in English at Colen, and began to seek meanes to have them dispersed in England ... and there was a certayn foul fusteluggs [old whore], dishonest of her body with base fellows, as was openly reported, whose name was Joan Knell alias Burcher; if I forget not, who beginning to be a great reader of Scripture herself became a principall instrument also in that tyme to devulge such Bibles as were sent, especially in the courte, where she became known to certayne women in authority; and to convey the bokes more safly, she used to bynde them in strings under her aparrell, and so to pass them into the courte; but her neerest frendship was with An Askew, whoe King henry afterwards caused to be burned for denying the reall presence in the Sacrament of the Aulter....[28]

In 1721 John Strype made use of this additional information. Doubtless he was correct in his supposition that Joan's reported

---

27 Davis suggests that Joan had become a colporteur through associating with Robert Necton and John Hacker in the Lollard conventicles of Essex (*Ibid.*, 228).

28 Robert Parsons, *A Temperate Ward-word to the ... Watchword of Sir F. Hastings* (Antwerp, 1599), RSTC 19415, 16-17.

immorality was 'but a calumny' manufactured by her enemies.[29] Furthermore, as has been argued above, Parsons was probably mistaken in assuming that Joan's personal interest in Scripture-reading began with her Bible-smuggling activities. Yet while the New Testament was read in her house in Steeple Bumpstead in 1528, Joan Bocher remained illiterate. John Foxe states that although she was *'in scripturis prompta'* she could neither read nor write.[30] This suggests that Joan – in true Lollard fashion – had memorised passages of Scripture.

The really important information here concerns her activities at court. In 1556, that able poet and layman, Miles Hogarde, referred to the circle of devout women that had gathered around Queen Catherine Parr as,
> these London ladies, & other the like, whose talke is nothig but of religion, of Peter, of Paule, & other places of Scripture.[31]

Doubtless this was the company to which Joan Bocher had gained access. Particularly important is Parsons' assertion that she was a close friend of Anne Askew. Evidently Anne's experience had a profound effect upon her. At her own trial before the Edwardine commission in 1549, Parsons records that – when sentence of death had been pronounced – she scornfully addressed the commissioners in the following terms –
> It is a goodly matter to consider your ignorance; it is not long agoe since you burned Ann Askew for a peece of bread, and yet came your selves soone after to beleeue and professe the same doctryne, for which you burned her: & now (forsooth) you wil needs burne me for a peece of fleshe, & in the end you will come to beleeve this also, when you have reade the Scriptures and understand them.[32]

Robert Parsons referred to Joan Bocher in two subsequent works. In his *A Warnword to Syr F. Hastings* of 1602 Parsons describes Joan as 'a simple woman, but yet heady and wilful by reading Scriptures in

---

29   Strype, *EM.*, II (i), 334-5.
30   John Foxe, *Rerum in ecclesia* (Basileae, 1559-63), 202-3.
31   Miles Hogarde, *The Displaying of the Protestantes* (London, 1556), STC 13557, sig. J5ʳ.
32   Parsons, 17.

English'.[33] More significant are his statements in *A Treatise of three Conversions* published in 1603 and 1604.[34] In Part II of this work, Parsons writes of 'Ioane of Kent (*alias* Ioane Knell) that had byn a handmayd of Anne Askew'.[35] In Part III Parsons, referring to Anne Askew, comments,

> And yf she had liued but few yeares longer, yt is very likely, she would have come to the point, that her deare syster, disciple & handmayd Ioane of Kent (*alias* Knell, *alias* Butcher) did. Whome she used most confidently in sendinge hereticall books hither and thither, but especially into court.[36]

Within the *Treatise* there is also a slightly more detailed account of Joan's interruption of Cranmer as he was pronouncing the commission's sentence. Parsons says that Joan 'reproached Cranmer greatly for his inconstancy in Religion', scornfully telling him -

> yt is not long agoe, synce yow condemned and burned that notable holy woman Anne Askue, for a peece of bread. And now yow will burne me for a peece of flesh. But as yow are now come to beleeue that your selues, which yow condemned in her, and are sory for her burning: so will the tyme come quicklie, that yow will beleeue that, which now yow condemne in me, and be sory also for this wronge done vnto me.[37]

Finally, in this treatise Parsons records the source of his information on Joan Bocher. He writes,

> I do assure the Reader in all sincerity, that I have it by relation and asseueration [solemn declaration] of a worshipful & honorable* Knight that afterward was of Q. Maryes priuy councell: and was either present, when these things were spoken by Ioane of Kent, or heard yt from them, that were present....[38]

In the margin against the asterisk is printed the name 'Syr Francis Inglefield'. Sir Francis Englefield was High Sheriff of Berkshire at the close of the reign of Henry VIII. Although a loyal member of Mary

---

33   Robert Parsons, *A Warnword to Syr F. Hastings* (Antwerp, 1602), RSTC 19418, 60-1.
34   Robert Parsons, *A Treatise of three Conversions of England* (St. Omer, 1603-4), RSTC 19416.
35   *Ibid.*, Part II, 592-3.
36   *Ibid.*, Part III, 496-7.
37   *Ibid.*
38   *Ibid.*, Part II, 593.

Tudor's household he was knighted by Edward VI, and upon Mary's accession he was made a privy councillor. After Mary's death he went into exile in Spain, but soon removed to Brussels in the Spanish Netherlands where he spent the remainder of his life. It was in Brussels that he became acquainted with both Nicholas Sanders and Robert Parsons.[39]

While Somerset was in power, Englefield still had access to the court; it was only after Northumberland gained the ascendancy that he, with other members of Mary Tudor's retinue, had to live in retirement. Therefore, Englefield may well have heard a first-hand account of what took place before the commissioners in S. Paul's on 30 April 1549. However, it is to be doubted that he was actually present in S. Paul's himself – although he may have been at Smithfield for Joan's execution the following year. Thus, the record of Parsons, although very late, is based upon the authoritative (albeit hostile) testimony of a contemporary witness.

Twice Parsons described Joan Bocher as a 'handmayd' of Anne Askew. Indirect confirmation of this is found in Hogarde's description of Joan as Anne Askew's 'pue fellowe'.[40] Parsons also states that Anne used Joan to distribute heretical books at court. One of the charges that Wriothesley and Rich levelled against Anne was that she was responsible for the heretical books that were discovered in the possession of certain noble ladies at the court of Henry VIII. John Bale states that Anne was barely twenty-five years of age when she was martyred in July 1546. She must, therefore, have been born in the year 1521. Furthermore, she must have been much younger (at least fifteen years) than her handmaid, Joan Bocher, who was already a widow in 1528. Bale also states that Anne had been forced into an unhappy marriage with a certain John or Thomas Kyme and that she had borne him two children before leaving him in Lincolnshire and coming to London. Therefore, the earliest possible date that Anne could have been in London is 1539, when she was eighteen.

In his *Ward-word* Robert Parsons depicted Joan Bocher as one of

---

[39]   *DNB.*, XVII.
[40]   Below, 57.

Tyndale's agents who smuggled his New Testament (or Coverdale's Bible) into the court of Henry VIII. This suggests that Joan became known at court before she met Anne Askew, through her Bible-smuggling activities in the late 1530s. Nevertheless, this brought her in touch with Anne Askew who later employed her as her personal maid, and made use of her contacts at court to smuggle in other heretical literature. If this is the correct interpretation of these statements, then Joan Bocher did not become acquainted with Anne Askew until after 1543. In order to have remarried and established herself in Kent before 1541,[41] she could hardly have fled from London later than 1539, and it is barely possible that Anne could have been in London before that year. Moreover, had Joan been in the service of Anne Askew in 1539, surely her mistress would have sent her back to Lincolnshire rather than into unknown Kent. Therefore, it is suggested that some time after her release from Canterbury prison in 1543 Joan Bocher made her way back to London. There she became acquainted with the recently-arrived Anne Askew who employed Joan as her maid and colporteur. In her capacity as Anne Askew's personal maid, Joan would almost certainly have been present at the execution of her friend and employer.

It is quite clear from all the references linking Anne and Joan that their relationship was far more intimate than that of mistress and maid. Mutual faith forged deep bonds of friendship between these two courageous women. Parsons describes Joan as the 'disciple' of Anne Askew, but it is to be doubted whether the older and more experienced woman learnt much theology from her mistress. On the other hand, Anne's superior education and deeper knowledge of the Bible renders it unlikely that she owed very much to her maid. Dickens argues that the real influence behind Anne Askew was her fellow martyr, the courtier John Lascells.[42] Doubtless, mistress and maid were a source of strength and encouragement to each other. Doctrinal discipleship there may not have been, but discipleship in suffering there undoubtedly was. When her turn came in 1549-50 Joan Bocher followed the example set by her young friend, Anne Askew.

---

[41] Below, 45-6.
[42] A. G. Dickens, *Lollards and Protestants in the Diocese of York, 1509-1558*, (Oxford, 1959), 33-4.

The second source of information on the activities of Joan Bocher at this period relates to her sojourn in Kent, where she came into prominence during the years 1541-3. At that time she made use of a royal pardon – probably that issued in February 1539 [43] – a copy of which was in her possession. This suggests that her activities at court had been detected, that her influential friends had obtained a copy of the pardon for her, and that she had fled to Kent – probably after the Act of Six Articles became effective in July 1539. Canterbury – the diocese under Cranmer's liberal jurisdiction – was the obvious choice. In view of her previous abjuration, Joan would have been foolish to have returned to Essex or anywhere within the jurisdiction of the Bishop of London. Besides, Kentish Lollard/ sacramentarian conventicles had close associations with those in Essex.[44]

In Kent, Joan probably remarried – for it is only in the records of her Kentish activities that the name of 'Baron' is found. The Canterbury priest John Milles in his evidence to the 1543 commission refers to her as 'Joan Baron, sometime called Joan Bucher of Westgate'.[45] Later, Milles referred to the evidence given by the 'parson of Westbere' and two of his parishioners who had heard her husband speak of Joan's previous abjuration at Colchester.[46] This suggests that Joan had married a man named Baron who belonged to the parish of Westbere, four miles north-east of Canterbury. However, the fact that her husband did not personally make a statement or appear before the commissioners perhaps indicates that he had died before 1543 and that, within a few years of her remarriage, Joan was once again a widow.

Corpus Christi College, Cambridge, MS CXXVIII contains the depositions made to the commission that Archbishop Cranmer established to enquire into the accusations of the Canterbury prebendaries – accusations that threatened his downfall. Particularly strong complaints were levelled against Christopher Nevinson, Cranmer's commissary and nephew by marriage. Nevinson was accused of favouring heresy through his lenient treatment of Joan

---

[43] Above, 24-5.
[44] Below, 117-8, 120-1.
[45] *LP.*, XVIII (ii), 313.
[46] *Ibid.*, 314.

Bocher. Thus, one of the tasks of the 1543 commission was to investigate 'Whether Johanna Bochier was delivered by favour of the Commissary or by the King's pardon'.[47]

According to a deposition dated 21 September 1543, the story began on the morning of Easter Day 1541 in the house in Northgate parish of John Toftes, a leading citizen of Canterbury. There, according to the conservative prebendaries, a heretical conventicle regularly gathered. There, on Easter Morning 1541, John Clercke and Joan Bocher, 'Brake their fast ... with a calf's head ... which would the same day have received their Maker'. When informed that Clerke and Bocher had eaten a calf's head that Easter morning, Nevinson the archbishop's commissary replied, 'If they have broken their fast today let them have their rights tomorrow'.[48] This noncommittal response evidently angered those who had brought the accusation.

Apparently John Toftes protected the two accused, standing surety for John Clerke and keeping Joan at his house. No doubt it was with his assistance that Joan, shortly after her detection, succeeded in escaping to Calais. Again this was an obvious choice. She could not safely return to London, and Westbere was on the river Stour, along which vessels plied regularly between Canterbury, Sandwich and Calais. On 23 September 1542 the Council of Calais wrote to the Privy Council:

> On the 4th inst., Joan Baron of Canterbury, accused here of heresy, was acquitted by verdict of 12 men. Have however repried [remanded] her for heresies objected to her at Canterbury, and ask whether to send her thither.[49]

Since the same jury convicted a certain Denys Tod of heresy on the same day, it would be interesting to know their reasons for acquitting Joan Bocher. It may be that Joan spent most of her time in Calais in custody because in 1543 John Milles referred to her as 'being a prisoner for 2 years, more or less'.[50]

---

[47] *Ibid.*, 291.
[48] *Ibid.*, 312-3.
[49] *LP.*, XVII, 453.
[50] Below, 47.

Evidently the Privy Council ordered her to be sent back to England where she was handed over to the ecclesiastical authorities at Canterbury. The archbishop's commissary was then forced to examine her – probably in the spring of 1543. Nevertheless, it is apparent from the deposition of the priest John Milles that Christopher Nevinson made three distinct attempts to dismiss the case before he finally succeeded in delivering Joan Bocher from the Westgate prison, Canterbury. According to Milles, Joan was imprisoned as a self-confessed heretic, she was held in custody for two years 'more or less', she remained unabjured and unrepentant, and then she was set at liberty by Nevinson. Thereafter she proclaimed her sacramentarian beliefs with even greater confidence and vigour. Milles wrote,

Pleaseth your Grace, most of the vulgar people think the foundation of these errors in these parts cometh by the fault of heresies not punished set forth by Joan Baron, sometime called Joan Bucher of Westgate, she being a prisoner detect of heresies, being in prison, set at liberty, free for any man to common with her, which is against the law of God and of our Sovereign King.

1. She being a prisoner for 2 years, more or less, no evidence was brought against her, though she manifestly denied the Sacrament of the Altar with many slanderous words, her own confession remaining with the spiritual officers.

2. When delivered by the temporal judge into the hands of your officers, your Commissary would have delivered her by proclamation as a 'gynteles' [genteel] person; whereupon I came in and said 'Mr. Commissary ye do not well to deliver her by proclamation, for her own confession hath condemned her'. Then said Mr. Commissary 'Be ye all able to prove that you have spoken?'…. Then said I, 'Sir her own confession is in your registry'. Then Mr. Commissary made answer and said, 'I have enquired for them but I cannot find them. But I will look them out, for shorting of the matter'….

Milles' deposition clearly indicates that Nevinson was stalling. Despite mounting pressure and the clear evidence of several witnesses, he was reluctant to proceed with an examination of the case against Joan. Eventually Joan Bocher's confession was produced and read to the court. Milles continues:

The next court day appointed for that matter, he declared her to be an heretic, both by her confession and also by witness; which thing she utterly denied. But then, said he, 'You cannot deny it', but said to her without any confession on her part of her fault or offences, or without any requiring of her part of any pardon, 'You have a thing to stick to which may do you good. I advise you to stick to it'. Then did she bring forth the King's pardon which was given to the Anabaptists for their deliverance, repenting themselves. Which pardon, what else it contained, be it in your judgement.

Milles further complained that John Toftes was permitted to plead in the consistorial court in Joan's defence even though he was not a court proctor. Finally, Joan's accusers submitted evidence that she was already an abjured heretic. Milles concludes:

Also, at that time came forth to the Court the parson of Westbere with 2 honest men of the parish, that said that they heard her husband say that she was abjured at Colchester. Then said Mr. Commissary 'Do you know it for truth that she was abjured?' 'No', said they, 'but thus said her husband'. Then said Mr. Commissary, 'I take you for no witness in this point', and so delivered her, she requiring no pardon, nor confessing her offence why the pardon should be ministered to her.[51]

Thus, Cranmer's commissary first attempted to secure the release of Joan by proclaiming her to be a 'genteel' person. Secondly, he was reluctant to produce Joan's original written confession in court – the key piece of evidence. Thirdly, he advised Joan to make use of her royal pardon – of which, he obviously had prior knowledge. Finally, he refused to accept as admissable evidence the testimony of the parson and parishioners of Westbere that Joan was already an abjured heretic. Obviously Nevinson had inside knowledge of the case and he may well have been acting on instructions from Cranmer. The fact that Joan Bocher was known to some of the ladies at court and possibly to Cranmer himself may well have qualified her for the status of 'gynteles'.

It is little wonder that John Milles was annoyed by such blatant bias in favour of a heretic. Later in the investigation, Milles replied to the interrogatories –

---

[51]   *LP.*, XVIII (ii), 313-4.

... I have had much communication of gentlemen and other of the deliverance of Jone Baron (at the table) by your commissary, whereas she nother would confess that she had denied the Sacrament of the Altar, whereby she should have asked the King's Majesty his pardon, nother yet asked pardon; but she having a pardon in her bosom, was bid deliver it (as she did) and thereby was delivered....[52]

Further testimony to Joan Bocher's heresy was borne by Edmond Shether in a letter to the Duke of Norfolk:

Also, the wittnes of Joh'n Bocher's words against the sacrament of the Altar be alive and shall shortly be put in a remembrance of the same.[53]

Finally, there was the deposition of Prebendary Robert Serles who, according to Strype,[54] was responsible for gathering the evidence against Cranmer and Nevinson, Serles deposed,

...that one Joan Boocher, as it is said, abjured of heresy at Colchester for opinions sustained against the Sacrament of the Altar; which hath since spoken and defended openly her erronious opinions in Canterbury before many, and yet she is quit by a pardon.[55]

Here within these depositions is surely evidence that – even as early as 1543 – Thomas Cranmer was privately sympathetic towards the sacramentarians in his diocese.[56] It was not without justification that Miles Hogarde, writing in 1556, could refer to –

Joane Butcher, whiche in the beginnying of oure new founde opinions was greatlye mainteined by Cranmere, in Cantorburye, & other places of Kent....[57]

---

52 *Ibid.*, 366.
53 *Ibid.*, 359.
54 Strype, *Memorials of Archbishop Cranmer* (Oxford, 1848-54), I, 257.
55 *LP.*, XVIII (ii), 331.
56 In April 1538 Cranmer had interceded with Cromwell on behalf of certain conventiclers from Smarden and Pluckley who had been indicted before the Quarter Sessions at Canterbury for favouring the 'new doctrine'. (Below, pp. 187-8). Doubtless they too were sacramentarians.
57 Hogarde, sig. J3^r.

There is no evidence from this period in her career to suggest that Joan Bocher's beliefs had yet developed in an anabaptist direction. The author of the article on Joan Bocher in the *Dictionary of National Biography* would seem to be mistaken in his assertion that, 'Before 1543 she had adopted opinions about the incarnation which conflicted with the contemporary notions of both catholic and protestant orthodoxy'.[58]

It is in the traditional Lollard role of colporteur that Parsons depicts Joan's activities in the 1530s. She is noted for her Bible-reading, Bible-smuggling, and friendship with the sacramentarian Anne Askew. At King Henry's court she mixed with those ladies whose interests were in personal religion and Pauline theology. Even the most committed lady in that circle was no anabaptist. In 1604 Robert Parsons examined the letter that Anne Askew's friend and fellow martyr, John Lascells, had written while in prison awaiting execution, which had been published by Foxe. Parsons argued that Lascells' attack on transubstantiation followed neither Luther, nor Zwingli, nor Calvin but derived from the extremist, Carlstadt.[59] However, John Lascells, Anne Askew, and their associates could equally be designated disciples of John Frith.[60] Their 'mature' Protestant understanding of the eucharist could well have been assisted by ertswhile Lollards such as Joan Bocher. We have already noted the developed views on the nature of that ordinance held by members of the Steeple Bumpstead conventicle.[61]

Certainly John Milles refers to Joan's possession of a pardon that was given to repentant anabaptists, but the pardon of February 1539 also included sacramentarians.[62] The general pardon, which distinguished between sacramentarians and anabaptists, was not promulgated until July 1540. There is no evidence that Joan had espoused a Melchiorite christology or any of the eight anabaptist tenets delineated in the pardon of 1540. Would Cranmer and Nevinson have so blatantly protected her in 1543 if she was known to be in sympathy with the Continental anabaptist movement? Like many former Lollards, Joan may well have

---

[58] *DNB.*, II; also Horst, 109.
[59] Parsons, *Three Conversions*, Part III, 496ff.
[60] A. G. Dickens, *The English Reformation* (London, 1964), 195.
[61] Above, 37, 40.
[62] Above, 24-5.

been an extreme sectarian and vigorously opposed to any erastian religious settlement, but that does not make her an anabaptist according to the terms in which anabaptism was defined in 1540.

Furthermore, in 1541 Joan was detected as a sacramentary, not as an anabaptist. As Davis remarks, 'It is as a sacramentarian and not as a Radical that Joan features in the evidence of 1543'.[63] John Milles, Robert Serles, and Edmond Shether all agree in their evidence that she spoke against the 'Sacrament of the Altar', and that she acted in conformity with her denial of traditional sacramental teaching. At no point did they refer to any additional heretical beliefs maintained by her – beliefs which would have been even more damning in the estimation of the civil and ecclesiastical authorities – beliefs which would have added weight to their complaints – beliefs which it would have been to their advantage to expose. Moreover, the deposition of the prebendaries also provides us with a glimpse into the doctrine and practices of the conventicle that gathered at John Toftes' house in Canterbury. It reads:

Jo. Toftes is noted as a common maintainer and harbourer of persons accused of heresies, and of persons who have made themselves priests... he kept Joan Boucher in his house after she was accused. He was surety for one John Clercke.... His house has been the resort of Bland, Tournour, the parson of Hothefild... he said in Easter week last that it was abominable idolatry to kneel before the Sepulture... that it was no honour to God to have lights set up, for Christ is 'Lux Mundi'. He assisted and defended Joan Boucher in the consistory of Canterbury when she was detected as a sacramentary. When asked by Andrew Kempe why he had spoiled the images, he said that he had done nothing but his Prince's commandment.[64]

Anti-clericalism, iconoclasm, abomination of ceremonial and ornamentation, sacramentarianism – these are all typically Lollard features which were adopted by the later Protestant reformers. Moreover, the other members of this Canterbury conventicle mentioned in the deposition – John Bland, vicar of Adisham, Richard Turner, vicar of Chartham, and 'the parson of Hothfield' – all became prominent

---

[63]   Davis, 411.
[64]   *LP.*, XVIII (ii), 312.

Kentish supporters of the Edwardine reformation.[65] By no stretch of the imagination could these men be described as anabaptists. Thus, both the London circle to which Joan belonged in the 1530s and the Canterbury conventicle to which she attached herself in the early 1540s were dominated by establishment Protestants rather than sectarian anabaptists. Joan's fervent sacramentarianism and vigorous sectarianism doubtless caused her to be widely known and highly influential among the former Lollards of east and south-east Kent.

If Joan Bocher did adopt Continental anabaptist doctrines – as seems probable – then such influences are more likely to have occurred after 1543. Perhaps her activities as a colporteur in the service of Anne Askew brought her into contact with the dormant conventicle of foreign anabaptists in London. Perhaps she was influenced by their book on the incarnation. At any rate, the burning of Anne Askew in 1546 may well have been the unnerving event that finally caused her to throw in her lot with the London radicals.

(c) The Radical
On 22 April 1549 Joan Bocher appeared before Cranmer and the commissioners in S. Paul's. According to Jordan and Ridley, Joan had been reported to the Privy Council by Kentish magistrates as a confirmed anabaptist.[66] This suggests that Joan had returned to Kent after the death of her mistress, and resumed her proselytising activities after the death of Henry VIII. Evidently the Council ordered her to be brought to London to be examined by the commission. This time, inspired by the example of Anne Askew, Joan Bocher was determined neither to abjure nor to make use of any royal pardon. Thus, she was the only heretic who – having been examined by the commissioners and found guilty – refused to abjure. Her case was then adjourned while the sentence was determined.

---

65 The 'parson of Hothfield' was Henry Goodrick (Goderick) who was a well-known Protestant preacher in the Ashford-Canterbury-Folkestone district. He may have been a servant of Thomas Cromwell before Latimer obtained a license for him to preach and he was appointed vicar of Hothfield *circa* 1534 (*LP.*, VII, 318; IX, 76; XIV (i), 480-1). Was he, perhaps, a third brother of Thomas Goodrich, Bishop of Ely?

66 Jordan, *loc. cit.*; Ridley, 162-3. Perhaps she was one of the two Kentish anabaptists who figured in Bishop Ridley's discussions with Bishop Gardiner in 1547 (Above, 33, 33n, 35).

On Saturday 27 April 1549 John Champneys was examined and recanted the heresy of which he was convicted, and then the following Tuesday (30 April) Joan reappeared before the commissioners for sentencing. The commissioners condemned Joan to suffer death by burning as a relapsed heretic, their findings and sentence being recorded in Cranmer's register. Here, the particular belief which she stubbornly maintained and for which she was punished is stated –

> That you beleve that the worde was made fleshe in the virgyn's belly, but that Christe toke fleshe of the virgyn you beleue not; because the flesh of the virgyn being the outward man synfully gotten, and bourne in synne, but the worde by the consent of the inward man of the virgin was made fleshe....[67]

Sentence of excommunication was passed upon her and she was handed over to the civil authorities for punishment. Peter Heylyn states that Cranmer took great care over Joan Bocher's examination and spent much time trying to persuade her to 'a better sense'. He says that it was when the Archbishop was on the point of pronouncing sentence that Joan loudly interrupted the proceedings reproaching Cranmer for his condemnation of Anne Askew.[68] Heylyn's source for this information is not Robert Parsons (used by Strype) but another Elizabethan recusant, Nicholas Sanders, whose *De origine ac progressu schismatis Anglicani* was published in Ingoldstadt in 1587.

Joan was imprisoned in Newgate while the Privy Council considered what action to take. Some members expressed doubt as to whether the death sentence could be imposed, since Somerset had repealed the Heresy Act. However, the Lord Chancellor (Sir Richard Rich) pointed out that the King might at will order her execution within the bounds of the Common Law. Somerset was not prepared to countenance this, and so she remained in prison for a year while many attempts were made to obtain a recantation. It is significant that the final decision to burn her was not taken until after Somerset had fallen from power.[69]

---

67   Folios 74-5 printed in Wilkins, *Concilia*, IV, 43-4.
68   Peter Heylyn, *Ecclesia Restaurata* (1661) (Cambridge, 1849), 186-7.
69   Jordan, *Threshold of Power*, 329.

The examination of Joan Bocher evidently persuaded the Reformers of the need to take further action to counteract the spread of such unorthodox views. On 20 June 1549 John Hooper published his *A Lesson of the Incarnation of Christ*. In this brief work Bishop Hooper marshals powerful arguments from Scripture to support traditional christology against Melchiorite and other radical interpretations.[70] Five days after the publication of this treatise Hooper wrote to Bullinger in Zurich. He complained of those bishops who would not permit Reformed preaching within their dioceses. In London this was being circumvented by the holding of public lectures at S. Paul's Cross four times a week. He continues:

> The anabaptists flock to the place, and give me much trouble with their opinions respecting the incarnation of the Lord; for they deny altogether that Christ was born of the virgin Mary according to the flesh.... Although I am unable to satisfy their obstinacy, yet the Lord by his word shuts their mouths, and their heresies are more and more detested by the people.[71]

Early in 1550, Roger Hutchinson published a much longer work on the subject.[72] This appears to have been inspired by his interviews with Joan Bocher in Newgate prison. Evidently Joan had still not been burnt at the time of writing, for Hutchinson makes no mention of her execution.

Horst states that 'during the year following her sentence Joan was imprisoned at the house of chancellor [Richard] Rich', and he adds, 'this arrangement may be a clue to her social standing'.[73] However, a closer examination of the evidence reveals that it was only after the Council had finally decided to burn Joan that she was then taken into the house of Sir Richard Rich in one last ditch attempt to persuade her to recant. On 6 November 1555, during his examination of John Philpot, Rich remarked
–

> I had myself Joan of Kent a sevennight in my house after the writ was out for her to be burnt, where my lord of Canterbury and bishop Ridley resorted almost daily unto her. But she was so high in the spirit, that they could do nothing with her for all their learning; but she went wilfully unto the fire....[74]

---

[70]   *Later Writings of Bishop Hooper*, ed. Nevinson (PS. Cambridge, 1852), 1-18.

[71]   Hooper to Bullinger, 25 June 1549; printed in *Original Letters,* ed. Robinson, (PS. Cambridge, 1842), I, 65-6.

[72]   Roger Hutchinson, *The image of God, or laie mans booke*, (London, 1550) STC. 14019.

[73]   Horst, 110.

[74]   Foxe, *AM.*, VII, 631. Sir Thomas More had taken convicted heretics into his home in a final attempt to convert them. Sir Richard Rich evidently followed the example of his late neighbour (*DNB.*, XLVIII).

Apart from that final week, Joan Bocher had spent the whole year from April 1549 to April 1550 in Newgate prison. Charles Wriothesley records:

> Memorandum: the 2 day of May, Joane Barne, *alias* Joane Bocher, *alias* Joan of Kent, was burnt in Smythfeild, which sayd woman was condempned the 29 [*sic*] of Aprill, 1549... and she had lyen in Newegate ever since, and could never be converted by noe godly man.[75]

The year between her condemnation and execution was spent in seeking her conversion. She was regularly interviewed and interrogated by the leading reformers – Nicholas Ridley, Hugh Latimer, Thomas Goodrich, Roger Hutchinson, John Philpot, Thomas Lever and Archbishop Cranmer himself are all known to have visited and reasoned with her. Heylyn states that, not only were these sessions all to no avail, merely confirming the heretic in her obstinacy, but they added to her notoriety and gave 'no small encouragement to others, for entertaining the like dangerous and unchristian errors'.[76] Doubtless, it was for this reason that the Council finally decided to burn her.

After the initial condemnation of Joan as a relapsed heretic in April 1549, Thomas Cranmer did all in his power to save her. Strype is at pains to emphasise that the archbishop was not present at the Council-meeting when the decision to burn her was taken – although Goodrich, Bishop of Ely, was in attendance.[77] He further states that when she was removed to the Lord Chancellor's house Cranmer and Ridley came and reasoned with her every day.[78] The main responsibility for the execution of Joan of Kent must lie with the Privy Council – and probably with powerful laymen such as Chancellor Rich and the Earl of Warwick. Rich had previously taken a leading part in the examination of Anne Askew and was to adopt a similar role in the Marian period, Warwick

---

[75]   Wriothesley, II, 37-8.
[76]   Heylyn, 187.
[77]   Strype, *EM.*, II (i), 334.
[78]   *Ibid.*, *Memorials of Cranmer*, II, 97ff.

had no time for dissenters in general and anabaptists in particular. Certainly the Duke of Somerset had been restored to the Council on 10 April, but he no longer held any real power. Thus, on 27 April 1550 the Council issued a warrant to the Lord Chancellor to prepare a writ ordering the Sheriff of London to proceed with the execution. It may be significant that Joan had been removed from Newgate two days before the Council took its decision – perhaps that is why Cranmer absented himself from that particular meeting.[79]

Jordan argues that Cranmer 'bore a direct moral responsibility' for the burning of Joan Bocher because 'he did nothing to oppose the dreadful action'.[80] Yet, what more could the Primate have done for Joan than he had done for her over the past decade? Neither Cranmer nor Somerset could protect her any longer without jeopardising their own positions. As Horst states, the burning of Joan was a defeat for Archbishop Cranmer and an indication of the growing power of Warwick. He rightly points out that it was not long afterwards that the Council accused Cranmer of tolerating the anabaptists of Kent and ordered him to deal with them.[81]

In the Latin edition of his martyrology John Foxe recounts how he begged John Rogers (the Bible translator – soon to be appointed lecturer at S. Paul's) to use his influence with Cranmer and Ridley to save Joan's life.[82] However, Rogers vigorously opposed anabaptism (Below p. 117) and refused to intervene.[83]

The sentence was duly carried out on 2 May at Smithfield. In a final attempt to convert her, Dr John Scory (soon to be consecrated Bishop of Rochester in place of Ridley) preached at her. Nearly all the chroniclers

---

[79] It may be that Cranmer was genuinely shaken by Joan's christological heresy and angered by her obstinacy. However, the fact remains that Cranmer was absent from the Council when the decision was taken – and such absences were very rare during the year from December 1549 to December 1550. See D. E. Hoak, *The King's Council in the reign of Edward VI*, (Cambridge, 1976).

[80] Jordan, *Threshold of Power,* 330.

[81] Horst, 111.

[82] Foxe, *Rerum*, 202.

[83] J. F. Mozley, *John Foxe and his Book* (London, 1940), 35-6.

record Joan's violent reaction.[84] Of particular note is the account of
Miles Hogarde which was published in London only six years after the
event. Hogarde implies that, at her last hour, Joan Bocher imitated the
actions of Anne Askew. He writes:

> In lyke sorte the grosse martyr, Joane Butcher handled the matter. And
> where as one Skorie then preached before the people, in tyme of her
> death, she reuyled and spytted at hym, makyng the sygne of the
> gallowes towards hym, boldly, affirming that al they that wer not of her
> opinion, shuld be dampned. Yea & she was so bold to say, that a M. in
> London wer of her sect. Such & the like was ye charitie of Anne
> Askewe, so ofte by Bale lykened to Blandina that true martyr of
> Christes church, in his furious boke.... The sayde Anne Askewe, was
> of suche charitie, that when pardon was offered, she defied them all,
> revyling the offerers thereof, with suche opprobrious names, that are
> not worthy rehersall, makying the lyke sygnes too the preacher at her
> death, as her pue fellowe & syster in Christ, Joane Butcher dyd, at
> Skorie aforesayde.[85]

Anne Askew had withstood several interrogations; before her
execution she had been racked by Rich and Wriothesley. Little wonder,
then, that at her final moments she had behaved with something less than
decorum. Likewise, Joan Bocher had been held in prison under sentence
of death for a year, she too (although far less educated than her 'pue
fellowe & syster in Christ') had resisted numerous interrogations.
Violent hysteria during the final ordeal was to be expected from such a
vigorous nonconformist. Burnet's comment is probably closer to the
truth –

> The woman's carriage made her be looked on as a frantic person fitter
> for Bedlam than a stake.[86]

Thus, the proto-martyr of Edward's reign was burned in Smithfield on
2 May 1550. That day the young King recorded in his diary:

> Joan Bocher, otherwise called Joan of Kent, was burned for holding
> that Christ was not incarnate of the Virgin Mary, being condemned the

---

[84]   When examining Roger Holland in May 1558 Bishop Bonner referred to Joan
       Bocher's deranged state of mind (Foxe, *AM.*, VIII, 479).

[85]   Hogarde, sig. E6ᵛ-E7ᵛ.

[86]   G. Burnet, *The History of the Reformation of the Church of England*, ed.
       Pocock, (Oxford, 1865), II, 202.

year before but kept in hope of conversion; and the 30 of April the Bishop of London and the Bishop of Ely were [*sic*] to persuade her. But she withstood them and reviled the preacher that preached at her death.[87]

Evidently, the execution was regarded at the time as a notable event – for it was recorded by most of the contemporary chroniclers. Charles Wriothesley recorded that 'she dyed in her evill opinion like a wretch'.[88] Martin Micronius mentioned her execution in a letter to Bullinger dated London, 20 May 1550.[89] It is also recorded in the 1552 edition of *A breviat chronicle*, by the Grey Friars chronicler, in Fabyan's *Chronicle* of 1559, and by John Stow – both in his *London Chronicles* and in the 1614 edition of his *Annals*.

John Foxe included an account of the execution of Joan Bocher in the original Latin edition of his martyrology which was published in Basle in 1559. However, it was not included in subsequent English editions. There are, in fact, only three passing references to Joan in the *Acts and Monuments*, and it is clear that Foxe attempted to dismiss her as a figure of little importance. For example, in V:704 he merely records that she 'died for certain articles not much necessary here to be rehearsed'. Clearly John Foxe considered Joan to have been a dangerous heretic whose opinions deserved to be suppressed rather than publicised. Nevertheless he deplored the drastic measures that were taken against her – measures that were later applauded by John Philpot. Foxe records Philpot as saying –

As for Joan of Kent, she was a vain woman (I knew her well), and a heretic indeed, well worthy to be burned.[90]

However, the opinion of Philpot, Foxe and the Protestant establishment was not shared by a large number of ordinary Londoners. Heylyn records (probably on the authority of Sanders) that the crowd

---

[87] *The Chronicle and Political Papers of Edward VI*, ed. Jordan, (London, 1966), 23.

[88] *loc. cit.*

[89] *Original Letters*, II, 560.

[90] Foxe, *AM.*, VII, 631. Foxe may not have known very much about Joan Bocher or any of the radicals examined by the heresy commission. Soon after the accession of Edward VI he had gone down from Oxford and entered the service of the Duke of Norfolk as a tutor in his Surrey household (Mozley, *op. cit.*). However, it could be that Foxe deliberately suppressed information concerning the English radicals because he disagreed with their theological views so strongly (Above 29).

which gathered at Smithfield for the burning of Joan insisted that Scory prove, 'that point for denial whereof the obstinate wretch had been condemned'.[91] The crowd's sympathy for her evidently encouraged Joan to make the bold claim that 'a M. in London wer of her sect'. Perhaps this was a wild exaggeration, but there is strong evidence to suggest that a number of Londoners as well as Kentish men agreed with her doctrine. John Standish, archdeacon of Colchester, writing in 1556, stated –

...Joane of Kent ... had favourers whiche bothe thought & sayd when she was burnt, that she was the Martyr of God.[92]

Evidently there were those who considered Joan Bocher to be a martyr *par eminence* and who referred to her as 'The Martyr' (of God).

No doubt it was as an immediate response to this popular sympathy for Joan that Edmund Becke composed his long poem entitled, *A brefe confutacion of this most detestable, & Anabaptistical opinion, that Christ dyd not take hys flesh of the blessed Vyrgyn Mary nor any corporal substaunce of her body. For the maintenaunce whereof Jhone Bucher otherwise called Jhone of Kent, most obstinately suffered and was burned in Smythfyelde the ii day of May Anno Domini MDL.*[93] Collier describes this composition as 'a curious specimen of argumentative divinity in verse'.[94] Doubtless, Becke (who was associated with Canterbury and may have known Joan personally) believed that he could more easily influence theologically untrained Londoners to favour orthodox christology by the employment of simple verse rather than dull prose. The following stanzas illustrate both the skill of Becke's composition and the power of his arguments –

Stanza 5

God promised to Eue, that the sead of a womanne
Shulde treade downe the head of the subtill serpente.
This promise was fully accomplyshed than
When Christ became man, and made the attonemente.

---

[91]   *loc. cit.*

[92]   John Standish, *The triall of the supremacy*, (London, 1556), RSTC 23211, sig. A7ᵛ-A8ʳ.

[93]   London, 1550. STC. 1709. Reprinted in J. P. Collier, *Illustrations of Early English Popular Literature* (London, 1863). Republished New York, 1966; vol. II [no pagination].

[94]   *Ibid.*

This seade was of his mother, and not from heaven sente;
How can it be called the sede of a woman truly,
Which taketh no substaunce, nor parte of her bodye?
Stanza 7
How could it be their sead, whiche toke not their substaunce,
But came downe from heaven, and was not of their kind?
The Scripture conteineth no such repugnaunce:
Who shalbe able by the same to proue or to finde
To warrant Christes humanyty, or beleue it in his mynd?
If ye make it vncertayne of whom he did take it,
It appereth by thys opinion the deuyll is awaked.
Stanza 18
Christ toke the sede of Abraham, he toke it not of Aungelles,
So that he became like to his brethren in al thinges,
Synne only excepte: thus playnly Paule telles.
Where came he by thys flesh which amongst us he brings?
Had he fethers as well as flesh, and came downe with wings?
Christ came to be a mediatoure: it was requisite that he
Shuld be partaker of the godhede, and of our humanitye.

We cannot know how effective this poetic apology proved. It may not have circulated very widely since only a single copy now survives. Undoubtedly the execution of Joan Bocher had a more sobering effect upon radical and sectarian Londoners than Becke's poem. Heylyn observes:

... this terrible execution did not so prevail as to extirpate and exterminate the like impious dotages, though it suppressed them for a time.[95]

The case of Joan Bocher also made an impact upon those who sought to maintain and defend traditional Catholic orthodoxy. In 1556, Miles Hogarde – apparently making use of Cranmer's register – listed the heretical extremes to which Protestantism had sunk. Among the anabaptists he mentions, 'Joane of Kent a great pratler of divinite... was worthely burned in Smythfielde'.[96] In the same year John Standish also referred to Joan as an example of Protestant extremism. Later, after the Elizabethan Settlement, Catholic recusants such as Nicholas Sanders and

---

[95]   *loc. cit.*
[96]   Hogarde, sig. B3[r.]

Robert Parsons used her condemnation and execution to illustrate their arguments. In the course of his debate with Bishop Jewel, Thomas Harding asked,

David George, that took upon him to be Christ... was he your brother? To come near home, Joan of Kent, that filth, who took forth a lesson further than you taught her, I trow, or yet preach, was she a sister of yours?[97]

By contrast, the English Familists continued to revere Joan as a martyr and blamed Cranmer and Ridley for her execution.[98]

Horst concludes that the account of Joan's trial and burning 'provides details about a nonconformist sect, probably anabaptist, with centres in London and Kent'.[99] While Horst's use of the terms 'sect' and 'anabaptist' convey impressions of a distinctive ecclesiology and precise theology which the evidence does not warrant, nevertheless it would appear that – by 1549 – Joan Bocher had (as Harding stated) 'taken a lesson further than the Reformers taught her'. By 1549 she had adopted a radical christology that was characteristic of Dutch and Flemish anabaptists: and it is evident that there were a number of people who shared her doctrinal opinions and sympathised with her nonconformity both in London and Kent.

A year after his previous letter, and nearly two months after the burning of Joan, Bishop Hooper again wrote to Bullinger in Zurich. He gives the following account of his movements –

Having returned to London on the fourteenth day, I am going, by the King's command, tomorrow or the next day into Kent and Essex.... That district is troubled with the frenzy of the anabaptists more than any other part of the Kingdom.[100]

Thus, those who held the opinions which Hooper had described to Bullinger in his letter of June 1549 were to be found, not only in London and Kent, but also in Essex – that is, in the three areas in which Joan Bocher had contacts. Hooper's description of the doctrines of these

---

[97]   John Jewel, 'The Defence of the Apology of the Church of England' in *Works of Bp. Jewel*, ed. Ayre (PS. Cambridge, 1848), III, 187.

[98]   Thomas Rogers, *The Catholic Doctrine of the Church of England*, ed. Perowne (PS. Cambridge, 1854), 350; Below, 331, 334.

[99]   Horst, 111.

[100]   Letter XXXIX dated London, 29 June 1550 in *Original Letters*, I, 86-7.

London anabaptists[101] can be summarised as follows:–
1. In christology they denied the human flesh of our Lord.
2. In soteriology they maintained a sinless perfectionism, with an associated freedom of the will for the regenerate.
3. In revelation they argued for a further revelation beyond that contained in Scripture.
Certainly Joan Bocher held the first of these and probably the second, but in the slender evidence available on her beliefs in the latter years of her life, there is nothing to suggest that she maintained the third.

Roger Hutchinson supplies the most detailed account of her christology. When he and Thomas Lever visited Joan in Newgate they quoted the text, 'The seed of the woman shall bruise the serpent's head'. Joan replied,

I deny not that Christ is Mary's seed, or the woman's seed; nor I deny him not to be a man; but Mary had two seeds, one seed of her faith, and another seed of her flesh and in her body. There is a natural and a corporal seed, and there is a spiritual and an heavenly seed, as we may gather of St. John, where he saith, 'The seed of God remaineth in him, and he cannot sin'. And Christ is her seed; but he is become man of the seed of her faith and belief; of spiritual seed, not natural seed; for her seed and flesh was sinful, as the flesh and seed of others.[102]

This dualist approach to christology finds a counterpart in John Champneys' exposition of the nature of the regenerate man.[103] Both have a Flemish counterpart in the Loist concept of the two *homines*.[104] Untrained lay teachers such as John Champneys and Joan Bocher

---

101 Letter XXXIII, 25 June 1549, *Ibid.*, I, 65ff.
102 Hutchinson, 145-6.
103 John Champneys, *The Harvest is at Hand* (London, 1548), STC 4956, sig. C1^r-C4^v, C6^v, D5^r-D6^v.
104 Davis, 410. The Loists derived their name from (E)Loy (Lodewijk) Pruystinck or Schaliedekker, a slater of Antwerp. Loy and some of his disciples disputed with Luther and Melanchthon at Wittenberg in March 1524. Among other heresies, he taught that sin is not committed so long as one does not so intend. Loy maintained that man's flesh and spirit are thoroughly independent, having no influence upon each other. Therefore the regenerate spirit of a man incurs no responsibility for the weakness of the flesh. Loy was burned at Vilvorde on 25 October 1545. In February 1546 three other leaders of the sect were executed, and its remaining members in Antwerp and Amsterdam seem to have merged with the Davidists (Williams, *Radical Reformation*, 351-4; ME., II, III). William Turner lists the Loists in his *Preseruatiue* (sig. A3^r).

generally accepted the simple traducianist view of the means by which sin is transmitted. For such folk the human flesh is inherently sinful. How, then, could a sinless Saviour effect the sinner's salvation if he received his flesh from Mary? It is significant that Joan should point out to Hutchinson that Mary's 'seed and flesh was sinful, as the flesh and seed of others'. Catholic dogma has made an unsatisfactory attempt to solve this problem with the doctrine of the immaculate conception. On the other hand, the religious experience of the regenerate Christian renders it easy to accept a naive dualist anthropology or christology, *i.e.* the natural man and the spiritual man, the inward man and the outward man, the corporal seed and the heavenly seed.

Equally evident from the extant sources is the fact that Joan believed in the freedom of the human will. Her indictment reads, 'That you beleue that ... the worde by the consent of the inward man of the virgyn was made fleshe'.[105] According to Hutchinson, she argued that 'Christ... became man of the seed of her faith and belief'.[106] Furthermore, Joan's use of *I John* 3:9 may be an indication that she, like Hooper's London anabaptists, maintained that the regenerate were incapable of sin.[107] Here, again, Joan Bocher's belief in human freedom (and, possibly, in human impeccability) finds echoes in the teaching of John Champneys and the free-willers of the following decade.

In a sermon preached before the Countess of Suffolk at Grimsthorpe in 1552, Hugh Latimer gave a rather different account of Joan Bocher's christology. He stated,
    I told you, the last time, of one Joan of Kent, which was in this foolish opinion, that she should say our Saviour was not very man, and had not received flesh of his mother Mary: and yet she could shew no reason why she should believe so. Her opinion was this, as I

---

[105] *loc. cit.*
[106] *loc. cit.*
[107] Hooper informed Bullinger that, 'They contend that a man who is reconciled to God is without sin and free from all stain of concupiscence, and that nothing of the old Adam remains in his nature; and a man, they say, who is thus regenerate cannot sin. They add that all hope of pardon is taken away from those who, after having received the Holy Ghost, fall into sin'.

told you before, the Son of God, said she, penetrated through her, as through a glass, taking no substance of her... so this foolish woman denied the common creed, and said that our Saviour had a phantastical body....[108]

Latimer may have known Joan during her latter years in Kent, he was certainly among the commissioners who tried and condemned her in 1549. Moreover, he had interrogated Joan while she was in Newgate. Therefore the evidence supplied by Latimer that she advocated a Docetic christology – although it conflicts with that of Hutchinson – must be taken seriously. Joan Bocher was an elderly illiterate woman; she may well have made contradictory statements to the various eminent men who interviewed her in prison. However, if on some occasions she did echo the gnostic teaching of Valentinus it need imply no more than a reaffirmation of her original Lollard aversion to mariolatry.

(d) Conclusion

The case of Joan Bocher is of unique importance in the history of English religious radicalism in the sixteenth century. Her importance lies, not merely in the fact that she was the only native-born Englishman or woman to suffer the extreme penalty for her beliefs during the Edwardine regime, but in the fact that the development of those beliefs can be traced. Here we find a woman with a typically Lollard background in the late 1520s associating with sacramentarian Protestants in London and Canterbury during the late 1530s and early 1540s, but who – by 1549 – had proceeded even further theologically than the English reformers cared to go. By the late 1540s this former Lollard had adopted a christology, anthropology, and ecclesiology which her opponents stigmatised as anabaptist.

One can also discern a gradual strengthening of her convictions – or, at least, of the vigour with which she proclaimed them. Shortly after her detection in 1528, Joan Bocher had followed the traditional Lollard practice and abjured her beliefs. There is no suggestion that she organised the Steeple Bumpstead conventicle or that she preached at its meetings, Joan simply made her house available for them. However, by 1541 she was expounding her sacramentarian doctrine to Kentish conventiclers and enjoying great influence among them. Nevertheless,

---

[108] High Latimer, *Remains*, ed. Corrie (PS., Cambridge, 1845), 114.

her behaviour before Cranmer's commissary can at best be described as equivocal. First she made a full confession, then she denied it, and finally she resorted to the royal pardon. By 1549 she was regarded as the most notorious anabaptist in Kent. Having been arrested and taken to London, Joan remained utterly obdurate both before the commission and under interrogation in Newgate. Her steadfastness during the ensuing year gained her both renown and popular sympathy. At the last – although possibly unbalanced and hysterical – she remained loyal to her convictions, and died the death of a martyr.

What had brought about this change from timidity to bravado? Almost certainly it was the example of her friend, Anne Askew. Joan's actions both before the commissioners in S. Paul's and before Scory at Smithfield were a conscious and deliberate imitation of those of her friend three years earlier. The similarities in their circumstances had not escaped Joan's notice. Like Anne she had been condemned by Cranmer and the English 'establishment', like Anne she had been imprisoned in Newgate, like Anne she had suffered at the hands of Sir Richard Rich. Therefore she was determined to face her burning like Anne. No doubt she hoped that, since the martyrdom of Anne Askew had served to publicise and gain sympathy for the cause she espoused, so her own martyrdom would do likewise.

Development is even more apparent in Joan's understanding of doctrine. However, her radical christology, implicit perfectionism and belief in human free will need not be entirely ascribed to the influence of Continental anabaptism. The Lollards' aversion for mariolatry, their extreme sacramentarianism, and the inadequacy of their soteriology made the extreme elements among them ready for such influences by the 1530s. The refined version of the doctrine of the celestial flesh which Joan explained to Roger Hutchinson strongly indicates the use of Continental apologetics. Utilisation of the Loist (or Spiritualist) concept of the two *homines* provided Joan with a rationale for her own experience of spiritual regeneration. This in turn facilitated belief in a full restoration of the original Adamic nature with its true autonomy, also the possibility of sinless perfection for the regenerate. Under the influence of Continental Spiritualism, Lollard exegesis of Scripture ceased to centre upon the Synoptic Gospels and the Epistle of James and turned to the Johannine literature. Traditional concepts of discipleship, *imitatio Christi,* good works and legal obedience tended to become absorbed in a new emphasis upon the regenerative work of the Holy Spirit, upon brotherly love, and the attainment of moral perfection. Nevertheless – as with the later Lollards, but unlike the magisterial reformers – Pauline soteriology remained a mystery to both English and Continental radicals.

In one aspect the teaching and practice of Joan Bocher shows no change or development. In 1528 she was a firm nonconformist and she remained a vigorous sectarian throughout her career. There seems to have been a reluctance among some of the later Lollards to support the magisterial reformation in general and the Edwardine reforms in particular. This is hardly surprising among people in whom generations of protest, persecution and social isolation would have bred a suspicion for all educated clergy and all religious establishments. On the other hand, these obstinate individualists would have had a natural kinship with sectarian refugees from the Continent – many of whom were from a similar artisan social background.

Undoubtedly, there was a cross-fertilisation of ideas between English Lollards and Continental radicals in the south-east of England during the 1530s, 40s and 50s. However, the very vigour with which such recalcitrant Lollards as Joan Bocher maintained their freedom of worship, and opposed the Protestant establishment, opened the way to heresy. The remaining Lollard conventicles were exposed to the influence of equally uneducated but more charismatic prophets and teachers from the Netherlands. Surely Davis is close to the truth when he writes,
> It was in this sort of continuing eclectic sectarianism in which some Lollards indulged that the Radical doctrines expressed by Thombe and Bocher could evolve with only the minimum of continental influence.[109]

As far as it can be discerned, the doctrine of Joan Bocher appears to have been less biblically orientated than that of her friend and exemplar, Anne Askew. Certainly, as far as the reformers were concerned, she expressed herself less convincingly and with less clarity. However, this

---

[109] Davis, 412.

is explained by her social origins. Joan Bocher was far less educated than Anne Askew. In fact she was an illiterate woman who had committed large portions of the Bible to memory. She was classed as a 'gynteles' person, not because of her birth or upbringing, but because of her associations with Bible-reading ladies at the court of Henry VIII. Parsons stated, 'beginning to be a great reader of Scripture herself... she became known to certayne women in authority'.[110] Dickens notes the wide social spectrum from which the members of those early Bible-reading circles were drawn. He writes,

In London there had developed heretical groups compounded of people with varied social and educational backgrounds and it became increasingly easy for working-class Protestants to gain indoctrination from educated leaders.[111]

In 1528 Joan Bocher was a Lollard heretic, fifteen years later she was still guilty of sacramentarian heresy, twenty years later (when sacramentarianism had been rendered respectable) she was found guilty of 'horrible' christological heresy. One is left wondering whether the real 'heresy' for which Joan suffered at the hands of authority was neither Lollardy, nor Sacramentarianism, nor Anabaptism. Indeed, was her crime doctrinal at all? Was it not rather her obstinate refusal to conform?[112]

---

[110] *loc. cit.*

[111] Dickens, *English Reformation*, 195.

[112] The articles on 'Joan Boucher', 'Johan Knel' and on 'London' (where Horst refers to 'John Knel') in the *Mennonite Encyclopaedia* are very inaccurate. Neff's article on Joan Boucher in Volume I perpetuates Foxe's inaccurate account of Cranmer's part in the execution of Joan – an account that has been discredited since the time of Strype. Van der Zijp's article on 'Knel, Johan' and 'Anna Cantiana' in Volume III is mistaken and doubtless based upon the account of the events of 2 May 1550 preserved in van Braght's *Het bloedig tooneel, of martelaers spiegel der Doops-gesinde* or 'Martyrs' Mirror'. However, the first edition of this martyrology was not published in Dordrecht until 1660. It may be that Joan Bocher was known as 'Knell' by her Flemish associates in London, Essex and Kent. No doubt these foreign refugees relayed the news of her martyrdom to the Continent where confusion over her numerous aliases caused a garbled version to be preserved. It is significant that Foxe in his *Rerum* calls Joan 'Ioanna Cantiana', and it was this work rather than his *Acts and Monuments* that was influential on the Continent (Mozley, p. 128). Johan Knell, Anna Cantiana and Joan Boucher were all one and the same person. Notwithstanding the graphic illustration in the *Mennonite Encyclopaedia* (Volume III, Illustrations Appendix, p. 4), nobody else was burned at Smithfield on 2 May 1550. Therefore, the connection which van der Zijp seeks to establish between Joan Bocher and Menno Simons is dubious to say the least.

II JOHN CHAMPNEYS

On Saturday 27 April 1549 – five days after Joan Bocher made her first appearance – John Champneys was brought before the heresy commission. The Grey Friars' Chronicler records,

> Item the xxvij day of Aprill, the whych was the satorday in Ester weke, the ante-baptystes wore in our Lady chappelle in Powlles before the byshoppe of Caunterbory with other comyssionors, and there one recantyd; and the nexte sonday, the wych was Lowe sonday, stode at the crosse and bore a faggott....[113]

Wriothesley is more explicit:

> the xxviii daie of Aprill, being the first Soundaie after Easter, one Champnes of Stratford, bore a fagott at Poules Crosse, which was an Anabaptist, whose opinion was, that after man was regenerate by baptisme and the Holie Ghost that he could not sine, which damnable opinion he abiured the daie before at Poules before my Lord of Canterburie, and was sorie for his error.[114]

Evidently one appearance before the commissioners was sufficient to dampen Champneys' enthusiasm for anabaptist doctrine. However, this was not the first occasion on which he had been in trouble with the authorities. Six years earlier (12 May 1543) the Privy Council – which included Thomas Cranmer – ordered John Champneys to be 'released from the Counter in the Poultry upon his recognizance to fulfil the order to be taken by the bp. of Bath, Sir Hugh Paullett and Sir John Saintclow.[115] The following week (21 May 1543) the Council ordered letters to be written to the bishop of Bath, Sir Hugh Paullet and Nicholas Fitzjames commanding them 'to examine an information exhibited by John Champneys and proceed to the reformation of the same'.[116] This suggests that Champneys had been imprisoned in the Counter for some infringement of the Six Articles,[117] but had secured his freedom by promising to provide information on illicit religious activities within the

---

[113] *Chronicle of the Grey Friars of London*, 58-9.
[114] Wriothesley, II, 10-11.
[115] *LP.*, XVIII (i), 311.
[116] *Ibid.*, 335.
[117] In the light of his subsequent treatise probably violent anti-clericalism.

jurisdiction of the bishop of Bath.[118] Such familiarity with the current state of Somerset nonconformity indicates that Champneys had but recently arrived in London.

(a) His Background

At the beginning of his only extant work, *The Harvest is at Hand,* Champneys describes himself as 'an unlearned man born in the county of Somerset, a little besides Bristol'.[119] This immediately suggests that he came from either Redcliffe or Bedminster, the two populous industrial parishes of Bristol that lay south of the river Avon in Somerset and within the diocese of Bath and Wells. Redcliffe in particular had a strong tradition of Lollardy.[120] However, the Champneys family was of longstanding in Somerset. Champneys had been living at Frome since the early Middle Ages, and were in possession of the Orchardleigh estate near Frome from the reign of Henry II.[121] Moreover, the family strongly favoured the Christian name 'John' and its sons had a 'pronounced tendency towards ecclesiastical careers'.[122] Towards the end of the fifteenth century a John Champneys migrated from Somerset to London. His grandson, another John, became Lord Mayor of London in 1534.[123] Our subject may have been a member of a junior and poorer branch of the family that had moved closer to Bristol. Perhaps he was attracted to London by the success of his kinsman. Certainly his book reveals considerably more literary ability than one would expect from an author who claimed to be but a 'poor unlearned layman'.[124]

In the last years of the fifteenth century there were several heresy prosecutions in Bristol, chiefly of poor laymen from the industrial

---

[118] Sir Hugh Paulet was Sheriff of Somerset in 1543, Nicholas Fitzjames was a member of the jury that condemned the Abbot of Glastonbury in 1539. Both were members of the Somerset aristocracy. *Victoria County History*, Somerset, ed. Page, II, 96.

[119] Champneys, sig. A3^v.

[120] K. G. Powell, 'The Beginnings of Protestantism in Gloucestershire', *Transactions of the Bristol and Gloucestershire Archaeological Society*, 90 (1971), 142-3.

[121] Henry Stapleton, *The Model Working Parson* (Privately published in 1976 by the author at Hoveton Vicarage, Norwich), 7. The line ended with the death of Sir Thomas Champneys (2nd Bart.) in 1840.

[122] *Ibid.*, 8-9.

[123] *Ibid.*, 10.

[124] Champneys, D8^r.

suburb of Redcliffe. Bristol was still regarded as a centre for heresy in the reign of Henry VIII. Sir Thomas More claimed that heretical books were so freely available there that they were 'throwen in the strete and lefte at mennes dores by nyghte'.[125] These 'poysoned bookes', as More calls them, were distributed in the city by Richard Webb of Chipping Sodbury. Webb was in contact with the London book-agent, Robert Necton. The book trade was the most important means of contact between English Lollardy and the various Continental reformation movements.[126] Any Lutheran, Reformed or Anabaptist influences reaching the Bristol Lollards would appear to have been brought overland from London, East Anglia or South-east England and not by means of the city's seaborne commerce.

Powell states,

> There is no evidence that Protestant ideas were at any period reaching Bristol directly from the Protestant lands of Europe. The trade of the port was in fact conducted almost entirely with Catholic countries....[127]

The city's reputation as a haven of unorthodoxy attracted the attention of several leading English reformers, including Tyndale and Latimer. George Wishart, the Scots reformer with Zwinglian sympathies, visited the city in 1539 and there, according to Mayor Ricart, he preached 'the most blasphemous heresy that ever was heard'.[128] Wishart was brought to trial in the city later that year and was sentenced to bear a faggot in the churches of S. Nicholas and Christchurch. The rural dean of Bristol accused him of persuading many of the common people of the town to adopt heretical opinions.[129]

The year 1539 was a critical one in the ecclesiastical history of Bristol. Hugh Latimer as Bishop of Worcester had done all in his power to avoid heresy trials in his diocese. However, in 1539, seeing that the political climate had ceased to favour the reform party in the Henrician church, he resigned the see. His successor was John Bell, a conservative lawyer whose episcopate from 1539 to 1543 witnessed a Catholic reaction and

---

[125] Powell, *loc. cit.*
[126] Above, 3-8, 17-21.
[127] Powell, *loc. cit.*
[128] *Ricart's Kalendar*, ed. Smith, Camden Society, N.S. V (London, 1872), 55.
[129] *VCH.*, Gloucester II, 25.

the prosecution of all those who would not accept Henry's Six Articles. Early in June 1539 a royal commission was established to investigate sacramentarianism in Calais, Cranbrook, and Bristol.

One of the more interesting cases recorded in Bishop Bell's 'Act Book' concerns the discovery of a conventicle that gathered in a mill at Upleadon on the Gloucestershire/Worcester boundary. In April 1541 members of the group were brought for trial at the episcopal court. The charges reflect typical Lollard beliefs: – sacramentarian views of the mass, denial of the real presence, deprecation of auricular confession, penance and various ceremonies, and abomination of images. There was also evidence of radical christological beliefs. It was alleged that some of the Upleadon conventiclers maintained that, 'our savyor Christ Jhesus received not flesshe and blode of the virgyne Marie and that he was never fleshe and blode'.[130] This suggests that the influence of the 'book on the incarnation of Christ' produced by foreign anabaptists residing in England *circa* 1538[131] had reached the Lollards of the West-country by 1541.

In 1540 the small diocese of Bristol was created, and the southern suburbs of Redcliffe and Bedminster were removed from the jurisdiction of Bath and Wells and incorporated in the new diocese.[132] Hitherto, Lollard heretics in the former diocese must have had an easy time. John Clerke was appointed to the see of Bath and Wells in 1523 and remained its bishop until 1541, yet only one heresy trial is recorded.[133]

It is against this background that we must view John Champneys' removal to London. It may be that his reasons for moving to the metropolis were entirely unconnected with his religious persuasions. On the other hand, the arrival of Bishop Bell in 1539, the investigations of the royal commissioners, the incorporation of Redcliffe and Bedminster within the new diocese of Bristol in 1540 with the closer episcopal scrutiny that this would entail, and the passing of Bishop Clerke in 1541

---

130 Powell, 147.
131 Above, 17-18.
132 *VCH.*, Somerset, II, Appendix II, 67.
133 Thomson, *op. cit*, 50-1.

– all brought great pressure to bear upon Bristolian nonconformists like Champneys. Any of these events could account for Champneys' departure from the Bristol area, and it is not unreasonable to suggest that he arrived in London some time between 1539 and 1541.

According to the record of his trial our subject belonged to the parish of Stratford-le-Bow.[134] Here the violently Protestant pamphlets that poured from the presses after the death of Henry VIII would have been easily obtained. Here, too, he may have witnessed a notable example of Protestant iconoclasm when in 1547 Colonel Edward Underhill removed the pix from the altar of Stratford's parish church.[135] The religious extremism that pervaded the London parishes in 1547 – 48 doubtless inspired Champneys to publish his own contribution to early Protestant propaganda.[136] Even before the old King's death, crudely printed Protestant pamphlets had begun to circulate in London.[137] Throughout 1547 and 1548 the tracts poured from the presses. There was tremendous vitality and power in this surge of fervent Protestant writing. For the most part, they were slender works, crudely printed, hastily written, unsystematic and imprecise in their doctrine. Their tone was radical, highly nationalistic – violently anti-Papal, anti-Catholic, anti-prelatical – and in some cases anti-clerical. The chief object of attack was the Roman mass. By misuse of this ordinance the Gospel had been repudiated and perverted by a priestly caste which was concerned only with the arrogation of power to itself.[138] Champneys' book clearly belongs within this *genre* of early Protestant propaganda.

However, by 1548 some writers were beginning to realise that freedom of expression was not producing the desired consensus but rather anarchy and iconoclasm. Philip Nicolls exclaimed,
What a number of books there be abroad in every man's hand of divers and sundry matters which are very greedily devoured.

---

134   Cranmer, register, f. 71; Wilkins, *Concilia*, IV, 39-40.
135   'Diary of Col. Edward Underhill', ed. Nichols, *Narratives of the Reformation*, Camden Society, Old Series 77 (London, 1859), 160-161.
136   Jordan, *Threshold of Power*, 138.
137   For example George Joye's tract against Stephen Gardiner (RSTC 14828.5) which appeared in 1546.
138   Jordan, *loc. cit.*

Nevertheless, he regretted the lack of discrimination exercised by readers who tended to prefer, 'trifling matters, finely handled'.[139] Like the authors of the previous year, Nicolls was still concerned about the restrictive practices of the clergy. While Henry VIII had delivered England from bondage to Rome, the prelatical and priestly class still attempted to impede the layman's search for Gospel truth by laying heresy charges against him.[140] Nicolls suggested that more of the unlearned laity, 'which never wrote before, should also set themselves to work bestowing the talent that God hath lent them to the most advantage'.[141] That is precisely what John Champneys did – perhaps he was inspired by Nicolls' suggestion.

(b) His Book

The full title of Champneys' work is *The Harvest is at Hand, wherein the Tares shall be bound and cast into the fire and brent.*[142] According to the colophon it was published in 1548. A more precise dating can be deduced from the author's petition to the Privy Council for a similar freedom to preach in public as the 'marked men' (the learned clergy) enjoy.[143] This suggests that his book was produced between 24 April 1548 – when only certain specifically licensed ministers were permitted to preach[144] – and 23 September 1548 – when all preaching was prohibited.[145]

The book was crudely printed and carelessly bound[146] by Humfrey Powell. Only three other works are known to have been printed by Powell in London, all between 1548 and 1549. Thereafter he obtained a royal license to print and publish books in Ireland.[147]

Champneys' main theme is the nature of the Christian ministry; particularly, the means that should be used to discern true ministers of

---

[139] Philip Nicolls, *Here begyneth a godly newe story* (London, 1548) RSTC 18576, sig. A3^v-A4^r.

[140] *Ibid.*, B6^v-B7^r.

[141] *Ibid.*, A4^v.

[142] Three copies are known to survive – at the British Library, the Folger Library and Yale University.

[143] Champneys, D7^r-D7^v.

[144] *TRP.*, I, 421-3.

[145] *Ibid.*, I, 432-3.

[146] sigs. A7^v-B2^r are repeated and bound together between sig. B2^r and B2^v.

[147] *Early English Printed Books 1475-1640*, ed. Sayle (Cambridge, 1900), I, 205.

the gospel, the source of true spiritual authority, and the coming exposure of the wicked false ministers in the current ecclesiastical establishment. These clerics he usually refers to as 'marked monsters', an epithet the author explains in his prologue –

> ...our feigned spirituality, whom I do most commonly name... marked monsters, not only because they are marked in their bodies and sometimes wear disguised monstrous garments, but because their doctrine is marked also....[148]

Presumably the reference to marked bodies refers to the tonsure (the highly conservative vicar of Stepney – which included Stratford – had been an abbot before the Dissolution[149]) and 'disguised monstrous garments' were presumably vestments. However, not all of those whom Champneys accounted monsters wore such garments, and as his theme develops it becomes apparent that the writer disliked all the learned clergy. Champneys asserts:

> ...our marked men now being destitute of the Spirit of Christ, thinketh to minister the gospel by their outward learning; for other knowledge they have not, but do therein now like as the Scribes and Pharisees did, which knew not that the law was spiritual....[150]

That the writer was also attacking Protestant preaching and Reformed exegesis is confirmed by the subsequent comments of Jean Veron.[151]

Nevertheless, Champneys accepted that there were some clergy 'which hath been of the mark, and be now truly converted'. Such ministers, he believes, will recognise the truth of his words and not be offended by this description of their fellow clerics.[152] Such ministers do not depend on 'outward' learning but on the Holy Spirit's inward instruction in the Scriptures. By contrast,

> Our shameless monsters would have men to believe, that their clerkly sophistical doctrine should sufficiently instruct the people in the knowledge of the holy scriptures, for they themselves know not what the regeneration of the spirit of christ is, but what the devil and the

---

148 Champneys, A2ᵛ.
149 *Narratives of the Reformation*, 157, 157n.1, 160n.1.
150 Champneys, B5ʳ-B5ᵛ.
151 Below, 102.
152 Champneys, A3ʳ.

subtlety of man's wit by outward learning knoweth.[153]

After a long introduction in which the author describes the ungodly and their fate, particularly having in mind the 'policy of popish priests' whom he compares with the priests of Baal, Champneys divides his book into seven further sections. These are signified by marginal annotations. The contents of each section can be analysed as follows:–

1. Introduction – Popish Priests (A3ᵛ - B2ᵛ):

Champneys states that he has written his little book as witness against the 'clerkly sophistical connivance' of the educated clergy. He acknowledges that he writes 'rudely' but he is convinced that the 'elect of god and regenerate in christ, doth delight more in every part of the truth being never so rudely written or spoken, than they do in a clerkly sophistical lie, although he be never so pleasantly uttered'. However, such lies abound. Since the high powers will no longer allow the clergy to 'use their old abominations', they have been forced to set forth 'new hypocritical doctrine' in order to send their congregations to sleep. However

...if the children did know perfectly what nurses they be that rock them, they would sleep no more in their cradles, but would rather lie in the bare plain ground with the elect people of god in christ.[154]

The reference to 'old abominations' is undoubtedly to Roman sacramental and liturgical practices, and presumably the 'new hypocritical doctrine' is the learned preaching of the Henrician reformers. In view of what Champneys writes subsequently, his statement about the children preferring to leave their cradles for the bare plain ground must be regarded as a hint at separation.

Doubtless it was with a touch of local pride that Champneys indicated that he was in sympathy with the work of Somerset, the Lord Protector. He prays for divine protection and assistance for 'the King's majesty, my Lord protector and all other members of the King's most honourable Council'. He prays that the present religious policies may 'prosperously take good effect', so that godliness may be increased in the realm, the people of God enjoy freely the liberty of the gospel, and the power of

---

[153]   *Ibid.*, A4ᵛ.
[154]   *Ibid.*, A5ʳ-A5ᵛ.

the marked priesthood be utterly destroyed.[155]

Like many other preachers and writers of the time, Champneys compares the young King Edward with the Old Testament King Josiah and looks to him to implement reforms in a similar manner. He compares the unreformed clergy with the prophets of Baal but believes their abominations to far exceed those of the latter. They have deluded the people into worshipping many more idols while claiming to be ministers of the gospel of Christ. They delight in temporal possessions and dignified titles, and like the prophets of Baal, they have procured the death of many true prophets. Moreover, they would still do so but for fear of the temporal authorities. While going as far in their abominations as they dare, they wish to be called the ministers of Christ merely because 'they can talk of gods word, and have many crafty arguments and sophistical disputations thereof'.[156]

However, the writer believes himself to be living in the last days. Soon the Lord Jesus will show himself from heaven rendering vengeance upon the ungodly and disobedient. Quoting *II Thessalonians 1* and *Revelation 20*, Champneys maintains that Christ has already come 'in spirit to be glorified in his Saints'. This is 'the binding of Satan and the first resurrection spoken of in the Apocalypse'. He explains that this means that, 'the true profession of the Gospel has been so much persecuted and hated ever since the Apostles time that no man might openly follow it'. However, 'now God will glorify all them that love it [the Gospel] ... And will clearly destroy the whole power of all the enemies thereof'.[157]

Thus, Champneys seems to have believed that God was about to openly intervene to restore the true Apostolic Church which had remained hidden since New Testament times. It is significant that this was one of the statements for which the author was condemned when he was examined before Archbishop Cranmer the following year. Evidently Cranmer, Cox, Latimer, *et al.* did not share his views on the

---

[155]   *Ibid.*, A7^r.
[156]   *Ibid.*, A8^v.
[157]   *Ibid.*, B1^v-B2^r.

underground church and the impossiblity of openly following the
Gospel prior to 1548.

2. The Nature of Man (B3ʳ-B5ʳ):
Such is the human condition that God's commandments were bound to
be broken and his Gospel corrupted, 'for the first man Adam [?bare] a
wicked heart, transgressed and was overcome, and so be all they that are
born of him'. Therefore those things which men hold in high esteem are
abominable in the sight of God.[158] Thus Champneys makes use of the
doctrine of original sin to explain the spiritual blindess of people in
general and the clergy in particular.

> Wherefore, it is undoubtedly to be believed, that all people remain in
> the old Adam, being of natural discretion, which be not regenerate of
> God, with the Spirit of Christ, are thus forsooth until this time the
> subjects of the devil and [?*abiectes*] from God. What wisdom or
> learning so ever they have, or what outward life so ever they live, and
> knoweth nothing of the things of God.[159]

He maintains the total depravity of human nature and man's utter
inability to work any spiritual good. Only through a spiritual
regeneration wrought by God the Holy Spirit can a man exchange his
outward righteousness for a real inward holiness, his external knowledge
for a true internal understanding.

> Howbeit no man, by any gift of nature may glorify God, or do
> anything which is godly: for it is God which worketh all goodness in
> us, both the will and also the deed. Wherefore, the only true and
> perfect remedy is for all reasonable people to seek of God in prayer,
> the regeneration promised in Christ. Whereby they shall have both the
> true understanding of his word, and also power in Spirit to live always
> according to the true profession of the Gospel.[160]

There is a hint of perfectionism in this last phrase. If Champneys has a
high view of the extent of sin, he has an even higher view of the power of
regeneration.

---

[158] *Ibid.*, B3ʳ.
[159] *Ibid.*, B3ᵛ.
[160] *Ibid.*, B4ʳ.

3. The Nature of Law (B5ʳ-B8ʳ):
Since 'our marked men are destitute of the spirit of Christ and have no true knowledge', they attempt to minister the Christian gospel by means of their outward learning. In this they are like the scribes and pharisees who were not aware that the law was spiritual. Champneys regards learned disputations over doctrine as 'vain jangeling about the law' – and clearly he has Reformed ministers in mind.

In this well-reasoned section the author argues that those who observed the Old Testament Law received the benedictions promised by that Law – but these blessings were material and 'did not help them to everlasting life'. The Law only serves to 'utter sin' and is no longer binding upon those 'to whom the promise was made (which is Christ)'. Such elect, regenerate people have no need of the Law, since they have 'the power in spirit.... To love all the elect people of god, according to the commandment of christ'. This is the fulfilling of the Law. Champneys adds, 'for the whole commandments of the law are included in the perfection of love'.[161] His use of the formula 'perfection of love' may be of significance in view of its importance in Davidist and Familist circles. Certainly Champneys emphasises love, and in particular love for the elect, as the chief evidence of regeneration.

As for the marked men who teach the Law but cannot observe it – '... they be very desirous of the benedictions of the law, and think themselves to be in the favour of god because they have abundance of all worldly things'. Such worldly teachers should be separated from the company of all Christian people.[162]

4. The Work of Christ (B8ᵛ-C1ᵛ):
Unfortunately this section is very brief. In the development of his theme Champneys evidently did not feel it necessary to produce a detailed statement on the Person and Work of Christ. Quoting liberally from Scripture, he simply argues that Christ has put away the Law and has established a new testament as promised by the Prophets. However, this new testament 'is made only to them that be regenerate in Christ'. All those who possess only natural understanding have 'no promise made

---

[161] *Ibid.*, B7ʳ.
[162] *Ibid.*, B8ʳ.

within any part of the new testament to be saved by Christ'. Whereas the, 'saved in Christ shall be all taught of God' – this is Christ's great promise.[163]

5. The Knowledge Christians Possess (C2^r-D7^r):
Unlike christology, here is a subject that fills the author with enthusiasm. Two questions particularly interest him, *viz.* how can one know those who really know the gospel and, more important, how can one know those who are the true ministers of the gospel.

To answer the former question, Champneys says, we must know what fruits a good tree bears that an evil tree cannot bear; that is, 'what good deeds they be which an evil man cannot do'.[164] He then gives a detailed description of four such fruits. The first of these is *love* – the love which the elect have for one another. In this important passage Champneys frequently uses the phrase 'perfection of love' and is fairly explicit in contending that the regenerate cannot sin. He cites *I John 3:9* as his authority – just as Joan Bocher did in Newgate the following year.[165]

First of all, the elect people of god, are known by godly love one to another according to the sayings of Christ... which godly love cometh only by the gift of the holy ghost. And falleth never away from them which be regenerate in Christ. So that envy and malice be sins which the people of God, being regenerate in Christ, cannot be infected withall... for the Spirit of God remaineth always in them that be regenerate in Christ, wherefore they cannot do contrary to the commandment of Christ, which is love, because they are born of God, and his seed remaineth always in them.[166]

By contrast the people of the world can have 'no such perfection of love' towards the people of God, since this is the chief gift of the Holy Spirit. Moreover, as the people of God bear a 'perfect love to all them that be obedient to the Gospel of Christ, so is there also in them a spiritual hatred... against all worldly affections and lusts, both in themselves and in all other people'.[167] Here Champneys cannot resist

---

163 *Ibid.*, C1^r-C1^v.
164 *Ibid.*, C2^r-C2^v.
165 Above, 61-3.
166 Champneys, C3^r-C3^v.
167 *Ibid.*, C4^r.

another dig at his pet aversions, for he adds – 'especially against the whole conversation of all marked men'. Similarly, this genuine hatred of worldly 'affections and lusts' is also a gift of the Holy Ghost only to be found in the elect people of God.

A second evidence is '*bearing of the cross of Christ*', which the writer defines as 'to have always a spiritual patience in all adversities, tribulations and persecutions, and to rejoice only in them'. Adversity and persecution, together with the spiritual comfort and joy which the elect derive from them, are another 'principle gift' of the Holy Ghost. Such an attitude cannot be imitated because it is 'clean contrary to the natural disposition of all worldly people'.[168]

A third good fruit is *child-likeness*. Quoting *Luke 13* and *Matthew 18* ('Except ye become as little children...') Champneys interprets this to mean that all who receive salvation in Christ, 'shall receive it only by grace given of God ... without any assistance thereunto of any of our own works'. Such people submit themselves as 'elect children wholly to be taught and led ... only by the spirit of Christ'.[169]

The final fruit is possession of *secret knowledge or understanding* – knowledge of 'a song as no earthly persons could learn since the time of Christ, but only the number appointed'.[170] Through this inward instruction the elect are able to discern 'both the people of God, and also the people of the devil'. The writer emphasises that this discernment is not based upon the outward appearance, for that is the basis upon which worldly people who 'worship the beast' make their judgements –
(The worldly) thinketh to know and to discern what sorts men be of by other outward, hypocritical works, wherefore they condemn the people of God in their judgements... because they seem not to them to be so holy in their outward appearance as the worldly hypocrites do.[171]
This last phrase may be significant because it suggests that the Christians with whom Champneys had associated tended to be either Nicodemite or antinomian in their practice. Since antinomianism was a

---

[168]   *Ibid.*, C5^r.
[169]   *Ibid.*, C5^v-C6^r.
[170]   *Ibid.*, C6^r.
[171]   *Ibid.*, C6^v.

favourite accusation levelled at the Edwardine reformers, the former attitude seems more likely to have been present in John Champneys and his associates.

Next comes a long section on 'the best means and way to know who be the true ministers of the gospel... if they be strangers unto us'. Champneys states that the surest way is to enquire closely whether they preach the Gospel in the same way that the Apostles did, that is, 'only by the instruction of the holy ghost and not otherwise'.[172] All those who preach without this instruction of the Spirit of Christ are deceivers and false ministers. The Christian Gospel cannot be purely and truly ministered by 'outward learning' –

> For all our marked men ... are puffed up with the delusion of the devil, and knoweth nothing that is good, but wasteth their brains about questions and arguments and strife of words, with many vain disputations after their corrupt minds, being clearly destitute of all true knowledge.[173]

Therefore, the most important thing is 'to be regenerate of god with the most holy spirit of Christ'. Champneys continues in this vein at some length during which two important features of his own position become apparent. First, there are signs that he holds to a separatist ecclesiology. He refers to 'the Elders of the congregations in the primitive Church' who 'would not suffer any of (the scrupulous Jews) to continue in the congregation which converted not after certain admonitions... but utterly expelled them out of the congregation'.[174] This certainly suggests sympathy with the concept of a gathered church governed by elders who exercised discipline in the congregation. Secondly, there are some important statements about the sufficiency and authority of Scripture. Quoting *Revelation 22* he urges his readers to note that those who add or remove anything from that which the apostles, evangelists, patriarchs and prophets wrote for us are accursed of God –

> For the Apostles of Christ were the last people that God appointed to write scripture, whose doctrine shall remain to the world's end.[175]

---

172 *Ibid.*, C7^r.
173 *Ibid.*, C8^v.
174 *Ibid.*, D1^v-D2^r.
175 *Ibid.*, D2^v.

Such sentiments one would not expect to find in a man whom Horst claims as a follower of Melchior Hofmann and David Joris.

Nevertheless, John Champneys had little time for 'long clerkly protestation' (?Reformed exegesis of the Scriptures) because this hinders the unlearned from that which is truly profitable *i.e.*, 'the true literal sense of the holy scriptures as they be written'. When such elect unlearned folk hear the true literal sense of Scripture proclaimed, God gives them understanding of it. Therefore, 'they delight not in such clerkly curiosity of men, but do utterly abhor it, because so many men have been deceived by it'.[176] By contrast the natural man cannot perceive the spiritual light of God's Word until he be 'regenerate of God'; thereafter he has 'no more pleasure in man's clerkly curiosity in doctrine'.[177] Here Champneys employs three apt illustrations. Whoever is taught by an unregenerate preacher is like a blind man who imagines that he will be enabled to see if another man's eyes are placed in his head. The elect unlearned long to learn the Scriptures by heart but when they listen to the long clerkly sermons of the learned the literal sense of Scripture is obscured, as if the words were being sung to them in a complicated song. The singer may sing with a fine descant but the hearer cannot clearly perceive the words that he desires to learn by heart. However, the regenerate recognise truly spiritual enlightenment from the Scripture when they hear it and will not refuse it, rather they will prefer it to the vain imaginations of men. Just as all reasonable men do not usually shut the doors and windows of their houses during daylight and burn candles. For as it is folly to burn candles when the daylight may suffice, so it is 'devilish madness' to trust in any man-made doctrine.

How foolish it seems to 'us which be regenerate in Christ', exclaims the writer, that people should seek the things necessary for their salvation from men rather than from God. This is particularly true at this present time since God is now offering the Gospel 'to all people which hath not openly blasphemed the holy ghost'.[178] However, few are taking advantage of this offer, and therefore 'his wrath will shortly be known'. Here again is evidence that Champneys believed himself to be

---

[176] *Ibid.*, D3^v-D4^r.
[177] *Ibid.*, D3^r.
[178] *Ibid.*, D5^r.

living at a unique juncture in world history – that period immediately prior to the *Eschaton* when the Gospel would be openly proclaimed. The writer maintains that the 'wonderful works of God' are being seen in his day –

> For what is a greater miracle than the whole and clear alteration of the heart of man, which may undoubtedly be perceived in all them which be regenerate in Christ.[179]

This section continues with a catalogue of the fruits of the Spirit to be found in the regenerate – yet not apparently discernible to the unregenerate since, 'no man is known by any outward appearance'. Finally, there is an enigmatic statement which caused Champneys a great deal of trouble at his interrogation the following year. While writing of the Christian's heavenly citizenship and earthly pilgrimage, he states that they do not work – 'with the respect of our own lucre, but for that we would not live idly, and also to have wherewith to help the impotent members of Christ'. They do not love worldly things, but receive 'all needful necessities of the body in worldly things ... without any scrupulosity or grudge of conscience'. He continues:

> For like as God doth forbid all men from the loving and inordinate using of worldly things, so likewise doth he permit all his elect people their bodily necessities of all worldly things.[180]

The authorities evidently took exception to this final phrase for it was quoted verbatim at Champneys' trial. It could, one imagines, be regarded as containing antinomian sentiments, an advocacy of community of goods amongst believers. In the political climate of 1549, with Ket and his followers in East Anglia forcibly resisting enclosures and proclaiming theories about the 'commonwealth' of England, such statements as the above may have been regarded as socially dangerous. However, bearing in mind what Champneys had already written about the love of worldly things – those 'benedictions of the law' which the false clergy possess, this statement is really quite innocuous. Champneys is simply explaining the attitude of the spiritually regenerate to material necessities and by implication contrasting it with that of the 'marked men'. The only point of any significance here is Champneys' earlier statement about the regenerate working to assist 'the impotent

---

[179] *Ibid.*, D5ᵛ.
[180] *Ibid.*, D6ᵛ.

members of Christ'. This suggests that the gathered congregation to which Champneys belonged assisted each other materially. It may indicate that they practised a 'community in consumption' of goods, but it is not evidence that they practised community of goods *per se*.

6. The Humble Petition (D7ᵛ-F6ᵛ):
The writer now reaches the crux of his argument and the objective at which his book was aimed. Champneys seeks to prove that the 'marked men' are deceivers, but to do so he needs the same liberty to preach openly that they enjoy. Therefore, he makes the following request:

> ... if it may please the King's majesty, by the godly advice of my lord protector's grace and other of his honourable counsel, to grant and permit like liberty to some one of them being of small reputation and learning, which be now regenerate with the spirit of Christ as was granted to Elijah in the time of Ahab, King of Israel.... That like trial as was between the said Elijah and all Baal's prophets, by the offering of sacrifice, may be now openly and only by the holy scriptures written, after the literal sense: Between one such of the elect in Christ and the whole multitude of them, now may confer their learnings together: or severally whether they list, and then to be openly and plainly known and seen, whether they can shew the word of God written after the true literal sense... yea or no: and if they cannot, all men ought to refuse and to despise their doctrine, how clerkly or eloquently soever it be uttered.... And on ye other side if the compiler hereof, a poor lay man, and of small literature, be not able by god's assistance, only by the power of the Spirit of Christ, to shew the word of God written in the true literal sense both for the clear discharge of his own conscience and conversation, and also of all other that be regenerate in Christ, let it be death unto him.[181]

Thus, in the summer of 1548, John Champneys, a poor Somerset layman – seeing himself in the role of Elijah and the representative of all regenerate conventiclers – issued a challenge to the learned clergy of London. He challenged them to explain simply, without any theological jargon, what the Christian Gospel was. If they could not do so then they would have shown themselves to be deceivers and ministers of the devil. As for the writer, he will 'shew the word of God' without the

---

[181] *Ibid.*, D7ᵛ-D8ᵛ.

assistance of scholarship but with the assistance of the Holy Spirit. If he fails to do so, then let him be executed.

In proposing this public confrontation Champneys was almost certainly motivated by eschatological considerations. Such an open humiliation of the established clergy and public vindication of the regenerate he considered essential pre-requisites before the *Eschaton.* Citing *Revelation 10: 7, 11: 18 & 19, 17: 17,* Champneys asserts –

Now in the days of the voice of the seventh Angel which beginneth to blow … the mystery of God shall be openly published…. That is, that the elect people of God shall only with the spirit of Christ and the word of God, written, clearly confute and confound the abominable cauteilous [crafty] delusion of all marked men…. For the time is come that God will utterly destroy them, because they have destroyed the godly people of the earth… their cauteilous dilusion shall prevail no longer.[182]

However, he appears uncertain whether this final exposé will be achieved through the agency of the magistracy – God's 'elect high powers' – or whether it will be as a result of the direct intervention of Christ at the *Parousia.* Quoting *Isaiah 10: 17,* he writes –

And where it is said that they shall be burned in one day: that signifieth that they shall be utterly confounded now at this present time, in the appearance of the second coming of Christ.[183]

According to Champneys the fact that the 'marked men' made use of temporal power to propagate their 'individual interpretations' of Scripture accounts for the hitherto universal dominance of such interpretations. Having the support of the political authorities, they forcibly suppressed the truth – 'for they made the fire to defend them against all those people which professed the true religion'.[184] This appears to be a reference to the persecution of Lollards by the Roman Church, but Champneys might possibly have had in mind the more recent burning of emigré Anabaptists in 1535 and 1538 by the Henrician authorities.

---

[182] *Ibid.*, F5^r-F5^v.
[183] *Ibid.*, F6^r-F6^v.
[184] *Ibid.*, E3^r-E3^v.

That John Champneys possessed a well-developed understanding of hermeneutics is evident from his next statement which provides both the parting shot in his battle for the authority of Scripture and the opening salvo in his contention for Christian perfection. He writes:

For of the holy scriptures there is but one true sense which is directly and plainly expressed in the letter thereof, being compared together: so that there is no part of it repugnant one against another.[185]

The misuse of Scripture by the natural man arises from the fact that he is unable to obey its literal commands and therefore believes not 'that the literal sense is always true'. Once again our author emphasises the importance of regeneration: the natural man cannot accept a literal interpretation of Scripture because he fails to take into account the fact that 'there is a new creation by God above nature'. Only those who are new creations in Christ have the ability to do 'that which the letter of the holy Scripture commandeth'.[186] This is the basic principle behind the writer's belief in the possibility of Christian perfection. Contrariwise, he believes it to be the 'most principalest part of our marked men's doctrine, to make the people believe that there was no such spirit given unto man whereby he should remain righteous always in Christ'.[187] Here Champneys reveals a streak of optimistic idealism which does not accord well with his belief in total depravity and which probably caused him to throw in his lot with the free-willers. He continues:

...every member of the mystical body of Christ hath one spirit and one intelligence of the word of God and one purpose of heart in all godliness; so that, advisably and willingly they do nothing against the will of god. Therefore the holy Scriptures in the true literal sense is sufficient for their outward instruction in all godly doctrine.[188]

Champneys' use of the word 'outward' in the above statement is noteworthy. One wonders whether there is not – as least potentially – a dichotomy between the outward letter and the inward spirit. Such a dichotomy was much more explicitly evident in the writings and actions

---

[185] *Ibid.*, E3^v-E4^r.
[186] *Ibid.*, E4^r.
[187] *Ibid.*, E4^v.
[188] *Ibid.*, E5^v.

of those who followed Melchior Hofmann, David Joris and Hendrik Niclaes.

Those who think that the word of God is insufficient for all instruction are denying both the sufficiency of Christ and also the perfection of the Holy Spirit:

> For Christ is included in the word, and the word in Christ. Wherefore to think the word insufficient, is to think Christ is insufficient, and also the holy ghost to be unperfect, which wrought always in them that wrote it, by whom also it hath been always preserved... for the Apostles left nothing unwritten which was profitable to our faith....[189]

This leads the writer to explain the warning given in the gospels concerning false Christs. He says that this does not mean that false teachers will call themselves by the name of 'Christ', but that they will claim for themselves that divine anointing which the term 'Christ' signifies. He continues,

> For Jesus was anointed of god: and had also the godly power in him. Wherefore he is called Jesus Christ, an only saviour anointed of God, for the justification of all his elect people from sin.[190]

Now, while this particular statement undoubtedly represents an inadequate expression of the divinity of Christ, suggesting a weak christology; yet this weakness is not of the Melchiorite docetic type. Rather, it is reminiscent of that rationalistic adoptionist christology which was found in England among some who were accused of Lollardy.[191]

Under the marginal annotation 'nota', the remainder of this section consists of a long digression on the nature of Christian perfection and on the current religious situation, all permeated as usual with attacks upon the wicked 'marked monsters'. Making a firm distinction between the gift of faith and that of the Holy Spirit, Champneys maintains that while the former makes us righteous, the latter makes us 'perfect both in knowledge and power to do the will of God in spirit'. Had Cranmer, Latimer and Cox been looking for theological instead of political and social grounds for condemning Champneys' teaching, they would

---

[189]   *Ibid.*, E6^r-E6^v.
[190]   *Ibid.*, E7^r.
[191]   Thomson, *op. cit.* 248.

surely have found it here. He clearly teaches that faith is insufficient and that further 'blessings' are required –

But faith of itself hath neither perfect knowledge of the holy Scriptures, neither power to do that which the Scripture commandeth: for that cometh only by the gift of the holy ghost after faith, sometime immediately... and sometime long after.[192]

The gift of the Holy Spirit is bestowed upon the elect *via* the 'prayer of faith' and the laying-on of hands of 'elect ministers'. Normally it is manifested in the gift of godly knowledge and the power to live perfectly rather than in the ability to perform miracles. The practice of the marked monsters in administering 'a certain oil or grease' at the confirmation of the ignorant is a devilish substitute and can never result in the bestowal of the Holy Spirit. Champneys compares this erroneous ritual with the erroneous doctrine of Mohammed who taught people to believe that the Holy Spirit in the likeness of a dove had instructed him. However,

the delusion of Mahomet's priests now at this present time is not so much to be marvelled at, as the delusion of our marked men, because Mahomet's priests do live according to their profession.[193]

In fact, these false clergy are so deceitful and crafty that – even though we may have some human affection for them – we must treat them as we would treat rotten teeth. Once again our author's sense of humour is revealed in his use of the two amusing illustrations that follow –

For a natural man which hath rotten teeth in his head, that doth never rest from painful ache, will seek a remedy: but if he have none, he will have his rotten teeth drawn out of his head, rather than have all his body continually disquieted. And even so likewise our Marked men are like unto rotten teeth: for they cannot minister the word of God as they ought to do. And as for the spiritual ache, which all godly people have by them we see plainly that the high powers have sought as much the reformation of them as may be, and yet they be as crafty as ever they were, disguising themself with sophistical hypocrisy, either new or old, as fast as ever they did, and the devil is

---

[192] Champneys, E7^v-E8^r.
[193] *Ibid.*, F1^r.

as familiar with them as ever he was. Wherefore God send us remedy of them shortly.[194]

The attempted reformation of the clergy referred to here is presumably the provision introduced by Cranmer for the instruction of the clergy. The reference to 'sophistical hypocrisy, either new or old' is also interesting. It represents Champneys' low opinion of theology – whether Scholastic or Reformed.

The writer's next analogy illustrates his belief that it is impossible to treat the rotten, unregenerate clergy by instructing them. He writes,

How-beit, most men be in like case with them as women be with their Parots: for women use much diligence to make their Parots to speak, and yet with all their diligence, they cannot make them to talk so reasonably as a reasonable creature can. And no more can a man make those ministers which be only appointed by men to declare the true meaning of the word of God, so plainly and truly as it ought to be, what soever be devised for them....[195]

Is this latter statement a derogatory reference to Cranmer's *Book of Homilies*?

Champneys concludes this section with a final thrust at those whose religious policies and programmes for reform were governed by the belief that it was possible for the established clergy to be reformed. Such an attitude reflects a failure to accept the plain prophetic teaching of Scripture.[196] Champneys' own radical solution (extraction of the 'rotten teeth') is based upon his interpretation of the contemporary situation which in turn is determined by his eschatological hopes.

It was part of the Divine purpose that the elect should be persecuted and hated in every age, from the time of the 'primitive church' until the time when God will 'glorify the gospel'. Nevertheless, the worldly are quite ignorant of all this devilish activity –

---

194   *Ibid.*, F2^r-F2^v.
195   *Ibid.*, F2^v.
196   *Ibid.*, F3^v-F4^r.

For the devil being changed into the likeness of an Angel of light hath given his power unto marked men his ministers. By whom all earthly people have been deceived... because the spiritual whore of Rome... did sit upon their doctrine, and was maintained thereby.[197]

However, the situation has now changed, these are unique times – the times, in fact, foretold in *Revelation 17*. God has disclosed the abominations of Rome to 'diverse Kings and high powers' and caused them to despise her. Yet, although Rome has been rejected, power still lies in the hands of the 'corporation of all marked men'. These Kings have –

given her kingdom and power unto the Beast, until that time the words of god be fulfilled. That is, now in the days of the voice of the seventh Angel, which beginneth to blow....[198]

In these days, as never before, the mystery of God shall be openly published as prophesied in *Revelation 10*. In this time of the Seventh Angel,

the elect people of God shall only with the spirit of Christ and the word of God written, clearly confute and confound the abominable cauteilous [crafty] delusion of all marked men.[199]

The time has come for their satanic power and glory to be destroyed –

For the time is come that God will utterly destroy them, because they have destroyed the godly people of the earth.... For their cauteilous delusion shall prevail no longer.[200]

7. The Joyful Time to Come (F6ᵛ-G1ᵛ):

In the manner of contemporary pamphleteers, Champneys describes the joys of the Millenium by stringing together without intervening comment a collection of quotations from the Prophets and the Book of Revelation. Beside a quotation from *Zechariah 8* the word 'nota' is again inserted in the margin – presumably because the writer regarded this text as furnishing scriptural grounds for the political authorities to take action against the clergy. He concludes with a ringing challenge to the learned clergy to conform to the example set by their master, the Devil, during

---

[197] *Ibid.*, F4ᵛ.
[198] *Ibid.*, F5ʳ.
[199] *Ibid.*
[200] *Ibid.*, F5ᵛ.

our Lord's wilderness temptations.

For in so much as he being the author of that profession of your incorporation, dignity, and power, confessed the truth of Christ and of his Apostles after that he was once confuted with the scriptures written. Be not you no longer more comberous and obstinate against the truth thereof now, than the devil was at that time and allege other things to be meant in the holy scriptures, than is expressed in the true literal sense thereof. For if ye do, all men will know shortly that you are worse, and more worthy of condemnation than the devil is: for belike he had not so much falsehed [*sic.*], or else he was not so foolish when he tempted Christ by the Scriptures, to allege other meanings therein, than was expressed in the letter thereof: neither he defended not his own imaginations against the holy scriptures written, as all you marked men have done a long time.[201]

8. A General Absolution (G2ʳ-G3ᵛ):

Having unfavourably compared the learned clergy of the Church of England with the prophets of Baal, the priests of Mohammed, and even the Devil himself, it is hardly surprising to find that the 'general absolution' which Champneys offers them is no absolution at all. The 'feigned spirituality' must simply accept their coming purgation from the body-spiritual. Their salt 'hath lost its saltness' and their submission to discipline and expulsion is essential if the body is to be recreated.

Wherefore now from henceforth suffer the people of God, wholly to purge out your old rotten leven, for otherwise we cannot be new dough in Christ: for a little of your leaven soureth a great piece of dough.[202]

The writer's antipathy towards the established clergy, which finds expression on almost every page of his book, continues to the very end. He states that the, 'marked men... shall not be forgiven, neither in this life, nor in the life to Come'.[203] Then the work closes with a stirring exhortation –

---

201   *Ibid.,* G1ʳ-G1ᵛ.
202   *Ibid.,* G2ʳ.
203   *Ibid.*

Wherefore God commandeth all his elect people to depart out of your company, and to separate themselves clearly from you, and not to touch any of your uncleanness.[204]

Undoubtedly Champneys is advocating the principle of separation here, but since he held high hopes that Somerset and the Council would respond to his exhortation, the separation he envisages is that of the nation from the clergy. Our author is anticipating the rule of the saints over society rather than the separation of the saints from society. Champneys may have been exposed to Continental anabaptist influences as Horst suggests,[205] but clearly he had learnt nothing from Münster and owed nothing to Menno Simons. That he was thinking in terms of a national separation and reformation is confirmed by his application of the reference to islands in *Isaiah 59* to this theme. He states,

For God will avenge him on you, and will shew no mercy to you, as he doth to other people. For you are the people whom god hath appointed to his wrath, within the Islands of this part of the world, whereby the name of the Lord might be feared.[206]

The author concludes his exhortation with a final reference to the simile with which he began his book –

Wherefore we ought to have no more in number of you, to remain as ministers of the gospel, but even so many as Elijah suffered of Baal's Prophets to live when he had confounded them, by offering of Sacrifice. Howbeit, it is to be thought that Baal's Prophets had not so much sophistical conveyance to make their excuse at that time, as you Marked men have now, or else subtle excuses were less regarded at that time, than they be now.[207]

Champneys then promises his readers a further book in which he intends to prove that the 'abomination and crafty delusion' of the learned clergy was worse than that found in any other nation since the beginning of the world. Such long and tedious historical surveys were fairly common at this time, but it is unlikely that John Champneys ever succeeded in adding to their number. For, within a year of publication

---

204   *Ibid.*, G2ᵛ-G3ʳ.
205   Horst, 114.
206   Champneys, G3ʳ.
207   *Ibid.*, G3ʳ-G3ᵛ.

he was standing in abject submission before S. Paul's Cross, bearing a faggot upon his shoulder, while Miles Coverdale preached at him.

An Assessment

It is readily apparent why, among all the books and pamphlets published between 1547 and 1550, this one in particular should have attracted the attention of the political and ecclesiastical authorities. John Champneys may have had humble origins but he was no mean writer. Although he was a man of 'small literature', he possessed a comprehensive knowledge of the Bible. His book is saturated in quotations from Scripture. These appear to be from the Matthews' Bible of 1537. Sometimes these citations are rather loose and abbreviated to suit the purposes of his argument. While constantly deprecating the subtleties of clerkly exegesis, Champneys occasionally engages in allegorical exegesis himself.

Furthermore, our author possessed some exegetical ability. Although here his objectivity is somewhat blurred by his estimate of the power of spiritual regeneration to bestow understanding of the true meaning of Scripture. No doubt the writer's own spiritual experience is reflected in this emphasis upon the indispensability of regeneration. However, he does attempt to preserve a balance between reason and experience by an equal emphasis upon the literal meaning as the sole legitimate interpretation. According to Champneys, all who are regenerate have the ability to understand the inner meaning of Scripture. Nevertheless, such interpretations must be conformable with the literal meaning of the text.

Above all, one is impressed by the manner in which the contents of this book are organised and presented. Clearly it was written by a man with a disciplined, ordered mind. The plan outlined in the introduction is carefully followed. The arguments are developed logically and with very few inconsistencies. The apt and amusing illustrations sharpen his arguments yet add a touch of humour and colour to a serious subject. It is easy to see why this poor Somerset layman was so frustrated and angry with the established clergy. Quite apart from any special spiritual enlightenment, John Champneys was more able than many of them. Reformers such as Coverdale recognised his potential and sought to recruit him into the ministry of the newly-established Protestant Church

– thus providing the platform he desired – but years of Lollard non-conformity had left their own indelible 'mark'.

John Champneys believed himself to be living in momentous times. Therefore he dared not dissipate his energies on the trite and trivial. Certainly there is nothing trivial about the contents of this book, neither is it unduly repetitive. He likened himself to Elijah, but the reader will perhaps detect within this bold, blunt manifesto something of the spirit of Amos.

(c) His Examination
In *The Harvest* Champneys had petitioned the Privy Council to sanction a public debate between himself and the learned clergy of England. Within a year of publication his wish had been granted, but not quite in the way he had expected. The following April our author stood before the bishops and other learned ecclesiastics in S. Paul's to answer for his 'heresy'. The circulation of such an inflammatory book as *The Harvest* in London in the autumn of 1548 may have been another factor persuading the Council to establish the heresy commission the following spring.

It is clear that Champneys' views met with little sympathy among the commissioners. Indeed, John Champneys was as prompt to make an abject abjuration of his opinions as Joan Bocher was recalcitrant in the maintenance of hers. His recantation of heretical statements, affirmation of orthodox teaching on these matters, and the sentences imposed upon him are all in the standard format of medieval heresy trials. The recantation begins,
... I John Champneis of Stratford on the Bowe, in the county of Middlesex ... confess and openly recognise, that in tymes past I ... taught and presumptiously in my booke sette forth in my name these and all other errours, heresies and damnable opinions following .... First, that a man after he is regenerate in Christe, cannot synne. Item secondly, that I have defended the said first article, graunting that the outward man might synne and the inward man cold not synne. Thirdly, that the gospel hath bene so muche persecuted and hated ever sythens the apostelles tyme, that no man might be suffred openly to follow hyt. Fourthly, that godly love falleth never away from them which be regenerate in Christ, wherefore they cannot do contrary to the commaundment of Christ. Fifthly, that, that was the most

principall of our marked mann's doctryne to make the people beleve that there was no suche spirite geven unto man, whereby he sholde remayne righteous alwaies in Christe, which is a most develishe errour. Sixthly, that God doth permitte to all his electe people their bodilie necessities of all worldly thinges....[208]

Evidently the commissioners had carefully perused *The Harvest*, for the phrasing of several of the charges is that of the author himself.[209] In view of this thorough examination of his book it is rather surprising that the six charges make no mention of Champneys' slanderous descriptions of the clergy. Neither do they contain any reference to his revolutionary eschatological expectations. However, both Champneys' anti-clericalism and his eschatological expectations were shared by large sections of the populace at this time. In fact, the commissioners were theologically and politically astute in restricting their charges to his teaching on the power of regeneration and the needs of the regenerate. Five of the six items relate to his teaching on the nature of regeneration.[210] Item one is a retraction of Champneys' fundamental doctrine – the power of regeneration to produce sinless perfection in the elect.[211] Conversely, Champneys was required to confess that the truly regenerate Christian may sin. Item two implies that Champneys had not yielded to the learned divines on this point without a struggle. Instead, he had modified his position by adopting the spiritualist dichotomy between internal and external sin.[212] Nevertheless, he was finally forced to confess that the inward and the outward man act in conjunction, that the regenerate man remains wholly a sinner. The third charge related to Champneys' justification of secrecy and inner religion,[213] but again he admitted that he was in error. Items four and five were variants on the first charge: that the regenerate always exhibit perfect love for each other in obedience to Christ's command; that the unregenerate clergy taught the 'devilish error' that the Holy Spirit did not preserve the Christian from sin.[214] Once again Champneys acknowledged that it was he who

---

[208] Wilkins, *Concilia*, IV, 39-40. The record of the trial is dated April 1548 (IV, 39) but this must have been a clerical error,.

[209] Champneys, B1ᵛ-B2ʳ, C3ʳ-C3ᵛ, D6ᵛ.

[210] *Ibid.*, C2ʳ-D7ʳ.

[211] *Ibid.*, C4ʳ.

[212] Compare *Ibid.*, C6ᵛ.

[213] *Ibid.*, B2ʳ.

[214] *Ibid.*, C3ʳ-C3ᵛ, E4ᵛ.

had been in error, not the learned clergy. The final charge concerned the regenerate man's continued need for the material necessities of life. This may have been included by the ecclesiastics among the commissioners as a sop to the secular authorities. Alternatively it may have been added to the charge-sheet by the sheriffs and secular officers sitting on the commission.[215]

The sentence imposed upon Champneys was in three parts. First, he was forbidden to preach, teach, or publish anything further without first obtaining a special licence from the authorities. Secondly he was commanded to gather in immediately as many copies of *The Harvest* as could be traced, and then to destroy them. Finally, Champneys was ordered to perform public penance at S. Paul's Cross the following day.[216] From the recognizance required for his bail, it appears that our subject had some wealthy sympathisers. The large sum of five hundred pounds was put up by Reginald Mohun of Cornwall (?Cornhill) who is simply described as '*generosus*'; and by Lawrence Clerke, a 'barber' from Whitechapel. Perhaps Champneys' two benefactors were members of that elusive coterie – the 'Christian Brethren'. Mohun's contribution may reflect the practical sympathy of a fellow West-countryman.

Several chroniclers record John Champneys' public penance at Paul's Cross on 28 April 1549, Stowe states that 'Myles Coverdale preached the rehearsall sermon' on this occasion.[217] Peter Heylyn, writing even later than Stowe (1661), states that this punishment had a profound effect upon Champneys.[218] Whether Heylyn was referring to the preaching of Miles Coverdale in particular or to the commissioners' examination in general is uncertain, but there are signs that he was correct. With regard to the first part of the sentence, there is no evidence

---

[215] Horst suggests that the authorities preferred the sixth charge because they 'found this an intimation that all goods may be held in common' (113). Champneys' original statement is tantalisingly obscure, but from the context he does not appear to be advocating the anabaptist principle of community of goods. Their objection can be explained in terms of the current political unrest in East Anglia where Ket and his followers were forcibly resisting enclosures and proclaiming the 'commonwealth' of England.

[216] Wilkins, *loc. cit.*

[217] Stow, *Annals* (1605 ed.) I, 596.

[218] Heylyn, I, 152-3.

that Champneys either produced or published the further work promised in his conclusion to *The Harvest*.[219] Ten years were to elapse before he ventured to circulate another publication, and that was in a different cause. That Champneys did diligently procure the recall and destruction of *The Harvest* may be inferred from the fact that only three copies now survive.[220] Several authorities testify that Champneys penitently bore his faggot at Paul's Cross on Low Sunday, 1549. Wriothesley records that Champneys was 'sorrie for his error'.[221]Despite the notice his case received, and unlike Putto the Tanner,[222] Champneys was not required to repeat this act of penance.

(d) His Subsequent Career

After generations of persecution the Lollards had 'developed their own tortuous casuistry which engendered abjuration rather than encouraged martyrdom'.[223] It has been suggested that Champneys' abjuration was of the same order, that it was 'not too difficult' for him to abjure.[224] However there is much to be said in favour of Peter Heylyn's account. He states,

… which punishment so wrought upon him that he relinquished all his former errors and entered into holy orders, flying the Kingdom for the better keeping of a good conscience in the time of Queen Mary, and coming back again with the other exiles after her decease.[225]

At first glance it might appear highly unlikely that the Edwardine bishops would ever have ordained a recently-abjured 'anabaptist' like Champneys. Nevertheless, such ordinations did take place. In December 1552 Nicholas Ridley ordained the former heretical tanner, Thomas Putto of Colchester, in S. Paul's.[226] Putto had appeared before the commissioners and abjured his heresy only three days after Champneys.

---

[219] Champneys, G3ᵛ.
[220] Above, 73 n. 142.
[221] *loc. cit.*
[222] Below, 110-1.
[223] E. G. Rupp, *The English Protestant Tradition*, (Cambridge, 1947), 2.
[224] Horst, 113-114.
[225] *loc. cit.*
[226] Ridley's ordination book cited in W. H. Frere, *The Marian Reaction* (London, 1896), 205-6.

Almost conclusive proof that Champneys was an Edwardine ordinand is supplied by the register of Matthew Parker. Among the one hundred and twenty deacons and forty-three presbyters who were ordained at Lambeth by Bishop Bullingham of Lincoln in the absence of the Archbishop on 10 March 1559/60 was 'Johannes Champneis'.[227] Since he was ordained presbyter at that time he must have been admitted to the diaconate already.

Did Ridley ordain Champneys as well as Putto? This must be considered unlikely. There is no mention of a 'Champneys' in Ridley's ordination book, and Frere notes 'the great care and fullness of the record of Ridley's Ordinations as contrasted with the slovenliness of those of Bonner's time.[228] A more likely episcopal sponsor is Miles Coverdale. On 20 December 1551, in his private chapel at Exeter, Coverdale ordained four men to the diaconate – one of these is listed as Thomas Champneys.[229] Was he our subject?

In the summer of 1551 Coverdale had been commissioned to accompany Lord Russell's expedition into Devonshire to preach to the rebels. On 30 August 1551 he was consecrated Bishop of Exeter, and the December ordinations were his first. Two of the four ordinands became priests a week later and were collated to benefices, but not Champneys.

It is suggested, therefore, that in the course of his examination before the heresy commissioners, John Champneys totally altered his opinion of the 'marked monsters' – the learned clergy of the religious establishment. He may well have been surprised to discover that Cranmer, Latimer, Cox, Coverdale, *et al.* did indeed know the scriptures and understand the Christian gospel. Since his own eschatological expectations had failed so dismally, he gave the Edwardine reformers his allegiance. After Champneys' public act of penance at Paul's Cross, Coverdale took him 'under his wing'. In 1551 Coverdale invited his Somerset protégé to accompany him to the West Country, where he ordained him.

---

[227] *Registrum Matthei Parker*, ed. Frere (Canterbury & York Society, Oxford, 1928), I, 343.
[228] Frere, *Marian Reaction*, 94.
[229] *Ibid.*, 216.

Heylyn's statement that Champneys 'fled the Kingdom... in the time of Queen Mary' is much more difficult to substantiate. There is no sign of any refugee named Champneys among the lists published by Garrett.[230] In February 1555, thanks to the intervention of the King of Denmark, the Privy Council granted Miles Coverdale a passport. He was given permission to take with him to Denmark two of his servants. One of these 'servants' was almost certainly his wife, the other could have been Champneys. Coverdale did not stay long in Denmark, becoming preacher to the Duchess of Suffolk's congregation at Wesel.[231] There are no records of any census of English refugees at either Wesel or Emden, and so Champneys could easily have been a member of either colony without being listed in Garrett.

Apart from the rehearsal sermon at S. Paul's Cross in April 1549 and the possible reference to our subject in Coverdale's Exeter register, the only other mention of Champneys in connection with Miles Coverdale is in John Bale's catalogue of English books. The second edition of this massive work was produced in Basle between 1557 and 1559. Among the latest additions is a list of Coverdale's works, and almost the last on that list is the following title: – *'Psalterium Joannis Campnesis Lib. I'*. Beneath the list Bale comments, *'nunc autem in Germania pauper ac peregrinus Manet'*.[232]

Heylyn must have had a reason for his assertion that John Champneys was a Marian exile. However, he was mistaken when he assumed that Champneys returned to England with the other exiles after the death of Mary Tudor. On 29 May 1557 the Privy Council sent a letter to the Earl of Shrewsbury – President of the Council of the North – informing him that 'the case of Champneis' had been referred to the Court of Exchequer and that he was to 'suffre no detriment thereby during his imprisonment'.[233] Four days later the Council sent another letter to the Commander in the North stating that Champneys' case had received

---

[230] C. H. Garrett, *The Marian Exiles* (reprinted Cambridge, 1966).
[231] *Ibid.*, 132ff.
[232] John Bale, *Scriptorum illustrium majoris Britanniae Catalogus* (second edition, Basle 1557, 1559) I, 721.
[233] *Acts of the Privy Council*, ed. Dasent, New Series VI (London, 1893), 92.

further consideration and they had resolved,

> that bothe he and suche as were taken in his companie shuld be furthwith set at libertie, binding first the said Champneis and oone Wall of London, girdeler, ... to make thier apparaunce... the next Terme in the Courte of theschequier to aunswere unto suche matter as is to be laide to thier charge....[234]

Unfortunately the records of the Court of Exchequer for the reigns of Edward and Mary are no longer extant, but clearly Champneys suffered no more than a period of imprisonment at the hands of the Marian authorities. These references could mean that Champneys did not 'fly the Kingdom' in the time of Queen Mary. Rather, that he fled north of the Trent where he organised a conventicle of like-minded Christians until they were apprehended by Marian officials. However, in view of the lenient treatment meted out to them it seems more likely that Champneys led a party of disillusioned refugees back to England in the summer of 1557. In an attempt to avoid detection they landed in Yorkshire (possibly Hull) but were immediately apprehended.[235]

After mentioning the flight of Champneys and his return from exile, Heylyn continues –

> At that time he published a discourse, in the way of a letter, against the Gospellers .... His discourse answered not long after by John Veron... but answered with scurrility and reproach enough, according to the humour of the Predestinarians.[236]

This work is no longer extant, but a reference in Tanner's *Bibliotheca* confirms that such a publication existed:

> Hic Champneis... in principio regni Elizabethae, scripsit, librum, suppresso autoris et typographi nomine, 'Contra dialogum Joh. Veroni de praedestinatione': cui respondet Veronus in 'Apologia' sua.[237]

---

[234] *Ibid.*, 96.
[235] There are other examples of refugees who returned to England before the end of Mary's reign, notably Elizabeth Young from Emden in 1557-8 (Foxe, *AM.*, VIII, 536-48), Thomas Bentham from Frankfurt (*Ibid.*, VIII, 788). Also Richard Yeoman, curate of Hadleigh, (*Proceedings of the Suffolk Institute of Archaeology*, III, (1863), 100-107).
[236] *loc. cit.*
[237] Thomas Tanner, *Bibliotheca* (London, 1748), 164-5.

The 'Gospellers' whose opinions Champneys opposed were those Calvinist preachers who held extreme views on the doctrine of predestination, among whom was Jean Veron, prebendary of S. Paul's.[238] In 1561 John Tisdale of London published five books by Veron,[239] but at least two of them must have been written earlier. Since Veron added his apology to the second edition of his *A fruteful treatise of Predestination*, Champneys must have written his book in reply to the first edition. In this apology Veron supplies interesting information concerning the circumstances in which Champneys' book was circulated. Having referred to Champneys' earlier abjuration, he continues –

Belike fearing now the like punishment, and that he should be compelled to revoke his Pelagian-like opinion, he durst not for all his proud boast set his own name to his railing and venemous book, nor yet suffer them to be sold openly or publicly in the book-binders shops, but cowardously suppressing both his own name and the name of ye unwise and foolish printer, got the whole impression into his hands, that so he might in hugger mugger send them unto his privy friends abroad whom belike he suspected to be of his affinity, and damnable opinion. Howbeit this could not be wrought so privily, but that within a while, some of his books came into my hands, whereby shortly after, the printer was known, and brought to his answer, whom this stout champion of Pelagius, hath left in the briars, and lest he himself should be faine to shew a reason for his doctrine, doth keep himself out of the way still, and dare not once show his face. If he be able to maintain his doctrine against my book let him come forth and play the man.[240]

Thus, from these sources we conclude that, in the year 1559, John Champneys composed an anonymous reply to Veron's *A fruteful treatise*. He had it printed privately and anonymously, and personally distributed copies of the book to those former associates whom he supposed would sympathise with his opinions. The book was entitled, *Against John Veron's Dialogue on Predestination*, and it may have been in the form of a letter. Unfortunately for Champneys – and more

---

[238] For an account of Veron see Philippe Denis, 'John Veron: The First Known French Protestant in England', *Proceedings of the Huguenot Society of London*, XXII, (1973), 257-263.

[239] RSTC 24680-24685.

[240] Jean Veron, *A fruteful treatise of Predestination* (London, 1561), RSTC 24681, sig. B8ʳ-C1ʳ.

especially for his printer – several copies fell into the hands of Jean Veron. He discovered the identity of the printer, who doubtless revealed the identity of the author. Whereupon Champneys, no doubt recalling the events at Paul's Cross ten years earlier, promptly went underground, leaving the unfortunate printer to face the consequences. Veron attached a hurried reply to the second edition of his *A fruteful treatise*, and later published a more comprehensive work on the subject entitled, *A moste necessary treatise of free wil.*

Unfortunately Veron does not quote at length from the work he seeks to answer. In fact, his 'Apology' makes only passing references to Champneys, while his considered treatment does not mention Champneys' book at all. Nevertheless, from Veron's comments it is apparent that Champneys had returned to his former opinion of the religious establishment. Veron remarks:

> Unto him, all those learned ministers, which do set forth and maintain this most wholesome and comfortable doctrine (which he calls as it pleaseth him) be the devil's most obedient children and trusty disciples. Whereas, all men may judge him rather to be an imp of Satan, since that he doeth by his blasphemous lies study, labour and travail all that in him lieth, to bring the godly learned ministers of this our time, as he did them that were in King Edward the sixth's days, into obliquy and hatred of the world....[241]

Heylyn was certainly correct in his use of the terms 'scurrility and reproach' to describe Veron's answer. At various points in this brief reply he refers to John Champneys as a 'most pestilent and pernicious sectary', as 'the blind guide of the free will men', and as 'an imp of Satan'. He ironically refers to him as 'this stout champion of Pelagius', as 'this high divine', as 'doctor Champenies' and as 'the gentleman'. Twice he contemptuously refers to Champneys' book as an 'unlearned fumbling together of the scriptures', and Champneys may well have begun his reply with a collection of Biblical texts that appear to teach the possibility of universal redemption. Veron refers to 'those universal propositions which so wittily are fombled together of Champneys'.[242]

---

[241] *Ibid.*, F1^v, see also B8^r.
[242] *Ibid.*, D8^v.

These seem to have included that old favourite, *I Timothy 2:4* and also *Psalm 145:14*. Then he may have put a series of four questions to Veron since – near the end of his apology – Veron writes, 'Now will I answer to the 4th question...'.[243]

Champneys' first question seems to have been connected with the relationship between foreknowledge and predestination. Something of Champneys' argument is preserved by Veron, who writes –

Now Champenies being a very Pelagian in this point... goeth about to mock away whatsoever I have spoken in my treatise, of election and reprobation, with the common [?armour] of the school-men.... God (sayeth this high devine) knowing from everlasting, before the world was made, who would incline to his will, and who would contemne it; hath according to his righteousness, foreordained the one unto life everlasting and the other unto eternal damnation. Who would have thought so much divinity to be in Champneys?[244]

As in *The Harvest*, Champneys made use of texts from the apocryphal books of *Wisdom* and *IV Esdras*, but Veron was not prepared to recognise their authority.

Question Two seems to have been about responsibility for human evil, and in particular false or blasphemous speech. If men can only speak that which is according to the will and appointment of God, what about lies? Veron replied,

'It is', sayeth this great divine, 'an open blasphemy to affirm and to say, that the publishing of lies, and falsehood is according to God's will and appointment ... that he suffereth the devil by such sectaries as Champneys is, to sow his lies abroad, it is because that he will have it so, partly for the trial of his elect.[245]

The third and fourth questions are even more difficult to deduce from the text of Veron's apology. The third seems to have arisen from a misunderstanding of some point made by Veron in his *Fruteful treatise*. Again it involved human responsibility. Veron asked Champneys to show him the place in his treatise where he had stated that, 'no man shall be condemned for his own actual sin, and wickedness, how blasphemous so ever it be'.[246] The final question may have been related to the recent Marian persecution. Is God responsible when those who imagine that they are serving him put his true servants to death?[247]

243 *Ibid.*, F3ʳ.
244 *Ibid.*, E5ᵛ-E6ʳ.
245 *Ibid.*, E7ʳ-E8ʳ.
246 *Ibid.*, E8ᵛ.
247 *Ibid.*, F3ʳ.

In the dedicatory epistle at the beginning of Jean Veron's considered treatment of the question of human freedom, he states that there were a number of free-willers still around –

I cannot but marvel at our pope pelagians and at the viperous brood of the free will men which do still to the great injury of the gratuite and free grace of God, so set out boast and advance the free will and strength of man.[248]

At one point in his apology Veron refers to Champneys as the 'blind guide of the free will men', and at another he writes of 'the free will men, whose standard bearer Champneys would fain be'.[249] This suggests that there was a fairly numerous group of Protestants, believing in human freedom and its associated perfectionist doctrine, in London in 1559-60. Moreover, Veron's statements indicate that John Champneys was either the leader and spokesman of the London free-willers, or that he was attempting (through his book) to rally them around his leadership. Since Veron also refers to him as a 'pernicious sectary', it would appear that Champneys had not resumed his ministry within the established church after the death of Mary Tudor. In fact, in 1559, this former deacon had attempted to organise a totally separated conventicle of London free-willers. However, the fact that he presented himself to Archbishop Parker as a candidate for admission to the priesthood (and was accepted) in 1560 indicates that his attempt failed. No doubt this was due to Veron's active opposition; it would be interesting to know his opinion of Champneys' subsequent ordination.

Unlike the majority of those whose ordination is recorded in Parker's *Register*, there is no record of Champneys being collated to a living. Possibly he went to a parish that was not in the gift of Archbishop

---

[248] Jean Veron, *A moste necessary treatise of free wil*, (London, 1561) RSTC 24684, sig. A5^{v}.

[249] Veron, *A fruteful treatise*, E8^{v}, see also A2^{r}-A2^{v}, I1^{r}.

Parker. Perhaps Champneys returned to the West Country; but after 10 March 1560 all is silent.[250]

(e) Conclusion

Horst is one of the few historians to have examined the contribution of John Champneys. He places our subject firmly among the English anabaptists.[251] However, a close examination of his book and his subsequent career suggests otherwise.

First, there is not the slightest evidence that the author of *The Harvest* advocated believers' baptism. While he undoubtedly sympathised with the concept of the gathered church, the only condition of entry therein is an experience of regeneration, and there is no sign that this was to be signified by baptism. Secondly, unlike two of the other 'anabaptists' examined by the commissioners in 1549, Champneys did not advocate the characteristic celestial flesh christology. Thirdly, there is no sign in Champneys of that pacifism which characterised Dutch anabaptism after the Bocholt conference of 1536. Over twelve years had passed since Münster, the Amsterdam uprising and their sequel at Bocholt, yet in

---

[250] The RSTC refers to a second extant work associated with Champneys. This is listed as, *The Copie of an answere made unto a certayne letter wherein the answerer purgeth him selfe and other, from Pelagius errors* [The Netherlands? 1563], STC 5742.10. The only known copy is in the Library of All Souls College, Oxford. Both author and printer are anonymous, and it is in the form of a letter. It was doubtless on the strength of these similarities and its title that William Prynne assumed that it was the anonymous reply to Veron's *A Fruteful treatise* and attributed the work to John Champneys (William Prynne, *A quench-coale*, London 1637, STC 20474, sig. c4^v). However, as the RSTC notes, *The Copie* makes no mention of either Veron or his books and consequently must be a different work. Moreover attribution of *The Copie* to Champneys is clearly erroneous since its anonymous author is certainly not an unlearned man 'of small literature' (Above p.84). On six occasions he quotes Augustine in Latin then translating into English (*e.g.*D4^v-D5^r), besides quoting and translating Cicero and Seneca and discussing Augustine's use of the word 'mathematicus' (C5^r margin). He checks Knox's citation of Augustine and finds it inaccurate (D1^r) and he quotes both Calvin and Melanchthon against Augustine in Latin (B1^r, B3^r-B3^v). Prynne had not personally read or examined the book but was dependent upon a respected informant – the Puritan controversialist Sir Humphrey Lynde (1579-1636) of Cobham, Surrey (Prynne, *A quench-coale*, D1^r) – and evidently he was misinformed.

[251] Horst, 114. In the revised edition of *The English Reformation* (1989) A. G. Dickens describes Champneys as 'a Melchiorite Anabaptist' (263).

1548 Champneys had high hopes of the English magistracy. He expected the secular authorities to co-operate with the Lord's servants in forcibly excluding the 'marked monsters' from the church. Later he submitted to episcopal ordination and became a recognised minister in the established church.

On the other hand, the part that Champneys envisaged for the magistracy in the realisation of the *Eschaton* is fully in accord with the native Lollard tradition. Furthermore, his virulent anti-clericalism is as much a characteristic of Lollardy as it is of anabaptism. The practice of abjuration was the norm for later Lollards as well as for the Spiritualists.[252] In both of Champneys' publications there are signs of the old indigenous sectarianism, and his nomenclature of 'marked monsters' or 'markid men' is certainly reminiscent of Lollardy's 'known men'.[253] Above all, the biblicism of John Champneys is firmly rooted within the Lollard tradition.[254] The only authority for doctrine that he accepts is the Bible, literally interpreted. He knows nothing about directly inspired prophets proclaiming additional authoritative revelations à la Davidist spiritualism. Finally, his later emphasis on human free will in opposition to the doctrine of predestination could reflect the attitude of later Lollardy as much as anabaptism.[255]

A. G. Dickens supplies a pertinent warning when he emphasises the ease with which 'the unwary' can mistake Lollardy for anabaptism.[256] Later he asserts,
   (Englishmen) had already found their special affinity with the linked ideas of conversion and the vernacular Bible.[257]
Those two 'linked ideas' are exactly the twin emphases found in John Champneys' *The Harvest*.

Nevertheless, there was some Continental anabaptist influence behind the formulation of his 1548 manifesto. Living in London at the time he did, and frequenting sectarian conventicles as he undoubtedly did, John

---

252 'Schwärmer' – a descriptive term that includes the followers of David Joris. Dickens, *Lollards and Protestants*, 10
253 Davis, 405.
254 See G. F. Nuttall, *The Puritan Spirit* (London, 1967), 39-42.
255 Below, 339-40.
256 Dickens, *Lollards and Protestants*, 10.
257 *Ibid.*, 135.

Champneys must have been confronted with foreign religious radicalism. His emphasis upon spiritual regeneration as the essence of Christian salvation, his over-optimistic estimate of its power to overcome the practical effects of original sin in the regenerate, his spiritualist interpretation of sinless perfection (its inward character) – all indicate Melchiorite influence. Similarly, his emphasis upon 'perfection of love' as the supreme evidence of truly Christian discipleship is reminiscent of Davidist teaching.[258] Finally the role that Champneys appears to envisage for himself in the realisation of the *Eschaton* in his own day suggests an almost conscious imitation of the demagogic Melchiorite prophets. These features of 'anabaptism' were recognised as such by the authorities in 1549. They are reflected in the charges brought against John Champneys by the heresy commissioners. It was, therefore, not entirely unjust that he should have been convicted of anabaptist heresy.

In conclusion it is suggested that the development of John Champneys' theological career was along the following lines. The early formative influences were exerted in the 1520s and 30s by the Lollards of the West Country. In sectarian circles in London in the 1540s he came under the influence of Melchiorite anabaptist doctrine. These two strands of religious radicalism fermented within Champneys, reaching a climax in London in 1548 with the publication of his apocalyptic challenge to the ecclesiastical establishment. His subsequent trial before the heresy commissioners proved to be a devastating anti-climax, and Champneys meekly accepted a lowly place within the Edwardine religious establishment. In exile in Germany *circa* 1556 Champneys became disillusioned with the quarrels of the refugees over ecclesiastical polity and the doctrine of predestination. He reverted to his former Lollard/anabaptist belief in human autonomy and perfectibility and returned to Marian England. In London in 1559 he once again attempted to make a public stand against the learned clergy, and once again they defeated him. In 1560 he rejoined the established church. Perhaps John Champneys ended his ministerial career serving as an itinerant Anglican lecturer – much as he probably began it as an itinerant Lollard preacher.

---

[258] Champneys, C3^r-C4^r.

III MICHAEL THOMBE

On 11 May 1549 a London butcher was brought before Archbishop Cranmer and three other commissioners at a sitting in Lambeth Palace, and there charged with anabaptist heresy. With a standard formula of recantation, Michael Thombe abjured two heresies –

> That rather Christ toke no flesshe of our Lady and that rather I beleue that I haue said that the baptyme of infantes is not profitable because it goith without faith:[259]

The celestial flesh christology was a characteristic of Melchiorite anabaptism and had been maintained by several Londoners convicted of heresy in the previous reign. The second charge indicates that Thombe was a true anabaptist. Thombe believed that baptism was profitable but only when the subject was capable of exercising faith, *i.e.* when he was an adult-believer. As consistent sacramentarians the Lollards maintained that the baptism of infants was unnecessary and unprofitable, but such reasoning did not imply rebaptism as did the views of Thombe.[260]

There is no record in Cranmer's register of the sentence imposed by the commissioners. However, Wriothesley records that on the following day, 'a butcher dwelling by Ould Fish Streete bare a faggot at Poules Crosse, which was an Anabaptist'.[261] Having submitted and done penance Thombe disappears from the records. His surname is certainly unusual. Perhaps he was one of the foreign anabaptists who had settled in London.[262]

---

[259] Cranmer, Register, folio 74^r; Wilkins, *Concilia*, IV, 42.
[260] Davis, 408.
[261] Wriothesley, II, 12-13.
[262] Dickens, *The English Reformation* (second revised edition) refers to him as John Thombe, states that he was naturalised in June 1549, and suggests that he came from the Netherlands (263n).

IV THOMAS PUTTO

That Cranmer's register does not supply an account of all the individuals who appeared before the commissioners on heresy charges in 1549 is proved by the case of 'one Puttoe, a tanner'. Wriothesley records,

Memorandum: the fifth daie of Maie, being the second Soundaie after Easter, one Puttoe,a tanner in Collchester in Essex, bare a faggott at Poules Crosse, which was an Anabaptist and was abiured the xxxth daie of Aprill at Poules, before my Lorde of Canterburie; his opynion was, he denied that Christ descended not [*sic*] into hell, which damnable opinion he now lamentith.[263]

Thus, in the week before the examination of John Champneys and the second appearance of Joan Bocher before the commissioners, Putto was tried in S. Paul's. The denial that Christ descended into hell was not a cardinal tenet of anabaptism.[264] However, since Wriothesley only listed one of the two charges against Michael Thombe, it may be that other charges were preferred against Putto. Strype recognised the inadequacy of the charge against a man who was tried and convicted by commissioners who were investigating anabaptist heresy. He therefore assumed that Putto either maintained Joan Bocher's heretical christology or advocated believers' baptism.[265] Certainly subsequent references indicate that Putto was as stubborn and defiant as Joan.

In 1556 Miles Hogarde referred to this series of heresy trials and mentioned the case of Thomas Putto. However he did not record any additional charges. Hogarde states,

Furthermore, there was one Puttoe a Tanner, which denied one of the articles of the Crede, whiche was that Christe descended not into he[ll], saying, he could not rede it in the worde written & therefore not worthy to be credited. But abiuring the same opinion he caried a fagot.[266]

From this it appears that Putto's objection to the credal formula derived from his own understanding and personal reading of the Bible rather than from any christological heresy.

Hogarde's account also indicates that another radical 'gospeller' appeared before the heresy commissioners at this time. He continues,

A Bricklaer taking upon him the office of preachyng, affirmed he myght laufully do it, though he were not called therunto by ye church. For 'Spirito vbi vult Spirat'.[267]

---

263 Wriothesley, II, 12.
264 Above, 28-9.
265 Strype, *EM.*, II (i), 336.
266 Hogarde, *op. cit.*, sig. B2^v-B3^r.
267 *Ibid.*, B3^r.

This sounds very much like John Harrydaunce the bricklayer-preacher from Whitechapel, who was in trouble with the Henrician authorities on numerous occasions for illicit preaching.[268]

A fortnight after his first act of penance Thomas Putto again stood at Paul's Cross, because it was adjudged that his demeanour had been unsatisfactory on the previous occasion. Wriothesley states,

> Memorandum: the nynetenth daie of Maie... Puttoe... because he stoode that tyme with his capp on his head all sermon tyme, to the peoples estymation unpenitent for his offence, was sent to my Lorde of Canterburie, who had further ioyned him in pennance to stand this daie againe....[269]

Although 'the awdience well accepted' Putto's repeated penance, within two months he was in trouble again. On 30 June 1549 the Privy Council paid Edward Sheffield twenty-six shillings and eight pence for 'bringing upp oone Putto, *alias* Tanner'.[270] This time Putto was taken into custody and brought to London for preaching without license. However, he seems to have been let off with a caution. On 28 April 1550 the Privy Council record states,

> It was declared that one Putto (who for his lewde preaching had been put to silence by ordre of the Counsaill) did nowe, neverthelesse, of his owne hedde preache as lewdely as he had doone before....[271]

This time the Archbishop of Canterbury and the Bishop of Ely were requested to examine and correct him, but once again he was treated with great leniency. On 15 July 1550 'Thomas Puttowe of Berechurche

---

[268] The most detailed account of Harrydaunce is to be found in G. R. Elton, *Policy and Police: the enforcement of the Reformation in the age of Thomas Cromwell* (Cambridge, 1972), 162-4. However, Brigden (*op. cit.*, pp. 161-2, 192-3) suggests that Elton treats him 'too lightly'. See also Claire Cross, *Church and People 1450-1660* (Glasgow, 1976), 73, 121.

[269] Wriothesley, II, 13.

[270] *APC.*, II, 298.

[271] *Ibid.*, III, 20.

in the countie of Essex' entered into a recognizance of one hundred
pounds upon condition that –

he behave himself like a good subject, and forbeare open preaching to
any other than his owne famylie betwene this and the Feast of All
Saintes, and then to appeare before the Counsaill to abide their further
ordre.[272]

Presumably Putto's conduct was satisfactory for, eighteen months later,
(13 November 1551) his bond was reduced to twenty pounds upon
condition that he 'nether preache nor read any more untill he be
thereunto laufully called and authorised'.[273] A year later (11 November
1552) Ridley ordained 'Thomas Putto, aged about forty, born at
Broomfield in Essex, for the previous five years resident at Mile End,
Colchester'.[274] Evidently the ecclesiastical authorities had come to the
conclusion that it was better to channel Putto's energetic preaching into
the service of the established church than attempt to silence him.
Conversely, Putto apparently came to accept that the Edwardine church
afforded adequate opportunities for Christian service.

Presumably Putto's ordination to the diaconate enabled him to preach
freely in and around Colchester. There is no evidence to suggest that he
was subsequently admitted to priests' orders or ever held a living. He is
not listed among the married clergy of Essex who were deprived of their
livings by Bishop Bonner.[275] On the other hand, the rector of Mile End,
Colchester, was among sixty or more Essex clergy who were deprived
during the Marian period.[276] Putto may have held a curacy – probably of
his home parish of Mile End – or simply have been given a licence to
preach freely within the archdeaconry of Colchester.

On 19 February 1554 the Privy Council ordered Lord Rich and Sir
John Wentworth, sheriff of Essex, to punish 'certayn lewde personnes'
in and around Colchester 'that have gone about to dissuade the Quenes
people there from frequenting suche Divine Service' as was appointed

---

272   *Ibid.*, III, 81.
273   *Ibid.*, III, 413.
274   Frere, *loc. cit.*
275   H. E. P. Grieve, 'The Deprived Married Clergy of Essex', *Transactions of the Royal Historical Society*, Fourth Series, XXII, 141-169.
276   *VCH.*, Essex, II, 33 n. l.

by law, *i.e.* the recently reinstituted mass.[277] That one of these 'lewde' preachers was Thomas Putto is evident from the charges that were preferred against him in 1556 and which were recorded in *The Oath Book of Colchester*.[278] On 27 April 1556 Thomas Putto, tanner, late of Colchester, was accused of gathering on 10 November 1554 twenty or more other people, with 'force of arms and swords', at Mile End, Colchester and elsewhere in unlawful conventicles. Putto was described as a 'most hateful enemy of Christ', who by 'enticements, persuasions and procurements entangled people in errors, infidelities and execrable opinions'. Moreover, he had 'taught some of the Queen's subjects to escape and others to resist the royal power and the doctrines of Christ and Holy Mother Church'. Six other men and seven women were charged at the same time with being 'obstinate and fugitive heretics who spurned the true doctrines of Christ and Mother Church'.[279]

Putto had evidently resumed his former trade soon after the accession of Mary. However, he continued to preach in illegal conventicles which he gathered in the countryside around Colchester and which were protected by armed men.[280] Furthermore, he appears to have encouraged detected heretics to escape overseas and others to openly resist the political and ecclesiastical authorities. Putto was tried some eighteen months after the initial offence was committed which suggests that he too either joined the refugees overseas or went 'underground' upon detection. Nothing is known about the outcome of his trial before the Colchester magistrates. Thomas Putto was accused of very serious crimes, and bearing in mind his age (he was at least forty in 1552), it would appear unlikely that he survived the Marian regime.

---

[277] *APC.*, IV, 395.

[278] ed. W. G. Benham (Colchester, 1907); Benham, '12 Colchester Persons indicted for Heresy in 1566 [*sic*]', *Essex Review*, L, (1942), 157-162.

[279] *Ibid.*, cited by Oxley, 225.

[280] This conventicle also met at West Mersea and at Dedham to hear the famous itinerant preacher, George Eagles. On 25 July 1556 John Jeffrey the elder, of West Mersea, and a clothier from Dedham whose surname is not recorded were indicted before the quarter sessions at Colchester. They were accused of 'gathering conventicles of twenty or more persons at West Mersea and Dedham with George Eagles, tailor'. However, by the time of the trial Jeffrey had died, and the Dedham clothier was merely fined five shillings (Essex Record Office QSR 2/15).

Oxley suggests that Putto's anabaptism of 1549 'did not go very deep'.[281] Subsequent references tend to confirm this assessment. Putto was addicted to preaching rather than to any specific anabaptist heresy. His rejection of the credal assertion that Christ descended into hell may simply have derived from his own understanding of the Bible. Moreover, his open defiance of the Marian authorities and readiness to preach to armed conventicles of Protestants suggests Calvinist influence rather than the pacifism or Nicodemism of the anabaptists.Undoubtedly Thomas Putto was a rugged individual, ever ready to take independent action and not averse to separatism. Nevertheless, he was a radical 'gospeller' in the mould of John Harrydaunce,[282] rather than a radical 'anabaptist' in the sense of Joan Bocher, Michael Thombe, or even possibly John Champneys.[283]

---

[281] Oxley, 166.
[282] Above, 110.
[283] Davis, (354-5) identifies Putto with Thomas Potto of Sawston, Cambridgeshire, a butcher who was charged with sacramentarianism under the Six Articles on 7 March 1540. However, all three places mentioned in connection with Thomas Putto the tanner – Broomfield, Berechurch and Mile End – lie within two miles of Colchester. Davis' identification must be regarded as conjecture.

B. THE HERESY COMMISSION OF 1551.

In January 1550 a general pardon was proclaimed. Like that of a decade earlier, anabaptist heretics were again excepted, and like the pardon of July 1540 anabaptism was again defined. The six opinions delineated are identical with those of 1540.[284] However, it is significant that the seventh, determinist, tenet which was defined as a principle of anabaptism in 1540, was now omitted.[285] Presumably this was due to the increasing influence of Reformed theology from the Continent.

Undoubtedly it was in the city and diocese of London where religious radicalism posed the greatest problems for the ecclesiastical authorities. This may well have been one of the factors behind the translation of Nicholas Ridley from Rochester to London, together with the integration of the diocese of Westminster into London, in April 1550.[286] Likewise, the formerly independent (and lawless) borough of Southwark was brought within the jurisdiction of the City of London the following month.[287] In the same month (May 1550) Bishop Ridley began a visitation of his new diocese. Several of his articles of enquiry reflect the bishop's concern over the presence of anabaptists. Article thirteen asked 'Whether any do preach or affirm all things to be common, or that we ought to have no magistrates?'[288] Article forty-eight asked 'Whether any speaketh against baptism of infants?'[289] Most significantly, Article forty-four suggests that there may have been some in the diocese who had already rejected the Act of Uniformity of 1549, separated from the established church, and organised independent churches –

> Whether any of the Anabaptists' sect or other, use notoriously any unlawful or private conventicles, wherein they do use doctrine or administration of Sacraments, separating themselves from the rest of the parish.[290]

---

284   Above, 28-9.
285   *Statutes of the Realm*, IV (i), 128.
286   Strype, *EM.*, II (i), 338-40.
287   Wriothesley, II, 38.
288   *Visitation Articles and Injunctions of the Period of the Reformation*, eds. Frere and Kennedy (London, 1910), II, 233.
289   *Ibid.*, 238.
290   *Ibid.*

Another step taken at this time by the authorities to curtail independent religious activity in London was the establishment of the Strangers' Church at Austin Friars. It has been estimated that there were by 1550 between six and eight hundred Dutch refugees in the City.[291] John à Lasco arrived from East Friesland on 13 May, and the Church was established under his supervision in June 1550.[292] The King noted in his diary,

> It was appointed that the Germans should have the Austin Friars for their church to have their service in, for avoiding of all sects of Anabaptists and suchlike.[293]

Lindeboom's assertion that a 'well-regulated body' such as the Strangers' Church 'constituted a counterweight' against anabaptist influence[294] is correct. Under à Lasco's influence the Strangers' Church produced a confession of faith and quickly began to exercise congregational discipline. Early in 1551 the church excommunicated George van Parris, a Flemish surgeon, for denying the deity of Christ. He was handed over to the recently re-established heresy commission and examined by Archbishop Cranmer and the commissioners in Lambeth Palace on 6 April 1551. Since van Parris knew no English the examination was conducted with Miles Coverdale acting as interpreter. The accusation states,

> that he beleveth that God the Father is only God, and that Christ is not very God, is noon heresy, and beyng by like interpretation declared unto him, that yt is an heresy; and being asked whether he will retracte and abjure the same opinion; he saith, no.

He was found guilty and the following day the commissioners sentenced him to be burned as an obstinate heretic. The sentence was duly executed in Smithfield on 24 April.[295]

The fate of van Parris did not, however, deter the anti-trinitarians among the foreigners – although the Davidists may have decided to keep their opinions to themselves. On 14 August 1551 Martin Micronius (à Lasco's assistant) informed Bullinger that 'the chief opponents of

---

[291] J. Lindeboom, *Austin Friars: History of the Dutch Reformed Church in London 1550-1950* (The Hague, 1950), 5, 5 n. 2.

[292] This was achieved due to the influence of the Duchess of Suffolk, and despite the strong opposition of Bishop Ridley; *ibid,* 6.

[293] Jordan, *Chronicle,* 37.

[294] Lindeboom, 10.

[295] Cranmer, Register, folio 78^r-79^r; Wilkins, IV, 44-5; Jordan, *Chronicle,* 58; Wriothesley, II, 47; Wilbur, 171.

Christ's divinity are the Arians, who are now beginning to shake our churches with greater violence than ever'.[296] The following year bishops Ridley, Hooper, Thirlby and Coverdale introduced a bill in the House of Lords, 'For the Preservation of the King's Majesty's Subjects from such Heresies as may happen by strangers dwelling among them'.[297] By the next year Micronius was more optimistic. Writing to Bullinger from London on 18 February 1553, he stated,

...no foreigner is now eligible to the rights of an English citizen, without having previously made a confession of his faith to the ministers of the foreign churches. Should this regulation last some years, this Kingdom will be delivered from great and various errors, which are usually introduced by foreign sectaries.[298]

Thus, by 1553, every foreign refugee holding radical religious opinions who wished to enjoy the privileges of denizenship had to resort to Nicodemism.

With regard to the rural parishes within Ridley's diocese, those of north-east Essex in the archdeaconry of Colchester were especially infected by religious radicalism.[299] Between 1548 and 1551 Jean Veron translated and published at least three of Bullinger's anti-anabaptist treatises.[300] Veron dedicated his version of *A moste necessary & frutefull Dialogue* (concerning magistrates), published 3 April 1551, to Sir John Gates – the High Sheriff of Essex. In his dedicatory epistle Veron gave his reasons for dedicating his work to a man he had never met. He writes,

The second cause that moueth me, to dedicate, this little worke unto you is that ye are... placed in authoritie for this our countrey of Essex, in the which, many of these Libertines and Anabaptists, are running in hoker moker, emonge the symple and ignoraunte people, to impell and moue theym to tumulte and insurrection agaynste the maiestrates and rulers of thys Realme.[301]

---

296 *Original Letters*, II, 574.
297 Quoted by C. H. Smyth, *Cranmer and the Reformation under Edward VI*, (Cambridge, 1926), 220.
298 *Original Letters*, II, 581.
299 Strype, *EM.*, II (i), 341-2.
300 STC. 4059, 4068, 4069.
301 Jean Veron, *A moste necessary & frutefull Dialogue*, (Worcester, 1551) STC 4068, sig. C2ᵛ-C3ʳ.

On 23 July 1551 Bishop Ridley wrote to Sir John Cheke asking him to use his influence to secure prebends for Edmund Grindal, John Bradford and John Rogers. Ridley described Rogers as a preacher who was actively detecting and confuting anabaptists in Essex.[302] Later, when he was in prison at Oxford, he wrote to Bradford bitterly criticising contemporary heretics some of whom denied the Trinity, some the divinity of Christ, some the baptism of infants, some original sin, some affirmed human free will, and some advocated re-baptism.[303]

In these circumstances, therefore, it is hardly surprising that on 18 January 1551 the heresy commission had been reconvened with Bishop Ridley prominent among its members.[304] Strype states that this was, in fact, a 'special commission from the King against Anabaptists and sectaries in Kent and Essex'. It consisted of no less than thirty-one persons – both clergy and laymen – and included Matthew Parker, Miles Coverdale, Christopher Nevinson and Nicolas Bullingham. They were authorised to 'correct and punish all Anabaptists, and such as did not duly administer the sacraments according to the Book of Common Prayer'.[305] However, having reconvened and strengthened the heresy commission, the Privy Council decided to examine the first group of suspects itself.

I THE ESSEX RADICALS

On 27 January 1551 Thomas Upcharde, weaver of Bocking near Braintree, was brought before the Privy Council. Upcharde had been arrested on the instructions of Sir Richard Rich after a large number of people had met in his house at Bocking on the Sunday before Christmas, 1550. On 26 January the Council asked Chancellor Rich to send up the 'man of Bocking' whom he had examined.[306] Upcharde was then taken before the full Council gathered at Greenwich. Here Upcharde confessed,

that [there] were certein Kenttishemen to the towne to ha[ve] lodged with goode man Cooke, and bicause Cookes wief was in childebed, thei cam to this Upcharddes howse, weare Cooke was th[en] at

---

[302] *The Works of Nicholas Ridley*, ed. Christmas (Cambridge, 1841), 331.
[303] *Ibid.*, 367.
[304] Above, 35; Wilkins, *Concilia*, IV, 44-5.
[305] Strype, *EM.*, II (i), 385; II (ii), 200.
[306] *APC.*, III, 196, 197, 198-9.

dinner, and by Cookes entreatie there thei were lodged. And upon the morowe, which was Soundaie, divers of the towne about xij of the clocke came in, and there thei fell in argument of thinges of the Scripture, speciallie wheather it were necessarie to stande or Kneele, barehedde or covered, at prayer; whiche at length was concluded in ceremonie not to be materiall, but the hartes before God was it that imported and no thing els;[307]

The Council decided that there was more to this gathering than Upcharde would have them believe – and doubtless they were right. The record continues,

and bicause it seemed suche an assembley, being of lx persons or moo, shulde meane some great matter, therefore both the said Upcharde, and one Sympson of the same sorte, was committed to the Marshalsie till further triall were had, and order taken that lettres shulde be sent bothe into Essex and Kent for thapprehension of these that arr accoumpted chief of that practise.[308]

A letter was then despatched to a sheriff of Essex, Sir George Norton, enclosing a list of the leading members of the Bocking conventicle, ordering their arrest and commanding him to, 'sende them hither that none of them have conference with other'. Included on the list were:– John Barrett, of Stamphorde, coweherde; Robert Cooke, of Bocking, clothier; John Eglise, of Bocking, clothier; Richard Bagge; Thomas Pygrinde; John Kinge; – Myxsto; – Boughtell; and Robert Wolmere.[309] A similar letter was sent to two sheriffs of Kent, Sir Edward Wootton and Sir Thomas Wyatt. They were commanded to arrest and send to London the following persons:– William Sibley and Thomas Yonge of Lenham, Nicholas Shetterton and Thomas Sharpe of Pluckley, John Lydley and – Chidderton of Ashford, and Cole of Maidstone, 'scholemaster'.

On 3 February 1551 seven of the Essex men and five from Kent appeared before the Council. Robert Cooke and Robert Wolmere were not there, and neither were the two Ashford men, Lydley and Chidderton; presumably they evaded capture. Even more surprising is the absence of Upcharde and Sympson who had been held in the

---

[307]   *Ibid.*, 198-9.
[308]   *Ibid.*, 199.
[309]   *Ibid.*

Marshalsea for the past week. The two groups were interrogated separately about the assembly at Bocking, but both confessed –

the cause of their assemble to be for talke of Scriptures, Not denyeng but thei had refused the communyon aboue ij yeres, vpon verie superstituouse and erronyose purposes: withe Divers other euill oppynyons worthie of great punyshement.[310]

Thus, the suspicions of the Privy Council were more than justified.[311]

Fragments of a later interrogation of the Kentish conventiclers (probably by the heresy commissioners) are preserved in a Harleian manuscript.[312] This reveals that a collection had been taken up among them to cover the expenses of the trip to Bocking. It also reveals that the doctrine of predestination was a major concern of the conventiclers at this time. It is reasonable, then, to suppose that the 'argument of thinges of the Scripture' which took place at Bocking concerned the merits of the 'new' teaching on predestination *vis à vis* free will. The controversies over kneeling and head-covering may be interpreted as an oblique reference to the new Prayer Book services. Although their attitude to the 1549 *Book of Common Prayer* may have been ambiguous, these leading conventiclers from Essex and Kent nevertheless admitted that 'thei had refused the communyon aboue ij yeres'. Champlin Burrage argued that this evidence was not sufficient to justify the conclusion that the two groups had separated from the established church.[313] In fact, the opposite interpretation could be placed upon these statements, *i.e.*, that the conventiclers had never been in communion with the Edwardine Church, that they had absented themselves from their parish churches since 1547 at least.

The prisoners were also found guilty of maintaining, 'Divers other euill oppyynons worthie of great punyshement'. Similar phraseology was used by John Knox and William Turner when referring to the

---

310 *Ibid.*, 206-7.
311 The parish of Bocking was a 'peculiar' of the archdiocese of Canterbury and therefore the responsibility of Archbishop Cranmer. This may have caused the Privy Council to take a greater interest in the affair, for the Archbishop's leniency towards conventiclers was well-known.
312 BL. MS., Harleian 421, folios 133-4.
313 Champlin Burrage, *The Early English Dissenters* (Cambridge, 1912), I, 51-2.

teaching of Robert Cooche, and by John Careless when referring to Henry Harte.[314] Therefore, these opinions may have related to human autonomy and impeccability – opinions which fervent predestinarians considered 'evil' and (when they were associated with separatism) punishable.

Hargrave follows Strype[315] in regarding these conventiclers as the earliest separatists from the Church of England. He states,

> The Freewillers made their initial appearance in the second year of the reign of Edward IV when they began forming an association in the southeastern part of England. In that year (1549) separatist conventicles were established at Faversham in Kent and at Bocking in Essex. In these activities the Freewillers were among the earliest separatists from the Church of England....[316]

However, neither this assessment nor that of Burrage takes sufficient account of earlier nonconformity in these districts, neither do they allow for any continuity with Lollardy. It was only twenty-two years since the Lollard conventicle at Steeple Bumpstead was discovered, and Bocking was only eleven miles from Steeple Bumpstead. Surely Oxley is closer to the truth when he notes,

> there was an old Lollard connection between Kent and Essex, and it is tempting to see in this conventicle Lollardy divided against itself by two different sources of Reforming doctrine.[317]

In 1428 William White of Tenterden escaped with some of his associates from Archbishop Chichele's persecution of Kentish Lollards. They did so by fleeing from the Weald of Kent to East Anglia, almost certainly *via* Colchester.[318] Kentish Lollards could take passage across the Thames Estuary from Faversham Creek either to Maldon or up the Colne to Colchester itself. Doubtless this was the route taken by William Sibley *et.al.* at Christmas 1550.[319] From Maldon or Colchester they

---

[314] Below, 252-3, 246, 203.
[315] Strype, *EM.*, II (i), 369.
[316] O. T. Hargrave, 'The Freewillers in the English Reformation', *Church History* XXXVII (1968), 271.
[317] Oxley, 165 n.1.
[318] Thomson, 122-3, 174-6.
[319] This was the route taken by John Frith in 1533. He was captured in Essex whilst in flight to the Continent from Kent (Foxe, *AM.*, VIII, 695).

would have travelled overland to Bocking – a journey of some fifteen miles. Five years later, during the Marian persecution, John Denley and John Newman, both of Maidstone in Kent, were arrested in Essex while 'going to visit such their godly friends as then they had in the county of Essex'.[320] Writing about the changing pattern of Kentish communications during the first half of the sixteenth century, Clark states,

> There was, in addition, considerable trading contact with East Anglia... the burgeoning ordinary contact between southern Essex and North Kent, through common interests in fishing, cloth manufacture, and agricultural exchange. The Tilbury ferry to Gravesend and the multitude of other cockboats plying the river made travel across the Thames estuary much easier than on the Kentish mainland itself.[321]

Having interrogated the prisoners, the Privy Council then pronounced the following sentences:–

> Whereupon Boughtell Barrey Coole william Sibley and Nicholas Shittrenden were commytted to [hiatus] Iohannes Eglins, Thomas Myxer, Ricardus Blagge, Thomas piggerell et Iohannes King de Bocking in Essex recognouerunt *etc.* in xl libras pro quolibet eorum. The Condicon tappeare whan thei shalbe called vpon, and to resorte to their ordinarie for resolucion of their oppynyons in cace thei haue any doubte in religion The like Recognisaunce taken of Thomas Sharpe of plukely and Nicholas Yong of lenham.[322]

Presumably Boughtell, Barrey, Coole, Sibley and Shittrenden were committed to prison, they being the most recalcitrant of the conventiclers. Those who were released upon a recognisance of forty pounds were, perhaps, less ardent exponents of free will and more ready to abandon separatism and 'resorte to their ordinarie'. Just over a year later, Thomas Cole was preaching before Archbishop Cranmer at Maidstone.[323] Therefore the conventiclers could not have been kept in prison for very long. Nevertheless, as far as Cole and Upcharde were concerned, the punishment seems to have had the desired effect. Furthermore, none of those who were released on bail figure in any subsequent record of religious unorthodoxy.

---

[320] Foxe, *AM.*, VII, 329.
[321] P. A. Clark, *English Provincial Society from the Reformation to the Revolution* (Hassocks, 1977), 11.
[322] *loc. cit.*
[323] Below, 145-53.

Of the eleven Essex men listed in these records we have further information on three of them.[324] Each of these three seems to have played a prominent part, both in this conventicle and in later Essex nonconformity.

(a) Thomas Upcharde

Evidently both Thomas Upcharde and Robert Cooke were men of some substance in Bocking. Cooke is described as a 'clothier' – a master weaver who employed other weavers – while later records refer to Upcharde as 'a weaver of Bocking'. It is therefore to be expected that the delegation from Kent had arranged to stay with Cooke, but due to his wife's incapacity they were put up at Upcharde's house.

Although Upcharde's term of imprisonment in the Marshalsea may have lasted but a few weeks, our next record suggests that he may have suffered a somewhat longer period of imprisonment under the Marian regime. In John Trewe's account of the King's Bench controversy there is a passing reference to Upcharde's release from that prison –

> Wherefore we gave them over, and meddled as little with them as we could, until Simson, Upchear and Wodman... were delivered out of prison.[325]

The date of these prisoners' release can be precisely determined from a reference in Foxe. Referring to Richard Woodman, Foxe states:

> At length the same day when master Philpot was burned, which was the 18th of December, he with four other prisoners was delivered and set at liberty by Bonner himself.[326]

Thus Upcharde was released from the King's Bench on 18 December 1555. Trewe's statement also implies that he had thrown in his lot with the predestinarians.

---

[324] Additionally, the Essex conventicler named Boughtell, whom the Privy Council sent to prison, may have been the Thomas Bowtell of Newport who was indicted for heresy and fled to Wiltshire in 1556 (D. M. Loades, 'The Essex Inquisitions of 1556', *Bulletin of the Institute for Historical Research*, XXXV (1962), 93-4).

[325] Richard Laurence, *Authentic Documents Relative to the Predestinarian Controversy* (Oxford, 1819), 57.

[326] Foxe, *AM.*, VIII, 333.

This is confirmed by the contents of a series of letters written from the King's Bench to 'T.V.' by John Careless.[327] Apparently Upcharde had written to Careless in the King's Bench, but Careless had delayed his reply in the hope of seeing him again – perhaps he had hoped for a similar release. Now, however, he suffers 'the bitter cup of inward afflictions' and does not expect to see Upcharde again in this life. Therefore he, 'can no longer forbear the scribbling of these few lines unto you'.[328] Since Careless died in the King's Bench on 1 July 1556, this correspondence must have taken place between January and June of that year.

John Careless was a fellow weaver; like William Tyms and other Essex radicals,[329] Upcharde had evidently come under his influence during his incarceration in the King's Bench. In his first letter, Careless, echoing the Apostle Paul, refers to Upcharde as 'mine own bowels in the Lord'.[330] However, it is clear from subsequent letters that Upcharde was only partially persuaded by Careless, that he still entertained strong doubts concerning Reformed soteriology.[331] In his second letter Careless advises,

But yet, my good brother, use a measure in this your godly mourning, and make not your faithful friends too much sorry for you. Let the persuasions of such godly lovers as you do daily company withal... move you to some godly mirth and rejoicing.[332]

Evidently Upcharde had joined the London underground congregation of predestinarians, which at this time was led by Thomas Fowle with the recently released Cuthbert Sympson serving as deacon. This congregation was in communion with various congregations of exiles on the Continent and used the Edwardine Prayer Book services.[333]

---

[327] Four letters from John Careless to T.V. were published by Coverdale in his *Godly Letters of the Martyrs* (STC. 5886; ed. Bickersteth, London, 1837): – I = pp. 445-7; II = pp. 447-9; III = pp. 475-6; IV = pp. 477-9. John Foxe included Letters II and IV with his material on Careless (*AM.*, VIII, 183-5, 189-91).
[328] Coverdale, 445-6.
[329] Below, 201-3.
[330] Coverdale, 446.
[331] *Ibid.*, 448, 475-6.
[332] *Ibid.*, 448-9.
[333] Foxe, *AM.*, VIII, 445-6, 454-61.

Careless' third letter to Upcharde was constantly interrupted and delayed – probably by the writer's deteriorating health. It contains the clearest evidence of the cause of Upcharde's doubts and depression. Careless writes:

I cannot express, my dear heart in the Lord, how my joys do increase, to see how God of his great mercy doth daily add unto his true church and poor afflicted congregation, such as he in Christ hath elected to salvation, before the foundation of the world was laid. ...And as this most true and heavenly doctrine doth bring all mirth, joy, peace, and quietness unto a Christian conscience, so doth it set Satan in a most sore rage and malice against the same...

Therfore, above all things, Satan seeketh to darken and make dim this doctrine of our salvation, yea, clean to quench it out if he could, and to bring us from this persuasion of God's Spirit unto distrust and infidelity ... Let us hold this fast, as the sure sheet-anchor of our soul:[334]

From the fourth letter we learn that Upcharde had responded to these exhortations and had written to thank Careless for his help. To this Careless responded,

Ah, my dear heart in the Lord, well is me that ever I was born, that God of his great mercy and infinite goodness hath used me (most miserable wretch) at any time, as his instrument to minister any thing unto you, either by word or writing... as your most loving and godly letter seemeth to import.[335]

Yet the writer realised that for him the time was now 'so short'. Thus, he concluded this final letter to his disciple with the promise that 'so long as my poor life doth last, my prayer shall supply that my pen doth want'.[336]

The next record of Thomas Upcharde dates from June 1557. At that date he is listed among the English exiles residing at Frankfurt. The record refers to 'Thomas Upcher, weaver of Bocking in Essex' who was living with his wife and two children in the house of Laurence Kent.[337] According to Garrett, Laurence Kent was a merchant from

---

[334] Coverdale, 475-6.
[335] *Ibid.*, 477.
[336] *Ibid.*, 479.
[337] *Proceedings of the Huguenot Society*, IV (London, 1894), 89.

Linford in Buckinghamshire who had been one of the earliest arrivals in Frankfurt, having been there since at least 3 December 1554.[338] In the early 1530s Lollards were still being burned in Buckinghamshire.[339] Kent's hospitality at Frankfurt may have arisen from earlier associations between Bocking and Buckinghamshire. Garrett suggests that Upcharde and his family may have originally fled to Wesel.[340] During the summer of 1557 he was a member of the delegation which went to Geneva under the leadership of Thomas Lever to seek the advice of the Genevan Church regarding the establishment of a new congregation at Aarau. Thereafter, Upcharde and his family moved to the new colony where they lodged in the house of Hans Gysins. It was while they were living at Aarau that his two sons, John and George, both died.[341]

Upcharde seems to have returned to England along with the main body of exiles for, on 25 April 1560, he was ordained deacon by Edmund Grindal, the newly-appointed Bishop of London.[342] In 1561 he was collated to the benefice of Fordham near Colchester, and some time later he became rector of S. Leonard's, Colchester. There is no record of the date of his resignation of Fordham and institution to S. Leonard's. [343]

According to Davids, Upcharde was in trouble with the authorities in 1570. This was probably in connection with the vestiarian controversy. Once again he was brought before the Privy Council, but this time he was discharged.[344] Bishop Grindal seems to have granted Upcharde an informal, verbal licence to minister without the surplice. Whereupon several other radically puritan ministers in the locality followed Upcharde's example. Later Grindal wrote:

---

[338] Garrett, 203-4.
[339] Foxe, *AM.*, IV, 580-2.
[340] Garrett, 316-7.
[341] *Ibid.*
[342] Strype, *Life of Grindal*, (Oxford, 1821), 58.
[343] T.W.Davids, *Annals of Evangelical Nonconformity in Essex* (London, 1863), 79 n.
[344] *Ibid.*

I was contented to bear with M^r. Upchire for the surplice, and upon that three or four more took upon them the like liberty, without licence.[345]
Davids states that Upcharde resigned S. Leonard's in May 1582 but continued to live in Colchester.[346] However, it seems more likely that he had been deprived of the living by Bishop Aylmer. In 1583 Thomas Upcharde was one of twenty-seven Essex ministers, some 'being allreadie put to silence', who petitioned the Privy Council for protection from Aylmer's next visitation.[347] They were all non-subscribers and advocates of that 'most excellent instrument of God' – Calvin's *Institutes*. It is evident, therefore, that Thomas Upcharde had joined the Classical Movement. He was not listed on the 1586 survey of Essex ministers whom Bishop Aylmer had suspended for non-subscription to the *Book of Common Prayer*.[348] This suggests that he died between 1583 and 1586.

All this evidence indicates that Upcharde's association with the reformed Church of England – an association which may have begun during his imprisonment in the King's Bench – remained an uneasy one. After initial uncertainties Upcharde seems to have fully embraced Calvinism, but this former leader of the Bocking conventicle was never really at home in Anglicanism.

(b) John Sympson
The Privy Council record states that, on 27 January 1551, 'one Sympson of the same sorte was committed to the Marshalsie' along with Thomas Upcharde.[349] Horst follows Burrage in identifying this Sympson with Cuthbert Sympson, the London tailor.[350] However, as Watts has noted, [351] he is much more likely to have been the John Sympson of Wigborough in Essex who was burned at Rochford in 1555. Although he lived some distance from Bocking, he evidently had

---

345 Cited in P. Collinson, *The Elizabethan Puritan Movement* (London, 1967), 66-7.
346 *loc. cit.*
347 *The Seconde Parte of a Register*, ed. A. Peel (Cambridge, 1915), I, 225-6. Davids (77-8) has mistakenly allocated this supplication to 1577 – the year of Aylmer's elevation to the see of London.
348 *Ibid.*, II, 163-5, 260-2.
349 *loc. cit.*
350 Horst, 125.
351 M.R.Watts, *The Dissenters* (Oxford, 1978), I, 12 n.2.

connections with the conventicle for he was a witness to the will of Robert Cooke, the Bocking clothier.[352] Presumably Sympson had been arrested separately – perhaps on the initiative of Rich – and sent to London with Upcharde. Doubtless he was released at the same time as the other conventiclers.

Foxe does not supply any information on the circumstances surrounding Sympson's subsequent arrest by the Marian authorities.[353] He links his name with that of John Ardeley, 'being both husbandmen in the town of Wigborough in Essex'. They were tried together on 25 May 1555, so presumably they were arrested in Great Wigborough at the same time. Foxe does, however, tell us that 'Simson was of the age of thirty-four'.[354] Moreover, he prints the seven articles that were objected against Sympson and Ardeley together with their answers. All of which, as Foxe doubtless recognised, were unexceptionable. For example, Sympson's answer to the third article contains an implicit acceptance of the principle of an established church – 'if the said Church of England be ruled and governed by the Word of Life, then the Church of England hath the faith and religion of the catholic church, and not otherwise'. In his response to the sixth article, Sympson accepted that the mass had some good liturgical features such as the 'Gloria in excelsis, the Epistle and Gospel, the Creed, and the Pater-noster'. Each of these were to be found in the Edwardine Prayer Book service.[355] On 11 June 1555 John Sympson was burned at Rochford and John Ardeley at Rayleigh.[356]

Of greater interest than the articles and answers that Foxe does publish is the letter that he omitted. Emmanuel College, Cambridge, MS 260 contains no less than four copies of a letter which John Sympson wrote from prison on 29 May 1555.[357] Since both Foxe and Coverdale drew extensively from this collection of *Letters of the Martyrs*, it must be

---

[352]   *Ibid.*
[353]   Foxe, *AM.*, VII, 86-90.
[354]   *Ibid.*, VII, 86.
[355]   *Ibid.*, VII, 87-8.
[356]   *Ibid.*, VII, 90, 765.
[357]   Emma. MS. 260 folios 47-8 contain the original autograph copy, folio 55 contains the second half of a transcript, folios 128-9 and 252b-253 contain two further complete transcripts. Each of these is in a different hand.

regarded as highly significant that neither chose to publish this particular letter. The reason for this omission can, perhaps, be detected in the letter's destination. Sympson entitles it:

An epistle or exhortation to the congregation dispersed in Suffolke, Norfolke, Essex, Kent and els where, John Simpson condemned for christs caus wisheth all unfained helth & perseuerence in the true faith.[358]

Doubtless the addressees were individuals or groups who had been in fellowship and communication with the Bocking conventiclers. As with the latter, many of Sympson's friends may have inclined towards separatism. Once again the traditional pattern of association between Lollards in Suffolk, Norfolk, Essex and Kent, which dates back to the time of William White, is in evidence.

The letter is full of exhortations to holiness of life and perseverance in the faith – 'wherefore deare brethern & sisters, fathers & mothers, & to all y^t [be] of christe church (I say) hold fast the [?insample] & folow with us, for ye ioye y^t is sett before us is verri confortable...'[359]. It concludes:

the xxixthof maie 1555,

Bi yor brother John Simpson

condemned for the truth

wyshing unfained helth and performance to ye end so be y^t

prai prai prai

Sympson then adds the following post-script:

Most hartily disyring you to write this [?]un to ye rest of o^{ur} britherne & sisters to ye prise of o^{ur} god. Amen.[360]

This explains the production of at least three transcripts. There may have been more taken since at least one copy reached its destination and provoked an immediate response.

On 11 June 1555 Edmund Tyrrel, an Essex magistrate, was returning to London having that day supervised the burning of Sympson and Ardeley. On the road he met and apprehended John Denley, gentleman, and John Newman, pewterer, both from Maidstone in Kent. They stated that they were 'going to visit such their godly friends as then they had in

358 Emma. MS. 260, folio 47^r.
359 *Ibid.*
360 *Ibid.*, f. 48^r.

the county of Essex'. Tyrrel also established that they had come from London.[361] When John Denley was searched a letter was found in his possession addressed to Sympson and Ardeley. Foxe chooses to print this brief and unexceptionable exhortation.[362]

Therefore it is suggested that, upon receipt of their copy of Sympson's letter, the Kentish conventiclers sent Denley and Newman to London to visit the condemned prisoner. On arrival they found that Sympson and Ardeley had already been despatched to Essex for execution. Whereupon they followed their brethren into Essex, Denley having previously written the prisoners a note in case they were prevented from speaking with them. Whether they reached Rochford or Rayleigh in time to witness the martyrdom of their friends must remain open to conjecture.

The extant material on John Sympson does not furnish any conclusive evidence concerning his doctrinal position. Had he survived longer he might have engaged in the King's Bench controversy over predestination;[363] had he survived the Marian persecution he might have followed Upcharde into the Church of England, but who can tell? One thing is certain, there was something about John Sympson's activities that caused the Edwardine authorities to imprison him, and something about his associations that caused Foxe and Coverdale to censor his literary remains.

(c) John Barre

In the Privy Council record John Barrett or Barrey was placed at the head of the list of those Bocking conventiclers who were 'accoumpted chief of that practise' and who were to be apprehended by Sir George Norton. It is somewhat surprising that a man whose occupation is listed as 'coweherde' should be mentioned before Robert Cooke, the Bocking clothier in whose house the Kentish delegation were to have lodged, or John Eglise (Eglins) another clothier from Bocking. Furthermore, Barre was one of only two Essex men to be committed to prison to join Upcharde and Sympson for their 'evill oppynyons'. All this suggests

---

[361] Foxe, *AM.*, VII, 329-31.
[362] *Ibid.*, 330-31.
[363] Sympson and Ardeley joined with John Bradford in sending money for the support of the family of Robert Smith early in 1555. This suggests that they were associating with the predestinarian party in the King's Bench (Foxe, *AM.*, VII, 369).

that John Barre – notwithstanding his humble occupation – was the leading figure in the conventicle; perhaps its teacher, reader or 'ministering brother'. Also noteworthy is the fact that he is listed as coming from 'Stamphorde' rather than Bocking. This was probably the village of Great Sampford, which is some eight miles from Bocking and less than five miles from Steeple Bumpstead. Doubtless, John Barre had been well-acquainted with the late Joan Bocher and other former members of that local Lollard conventicle.

The next probable reference to this man occurs in a letter which John Bradford wrote after he had been transferred to the Counter from the King's Bench. It is dated 16 February 1555 and was directed to the exponents of free-will, with whom he had been in literary and verbal contention while in the King's Bench. The letter is addressed as follows:

> To his dearly beloved in the Lord, Henry Hart, John Barr, John Lidley, Robert Cole, Nicholas Sheterden... and to all other that fear the Lord and love his truth, abiding in Kent, Essex, Sussex and thereabout....[364]

It is clear from the contents of the letter that Bradford believed all those whom he had named to be committed to the free-will position.[365] Again, it is significant that John Barre's name appears second on a list of thirteen individuals – second only to that of Henry Harte.

John Barre is next mentioned in the deposition of a certain Henry Crinel of Willingham (Cambridgeshire), who recalled an incident that occurred on or about October the first in the same year.[366] Just after Michaelmas, 1555, John Barre was sent to Colchester to confront the Familist evangelist, Christopher Vitells. Crinel deposed:

> Furthermore; at the same time one John Barry, servant unto Mr. Lawrence of Barnehall in Essex, come to the same inn [the King's Head at Colchester] to reason with the joiner about the divinity of Christ, which Vitells denied to be God. And after they had entered conference ... he put Barry to silence, and blanked him. So that he

---

364 *The Writings of John Bradford, M.A.*, ed. Townsend, (P.S., Cambridge, 1853), II, 194ff.

365 Below, 198-9.

366 Strype, *Annals of the Reformation* (Oxford, 1824), II (ii), 284-6.

had not a word to say; to the great offence of divers; and especially of two women gospellers, who came with Barry, to hear him and Vitells confer about this matter.[367]
Here we have a confrontation between the old English nonconformity as represented by Barre and a new and more radical sectarianism from the Continent as championed by Vitells. The devastating defeat of the former probably had increasingly serious repercussions among the conventicles of free-willers.

By this time Barre had moved from Great Sampford, changing his employment but not his status. His new employer, John Laurence of Barnehall, was extremely sympathetic towards his servant's views and ministry.[368] In the last two pieces of evidence concerning Barre his name is linked with that of Laurence.

In January or February 1557 the priest, Stephen Morris, submitted a written deposition to Bishop Bonner entitled, 'The principal Teachers of Heretical Doctrine in London'. Morris placed Laurence and Barre at the head of his list. It reads:
> The first, master Laurence of Barnhall, John Barry, his servant; and John Jeffrey, brother-in-law to master Laurence; these three do lie and abide, when they be in London, at an ale house in Cornhill.... These three are the greatest, and do most harm in persuading the people.[369]
Morris' deposition is substantiated by a transcript of a letter written by Laurence and Barre which is preserved within Bodleian MS. 53. This indicates that the pair were regular visitors to London and that they were in communication with the 'official' underground church there. It is interesting that Morris does not link Barre's name with Henry Harte whom he also mentions in his deposition as 'the principal of all those that are called free-will men'.[370] That Laurence and Barre were also free-willers is quite evident, not only from Bradford's letter of February 1555, but from their own letter written some three years later. Possibly the Essex men felt stronger ties with the predestinarian congregations of

---

[367] *Ibid.*, 285-6.
[368] Barnehall was (and remains) an ancient moated manor house in the parish of Downham near Wickford (*The Place Names of Essex*, ed. Reaney, Cambridge, 1969, p. 154).
[369] Foxe, *AM.*, VIII, 384.
[370] *Ibid.*

London and Colchester than with the radical conventicle led by Henry Harte, with its Kentish connections.[371] Was Essex nonconformity already becoming polarised between Puritanism and Familism?

Among other items, Bodleian MS. 53 contains some correspondence between Laurence and Barre and Augustine Berneher – the Swiss servant of Hugh Latimer. The opening paragraph of Laurence and Barre's letter to Berneher[372] includes the following remark:

You made us verily to maruell y^t yo^u were so importunate upo us: to receaue yor writing…. But whereas as we looked for ij [?things], y^t is for an answer of a writing we left with yo^u or some of yor copany at Bartholomewtide. & for ye proff of ye affirmatio y^t yo^u & others made whe we were last w^t you: (wch was) y^t god before ye world… did then also reprobate some to eternall Death but yo^u have nyther [?supplied] ye one, nor yet proud [proved] the other:[373]

The 'writing' which Berneher was so eager that Laurence and Barre should read is also preserved in this collection of manuscripts. Berneher entitled his treatise 'Certain testimonies, taken out of God's book, which do manifestly shew to the indifferent reader this proposition, (God hath generally chosen all men to salvation) to be untrue and against God's word'.[374] Berneher's reply to Laurence and Barre's letter is also preserved;[375] these transcripts having been taken and collated *circa* 1560.

It is evident from the above citation that Laurence and Barre had visited the London underground congregation of predestinarians and left a statement of faith with them. This asserted that God had elected all men to salvation – a doctrine that was also taught by the Kentish Free-willer, Humphrey Middleton.[376] On a subsequent visit Berneher and

---

[371] Below, 204-5. John Laurence's father-in-law (John Jeffrey the elder) came from West Mersea. He organised illicit conventicles there in 1555-56. George Eagles and Thomas Putto were associated with these conventicles where they used the Edwardine Prayer Book services (Above, 112 n.280; Foxe, *AM.*, VIII, 410-11, 417).

[372] Bodleian MS.53, folios 138^r-139^v. See Appendix Document III.

[373] *Ibid.*, f. 138^r.

[374] *Ibid.*, ff. 126^r-137^v.

[375] *Ibid.*, ff. 140^r-146^r.

[376] Below, 179-80.

other members of the congregation had solemnly affirmed their belief in double predestination. At that time Berneher had given Laurence and Barre a copy of his 'Certain testimonies', imploring them to consider it carefully. The letter preserved in Bodleian MS. 53 was Laurence and Barre's reply.

The date when these events took place can be determined with fair precision. At the time of this correspondence Berneher appears to be leading the London congregation. Berneher succeeded John Rough as leader of the 'official' congregation when Rough was captured in December 1557.[377] However, for some unknown reason this situation was regarded as unsatisfactory, and Thomas Bentham was commissioned by his fellow exiles to lead the congregation. In the Spring of 1558 he courageously returned to England to undertake this hazardous task.[378] Therefore, Laurence and Barre's letter must have been written early in the year 1558, after the apprehension of Rough and before the arrival of Bentham. They must have left their statement of faith with the church at Bartholomewtide (August) 1557 – a time when the church was leaderless, Rough not yet having arrived from Friesland. Their subsequent visit to London may have taken place at Christmas 1557, Rough having been captured on 12 December.

It is clear that Barre and his employer maintained the usual free-willer views on election and sanctification, and that they, like Robert Cooche,[379] strongly objected to the predestinarians' teaching on reprobation and the secret will of God. They write:

> For we hold y^t all thos wch walk in euill waies be out of election as yo^u know... for we hold none to be in ye electio but thos y^t be sanctified by ye spirite & folowe ye truth as y^t [?holighest] faythe.[380]

Like Cooche two years earlier, they argue,

> Fore yo^u speake of gods secritt will, wch was [never] revealed, & are yu not ashamed to affirm y^t in respect of gods comandyment it was not gods wyll yf Adam shuld syn but in respect of gods secrett will

---

[377] Foxe, *AM.*, VIII, 444.
[378] *Ibid.*, VIII, 559; Strype, *EM.*, III (ii), 132.
[379] Below, 251, 253.
[380] Bodleian MS. 53, ff.138^r-138^v.

god would have Adam to synne A blasphemy against god, making him ye auto^r of syne...[381]

Referring to eternal reprobation, they ask Berneher to produce one single text of Scripture to support this doctrine, and then they add –

Or els yo^u will make nu yor folly & say it is in ye greek [tongue]: as yo^u haue... in yor book & yo^u codemne all ye english translations: wch were translated by as well Lerned men as yo^u be.[382]

The letter concludes:

For we hate not yo^u as god noweth but yor opinions we hate... fare ye well... if by any means we could do yo^u good – John Laurence John barre.[383]

Notwithstanding Stephen Morris' deposition, it appears that Laurence and Barre had avoided arrest. Like many of their free-willer brethren in Kent there is no record of them suffering imprisonment under the Marian regime. On the other hand, we have no further knowledge of them after early 1558.[384]

(d) Conclusion

Thus, these slender sources depict Essex radicalism in the process of transition. While maintaining their traditional associations with radicals in Kent and elsewhere in East Anglia, these nonconformists were more prepared to entertain the opinions of learned men regarding predestinarian doctrine and Prayer Book worship. This provoked a visit from a delegation of their Kentish brethren – a visit that was clearly pre-arranged. Apart from the fines and imprisonment that some of its leading members suffered, the result of the Bocking conventicle of 1550 appears to have been inconclusive – the two groups agreed to differ. Between 1548 and 1558 many of the Essex men, while continuing to exhibit a tendency towards separatism, came to accept the doctrine and liturgy of the reformed Church of England. Therefore, it is not surprising that during the Marian persecution clandestine congregations gathered in Essex to hear the Edwardine services. Prayer Book worship was led by deprived ministers like Thomas Whittle, former vicar of Kirkby-le-

---

[381] *Ibid.*, f.138^v.

[382] *Ibid.*, f. 139^r.

[383] *Ibid.*, f. 139^v.

[384] The 1563 edition of Foxe states that Laurence and his wife were forced to leave Barnehall because of persecution (*AM.*, VIII, Appendix, III).

soken,[385] William Tyms, deprived curate of Hockley,[386] by John Rough at the King's Head in Colchester,[387] and by Thomas Putto at Mile End, West Mersea and Dedham.[388] Furthermore, one of the leading conventiclers, Thomas Upcharde, was subsequently ordained and held benefices in Essex before reverting to nonconformity. While some of the Essex conventiclers continued to espouse traditional views on free-will and sanctification, it is significant that nowhere do we find an Essex radical accused of 'anabaptism'. Nevertheless, by 1555 Essex separatists – especially the free-willers – were coming under pressure from Continental spiritualism in the form of Familism.

Undoubtedly Davis is correct when he states that the Marian Protestant conventicles were 'unlike that of Bocking in 1550 or those around Colchester in 1556 where Vitells was gaining converts'.[389] Davis later maintains,

> The distinction between the early brotherhoods and conventicles and the Protestant congregations of the Marian persecution, must clearly be made since the latter were churches in that they were served by pastors and celebrated the Edwardine services.[390]

To these distinguishing features must be added the Lollard conventiclers' preference for free-will theology and recognition of a lay ministry. However, in Essex (and, doubtless, in other former Lollard strongholds) the distinction was blurred as many of the earlier conventiclers came to accept Reformed doctrine and ecclesiology. Yet, not every conventicler made this transition – certainly not in London, Kent and Sussex.[391] Here there were those who, even after 1559, continued tenaciously to practise that extreme Lollard sacramentarianism which preferred informal worship led by lay ministers, and which emphasised human freedom and the Christian's duty to seek moral perfection.

---

[385] *APC.*, V, 150; Foxe, *AM.*, VII, 715-50.
[386] Foxe, *AM.*, VIII, 107-21.
[387] *Ibid.*, VIII, 384, 459.
[388] Above, 111-12.
[389] Davis, 344-5.
[390] *Ibid.*, 348.
[391] Watts, I, 14.

II THE KENT RADICALS

Of the seven Kentish men summoned by the Privy Council on 27 January 1551, only five appeared before them on 3 February. Presumably the two Ashford men, Lydley and Chidderton, escaped arrest. The record implies that these seven men formed the Kentish contingent that travelled to Bocking at Christmas 1550.[392] Strype, making use of the fragmentary depositions which were later printed by Burrage, states that the entire Kentish congregation 'went over unto the congregation in Essex, to instruct and to join with them'. Burrage developed this notion, suggesting that it was 'on account of impending persecution [that] the Kentish conventiclers removed to Bocking in Essex'. More recently this interpretation has been accepted by Dickens and by Cross who states, 'Before the end of 1550 this group migrated as a body to Essex'.[393]

However, since the Harleian fragment clearly relates to an interrogation that occurred after the gathering at Bocking, and since several leading Kentish sectaries mentioned in the fragment (Henry Harte, Humphrey Middleton, George Brodebridge, and Cole of Faversham) are not stated to have visited Bocking, it is more likely that the men listed in the Privy Council record comprised the entire Kentish delegation. It is hardly likely that the whole congregation including wives and children would have expected Robert Cooke to give them hospitality. Whereas half-a-dozen or so representatives of the congregation, arriving in Bocking to attend a pre-arranged conference, might well have expected the wealthiest man in the Essex conventicle to provide them with board and lodging.

As a result of their appearance before the Privy Council, Cole of Maidstone, William Sibley of Lenham and Nicholas Shetterton of Pluckley were sent (with Boughtell and Barre) to join Upcharde and Sympson in prison. Thomas/Nicholas Yonge of Lenham and Thomas Sharpe of Pluckley were released on bail upon the same recognisance and under the same conditions as their Essex compatriots.[394] However, the admitted separatism and 'divers other euill oppynyons' of the Kentish prisoners persuaded the Privy Council to order further investigations into Kentish nonconformity. Strype states that this took

---

[392] *APC.*, III, 206; Above, 117-19.
[393] Strype, *EM.*, II(i), 369-70; Burrage, I, 51; Dickens, 238; Cross, 98.
[394] *APC.*, III, 206-7.

place in 'the ecclesiastical court',[395] whereas Clark assumes that this further inquiry was entrusted to the sheriffs of Kent – Sir Edward Wotton and Sir Thomas Wyatt.[396] Strype is almost certainly correct. The special commission of 18 January 1551 was convened to investigate 'anabaptist' heresy in Essex and Kent. It allowed for any three of the thirty-one commissioners 'of which the Bishops of Ely, Norwich, Rochester, Nic Wotton, Petre, Cecyl, Cox, Hales, or May to be one' to examine suspects.[397] The Kentish radicals were probably interrogated by the Dean of Canterbury (Nicholas Wotton), by the Archbishop's commissary (Christopher Nevinson), and by the judge Sir James Hales of Thanington. It was probably conducted in the Canterbury consistorial court in February or March, 1551. The Harleian fragment reveals that an interrogation consisting of at least forty-six articles was administered to several witnesses as well as to confessed conventiclers. It is evident, therefore, that the investigation was very thorough.

The depositions of the first four witnesses were almost entirely taken up with the teaching of Henry Harte – teaching which is examined in detail elsewhere.[398] At a meeting of the congregation 'about bartholomewtide laste' (24 August 1550) Harte had vigorously criticised the doctrines of election and reprobation. Furthermore, he had deprecated the teaching of scholarly theologians and the preaching of trained ministers because 'lernyd men were the cause of grete Errors'.[399] John Grey, the witness, further deposed that 'on Lammas daye laste paste' he had heard Cole of Faversham criticise the doctrine of predestination saying that it was 'meter for divilles than for christian men'.[400] This meeting was also referred to by one of the later witnesses – John Plume of Lenham. He confessed that he was a member of the congregation and testified that,

> ...vmfrey Middilton beyng in Coles house at faversham apon Lammas daye he saide that Adam was elected to be salued And that all men

---

[395] *loc. cit.*
[396] Clark, 77.
[397] Strype, *EM.*, II(i), 385, II(ii), 200; Wilkins, IV, 66-7.
[398] Below, 192-3.
[399] Burrage, II, 1-2.
[400] *Ibid.*, II, 1.

being then in Adams Loynes were predestynate to be saluid and that ther were no reprobates.[401]

There had, therefore, been another meeting of the conventiclers earlier in the same month (1 August 1550). This had been held in Cole's house at Faversham, and once again the main topic had been the doctrine of predestination. Thus, within the space of a month, the Kentish conventiclers had gathered at least twice to consider the 'new' theology. Henry Harte had scorned the learning of Reformed scholars, emphasised human autonomy, and proclaimed that 'his faithe was not growndid apon Lernyd men for all errors were broughte in by Lernyd men'.[402] Cole of Faversham had also vigorously repudiated the doctrine of predestination, while Humphrey Middleton particularly objected to the concept of reprobation, believing that all men were predestined to salvation. Perhaps it was at one of these meetings that the congregation resolved to send a delegation to their brethren in Essex the following Christmas.

The four witnesses who made the first of the extant depositions were:– John Grey, Laurence Ramsey, William Forstall and Edmund Morris. Some interesting additional information is available on each of them. All four were later involved in the defence of the deprived vicar of Adisham, John Bland. The signatures of Forstall and Morris appear on a letter written in his defence in 1554 by some of Bland's former parishioners. Laurence Ramsey was the former parish clerk of Adisham. On 28 December 1553 he was arrested with Bland and taken with him to Canterbury gaol, but was later released on bail. John Grey, who came from the neighbouring parish of Wingham, supported Ramsey's stand against Bland's Marian opponents in Adisham.[403]

Thus, these four witnesses, who came from parishes some six miles east of Canterbury, had heard Cole of Faversham and Henry Harte inveigh against the predestinarian teaching of learned men at a meeting in

---

[401]   *Ibid.*, II, 3.
[402]   *Ibid.*, II, 2.
[403]   Foxe, *AM.*, VII, 289-91.

Faversham (eight miles west of Canterbury) the previous August. Since they were all supporters of the former schoolmaster, John Bland,[404] now a learned Reformed minister of the Church of England, they were bound to take exception to the sentiments they had heard in Faversham. Here then, we find four non-separatist sympathisers with predestinarian doctrine who were prepared to testify against their separatist, free-willer brethren. Oxley's assessment of the Bocking conventicle as 'Lollardy divided against itself by ... Reforming doctrine'[405] is equally applicable to the gathering of Kentish conventiclers at Faversham the previous summer.

Actually, Edmund Morris's deposition is not recorded on the extant manuscript. The next heading reads,

The depositions of m[r] Thomas Broke Roger Lynsey and Rycharde Dynestake Clarke productid apon the xiij and xiiij[th] articles of the Interrogatories aforesaid.[406]

From a later testimony concerning Humphrey Middleton it appears that the thirteenth and fourteenth articles dealt with sentiments expressed at the gathering in Cole's house at Faversham on 1 August 1550. Therefore these three witnesses may have been local Faversham dignatories. However, again there seems to be a hiatus in the manuscript, with the depositions of these witnesses omitted. For, the next lines read – 'Item Examyned apon the xxj[th] article he saithe that...'[407] The name of the testifier who gave the evidence that follows is not mentioned, but he and the remaining two witnesses whose testimonies are preserved on the fragment – William Greenland and John Plume – appear to have been committed members of the conventicle.

The testimony of the anonymous witness continues,'... he saithe that aboute xij monethes Sythen George Brodebridge saide and affirmed that goddes predestynation is not [? cer] teyne but apon condytion etc'.[408] This must refer to a different meeting of the conventicle held in the spring of 1550. Like Humphrey Middleton, George Brodebridge maintained a highly modified version of the doctrine of predestination. The deposition continues,

---

[404] Bland was the teacher of Edwin Sandys, Elizabethan Archbishop of York (Foxe, *Ibid*).
[405] *loc. cit.*
[406] Burrage, II, 2.
[407] *Ibid.*
[408] *Ibid.*

Item Examyned apon the xxxix[th] and xl[th] articles he deposithe and saithe that the contentes of those articles hathe byn affirmed amonge them for a generall doctryne.[409]
From the evidence of the next witness, William Greenland, we learn that the fortieth article referred to the conventiclers' rejection of gambling.

The next 'item' is difficult to interpret, but when linked with Greenland's depositions on the same articles, it becomes evident that it referred to the meetings of the conventicle and the visit to Bocking –
Item Examyned apon the xlj[th] and xlij[th] articles he deposithe and provithe the congregation and the same And ther goyng into Essex.[410]
Finally, this unknown witness responded to the forty-sixth article by deposing that, 'Cole of Maidstone saide and affirmed that children were not borne in originall Syne'.[411] He does not state when or where Cole made this affirmation. Nevertheless, it is clear that in 1550-51 the Maidstone schoolmaster was in sympathy with the Kentish free-willer conventicle. Moreover, the fact that he was included in its delegation to Bocking suggests that he was a respected member of the congregation and a trusted exponent of its opinions.

Next follows the evidence of 'Willelmus grenelande' whose deposition reads:
Item in aunsweringe to the xl[th] article he saithe that to playe at annye game for money it is Synne and the worke of the Fleshe.
Item in aunsweringe to the xlj[th] and xlij[th] and xliij[th] articles he confessithe the congregation and their Meatinges at divers places and ther goyng into Essex And also that he hathe contrybuted.[412]
The previous witness had stated that all the members of the conventicle accepted as an undisputed tenet the belief that gambling was 'Synne and the worke of the Flesshe'. John Trewe – the Sussex free-willer – stated that the controversy in the King's Bench began when he and his associates protested at the manner in which their predestinarian fellow-

---

409 *Ibid.*
410 *Ibid.*, II, 3.
411 *Ibid.*
412 *Ibid.*

prisoners whiled away the time by gaming.[413] Greenland appears to have confessed to being a member of the 'congregation', to have attended their gatherings at various places in Kent, and not only to have been aware of the visit to Bocking but also to have contributed towards the delegates' expenses.

The final deposition preserved on the Harleian fragment is that of John Plume of Lenham. His evidence begins:

Item Examyned apon the iiij[orth] and v[th] articles apon his othe Saithe that he beyng emonge the congregators he hathe herde it divers tymes affirmed as a generall doctryne that they oughte not to Salute a Synner or a man whome they knowe not And that Luste after lvill was not Synne, if that were not committed.[414]

It is noteworthy that this member of the Kentish conventicle was prepared to give his evidence upon oath. Some five years later, prospective members of Henry Harte's conventicle of free-willers in London had to swear an oath before gaining admittance.[415] Such a practice is unlikely to have occurred had these conventiclers been strongly influenced by the Mennonite version of anabaptism.[416] Plume then informed his interrogators of another generally accepted tenet of the conventiclers – that they should not have any dealings with flagrant unbelievers, or even with those of whose faith they were uncertain. This rigid exclusivism would doubtless have caused even more offence to fellow Protestants than their separatism. The use of the phrase 'a man whome they knowe not' is reminiscent of the Lollard concept of 'known men'. In Plume's deposition on the fifth article we find the conventiclers' answer to a familiar problem for all who espouse perfectionist doctrine – what exactly constitutes a sin? Only those who proclaimed the necessity to strive for sinless perfection and the ability of the true Christian to attain it would make such an unscriptural distinction between the thought and the act.[417]

---

[413] Laurence, 37-8. Below, 356.
[414] Burrage, II, 3.
[415] Below, 204-5.
[416] Above, 28-9; *Complete Works of Menno Simons*, ed. Wenger (Scottdale, 1956), 517-21.
[417] It is interesting that John Champneys, while maintaining this distinction, adopted the exact reverse position. (Above, 95).

Next, Plume was examined on the thirteenth and fourteenth articles. Here he gave evidence concerning Humphrey Middleton's views on predestination expressed at the Faversham meeting of 1 August 1550.[418] Responding to the ninth article, Plume stated that 'it is a generall affirmation emonge them, that the preachinge of predestynacyon is a dampnable doctryne'.[419] Finally, in answer to the sixteenth article, Plume deposed that, 'Nicholas Yonge saide that they wolde not comunycate w^t Synners.[420] Yonge, like Plume, came from Lenham. They may well have discussed together the question of participation in the new Prayer Book communion service at the local parish church. Yonge's statement reveals the determined separatism of the committed conventicler. Apart from Cole of Maidstone, Yonge is the only other member of the Kentish conventicle mentioned on the Harleian fragment who visited Bocking. In the Privy Council record he is referred to either as Thomas or Nicholas Yonge of Lenham. He appeared before the Council on 3 February 1551 and was released on bail.[421]

After Plume's deposition the manuscript record abruptly terminates. Although the extant depositions are brief and disconnected, they nevertheless furnish us with an invaluable glimpse into the beliefs and practices of the Kentish radicals in the years 1550-51.

The next mention of religious radicalism in Kent occurred some eighteen months later. In the record of the Privy Council meeting held on 27 September 1552 reference is made to a letter to be despatched to the archbishop of Canterbury (who was presumably in residence at Lambeth) ordering him to –
> examine the sect newly sprong in Kent whereof there is nowe a booke of examinacions sent hym, and to common with the man and woman, bearers of the lettre, who can enforme hym sumewhat of the matter, and to take suche ordre in the same according to his Commission as theese errours be not suffred thus to ouer spred the Kinges faithfull subjectes.[422]

---

[418] Above, 137-8.
[419] Burrage, II, 4.
[420] *Ibid.*
[421] *loc. cit.*
[422] *APC.*, IV, 131.

In his comment upon this letter Strype emphasises that this sect was said to be 'newly sprong' in Kent. He writes:

What this sect was, appeareth not. The anabaptists were taken notice of, and a commission issued out against them, some years before. These were sectaries more new, and wherof the council very lately was informed. It may be they were of the family of Love, or David George's sect...[423]

The 'anabaptists' to which Strype refers were the Kentish conventiclers against whom the depositions preserved in Harleian MS. 421 were laid. Strype's identification of this 'new' sect with the Family of Love appears to be the sole evidence upon which those who argue for the presence of Familists in England before 1555 base their case. However, the Familist evangelist Christopher Vitells began his ministry in Colchester not Canterbury, his earliest contacts seem to have been in Essex and Cambridgeshire rather than Kent.[424] Moreover, a different interpretation can be placed upon the Privy Council's letter to Cranmer of September 1552. The Council not only sent the archbishop a letter but also 'a booke of examinacions' which related to this sect. It is not unreasonable to suggest that this book comprised the evidence collected by the heresy commissioners in 1551, a fragment of which has been preserved in Harleian MS. 421. Thus, it is suggested that in September 1552 the Privy Council received further information concerning the Kentish conventiclers. Perhaps the man and woman, who acted as witnesses and bearers of the letter to Cranmer, testified that the conventiclers had again gathered on the holidays of Lammastide and Bartholomewtide that August. As far as Northumberland and the other members of the Council were concerned (no ecclesiastics were in attendance), these separatists from the reformed Church of England were a new sect. They searched out the information they already had upon them, and then sent the book of depositions together with the two new witnesses over to Cranmer ordering him to do his duty.

The archbishop immediately began preparations to travel into his diocese. However, on 8 October 1552 he received another communication from the Council ordering him to 'stay his going in to

---

[423] Strype, *Memorials of Thomas Cranmer* II, 410.
[424] Below, 301-4.

Kent till Tewseday next' because they wished to confer with him. At the next meeting of the Privy Council held on 11 October Cranmer was in attendance, but thereafter he was absent until 21 February 1553.[425] On 28 October 1552 Northumberland wrote to Sir William Cecil, expressing the wish that the King would appoint John Knox to the bishopric of Rochester because, 'he would be a whetstone to the archbishop of Canterbury, and a confounder of the Anabaptists lately sprung up in Kent'.[426] In this letter the 'sect newly sprong in Kent', the subject of the Council's letter to Cranmer the previous month, is termed 'Anabaptists'. Clark correctly observes:

> Terrified by fear of popular disorder, the government was only too willing to depict them as the progeny of the Münster Anabaptists.... But as far as we can tell, domestic religious influences, including residual Lollardy, were probably much more important than any foreign virus.[427]

Judging by the, admittedly slender, extant evidence, Northumberland was right to suppose that the tolerant Cranmer needed a rugged 'whetstone' like Knox to ensure that he dealt firmly with the Kentish radicals. Strype states that the archbishop, together with other heresy commissioners, sat at Ashford and examined several suspects, but he does not appear to have any record of these interrogations.[428] According to Strype, Nicholas Ridley accompanied Cranmer to Kent. J. G. Ridley doubts whether Ridley took part in the Ashford examination and suggests that the Bishop of London never went to Kent at all.[429] However, Strype clearly records the presence in the 'repository' of a commission issued in October 1552 to Cranmer and Ridley to examine and punish 'erroneous opinions in religion'.[430]

There is, additionally, some evidence in Foxe which indicates that Cranmer took stronger action against the Kentish radicals in 1552-3 than generally has been supposed. In the Latin edition of his martyrology

---

[425]   *APC.*, IV, 138, 140, 222.
[426]   *Calendar of State Papers, Domestic Series*, 1547-1580, ed. Lemon (London, 1856), 46.
[427]   Clark, 76-7.
[428]   Strype, *EM.*, II (ii), 19. In the single trial recorded by Foxe (*AM.*, VIII, 41-3) charges of 'anabaptist immorality' were disproved.
[429]   J. G. Ridley, *op. cit.*, 283-4, 284n.
[430]   Strype, *EM.*, II (ii), 209.

Foxe supplies some further information on the Ashford Free-willer, Humphrey Middleton.[431] He states that Middleton, together with other Kentish sectaries, was imprisoned at Canterbury during the final year of the reign of Edward VI. Moreover, he asserts that they were rigorously examined by Cranmer and the Commissioners.[432] Middleton came from Ashford, and it is not unreasonable to suppose that among his fellow-prisoners may have been the two Ashford men who visited Bocking in 1550, but who failed to appear before the Privy Council in 1551 – Lydley and Chidderton.

Furthermore there is the evidence from Thomas Cole's Maidstone sermon of 1553 that (apart from Cole himself) two anti-trinitarians had been examined and had abjured their opinions. These two men probably came from Maidstone.[433] Finally, there is Bishop Ridley's assertion that the Kentish radical, Henry Harte, was well-known to the Archbishop and had often been admonished by him.[434]

All this suggests that in the autumn of 1552 Cranmer and Ridley conducted a series of heresy trials at Ashford which resulted in the imprisonment of the local radical leaders at Canterbury. Later, in the spring of 1553 Cranmer conducted a similar investigation at Maidstone.

Further evidence that Cranmer took positive action against the conventiclers is provided by Thomas Cole's sermon at Maidstone on the first Sunday in Lent 1552/3. The full title given to this address, which was printed in London later in 1553 is – *A Godly and Frutefull Sermon made at Maydstone in the county of Kent the fyrste sonday in Lent, in the presence of the most Reuerend father in God Thomas Archbishop of Canterbury etc. by M. Thomas Cole scholemayster there, againste dyuers erronious opinions of the Anabaptistes and others.*[435] After his attendance at the Privy Council meeting on 21 February 1552/3, Cranmer was again absent from meetings of the Council until 25 March. During this second period of absence from the capital the archbishop doubtless visited Maidstone and heard Thomas Cole's attempt to justify himself.

---

[431] Foxe, *Rerum*, 202-3.
[432] Below, 179-80.
[433] Below, 147, 156.
[434] Bradford, *Works*, II, 173.
[435] Thomas Cole, *A Godly and Frutefull Sermon made at Maydstone* (London, 1553) STC 5539, sig. A1[r].

Cole's sermon supplies some valuable information on the Kentish conventiclers.[436] On the first page of the text a slightly different title is given,

A Sermon Made at Maydstone... agaynst dyuers errours of the Anabaptistes and such sectes where soeuer they be, as in christen religion call theym selues Brothers and Systers, and dyuide theym selues from other christian people.[437]

In these headings a clear distinction is made between those whom the authorities called 'anabaptists' and other more familiar sects. Indeed, as the sermon proceeds the reader begins to wonder whether Thomas Cole had any knowledge of anabaptists *per se*. Most of the errors that Cole preached against are those recorded on the Harleian fragment – errors of exclusivism and separatism practised by scattered conventicles of recalcitrant Lollards.

Cole likens these doctrinal errors to attractive, but poisonous, flowers which Satan places in the path of those who earnestly seek to know God and live righteously. By smelling their poisonous odour the 'godly lyuer' becomes an 'euell speaker' and so receives the grace of God in vain.[438] In the course of his sermon Cole described eleven of these 'stynkyng flattering floures of the dyuell' together with two 'triflig floures of scism', and warned his congregation to beware of each of them. In so doing he supplied posterity with a first-hand account of the features of Kentish religious radicalism.

Somewhat surprisingly, the first error that Thomas Cole mentions appears to be a fundamental principle of religious latitudinarians rather than a tenet of earnest conventiclers – 'That all menne be so saued, that none at length shalbe dampned'.[439] However, this could relate to Humphrey Middleton's statement at Faversham that all were elected in Adam to salvation and none to reprobation. In which case, Cole has

---

436 Only two copies of this printed sermon survive. One is in the Library of Emmanuel College, Cambridge; the other in the Folger Library, Washington. Printed by Reginald Wolfe, the text runs from sig. A2^r-E3^v.

437 Cole, *A Godly and Frutefull Sermon*, sig. A2^r.

438 *Ibid.*, B3^r-B3^v.

439 *Ibid.*, B3^v.

misrepresented Middleton and the conventiclers. On the other hand it may simply have been an opening gambit devised to stress the seriousness of heresy and the importance of his subject. Cole replies:

> This floure seemeth to haue a goodlye colour.... For it seemeth to be buylt upon the mercy of God, but so, that utterly it destroyeth his iustyce, breedeth in manne a false securitie, cleane rooteth oute of hys hearte the feare of God and obedience to hys woorde:[440]

If the 'flower' of universal salvation will not serve Satan's purposes, then he will produce another which has exactly the opposite implication and which is equally dangerous – 'That there is no predestination of God'.[441] Cole argues that such a doctrine must mean that none can be saved, because only those who are elected in Jesus Christ 'are sealed to eternall lyfe'. He continues:

> Nowe as it is a wycked errour to deny the Predestination of God, and our election in Christ ... so it is a moste damnable heresy... to affirme and holde that by predestination God is the author of syn.[442]

This is reminiscent of the later statements of Laurence and Barre.[443] Evidently the argument that the doctrine of predestination made God responsible for sin had already become a standard weapon in the armoury of the Free-willers.

The third flower that the devil had 'ready in store' was that, 'Christ died for his owne synnes as well as for the sinnes of the people'. Then Cole adds, 'How the diuel hath wrought by this flour, ye haue an exaple before youre eies'.[444] This is a reference to two men who must have been abjured heretics and who were presumably standing before the congregation in penitential garb while Cole preached this sermon.[445] Perhaps they had been examined the previous autumn by Cranmer, Ridley, and the heresy commissioners. It appears that these two miscreants had denied the divinity of Christ. Such extreme radical opinions had been held by some Lollards; Thomson describes them as

---

440 *Ibid.*, B3^v-B4^r.
441 *Ibid.*, B6^r.
442 *Ibid.*, B7^v.
443 Above, 133-4.
444 Cole, C1^r.
445 *Ibid.*, C3^r,D3^v.

the 'rationalist' element in Lollardy.[446] Similar extreme christologies were discovered among Kentish radicals during the Marian persecution.[447] Cole exclaims:

O subtyll dyuell, that so canste enchaunte the myndes of symple menne, to make theym so iudge of the immaculate lambe Jesus Chryst.[448]

Then he introduces the fourth error with the phrase, 'But nowe... hee [Satan] passeth frome the boddye of Chryste, and blasphemeth hys holly Spirite'.[449] It is surely significant that, when dealing with the christological errors of the Kentish radicals, Thomas Cole (who had been a conventicler himself) makes absolutely no mention of 'Melchiorite' christology. He was evidently unaware of any 'anabaptists' who maintained the doctrine of the celestial flesh; the only aberration he knew placed undue emphasis upon the humanity of Christ.

The fourth error, which Cole dismisses as unspeakably abhorrent, was that ' a manne hauynge the spirite of God, maye haue his neyghboures wyfe in common'.[450] Here we have an attack upon the one tenet of anabaptist extremism of which all Englishmen were aware since events at Münster made the doctrine infamous. It is noteworthy that Cole immediately asserts:

I knowe none infected with these aforesayd errours (these men except) but if there be anye, God bryng theym into the way of truth.[451]

If by 'aforesayd' Cole meant the third and fourth items, then this assertion may be accurate. However, if he intended to convey the impression that he was not acquainted with any who denied the doctrine of predestination, then his statement was patently false.

The fifth pernicious 'flower' to be condemned was that, 'the inwarde manne synneth not, whan the otter man synneth'.[452] Internalisation of the concept of sinless perfection was an expedient forced upon many who embraced perfectionist teaching when they became aware of the persistence of sin in the spiritually regenerate Christian. It is found in the

---

446   Thomson, 244, 248.
447   Strype, *EM.*, III (i), 540-2.
448   Cole, C1^v-C2^r.
449   *Ibid.*, C2^r.
450   *Ibid.*
451   *Ibid.*, C3^r.
452   *Ibid.*

teaching of Joan Bocher and John Champneys as well as among Continental spiritualists, particularly the followers of David Joris.[453] According to John Plume's deposition, the Kentish conventiclers affirmed as a general doctrine the opposite view.[454] However, both interpretations represent attempts by perfectionists to surmount the same problem.

According to Cole, Satan's next floral distractions had been extremely common. They had 'in tyme paste' deceived many;

Thys flour is, that by free wyll, sprong of our own nature, we may beleue the gospel, and doo all thynges pleasyng to God.

Or else hee bryngeth an other floure not unlyke to ye same... That by our fre wil, we may saue our souls.[455]

He may have had in mind the soteriology of the Roman Church, but in the context of Kentish radicalism the former flower continued to flourish within the conventicles of the Free-willers. Did the preacher wish to leave his congregation with the impression that the influence of the Free-willers had declined?

Next, Cole deals with those opinions which undermine God's established order in society – particularly the established ecclesiastical order. He observes:

And bicause nothyng can sooner deceyue manne than... that he hath some colour of goodnes: therefore [Satan] tempteth man to make new inuentions to hymselfe, and mislyke all publik and common order:

Saying, that to inuent orders in religion, and to mislyke al thyng y^t we inuent not our self is not euyl; or y^t it is lauful to euery man to make peculiar orders to himselfe, in contempt of the comon order.[456]

Evidently this criticism was aimed at the conventiclers' refusal to conform to the orders of worship prescribed in the *Book of Common Prayer*. The debate on ceremonial at Bocking may have been another manifestation of the Kentish conventiclers' predilection for nonconformity.

---

[453] Above,61-4, 94-6; Menno Simons, *Works*, 217-8; Williams, 352-3, 479-80.
[454] Above, 141-2.
[455] Cole, C4^r-C4^v.
[456] *Ibid.*, C5^r-C5^v.

In his treatment of the eighth error Cole attacks the conventiclers' exclusivism–

> But if the diuell can not cause men by his crafty illusyons, to condemne thynges done by the superyour powers... than hee laboureth to poyson men with the stinkyng floure of separation or segregation from other, as from wycked and damned men, not worthy to communicate the sacramentes, or to eate and drynke with theim.[457]

The leading members of the Bocking conventicle admitted to the Privy Council that they had not communicated for more than two years, Thomas Cole himself being among those that made this admission. This statement also corroborates the deposition of John Plume that the conventiclers maintained as a general doctrine the avoidance of all social contact with unbelievers. It also tends to confirm Plume's assertion that Nicholas Yonge refused to 'comunycate w^t Synners'. However, it is equally significant that Cole in condemning the conventiclers' nonconformity, separatism and exclusivism makes no mention of the rite of believers' baptism. Had the Kentish radicals practised, or even advocated, re-baptism as the means of initiation into their conventicles then surely Cole would have condemned it here. In fact, Cole's chief concern is to assert the responsibility of the properly constituted authorities to prescribe the order of worship and maintain the discipline of a local church. He proclaims:

> ...But if the churche or authorised disciplinatours be in this their office negliget, and wyl not excommunicate suche as be notorious & manyfest euylworkers, than must the priuate man comitte the matter to god, desyryng hym to redresse suche an abuse, beyng contented to lyue in the churche, and receyue the sacramentes, without separation, assured that the wyckednes of the wycked, can not make an holy thyng unholy or unprofitable to hym...[458]

Perhaps these remarks were intended for Archbishop Cranmer's benefit. Undoubtedly they reflect a remarkable transformation in the attitude of the preacher, and that would doubtless have given the archbishop considerable satisfaction. However, Cole's final remark on this subject again reveals his anxiety to justify himself and must have cast doubts upon his sincerity. He concludes, 'But truly I know none that useth any

---

[457] *Ibid.,* C5^v-C6^r.
[458] *Ibid.,* C7^r.

suche separation: yf there bee any, God reduce theim into the way of truthe'.[459]

Under the ninth heading Cole lumps together several doctrinal errors relating to sin which he claims are 'to pestylent to be founde among christians'.
Namely to deny that childern be borne in originall synne: or that a manne after baptisme can not fall into deadely synne: or beynge so fallen, canne not be renewed agayne by repentaunce: or to denye the baptisme of infantes.[460]
Having named them, the preacher artlessly pleads lack of time to provide the confutation from Scripture that would 'deface these floures', and then hastily passes on to the tenth enticement. However, in the spring of 1551 a witness had deposed that Cole himself affirmed that children were 'not borne in originall Syne'. In 1549 John Champneys had recanted the opinion that 'a man after he is regenerate in Christe, cannot synne'. In 1535 a number of Dutch refugees were condemned for their belief that 'hee who after his baptism sinneth wittingly, sinneth deadly, and can not be saved'.[461] The question of post-baptismal sin constituted a major problem for those Continental radicals who were influenced by the teaching of Melchior Hofmann.[462] Denial of the necessity for infant baptism is a natural adjunct of extreme sacramentarianism, and was a common charge levelled at Lollards.[463] Thus, notwithstanding Cole's insinuation that these errors were not held by any Christian believer, there is considerable evidence to the contrary. Indeed, not more than three years had elapsed since Cole publicly advocated at least one of these opinions himself.

The preacher returned to the subject of the established order in his revelations concerning the tenth devilish plant. This is stated to be, 'That it is laufull to be a publyke preacher in a christian comon welth, without the authoritie of the christen magistrates'.[464] Clearly this was aimed at leading conventiclers such as Henry Harte who disliked the settled ministry of officially approved 'lernyd men', preferring the traditional

---

[459] *Ibid.*, C8^r.
[460] *Ibid.*
[461] Above, 10.
[462] Horst, 113.
[463] Thomson, 245.
[464] Cole, C8^r.

Lollard custom of occasional preaching by itinerant laymen. By this means able laymen whose orthodoxy was questionable, such as Harte, maintained their platform. Having thrown in his lot with the Reformed establishment, Cole now regarded lay preaching as a challenge to the current Christian order. Firmly he instructed his congregation, 'And knowe you, that it is not laufull in a christian common weale to be a publyke preacher, without the authoritie of the hygher powers'.[465]

The eleventh 'flower' appears to be an even more specific condemnation of the teaching of Henry Harte. Cole proclaims:

An other flowre the dyuell hathe in store, wherwith he woulde perswade man, that in this lyfe he may attayne suche a perfection, that he shall synne in nothynge. And this is that dotyng floure, that a ma may kepe the comandementes of god so perfectly and absolutely that he shall synne in nothynge, nor haue nothyng wherof to aske Gods mercy... whiche sauoureth more of imagination tha of knoweledge.[466]

Harte was reported by Laurence Ramsey to have taught that no man was so reprobate, 'but that he maye if he will kepe the commandementes and be saluid'.[467] A similar emphasis upon obedience to the commandments in Scripture had been found in Harte's earlier publications.[468]

Finally, the preacher drew the attention of his congregation to two 'trifles' by which Satan sought to provoke schism and contention. The first of these contentious practices he describes as follows:

Therefore hee moueth muche strife, by the particular callyng of Brother & Syster, as thoughe Christes churche were dyuided, or that God fauoured suche particularitie and diuysion.[469]

Here we find a manifestation of the conventiclers' exclusivism – they referred to each other as 'brother' or 'sister'. In 1551 John Plume had testified to the negative aspect of this when he stated that they refused to 'Salute a Synner or a man whome they knowe not'. Since Cole no longer adhered to the tradition of the gathered congregation, he regarded

---

[465] *Ibid.*, C8^r-C8^v.
[466] *Ibid.*, C8^v.
[467] Burrage, II, 2.
[468] Below, 188-9.
[469] Cole, D1^v.

the selective use of such terms as arrogant and divisive. Therefore he affirmed:

> Whosoeuer therfore doth call any man or woman brother and syster otherwise then he calleth all other christian men, 'Peccat in unitatem ecclesiae'.[470]

The other 'triflig flour of scism' is stated to be the belief, 'That it is deadly syn to play at any game for money'.[471] This corroborates the evidence of William Greenland recorded on the Harleian fragment. Cole's assertion that the conventiclers' repudiation of gambling was a source of contention and irritation proved to be correct a year or so later in the King's Bench.[472] Here he explains:

> By this he [Satan] laboreth to thrust into mas heart such a precisenes, that at length a good ma might iudg euery thing although it wer but indifferent, to be damnable sin.[473]

How ironic that a man, who ten years later was to be known as a leading Puritan nonconformist,[474] should here criticise the social morality of the Free-willers as over-precise!

The conclusion to Thomas Cole's sermon was somewhat lengthy (sig. D3^r-E3^v). Here once again he sought to extricate himself from his former associates. Solemnly Cole affirmed:

> For God is my witnes, before whom I stad I neuer helde or taught any of these or such lyke erroures, neither do I knowe anye that doth holde or mayntayne any of theym, besydes these two simple men, whiche are here punished for their offences: by whom ye may learne to beware of lyke daunger.[475]

Viewed from the distance of four hundred years, it is difficult to avoid the conclusion that Thomas Cole's Maidstone sermon was replete with deviousness and dissimulation. At the very least the preacher was guilty of extreme casuistry. On the other hand it may be, as Watts suggests,[476] that Cole had consistently denied all the accusations levelled at him, that these protestations were genuine. Nevertheless, one is still confronted

---

470   *Ibid.*
471   *Ibid.*, D2^r.
472   Below, 264.
473   Cole, D2^r.
474   *Correspondence of Matthew Parker*, ed. Bruce (PS., Cambridge, 1853), 263-4; Collinson, 68.
475   Cole, D3^v.
476   Watts, I, 11.

with the fact that this schoolmaster from Maidstone was a member of the Kentish delegation that attended the Bocking conventicle at Christmas 1550. Furthermore, it is evident that the Privy Council in 1551 had remained unpersuaded by his explanations and protestations, for they sent him to prison. Whatever the truth of the matter, it is certain that Archbishop Cranmer would have known the full story. At least he must have derived satisfaction from listening to such an able convert deliver such a well-constructed sermon.

With the accession of Mary Tudor, Cranmer's half-hearted attempts at persuasion were superseded by harsher measures against Kentish sectarianism. Clark notes that 'the incidence of Marian martyrs in the county bears some crude topographical correlation with the known cases of later Lollardy'.[477] At least three of the Kentish martyrs had frequented the conventicles of the Free-willers: – Nicholas Sheterden, Humphrey Middleton and George Brodebridge.[478] From the evidence relating to the King's Bench controversy of 1554-6 it is clear that the majority of Kentish radicals – notwithstanding Thomas Cole's defection – continued to maintain human autonomy and impeccability after regeneration. Furthermore, there were other even more heterodox, religious radicals from Kent who suffered for their faith during the Marian persecution.

The visitation conducted by Nicholas Harpsfield, Cardinal Pole's commissary, in 1556 uncovered several 'unitarians'. At Sittingbourne a man named Newland declared that 'whoever says that Christ sits on the right hand of the Father they be fools'.[479] Harleian MS. 421 contains the record of four trials that took place before Archdeacon Harpsfield between 29 May 1556 and 20 July 1556, three of which were printed by Strype.[480] John Philpot of Tenterden, later burnt at Wye, maintained a highly individual interpretation of the Scriptures. He confessed to sacramentarian heresy and sectarian schism, but argued that communion was unnecessary. Moreover, he agreed with the invocation of saints and

---

[477] Clark, 101.
[478] Also, probably, John Fishcock of Headcorn who was burned at Canterbury on 19 June 1557. His confession, not printed by Foxe, reflects a similar exclusivist concern for real righteousness and a pure church (BL. Harl. MS. 421, ff. 101^r-104^r; Foxe, *AM.*, VIII, 326).
[479] Oxley, 166n.
[480] Strype, *EM.*, III (i), 540-2; Davis, 414-7.

the offering of prayers for the dead. These opinions may represent the confusion of a simple man rather than the results of mature reflection. William Prowtynge/Powting of Thurnham, later martyred at Canterbury, confessed:

that before his imprisonment he refused to come to the church, because the service is in a tongue that doth not edify. And he thinketh it contrary to God's word... And saith, that he doth not believe that there is in the real natural body of our Saviour Jesus Christ the form of bread... And saith further, that it is no article of our faith, that there is one God and three Persons, but one God Almighty: in whom he believeth, and saith, that Christ is not almighty of himself, but received all power from his Father, and is made God over all things unto us. And saith, that he was not God of the same substance of God from the beginning. And as for the Holy Ghost, he saith, that he believeth he is not God, but believeth he is the Spirit of God the Father only, given to the Son , and not God of himself....[481]

There is no evidence to suggest that this strongly anti-trinitarian sacramentarian had attended any of the Free-willer conventicles. Indeed, the first part of Prowting's confession suggests that he attended his parish church during the Edwardine period, only absenting himself when the Latin service was reintroduced.

John Symes/Simms of Brenchley was charged with the following articles –

That they that did not understand the Latin tongue should not have the service of the Church in the same tongue, because it doth not edify. That those that were lately burned were saved. That there is not the real body of our Saviour Jesus Christ under the form of bread. That it is against Scripture to burn heretics... And lastly, that he did not believe that Christ is consubstantial, that is to say, God from the beginning, and of one substance with the Father; and that there is one God, and three Persons. But he believeth the Father, the Word, and the Holy Ghost is one God, but not three Persons.[482]

A similar subordinationist christology was detected in the confession of the sacramentarian, Robert Kynge/King of Petham. Besides being charged with opposition to the Latin service and denial of the corporeal

---

[481] Strype, *Ibid.*, 540-1.
[482] *Ibid.*, 541.

presence in the sacrament, King was accused of saying that if any man could show him in Scripture the word 'consubstantial', then he would believe that Christ is consubstantial and of one substance with the Father, otherwise he would not. Furthermore, that if any man could show him the word 'person' in the Scripture in the same sense, then he would believe that there are three Persons and one God, otherwise he would not. Next, King was said to have 'doubted whether it can be proved by scripture, that the Holy Ghost is God, or no'. Finally, he was accused of saying that, 'it is not lawful to put a man to death for his conscience sake'.[483]

These anti-trinitarian, subordinationist opinions have more in common with the doctrines currently being proclaimed in and around Colchester by Christopher Vitells, than they have with the 'Melchiorite' christology advocated by Joan of Kent and the Dutch anabaptists. George van Parris had suffered martyrdom for similar views in 1551. Earlier, in 1548, the priest John Assheton had abjured almost identical heresies. The two penitents who stood before the congregation at Maidstone on the first Sunday in Lent in 1553 while Thomas Cole preached at them, had also been found guilty of holding unitarian opinions. In the 1560s the deprived Marian curate of Maidstone, John Day, declared that some of those who had suffered martyrdom in the town, 'did deny the humanity of Christ and the equality of the Trinity'; Day added, 'no man doubts that such are heretics'.[484]

Although John Philpot of Tenterden and William Prowting of Thurnham suffered martyrdom, none of these four cases is reported in any detail by Foxe. Symes and King are not mentioned, Philpot and Prowting are listed together with eight other Kentish men and women who were burned in January 1557. Foxe avoids publishing their articles of faith by stating –
What the ordinary articles were, commonly objected to them of Canterbury diocese, is before rehearsed,... To these articles what their answers were likewise, needeth here no great rehearsal, seeing they all agreed together, though not in the same form of words, yet in much like effect of purposes... And though they did all answer

---

[483] *Ibid.*, 541-2.
[484] BL., Harleian MS. 416, folios 123^v-124^r.

uniformly in some smaller things, as their learning served them, yet in the most principal and chiefest matters they did not greatly discord.[485] Similar omissions are noted by Davis in Foxe's account of the trial and burning of seven heretics in the diocese of Rochester in June and July 1555.[486] Davis comments:

It is difficult to account for this treatment since it is clear that Foxe had access to the consistorial material which contained the *acta*.... Foxe was not one to let genuine martyrs slip into obscurity, unless they did not conform to his pattern of belief and his ideal of conduct. The likelihood is that these shadowy figures had held Radical doctrines that did not fit into Foxe's preconceived picture of the two churches.[487]

Thus, it is evident that there were in Kent in the 1550s not only conventicles of separatist Free-willers, but also articulate individual free-thinkers who were considerably more radical in their theology. These anti-trinitarians may have been known to the conventiclers, but it is doubtful whether they frequented their conventicles since they do not figure in any of the 1551 depositions. Prowting, Symes, King *et al.*, maintained opinions derived from what Davis calls 'the eccentricities of rationalist Lollardy'.[488] In the fifteenth century Bishop Reginald Pecock detected two distinct forms of Lollardy – the evangelical 'Bible men' who gathered in conventicles and whom Pecock called 'Doctourmongers', and the more rationalist and sceptical individuals whom he labelled 'Opinion-holders'.[489] Both forms were still in existence in Kent in the mid-sixteenth century.

The Protestant Reformation had divided Kentish Lollardy as much as it had its Essex counterpart. Thus, in the spring of 1551 we find predestinarian sympathisers with the Edwardine church testifying

---

485   Foxe, *AM.*, VIII, 300.
486   *Ibid.*, VII, 318-21.
487   Davis, 296. Foxe did, however, publish the confession of Patrick Packingham who was tried with Denley and Newman (*AM.*, VII, 331) and burned at Uxbridge on 28 August 1555 (Strype, *EM.*, III (i), 360). It was compiled in response to one or more Protestants who had written to him in Newgate advising him that he was in 'blasphemous error'. Clearly Packingham was a subordinationist, if not an anti-trinitarian. He was also evidently a perfectionist and thus, presumably, a Free-willer (*AM.*, VIII, 722-3). See also Wilbur, 172.
488   Davis, 201.
489   Thomson, 244.

against local separatist Free-willers. However, in 1553, we find a member of the latter group – Thomas Cole – denouncing two of the 'unitarians'. As Davis observes, there is nothing to indicate that the congregation described in the depositions of 1551 (and by Cole in 1553) was any different in structure from the conventicles of later Lollardy. He continues, 'the point of division among the congregations that had come down from Lollard conventicles, as in East Anglia, was the attitude adopted by the sectarians towards the Edwardine orthodoxy'.[490]

The divisions produced by the religious policies of the Edwardine régime were succeeded by the persecutions suffered under Mary. As a result of these twin attacks Kentish sectarianism disintegrated. All the remaining exponents of free-will and separatism were either killed or silenced by the Marian persecution. In Kent, unlike East Anglia, there is no evidence of Familist activity in the Elizabethan period.

A considerable amount of information is available on individual Kentish radicals. Members of the Kentish delegation named in the proceedings of the Privy Council in 1551, Kentish conventiclers mentioned in the depositions to the heresy commissioners later that year, and Kentish Free-willers listed in John Bradford's letter of 1555 appear at widely scattered locations, on dates ranging from 1511 to 1586, in a variety of sources.

(a) Privy Council Record
Of the seven Kentish men mentioned in the proceedings of the Privy Council we have further information on four of them:– Nicholas Shetterton, John Lydley, – Chidderton, and Cole of Maidstone.

1.Nicholas Shetterton/Sheterden of Pluckley.
Sheterden was among the Bocking conventiclers who were committed to prison by the Privy Council on 3 February 1551 for their evil opinions and separatist practices.

The next reference to him occurs in a letter which John Bradford wrote from prison to, 'my friends and brethren in the Lord, R[obert]

---

490   Davis, 422.

Cole and N[icholas] Sheterden'.[491] He begins, 'Your letter though I have not read myself... yet I have heard the sum of it, that it is of God's election'.[492] Evidently Bradford, Philpot, Ferrar and the other reformers imprisoned in the King's Bench had received a letter from Cole and Sheterden on the subject of predestination. The contents of Bradford's reply indicate that he wrote it before he had completed his *Defence of Election*, which is dated 11 October 1554. It appears that Sheterden was arrested before the end of September 1554, in which case Cole and Sheterden's letter must have been written in the summer of 1554 – perhaps in the month of August, possibly from Faversham. Their letter may have resulted from a communication from John Trewe and the Sussex Free-willers in the King's Bench. Trewe seems to have had Kentish connections and was evidently known to them.[493] In his reply, Bradford argued that justifying and regenerating faith was the evidence of eternal predestination. He continues:

> Search your hearts whether you have this faith. If you have it, praise the Lord, ... But, if you feel not this faith, then know that predestination is too high a matter for you to be disputers of it, until you have been better scholars in the school-house of repentance and justification, which is the grammar-school, wherein we must be conversant and learned, before we go to the university of God's most holy predestination and providence.[494]

Sheterden appears to have been detected by Archdeacon Harpsfield during a visitation in the summer of 1554. At his examination before the suffragan bishop of Dover, Richard Thornton, *circa* June 1555, he claimed to have been in prison for three quarters of a year.[495] Therefore, in August or September 1554 Sheterden was arrested on the instructions of Harpsfield and imprisoned in the Westgate at Canterbury.[496] Bradford may not have heard of Sheterden's arrest when he wrote his reply, but some time later he addressed a further letter to Robert Cole only.[497] On 16 February 1555 Bradford included Sheterden among the

---

491   Bradford, II, 133-5.
492   *Ibid.*, II, 133.
493   *Ibid.*, II, 243-4; Below, 174.
494   *Ibid.*, II, 133.
495   Foxe, *AM.*, VII, 308.
496   *Ibid.*, VII, 306.
497   Bradford, II, 215-6.

Free-willers to whom he addressed his general letter of reconciliation.[498]

Foxe published a detailed account of his examinations before Harpsfield, Thornton and Stephen Gardiner, together with Sheterden's notes against the 'false Worship and Oblation of the Sacrament', a prayer written just before his martyrdom, and five of his letters.[499] In his initial debate with Archdeacon Harpsfield and Commissary Collins, 'for the which they sent him to prison', Sheterden made a remark which reveals his (and perhaps the majority of Kentish Free-willers') opposition to anabaptism. Quoting from *John 3* the Commissary sought to 'prove to me that Christ's manhood was in two places at one time'; Sheterden replied:

> This place and other must needs be understood for the unity of the person, in that Christ was God and man ... If ye will needs understand it to be spoken of Christ's manhood, then must ye fall into the error of the Anabaptists, which deny that Christ took flesh of the Virgin Mary; for if there be no body ascended up, but that which came down, where is then his incarnation? for then he brought his body down with him.[500]

Here is one Kentish radical who rejected the 'Melchiorite' christology expounded by Joan of Kent, and there seems no reason to doubt that Sheterden's associates did likewise.

In his subsequent examination before Bishop Thornton of Dover, Sheterden proved to be not only articulate and courageous but also something of a barrack-room lawyer. If he had shown a similar boldness before the Privy Council in 1551 then it is easy to understand why they sent him to prison. First, he insisted upon seeing the credentials of his interrogators. Then he refused to answer to any of their articles until they gave him a reason for his arrest. Sheterden continues:

> I answered, that I had been a prisoner three quarters of a year, and as I thought wrongfully: reason would, therefore, that I should answer to those things wherefore I was prisoner... 'For when I was cast into prison, there was no law but I might speak as I did: therefore, in that

---

498 *Ibid.*, II, 194.
499 Foxe, *AM.*, VII, 306-18.
500 *Ibid.*, VII, 307.

point, I could be no more suspected than you [Thornton] which preached the same yourself not long before'.[501]
The prisoner continued to refuse to answer their articles or submit to their judgment. Foxe comments, 'Upon this it appeareth the letters were written to the bishop of Winchester, by whom he was sent for afterwards and examined'.[502]

Having, presumably, been taken to London, Sheterden continued to prevaricate, refusing to respond to Gardiner's statements on the sacrament. Gardiner then turned to the subject of ceremonial and the use of images. Here Sheterden confounded the Bishop with his knowledge of the English Bible. After much discussion, Gardiner terminated the examination, dismissed Sheterden's appeal, and ordered him to abjure or suffer the consequences.[503] Sheterden was returned to Canterbury gaol.

Some time prior to his examination before Richard Thornton a letter from Sheterden to his mother had been intercepted.[504] This appears to have been the first of the collection of five letters published by Foxe. In this letter Sheterden sought to persuade his mother to leave the old ways of superstition and idolatry and obey the Scriptures. He exhorts:
Beloved mother, as I have oftentimes said unto you, even so now I beseech you from my very heart-root in Christ, to consider your own soul's health [that] is offered you; do not cast it off: we have not long time here....[505]

From the first of the two letters to his brother, Walter Sheterden, it appears that a wealthy uncle had visited him in prison at Canterbury and offered to leave him a large portion of his estate if he would give up his opinions.[506] His brother, who stood to gain financially from Nicholas'

---

[501] *Ibid.*, VII, 308. The heresy laws were not revived until December 1554.
[502] *Ibid.*, VII, 309 n.l.
[503] *Ibid.*, VII, 310-12.
[504] *Ibid.*, VII, 308.
[505] *Ibid.*, VII, 314.
[506] This was probably the Isaac Shetterden who died in 1573 leaving property in London, Great Chart and Shadoxhurst near Ashford (*Prerogative Court of Canterbury Wills 1558-1590* ed. Duncan, London, 1898, III, 280).

obduracy, had commented on his brother's lack of formal education –
and indeed Nicholas Sheterden could not read Latin.[507] He replied:

> For though I be not learned (as the vain men of the world call
> learning), yet, I thank my Lord God, I have learned out of God's book,
> to know God from his creatures, and to know Christ from his
> sacraments, and to put a difference between the merits of Christ's
> passion and his Supper, and a difference between the water of baptism
> and the Holy Ghost, and not to mix and mingle all things confusedly
> together.[508]

In the second letter, Sheterden urges his brother to seek a new life of
righteousness rather than temporal riches. This exhortation to Christian
discipleship, righteous living, and spiritual regeneration is very similar to
those found in the writings of Henry Harte. Sheterden writes:

> And now let us assay a new life, and trade our members in virtue... if
> we now return and lay hand of his word in deed and verity, as we have
> long time done in talk and liberty, then will God heap upon us such
> certificate of conscience, as shall kindle our consolation in him... Dear
> brother, my heart's desire and prayer to God is, that we may together
> enjoy the bliss of eternal inheritance by one spiritual regeneration and
> new birth as we are joined by nature.[509]

Perhaps the most illuminating letter from a doctrinal standpoint is the
one that he wrote to his wife from prison after she had sent him some
raisins and figs. This is the only extant record of his communication with
a fellow believer. The outstanding feature is Sheterden's use of highly
metaphorical language to describe the relationship between the physical
and the spiritual in human existence. At various points in the letter he
refers to the body as 'Esau the elder brother by nature', 'the servant and
stranger', 'your churlish servant Nabal', and as analogous with the
Gibeonites. Sheterden counsels his wife to use moderation in self-
denial–

> Now, my beloved... I know ye do complain of your servant the Flesh,
> that he is rebellious, disobedient, and untoward... but he lacketh both
> meat and drink, and other necessaries meet and due for a servant...

---

[507] Foxe, *AM.*, VII, 311.
[508] *Ibid.*, VII, 315.
[509] *Ibid.*, VII, 316.

Perhaps Mistress Sheterden was engaging in prayer and fasting on behalf of her husband, but such austerities fit in with the general impression of the conventiclers' more rigorous approach to the Christian life. Sheterden continues:

... if he [the body] do his service negligently (as, no doubt, sometimes he will), yet then ye may boldly correct him with discretion; and sometimes, if he do not his task, ye may make him go to bed supperless: but yet beat him not with durable strokes, neither withold his meat in due time, and pinch him not by the belly continually, but let him have something to joy in: only watch him, and keep him from doing harm. Though he be but a stranger in the life that is in God, yet be good to strangers... for we were all strangers in darkness, and captives in sin, as well soul and spirit, being in Egypt, as now the flesh is yet unbaptised with the terrible Red Sea of death.[510]

Here we find the same dichotomy between the Flesh and the Spirit as there is in Champneys' treatise.[511] The final sentence indicates that Sheterden believed that the spiritually regenerate Christian was inwardly liberated from sin and capable of an inner perfection. However, Davis probably reads too much into these remarks when he asserts that 'apart from the sectarian implication, the emphasis on the two natures, on the flesh and the spirit, and the appeal to wisdom strongly suggest Radical influences in the shape of the two *homines*, and the "inner light" of revelation'.[512]

Sheterden's final examination took place before the Bishop of Dover on 26 June 1555. He was examined along with four other prisoners:– John Frankesh, deprived vicar of Rolvenden; John Bland, formerly vicar of Adisham; Humphrey Middleton, a fellow conventicler; and one Thacker, who recanted at this eleventh hour. According to Foxe, seven articles were administered to them, Sheterden and Middleton answering together in complete agreement. The four confessors were then condemned as heretics and handed over to the secular authorities.[513]

---

510   *Ibid.*, VII, 317.
511   Above, 86-7, 95.
512   Davis, *op. cit.*, 428-9.
513   Foxe, *AM.*, VII, 304, 312.

The day before he suffered, Sheterden wrote the most moving of his five extant letters – and even the discerning Coverdale could not resist printing it.[514] This was again addressed to his mother. Sheterden writes:
> ...God grant you to see my face with joy: but, dear mother, then beware of that great idolatry, and blasphemous mass. O let not that be your god, which mice and worms can devour. Behold I call heaven and earth to record, that it is no god... O give over old customs, and become new in the truth. What state soever your fathers be in, leave that to God; and let us follow the counsel of his word... but yet cast off all carnal affections, and love of worldly things; so shall we meet in joy at the last day, or else I bid you farewell for evermore.[515]

Here we find the same ardent abomination of Catholic sacramentalism that is the main feature of the Lollard sacramentarian tradition. Here is the same emphasis upon obedience to the Scriptures, Christian discipleship, and ethical righteousness found both in that tradition and in the writings of the Free-willers.

The final piece of writing preserved by Foxe is entitled 'The Christian Prayer of Nicholas Sheterden before his death'. It includes the following statement –
> ...and lo, I leave here all the pleasures of this life, and do now leave the use of them for the hope's sake of eternal life purchased in Christ's blood, and promised to all them that fight on his side, and are content to suffer with him for his truth...[516]

Once again there are echoes of Christian discipleship, of an active striving after moral righteousness and Christian obedience. Nowhere in Sheterden's literary remains is the word 'election' used, nowhere is there that passive acceptance of God's will characteristic of many determinists. Christ's atonement is effective only for 'them that fight on his side'. Of course Sheterden and Middleton were imprisoned at Canterbury, and so they were far removed from the predestinarian controversies in the King's Bench. Nevertheless, members of the former Protestant establishment such as Bland and Frankesh were in prison with them. It is suggested, therefore, that Nicholas Sheterden

---

514   Coverdale, *op. cit.*, 510.
515   Foxe, *AM.*, VII, 316-7.
516   *Ibid.*, VII, 313.

remained a fervent believer in human free will and impeccability to the end. It must remain an open question whether he continued to advocate separatism.

Foxe's account concludes, 'And so, being given to the secular power, they were burned at Canterbury the 12th of July, at two several stakes, but all in one fire together'.[517] Thus, on 12 July 1555, two unlearned lay separatists who advocated the doctrine of free will suffered martyrdom alongside two learned ordained members of the Reformed Church of England. Doubtless the significance of this conjunction did not escape the bystanders in Canterbury that day.

2. John Lydley/Ledley of Ashford
In 1551 the Kentish sheriffs failed to apprehend the two Ashford men, Lydley and Chidderton – but they were evidently among the delegates at Bocking. Lydley is next mentioned in the list of addressees to whom Bradford sent his letter of 16 February 1555. At that time he was believed to be one of the Free-willers 'abiding in Kent, Essex, Sussex and thereabout'.[518] In the 1563 edition of *The Acts and Monuments* Foxe stated that John Lydley and his wife were forced to leave Ashford because of the persecution.[519] This may have been in the summer of 1555 after the burning of their associates, Sheterden and Middleton.

Lydley, like many others, sought refuge in the anonymity of the metropolis, and there joined one of the underground congregations. Strype prints a letter written by a former Free-willer to the London congregation of Free-willers. This unknown convert to predestinarian teaching remarks:
> For I consider[ed] the loss of mine own friends, and their displeasure... And although I thought I should lose many friends: yet it hath pleased God to raise up many friends to me for one. And I thank God, that they, whom I thought would have been mine enemies, are become my friends in the truth: as in sample, by our brethren Ledley and Cole, and such like. If it had lyen in their own

---

[517] *Ibid.*, VII, 312.
[518] Bradford, II, 194.
[519] Foxe, *AM.*, VIII, Appendix III, (1563 ed. pp. 1677-9).

wills, they would have been enemies to that excellent truth which they do now allow. Praised be God for them....[520]
Evidently John Lydley had embraced predestinarian teaching and joined the 'official' underground congregation in London. When Lydley and his wife fled to London they probably joined their former associate Robert Cole of Faversham and his family, and were influenced by him.

By 1557 Robert Cole(s) and John Lydley (Ledley) were key members of the London predestinarian congregation. According to Stephen Morris' deposition they were among the principal teachers of heretical doctrine in London – 'John Ledley, and Robert Coles, are great counsellors, and do resort much unto the King's Bench, unto the prisoners, about matters of religion'.[521] Evidently Coles and Ledley acted as intermediaries between the members of the underground congregations who were at liberty and those in the King's Bench. Having formerly been Free-willers they were well-placed to act as 'counsellors' to those prisoners currently engaged in the controversy over predestination. Morris further deposed that Coles and Ledley instigated the importation by William Punt of 'a barrel-full of books' against 'the sect of the Anabaptists'.[522] The association of Coles and Ledley with William Punt is interesting. Morris describes Punt as 'a great writer of devilish and erroneous books of certain men's doings.' This refers to a martyrology later used by Foxe. According to Strype, Punt wrote an inaccurate account of the sufferings of Protestant prisoners from Essex; he crossed to the Continent, had his manuscript printed, brought the books back to England and distributed them.[523] It would appear that Coles and Ledley made use of Punt's experience in order to obtain propaganda with which to combat the Free-willers. On Palm Sunday 1556 Punt landed in Essex from the Continent with his 'barrel-full' of copies of a book against the Anabaptists.[524] It is significant that the two former Free-willers were now so anxious to persuade their fellow conventiclers of the error of their ways that they caused this anti-anabaptist book to be printed and distributed. Possibly

---

[520] Strype, *EM.*, III (ii), 329.
[521] Foxe, *AM.*, VIII, 384.
[522] *Ibid.*
[523] Strype, *Annals*, I (i), 378ff.
[524] *loc. cit.*

William Punt wrote the work himself; although Dickens suggests that it was a further edition of William Turner's *A preseruatiue, or triacle, agaynst the poyson of Pelagius.*[525]

Morris' deposition continues:
And the said Robert and John went over at the same time, about questions of religion, to the learned that were over, to know their counsel in those matters, and so to turn back again upon the same.[526]
Thus, Coles and Ledley left England with Punt early in 1556, and while the latter was procuring the printing of the book, Coles and Ledley acted as messengers for the London congregation. They visited the learned exiles, seeking their advice about 'questions of religion'. Now, in the spring of 1556 the controversy over predestination reached its peak, largely due to the vigorous assertion of the Calvinist doctrine of reprobation by John Careless from within the King's Bench. It is suggested, therefore, that the 'questions of religion' to which Coles and Ledley sought answers from the learned reformers in exile related to the predestinarian controversy. They possibly arose from the articles of faith which John Careless had recently drawn up and circulated.[527]

We have no further information on John Lydley. Unlike his companion Robert Coles, there is no sign that he was ordained into the ministry of the Church of England. Perhaps Lydley and his wife returned to Ashford after the accession of Elizabeth.[528]

3. Chidderton of Ashford
Apart from his visit to Bocking in 1550, the only other possible reference to this man is in Foxe. Towards the end of the year 1556 fifteen Kentish men and women were imprisoned in Canterbury Castle. Foxe writes:

---

[525] Dickens, *The English Reformation*, 274.
[526] *loc. cit.*
[527] Below, 202, 278-9.
[528] John Lydley contributed to a collection of prayers compiled during the Marian persecution which became known as 'Ledley's Prayers'. They were published in 1560 and subsequently re-printed on several occasions (*STC* 10617, 17776).

In the beginning of November [1556] were together in the castle of
Canterbury fifteen godly and innocent martyrs, of which number none
escaped with their lives, but they were either burned, or else famished
in prison ... five were pined and famished most unmercifully in the
strict prison ... whose names were these: John Clark, and Dunston
Chittenden (which two were yet uncondemned)...

Foxe concludes his account by printing a copy of a letter which was
thrown out of a window in the castle by some of the prisoners and which
described how they had been denied food.[529] At the time this letter was
written Chittenden was already dead. There is also a reference in Foxe to
'one goodwife Chittenden' who fled from Kent because of the
persecution.[530]

Therefore, 'Chidderton of Ashford' may have been the Dunstan
Chittenden who, before being brought to trial, died from starvation in
Canterbury Castle between November 1556 and January 1557. His wife
may have fled to London after her husband's arrest.

4. Cole of Maidstone, schoolmaster

In his *Athenae Cantabrigienses*, Cooper listed Thomas Cole as coming
from Lincolnshire, as being a member of King's College, as gaining his
B.A. in 1546 and M.A. in 1550, and as schoolmaster at Maidstone in
1552.[531] However, Gray's corrections reveal that, although Thomas Cole
was admitted to a Cambridge D.D. in 1565, there is no evidence that he
graduated from Cambridge; Cooper had confused Thomas Cole with
Robert Cole.[532] In his *Alumni Cantabrigienses*, Venn only lists Thomas
Cole's D.D., but adds in brackets the quotation – presumably from a
Cambridge University register – 'M.A. Oxford 14 years'.[533] This would
mean that Thomas Cole gained an Oxford M.A. in the same year that
Robert Cole was admitted to a similar degree at Cambridge. However,
while Wood mentions Thomas Cole, Foster does not include

---

[529] Foxe, *AM.*, VIII, 253-4; Coverdale, 526-7.
[530] Foxe, *AM.*, VIII, Appendix III.
[531] *Athenae Cantabrigienses*, ed. Cooper (Cambridge, 1858), I, 295-6.
[532] *Ibid.*, III, ed. Gray (Cambridge, 1912), 79. Garrett has perpetuated this error (p. 122).
[533] *Alumni Cantabrigienses*, ed. Venn (Cambridge, 1922), I (i), 368.

him among the Oxford *alumni*.[534] Garrett suggests that Thomas Cole might have been the brother of William Cole, Fellow of Corpus Christi College, Oxford from 1545.[535] Strype states categorically that Thomas and William Cole were brothers.[536] According to Garrett, William Cole came from Grantham in Lincolnshire and lived from 1527 until 1600. In 1553 he went into exile, and later assisted with the translation of the Genevan Bible. In 1568 he became the first married president of Corpus Christi – an office he held for thirty years until he was appointed Dean of Lincoln in 1598.[537]

It is suggested, therefore, that Cole of Maidstone was the younger brother of William Cole of Grantham, Lincolnshire. He followed his brother to Oxford, possible becoming a member of the same college, and graduated M.A. in 1549/50. Thus, Thomas Cole would have been no older than twenty-one when he came to Maidstone, and the schoolmastership would have been his first appointment. Moreover, he was the first master of the new Maidstone Grammar School.[538]

The royal charter incorporating the Town of Maidstone and establishing its grammar school was secured early in 1549. One of the most prominent citizens in the town at this time was a certain 'John Denlye, gent.'. He had acted as an agent for the town in the negotiations with the Duke of Somerset that secured the royal charter. Previously he had taken a leading part in the sale of property confiscated from the College of All Saints – the proceeds then being used by Maidstone Corporation to purchase the Fraternity Hall for use as a grammar school.[539] There is no reason to doubt that it was the same John Denley who, in 1555, responded to the letter of the Essex Free-willer, John Sympson. Denley and Newman were apprehended in Essex shortly after the burning of Ardeley and Sympson. They confessed that they were

---

[534] *Fasti Oxonienses*, ed. Wood (London, 1815), I, 147 nn. 2-4; *Alumni Oxonienses*, ed. Foster (Oxford, 1891).
[535] Garrett, 123.
[536] Strype, *Life of Parker* (Oxford, 1821), II, 222.
[537] *loc. cit.*
[538] Frank Streatfeild, *An Account of the Grammar School in Maidstone*, (Oxford, 1915), 10-13.
[539] *Ibid.*

visiting their 'godly friends' in that county.[540] Denley was examined in S. Paul's by Bishop Bonner and burned at Uxbridge on 8 August 1555.[541]

Therefore, it is suggested that the young Thomas Cole – who perhaps gained the Maidstone schoolmastership on the recommendation of Somerset – arrived fresh from Oxford in 1549 and immediately came under the influence of one of the town's leading citizens, John Denley. The latter sympathised with the Kentish radicals and introduced Cole into their conventicles.

The Privy Council record of February 1551 includes Cole among those who had abstained from communion for more than two years. This indicates that he had not communicated at All Saints Parish Church since his arrival in Maidstone *circa* 1549. Moreover, he quickly espoused at least one of the conventiclers' tenets – that infants were not tainted with original sin. By the end of 1550 he was a leading member of the Kentish delegation to Bocking, and shortly after that he was made to suffer for his separatist activities.

It is not known how long Cole spent in prison, but he evidently came to see the error of his ways and underwent a rapid change of allegiance. Thomas Cole's flirtation with Kentish religious radicalism had been short-lived, but he was nevertheless a prize convert. His conversion to the established church must have had a profound effect upon the Kentish separatists. Perhaps, as Horst suggests, he pioneered the path that other Kentish conventiclers were to take during the following years of persecution.[542] Two years later he was preaching before Archbishop Cranmer in All Saints, Maidstone. The Archbishop may have taken the young enthusiast under his wing, in the same way that Ridley sponsored Thomas Putto the tanner and Coverdale influenced John Champneys. It would appear that Cranmer had ordained Thomas Cole or at least issued him with a license to preach. Cole's Maidstone address may well have served as a test-sermon, indicating to the ecclesiastical authorities his suitability for preferment in the established Church of England.[543]

---

540 Above, 128-9.
541 Foxe, *AM.*, VII, 328-34. See also *APC.*, IV, 373, 375.
542 Horst, 124.
543 There is no record of Thomas Cole's ordination, but none of Cranmer's ordinations have been preserved.

Shortly after this he was appointed Dean of Salisbury, but it is doubtful whether he was able to take possession of his deanery. Within a few months Edward VI was dead, and the two Cole brothers fled to the Continent upon the accession of Mary Tudor.[544]

By September 1554 Thomas Cole had arrived in Frankfurt. In February 1555 the English congregation appointed him to serve on the committee that was to 'drawe forthe' an order of worship 'meete for their state and time'. After a few modifications their production became the Order of Geneva. Cole was a consistent member of Whittingham's party and signed its letter of secession in August 1555. He remained in Frankfurt, however, when the rest of the party moved to Geneva in September 1555. Garrett suggests that he acted as an observer for Whittingham.[545]

On the accession of Elizabeth, Thomas Cole returned to England, and on 9 November 1559 he was admitted to the rectory of High Ongar, Essex, on the presentation of Lord Richard Rich. Doubtless Cole relished the irony in this presentation, for it was Rich who was behind the arrest and trial of the Bocking conventiclers some nine years earlier. On 3 January 1560 Bishop Grindal of London collated him to the archdeaconry of Essex, and on 20 February following appointed him to be his commissary in the archdeaconry of Colchester. On 7 December 1560 Grindal collated him to the prebend of Rugmere. Thomas Cole was present in the convocation of 1562 and subscribed to the thirty-nine articles, and also to the petition for discipline.[546] A former exile, writing to a Swiss friend in 1571 and mentioning the death of Cole, referred to his 'remarkable eloquence in the pulpit'.[547] The 1553 Maidstone sermon certainly bears out that observation. Cole's eloquence ensured that he was much in demand as a preacher. He preached the annual sermon at S. Mary Spital in the April of 1560, 61 and 63. His name was again proposed for the Spital sermon of 1566, but Archbishop Parker vetoed the suggestion because he suspected Cole of nonconformity.[548] Collinson describes him as 'a flagrant nonconformist',[549] but there is no

---

544 Garrett, 122; Streatfeild, 15-16.
545 Garrett, 122-3.
546 Cooper, *loc. cit.*
547 *Zurich Letters*, ed. Robinson (PS. Cambridge, 1852), I, 256.
548 Cooper, *loc. cit.*; Parker, *Correspondence, loc. cit.*
549 Collinson, 68.

evidence to suggest that he suffered for his opinions or deemed it necessary to resign any of his offices.

On 1 March 1564 he preached before the Queen at Windsor, his sermon being printed and published later that year.[550] At this point in his career it is evident that Thomas Cole was no compliant time-server. Boldly he urged the Queen to embrace 'that chaste estate of Matrimonie', also to tread under foot all 'golden idols' and 'burne them with Copes and al other Popish dregges'.[551] This boldness apparently did his career no harm, because on 13 July 1564 he was admitted to the rectory of Stanford Rivers, Essex, on the presentation of the Queen herself.[552] In the same year he commenced the Cambridge D.D. It is noteworthy that at this high point in his career, with all his interests apparently concentrated in London and Essex, Thomas Cole was still in contact with 'divers gentlemen in Kent'.[553]

When Edmund Freke was elevated to the see of Rochester in 1570/1, Thomas Cole was again preferred to the deanery of Salisbury. However, in June 1571 he contracted quinsy in London and, after only two days' illness, died very suddenly. He died on the day 'preceding that on which he had determined to go from London to Salisbury to receive induction, attended by many friends and domestics'.[554] Thomas Cole was under fifty when he died; he seemed destined for a bishopric, yet never attained the deanery to which he was twice appointed.

(b) Harleian Fragment
Of the eight men mentioned on this manuscript as being members of the Kentish conventicle, there is further information on four of them.
5. Cole of Faversham
A note in the 1563 edition of Foxe provides almost conclusive evidence that the Robert Cole who became rector of S. Mary-le-Bow, London, after the accession of Elizabeth was Cole of Faversham, the former Free-willer –

---

[550] Thomas Cole, *A Godly and Learned Sermon made the laste Lent at Windesor before the Queen's Maiestie*, (London, 1564), STC 5540.
[551] *Ibid.*, A8ʳ-A8ᵛ, F1ʳ.
[552] Cooper, *loc. cit.*
[553] Parker, *Correspondence*, 303 n.3.
[554] *Zurich Letters*, I, 242.

Out of Feversam was persecuted one Robert Coles, wyth his wyfe and chyldren, who is now person of Bow in London.[555] Robert Cole came from Biggleswade, Bedfordshire, and was educated at Eton College. He was admitted to King's College, Cambridge, on 13 August 1542. His age is given as eighteen, and therefore he must have been born *circa* 1524. He was matriculated in 1544 , admitted B.A. in 1546/7, M.A. in the Easter term of 1550, and is said to have been a Fellow of King's College from 1545 to 1551.[556] However, by 1 August 1550 Cole was residing at Faversham in Kent. How he came to be in Faversham is a matter for conjecture. Having gained his M.A. soon after Easter 1550, he may have obtained a teaching post at Faversham similar to that taken up a year earlier by his namesake at Maidstone. However, the proposed grammar school at Faversham was not finally established until *circa* 1580. It is equally possible that Robert Cole married into a Faversham family and eventually forfeited his Fellowship.

At the heresy commission's investigations into Kentish radicalism in 1551, John Grey deposed that on 1 August 1550 Cole of Faversham said and affirmed that 'the doctrine of predestynation was meter for divilles then for christian men'. John Plume's evidence indicates that this affirmation occurred during a meeting of conventiclers in Cole's house at Faversham.[557] There is nothing to suggest that Robert Cole was a member of the delegation that travelled to Bocking the following Christmas, although the delegates may have gathered at his house before taking ship across the Thames estuary.

The name of Robert Cole figures prominently in the correspondence of John Bradford. It was probably from Kent in the summer of 1554 that Cole and Sheterden wrote to Bradford about the doctrine of predestination.[558] Cole may have become acquainted with John Bradford at Cambridge; Bradford was admitted to St. Catherine's College in August, 1548, to his M.A. by special Grace in 1549, and elected Fellow of   Pembroke   the   same   year.[559]   Perhaps   the

---

[555]   Foxe, *AM.*, VIII, Appendix III, (1563 ed. pp. 1677-9).
[556]   Venn, I (i), 367.
[557]   Above, 137-9.
[558]   Above, 158-9.
[559]   Venn, I (i), 199.

predestinarian controversy then raging, both in prison and out of prison, in London and out of London, caused Cole to take the initiative and revive the acquaintance. Alternately, John Trewe (the Sussex Free-willer imprisoned in the King's Bench) may have contacted them. The Sussex Free-willers had close connections with their Kentish counterparts.

Sheterden was arrested shortly after the despatch of their letter, but Cole seems to have remained in Kent for a few months longer. In his general letter to Free-willers in Kent, Essex and Sussex dated 16 February 1555 Robert Cole is listed among the addressees, so presumably he was still at liberty in Kent at that time.[560] Shortly after this letter Bradford wrote to John Philpot. He remarks:

> My good brother, Robert Cole, hath written to me in this matter, to labour to persuade them with my letters. Therefore I purpose to write something to Trew and Abyngton thereabouts, which you shall see.[561]

The matter Cole had referred to was the dissension in the King's Bench between the Predestinarians and Free-willers. Cole appears to have been in contact with John Trewe and Thomas Abyngton – leading Free-willers from Sussex – who were also held in the King's Bench. This suggests that Cole was now in London. A further letter among Bradford's correspondence appears to support this. It is addressed to Robert Cole and is, perhaps, Bradford's reply to the letter referred to above. Bradford exhorts:

> Mine own heart in the Lord, desire our brethren that every one would bend himself to bow: let us never break, 'Love suffereth long...' God keep us from dissension.[562]

The 'brethren' referred to here were probably the London underground congregation for whom Cole, Ledley and Punt were later to act as messengers.

Therefore, from this correspondence it is concluded that between March and June 1555 Robert Cole, his wife, and children fled to London and became associated with the underground congregations. His acquaintance with Bradford enabled him to assume a mediating role between the two parties. However, Cole's own thinking was in process

---

[560]   *loc. cit.*
[561]   Bradford, II, 243-4.
[562]   *Ibid.*, II, 215.

of transition. In London he turned away from the separatism of the Kentish conventiclers and found a place in the 'official' underground church. On the doctrine of predestination he seems to have been partially persuaded by Bradford. Perhaps Bradford's martyrdom on 1 July 1555 cemented Cole's convictions because, by the time of the next reference (late 1555 or 1556) Robert Cole and John Ledley are described as former Free-willers.[563] The anonymous prisoner who had embraced predestinarian teaching makes a second reference to Cole in his letter to the Free-willer congregation. He writes, 'My brother Robert Cole did give you a good report to me and to my prison fellows'.[564] Evidently Cole was still in contact with his former associates among the Free-willer congregation.

The deposition of Stephen Morris in early 1557 confirms that Cole was continuing to act as an intermediary between the prisoners and the underground congregation.[565] Morris further deposed that in the spring of 1566 Cole travelled to the Continent along with Ledley and Punt in order to seek the advice of the exiles. Garrett argues that Cole's inclusion on John Bale's list of exiles indicates that he must have remained abroad for a longer period than John Ledley.[566] In the 1563 edition of Foxe the name of Robert Cole is linked with that of Thomas Bentham, the last minister of the underground church in London.[567] Since the context is a list of ministers and deacons of the 'official' congregation, this suggests that Robert Cole served as Bentham's deacon. It may be, therefore, that Cole remained on the Continent – perhaps at Basle – and returned to England with Bentham in the spring of 1558.[568]

In this edition Foxe also recounts the narrow escape that Cole had when he suddenly encountered 'hys mortall enemye' – a local magistrate

---

563 Above, 165-6.
564 Strype, *EM.*, III (ii), 334.
565 Above, 166.
566 Garrett, 121-2.
567 Foxe, *AM.*, VIII, 788 (1563 ed. p. 1700).
568 If Robert Cole did prolong his stay on the Continent it must have been after a subsequent visit because in *circa* August 1556 he delivered Augustine Berneher's book on election to Henry Harte (Bodleian MS 53 F. 141^r. Below 353).

named Petit – in 'a narrow lane, nor farre from Feversam'.[569] It is impossible to detect when this incident took place, but it is more likely to have occurred before Cole fled to London in 1555. The magistrate can, however, be identified. He was Cyriac Pettit, a member of the local gentry and a strong sympathiser with the Marian cause.[570] It is, moreover, clear that at the time of Elizabeth's accession, Robert Cole was holding office in the London underground congregation.

In his account of the preachers of the Spital sermons for Easter 1559 Strype lists Bentham as the preacher for Easter Monday and Cole, 'another exile', as the preacher for Easter Tuesday.[571] The conjunction with Bentham suggests Robert Cole rather than Thomas; William Cole was still in Geneva at that time. Robert Cole was among the large number of ordinands who were ordained by Bishop Bullingham of Lincoln (acting on behalf of Archbishop Parker) at Lambeth on 10 March 1559/60.[572] Thirteen days later he served as proctor for the bishop-elect, Thomas Bentham, at his consecration to the diocese of Lichfield.[573]

On 23 December 1559 Robert Cole was collated by Archbishop Parker to the rectory of S. Mary-le-Bow, London.[574] Cole appears to have been given a benefice before he was formally ordained deacon on 10 March 1560. Earlier in the month of December 1559 he had taken part in the consecration of five new bishops in Bow Church. His subsequent presentation to that living appears to have been merely the formalisation of an already existing arrangement. However, within a year he was anxious to obtain another benefice. On 18 November 1560 William Winthrop wrote to John Foxe, the martyrologist, at Norwich seeking preferments in Parkhurst's diocese for certain 'sober learned young men'. Furthermore:

He prayed him likewise to procure some living of 50L, a year, or upward, for Robert Cole, being minded to give up where he was.[575]

Perhaps Cole, being a family man, was pressed for money and needed a richer living. Alternately, the former radical may have grown restless

---

[569] *loc cit.*
[570] Strype, *EM.*, III (i), 476.
[571] *Ibid., Annals*, I (i), 299.
[572] Parker, *Register*, I, 342.
[573] *Ibid.*, I, 89.
[574] Cooper, I, 364.
[575] Strype, *Annals*, I (i), 310.

under the restrictive eye of his patron. Yet it is strange that he should have sought a benefice from Bishop Parkhurst in the diocese of Norwich rather than from his former associate Bishop Bentham in the diocese of Lichfield.

Evidently this application was unsuccessful. When Robert Cole's name next appears in the records some four years later, he had come to accept the situation. In March 1564 the ecclesiastical commissioners, under pressure from the Queen and her archbishop, determined to regulate the costume and practices of the London clergy. In particular they determined to insist upon the wearing of the surplice at all public services and the strict observation of the *Book of Common Prayer*. To ensure that their wishes were understood and obeyed the Archbishop, Bishop Grindal and members of the commission ordered the clergy of London to assemble at Lambeth on 24 March. There, they exhibited – somewhat ludicrously – a clergyman dressed in the required attire. It was the former separatist and Free-willer, Robert Cole. Strype continues:

> ...the Bishop's Chancellor spoke thus: 'My Masters and the Ministers of London, the Council's pleasure is, that strictly ye keep the unity of apparel like to this man', pointing to M^r. Robert Cole (a Minister likewise of the city who had refused the habits a while, and now complied, and stood before them canonically habited) 'as you see him; that is, a square cap, a scholar's gown priest-like, a tippet, and in the church a linen surplice'.[576]

Two years later (12 April 1566) Archbishop Parker, in a letter to Cecil, mentioned the difficulties that the radical puritan clergy and churchwardens of London were still causing him –

> As for mine own peculiars, fourteen or fifteen be all in order. Some did refuse, but now they be induced, and they be counted sortly learned with the best of them, as one Cole of Bow church, and one Beddell of Pancras.[577]

In fact, Robert Cole had to wait nearly five years for his compliance to be rewarded. It was not until 15 January 1569 that he was collated by Archbishop Parker to the rectory of All Hallows, Bread Street, which he

---

[576] *Ibid., Grindal*, 144-5.
[577] Parker, *Correspondence*, 278.

then held in plurality with S. Mary-le-Bow.[578]

The impression conveyed by these sources is of a radical puritan minister who began his ministry in 1559/60 with a determination to maintain his principles, but who quickly became subservient to those who controlled his livelihood. That Robert Cole allowed himself to be exhibited before the clergy of London after his initial refusal to conform suggests total dependence and abject compliance. Or did Cole heed the advice he had received from John Bradford some ten years earlier that everyone should 'bend himself to bow' rather than 'break' and thereby nurture dissension? Either way, for a man of his background and education who had risked his life ministering to the London congregation during the years of persecution, Robert Cole seems to have been treated very shabbily by the Elizabethan religious establishment.

Cooper states that Cole died 'about April 1577'.[579] If so, then he was little more than fifty at the time of his passing. According to Venn he ceased to be rector of his two parishes in 1576.[580] However, according to the puritan survey of *circa* 1586, Cole was still the incumbent of S. Mary at Bow but not of All Hallows, Bread Street.[581] It may be that he had resigned the latter benefice in 1576. In 1571 Robert Horne had heard Cole preach – presumably because he considered him to be a trustworthy 'Anglican' like Aylmer and Jewel.[582] Yet, on 24 June 1584 Thomas Barber was suspended from the office of lecturer at Bow Church by the Bishop of London for not subscribing to the *Book of Common Prayer*. In a subsequent supplication on behalf of Barber it is stated that 'of long time' he had preached in S. Mary at Bow four times a week, and that many people from all parts of London and many visitors to the metropolis had flocked to hear him.[583] It is possible that, after the death of Archbishop Parker in 1575, Cole finally succeeded in

---

[578]   Cooper, *loc. cit.*; Venn, *loc. cit.*
[579]   *loc. cit.*
[580]   *loc. cit.*
[581]   *The Seconde Parte of a Register*, II, 180, 182.
[582]   *Ibid.*, I, 80-1, 81 n.2.
[583]   *Ibid.*, II, 219-21, 262.

securing a benefice beyond the reach of Bishop Aylmer.[584] While he continued to enjoy the living of S. Mary-le-Bow Thomas Barber officiated and preached in his place.[585] In which case Robert Cole died in peaceful provincial obscurity many years later than 1577.[586]

6. Henry Harte
See below 184-236.

7. George Brodebridge
Foxe states that George Brodebridge of Bromfield, together with four other prisoners, was examined before Richard Thornton, Bishop of Dover, on 3 August 1555. Brodebridge's recorded answers indicate that he was a vigorous sacramentarian – 'as for your holy bread, your holy water, and your mass, I do utterly defy them'. All five prisoners were pronounced guilty of heresy and condemned, and all five suffered together in one fire at Canterbury *circa* 6 September 1555.[587] Bromfield was a parish some five miles south-east of Maidstone, lying between Maidstone and Lenham. Therefore Brodebridge came from the heart of the region in which most of the Kentish conventiclers lived.

8. Humphrey Middleton
In the 1551 investigation John Plume of Lenham deposed that at Faversham on 1 August 1550 Middleton said that 'Adam was elected to be salued And that all men being then in Adams Loynes were predestynate to be saluid and that ther were no reprobates'.[588] Clearly Middleton's rejection of predestinarian doctrine was carefully thought-out and lucidly expressed. It is a pity that we do not have more information on his beliefs.

---

[584] *Lincoln Episcopal Records* 1571-1584, ed. Foster, Canterbury and York XI (London, 1913), 323.
[585] It may be significant that of the one hundred and twenty-two London parishes listed in the 1586 survey Cole's is one of only two without the mysterious abbreviation 'r' against it (*loc. cit.*).
[586] During the Marian persecution Robert Cole (in association with Lydley) compiled a collection of prayers which were published in 1560 and subsequently reprinted on several occasions until well into the 1590s (R. Cole, *Godly meditacions*, London, 1560, STC 17776).
[587] Foxe, *AM.*, VII, 383.
[588] *loc. cit.*

Strype suggested that he was one of the leaders of the conventicle, perhaps its teacher.[589] This may have been the case for, in Foxe's account of an incident that occurred at Canterbury in the last days of Edward's reign, Middleton was evidently the leader and spokesman.[590] Middleton, with other conventiclers, was arrested by Archbishop Cranmer and the heresy commissioners late in 1552 or early the following year. Before they could be brought to trial, King Edward died. However, Middleton and his fellow prisoners were subjected to vigorous interrogation by the commissioners. Foxe records Middleton's prophetic reply to Cranmer –

Come, O reverend Sir, for the present it is permitted to you to pronounce concerning us but … I announce that your turn will come very soon after this.

Foxe adds that the prophecy was rapidly fulfilled. The King died 'not many days later', the Kentish prisoners were released, and 'the bishop did truly reconcile chains and prison'.[591]

Middleton is listed among the addressees in Bradford's letter to the Free-willers of 16 February 1555.[592] Later that year he was re-arrested, presumably during Archdeacon Harpsfield's visitation of the summer of 1555 – the same visitation that netted Brodebridge. Foxe states that Middleton came from Ashford. He was examined together with Bland, Frankesh and Sheterden by Richard Thornton at Canterbury on 25 June 1555. Sheterden and Middleton responded to the seven articles together, both refusing to answer to the three which dealt with the mass. Middleton affirmed that he believed in 'My living God, and no dead God'. Foxe's account concludes, 'they were burned at Canterbury the 12 of July [1555], at two several stakes, but all in one fire together'.[593]

---

[589] Strype, *EM.*, II (i), 370.
[590] Above, 144-5.
[591] Foxe, *Rerum*, 202. I am grateful to Mr. Theo Donner, late of St. John's College, Cambridge for his help with the translation of Foxe's Latin.
[592] *loc. cit.*
[593] Foxe, *AM.*, VII, 312.

(c) The Addressees in John Bradford's Letter to the Free-willers[594]

Of the thirteen individuals named by Bradford, nine can be identified. Three remain to be considered.

9. Richard Prowde

In the official list of English refugees at Aarau Richard Prowde is described as an 'edelman' living in the house of Mauritz Meggers. Hans Dür adds that he was born in Canterbury and lived at Faversham.[595] Presumably he was a junior member of the Proude family of Canterbury who also owned the manor of Goodnerstone near Faversham.

The first known reference to him occurs in a letter written by John Bradford to Mistress Joyce Hales which is dated 8 August 1554. Prowde had just informed him that Joyce Hales' father-in-law, Sir James Hales of Thanington, near Canterbury, had drowned himself shortly after being released from prison by the Marian authorities.[596] Joyce Hales was the wife of Humphrey Hales, the eldest son of Sir James; they lived in Canterbury and supported the Edwardine reforms. As a fellow member of the Kentish minor gentry, it is hardly surprising that the Hales family asked Richard Prowde to break the news to Bradford.

A few months later, John Bradford included Prowde among the Free-willers to whom he wrote his conciliatory letter concerning predestination. Foxe states that Richard Prowde, like Robert Cole and his family, was forced by persecution to flee from Faversham.[597] This must have been after February 1555 and possibly at the same time as Robert Cole. Presumably he went to London initially, but by 1557 he was in exile at Aarau where he remained until 1559.

On 31 March 1560 he was ordained by Bishop Grindal,[598] and at some date unknown was collated to the living of Burton upon Dunmore, Warwickshire. Strype publishes a letter which Prowde wrote from that

---

[594] Bradford, II, 194-8.
[595] Garrett, 262, 356.
[596] Bradford, II, 108-117, 85 n.4.
[597] Foxe, *AM.*, VIII, Appendix III.
[598] Strype, *Grindal*, 58.

parish to Lord Burghley in 1579. In it Prowde rebuked Queen Elizabeth's Secretary of State for his failure to go into exile under Mary and for his 'going along with this present queen' in the matter of vestments and ceremonial.[599] The letter is signed – 'Rychard Prowde, parson of Bowrton upon Donsmore, although unworthy of so great calling, having no greater learning. 13 of May 1579'.[600] It would be interesting to know whether Prowde suffered for his temerity.

In the Puritan survey of 1586 Prowde is listed as a 'sufficient' preacher who was 'in danger' because he had refused subscription to the *Book of Common Prayer*.[601] He was associated with the Warwickshire conventicles, and died in 1596.[602]

10. William Porrege

The Porrege brothers probably came from Sandwich. In his letter to Joyce Hales dated 8 August 1554 Bradford remarks – 'I received your letters by William Porrege', and later, 'As for William Porrege's report…'.[603] When taken with Foxe's account of his activities, it would appear that William Porrege served as a messenger between the exiles on the Continent and the London underground congregation.[604] His route seems to have taken him from Calais to London *via* Dover, Sandwich and Canterbury. Six months later John Bradford included both William and Richard Porrege among the Free-willers to whom he addressed his letter on predestination.

John Foxe recounts the 'happy deliverance of Thomas Sprat, tanner, and William Porrege his companion, now minister'.[605] He states that Sprat, 'went to Calais, from whence he used often with the said William Porrege, for their necessary affairs to have recourse into England'. This suggests that the two men fled to Calais and made use of the English outpost as a base from which to conduct their activities. Their dramatic

---

599 *Ibid., Annals* I (ii), 148; II (ii), 290-2, 662-5.
600 *Ibid.*, II (ii), 665.
601 *The Seconde Parte of a Register*, II, 172.
602 I am indebted to Professor P. Collinson for this information.
603 Bradford, II, 108, 117.
604 Garrett, 258.
605 Foxe, *AM.*, VIII, 576-8.

deliverance from almost certain capture occurred 'about the fourth year of queen Mary's reign,' that is, *circa* 1557, when they were travelling between Dover and Sandwich.[606]

William Porrege was ordained by Bishop Grindal in January 1560, being among those who were 'no scholars, or of any University, but men of sober conversation, and that could read English well'.[607] On 27 August 1560 he was collated by Archbishop Parker to the rectory of Grimston, near King's Lynn, in the diocese of Norwich.[608] Presumably Porrege was left well alone in his rural parish remote from London since nothing more is heard of him.[609]

11. Richard Porrege

Apart from the fact that he was listed among the Kentish Free-willers by John Bradford in February 1555, the only other information concerning him is that he was 'Jurate of the town of Sandwich' in 1574.[610]

Richard Prowde and the Porrege brothers seem to have been closely associated with Humphrey and Joyce Hales. These members of the minor Kentish gentry were apparently sympathetic towards the Kentish Free-willers. Doubtless their opinions were as influential among Protestants in the Canterbury area as were John Denley's in the Maidstone region. It is significant that John Bradford dedicated his treatise entitled *Defence of Election* to Joyce Hales.[611]

---

[606] *Ibid.*

[607] Strype, *Grindal*, 54.

[608] Parker, *Register*, I, 186.

[609] William Porrege probably supplied Foxe with the account of Cranmer's conduct of the heresy investigation at Ashford in 1552/3. The account is very sympathetic towards the accused (Foxe, *AM.*, VIII, 41-3).

[610] Garrett, 258.

[611] Bradford, I, 307-10.

C. HENRY HARTE

According to Dickens, Harte was 'perhaps the most influential English sectary' of the period.[612] Nevertheless, he is – as Martin states – 'a man more labeled than examined' by historiography to date.[613] One reason for this inadequate treatment may be the fact that, despite the frequency with which his name appears in the records, he is extremely difficult to identify. Horst suggests that he may have been the Henry Harte who was married to Ciceley Bowes, elder daughter of Sir Martin Bowes, a lord mayor of London.[614] Davis identifies him with the Henry Harte who is listed as a parishioner of Chart Parva near Pluckley in Kent in the Harpsfield visitation records of 1557 and 1558.[615] Among the wills proved in the Canterbury diocesan courts in the sixteenth century there are several for men from both Pluckley and Little Chart bearing the surname Hert, Hart, or Harte. The parish registers confirm that the Harte family was numerous in these parishes, also that they favoured the Christian name 'Henry'.[616] It is clear that our subject had strong Kentish associations – and particularly with the conventiclers of the area in which Pluckley is situated (Nicholas Sheterden came from Pluckley). However, it is not possible to make a positive identification of our subject among several individuals of that name in these parishes at that time.

Among the Hert/Hart(e) entries in the Canterbury Archdeaconry Act Book, one is for the administration of the estate of a Henry Harte of Pluckley in 1557.[617] He appears to be the most likely candidate. His will was proven on 6 March 1557, and in it he bequeathed six pounds to his natural daughter, Joanna. This may be the Henry Harte of Little Chart listed by Nicholas Harpsfield because one of the earliest entries in

---

[612] Dickens, *The English Reformation*, 238.

[613] J.W.Martin, 'English Protestant Separatism at its Beginnings: Henry Hart and the Free-will Men', *Sixteenth Century Journal*, 7 (1976), 56.

[614] Horst, 123 n.102.

[615] Davis, 423; *Archdeacon Harpsfield's Visitation*, ed. Whatmore (Catholic Record Society, London, 1950), I, 168; II, 321.

[616] Kent Archives Office, P82/1/1a Fl^v; P82/1/1c F.6^v; P82/1/1b F.2^r; P82/1/2 F.1^r; P82/1/1d F.5^r. The earliest entries in the Pluckley register date from 1560.

[617] *Ibid.*, PRC 3/15 F.22^r.

the first Little Chart parish register is the following under the year 1539 –

item ye doughter off harry hartt was crisnyt ye xiij day off november.[618]

Unfortunately the entries for the years 1556, 57 and 58 are incomplete and contain no mention of the burial of a Henry Harte. However, under the year 1560 the Little Chart register contains the following entry –

the xxvth day October was buried [?Elinor] the wyfe of Harry Hart.[619]

Twenty years earlier six men from Smarden and Pluckley had been indicted to appear at the Canterbury sessions for gathering in 'unlawful assemblies'. They appealed to Archbishop Cranmer who then wrote to Thomas Cromwell on their behalf. One of the two men listed as coming from Pluckley is a Henry Harte.[620] It is not unreasonable to suppose that these 'unlawful assemblies' were earlier meetings of the conventicle referred to in the records of 1550-51, also that the 'Henry Harte' who figures in both sources is the same man. If our subject did come from Pluckley, then he – like many of the Kentish conventiclers – belonged to a region with a strong Lollard tradition. In Archbishop Warham's persecution of Lollards in 1511-12 nearly all those detected came from the Maidstone – Ashford – Tenterden area.[621]

I. His Career

Our subject is probably to be identified with the 'Henry Hert, carpenter of Westminster' who associated with James Brewster, carpenter of Colchester, condemned as a relapsed heretic and burned at Smithfield on 18 October 1511. Brewster worked with Hert at Westminster. He 'had much conference with Henry Hert, against oblations and images' and they agreed that it was better to give money to the poor than spend it on pilgrimages.[622] Both were clearly Lollards. Even at that early date the

---

[618] *Ibid.*, P82/1/1a F.1^v.
[619] *Ibid.*, P82/1/1c F.6^v.
[620] *LP*, XIII (i), 319. Harte may have moved across the parish boundary into Pluckley because Lancaster, the vicar of Pluckley, sympathised with Cranmer. Certainly 'unlawful assemblies' would have stood more chance of toleration and survival in Pluckley than in neighbouring parishes.
[621] Thomson, 189.
[622] Foxe, *AM.*, IV, 216.

'company and conference of Henry Hert' was considered sufficient grounds to suspect heresy. Perhaps he had been forced to leave Kent by Archbishop Warham's persecution.

If Henry Harte was a carpenter that would explain William Turner's allusions to a 'woode spirite'.[623] If Harte's trade was based at Westminster that would account for his connections with Robert Cooche and the court of Henry VIII.[624] He may well have been highly mobile – an itinerant carpenter like Christopher Vitells, the Familist joiner of London and Colchester, a generation or so later. Like Vitells, Harte had contacts in London, Colchester and East Anglia – but unlike Vitells he also had a number of supporters in Kent.

If Henry Harte was an active Lollard in 1511, then he must have been born *circa* 1490, if not earlier. He would have been an elderly man by the time of John Bradford's reference to 'my father Hart' in 1554.[625] In which case he may well have returned to Pluckley and there died from old age in 1557.

After 1511, no further reference to an English religious radical named Henry Harte occurs for twenty-five years. In the summer of 1536 the conference of anabaptists at Bocholt was arranged through the auspices of an Englishman named 'Henry'.[626] This Englishman was of 'like mind' with David Joris and had 'long urged and implored' that there be such a conference in order to forge unity among the leaders of anabaptism in The Netherlands. Arnold writes:
> …an Englishman by the name of Henry, who previously was of like mind with him [Joris] had long urged and implored because of the great disunity, that their teachers or ministers, as they were called, should go there [Bocholt] at his cost, with the intention of finally reaching an agreement.[627]

The source from which Arnold derived this information was a biography of David Joris. He states that the sponsor of this conference (from

---

[623] Below, 189-90.
[624] Below, 190-1, 242-3.
[625] Below, 194.
[626] Above, 14-15.
[627] Arnold, *op. cit.*, II, 711.

which Joris emerged as the dominant figure) had previously known and sympathised with Joris. In fact some years earlier David Joris had stayed in England. Bainton writes:

> In the year 1520 Joris went to England in the service of Lord William Sandys, treasurer of Henry VIII to paint the windows of the chapel in his country house, 'The Vine' at Basingstoke in Hampshire. His work can still be seen. After two years his health forced him to go home...[628]

Henry Harte was a fellow artisan, much the same age as Joris. They may have met while working on the same building project at Basingstoke. Nevertheless, Horst's tentative identification of the sponsor of the Bocholt conference with Henry Harte must be regarded as highly speculative,[629] especially if our subject is the Henry Harte of Pluckley.

On 29 April 1538 Archbishop Cranmer wrote to Thomas Cromwell from Lambeth interceding for 'certain men of Smarden and Pluckley in Kent'. His letter continues:

> [They] are indicted for unlawful assemblies at the last session at Canterbury, and (as they report unto me) of none occasion or ground else, but because they are accounted fauters [favourers] of the new doctrine, as they call it; beseeching your lordship therefore, that if it cannot be duly proved that they are worthy thus to be indicted, they may be released of this their indictment. For if the King's subjects within this realm which favour God's word, shall be unjustly vexed at sessions, it will be no marvel though much sedition be daily engendered within this realm.[630]

On an attached paper six names of indicted persons are listed. The first of these is Henry Harte of Pluckley.[631]

This letter was written in the context of a running dispute between the Archbishop and several conservative Kentish magistrates who opposed the Henrician reforms.[632] Henry Harte and his fellow conventiclers were probably detected to Sir John Baker of Cranbrook, one of Cranmer's leading opponents.[633] During the decade 1537-47 the chief

---

[628] Bainton, *op. cit.*, 3.

[629] Horst, 79.

[630] Cranmer, *Works*, ed. Cox (PS., Cambridge, 1844, 46) II, 367.

[631] *Ibid.*, II, 367 n.3.

[632] *Ibid.*, II, 349-56, 367 n.4.

[633] *Ibid.*, II, 349 n.11.

reforming influence in the diocese of Canterbury appears to have been the Archbishop's own chaplains and licensed preachers. These included Nicolas Ridley (then Vicar of Herne), his brother Lancelot, John Scory, Richard Turner vicar of Chartham, John Bland vicar of Adisham, Henry Goodrick vicar of Hothfield, Michael Drum, and a man named Lancaster who was vicar of Pluckley.[634] The fact that the local parson sympathised with Cranmer's reforms may have been the reason why radicals like Harte and Sheterden settled in Pluckley. Cranmer and his preachers were also opposed by conservative clerics such as Richard Parkhurst vicar of Lenham, Robert Serles vicar of Charing, John Willoughby vicar of Chilham, and the Canterbury prebendaries John Milles, William Gardiner and Edmund Shether.[635]

The first definite evidence for Henry Harte the Free-willer leader dates from the year 1548, when his *A Godly Newe short treatyse* was published.[636] This must have been well received because less than three months later a new and improved edition of the work was published under the title, *A Godlie exhortation to all suche as professe the Gospell*.[637] Although its opening passages emphasise the need for spiritual regeneration, the greater portion of Harte's treatise consists of ethical exhortation couched in the language of Scripture. He implores his readers to eschew worldly pleasures and live devout, sober lives:

> Brethre, I beseche you for the dere mercy of God, esteme your salvatyo and health, w^c is precyous ... haue copassio on youre owne soules, and shewe loue and charty to the poor opressed, the lame blinde and nedye loke upon your selfes wyth an inwarde eye and see that your soules be refreashed that they may liue... whye esteme ye so much the vayne pleasures of thys worlde?... O, therfore I besych you, doo no more wyllfully euyll: Soo can synne nowe doo ye no harme.[638]

---

[634] Strype, *Memorials of Cranmer*, I, 249.

[635] *Ibid.*, I, 229-60; Above, 45-9.

[636] (London, 23 October 1548) STC 12887. Printed by Robert Stoughton. At least six copies are extant.

[637] (London, 1 January 1549) STC 10626. Printed by John Day and William Seres. Only one copy is known to survive in the Library of Emmanuel College, Cambridge.

[638] Harte, *Newe short treatyse*, sig. B2^r-B^v.

Similar themes are to be found in a much longer work which was published in Worcester a few weeks later. In fact, Harte's *A Consultorie for all Christians*[639] may well have been written before his *Newe short treatyse*. The *Consultorie* is the first book known to have been published by John Oswen after he moved from Ipswich to Worcester. Oswen published his last book in Ipswich on 10 August 1548 and presumably moved to Worcester shortly afterwards, taking the manuscript of Harte's *Consultorie* with him.[640] Furthermore, the title and comparative brevity of Harte's treatise indicates that it was a 'new' and 'short' successor to an earlier and longer work. Perhaps it was Oswen's apparent failure to publish the *Consultorie* that caused Harte to write his second book. Equally it may have been the success of Harte's *Newe short treatyse* which caused Oswen to throw caution to the wind and publish the *Consultorie*. If this is the case, then the *Consultorie* is Henry Harte's first, and most important, manifesto.

The publications of Henry Harte evidently made an impression in high places and provoked a rapid response. In 1549, William Turner – physician and chaplain to the Duke of Somerset – was appointed to a lectureship at Isleworth.[641] He used the opportunity to mount an attack on 'two of the opinions of Pelagius'. The dedicatory epistle in Turner's *A preseruatiue or triacle* contains information which enables a reconstruction of the events that provoked the composition of this treatise.[642] Turner writes:

> I thought to haue bene at good rest, and quietnes from contentious striuinges, wherewith I had bene muche troubled in tymes past.... But beholde sodenly sterte oute a woode spirite, muche periliouser than all the beastes, that I had to do with before: not because he is stronger then the other: but because his poyson, that he intendeth to spoute

---

639 (Worcester, 30 January 1549) STC 12564. Printed by John Oswen. Three copies are known – two in the Cambridge University Library and one in the British Library.

640 *Early English Printed Books 1475-1640*, ed. Sayle (Cambridge, 1900), II, 1302-3, 1305-6; Dickens, *The English Reformation*, 222, 355n.

641 *DNB.*, XIX. On Turner see Whitney R.D.Jones, *William Turner. Tudor naturalist, physician and divine* (London, 1988).

642 William Turner, *A preseruatiue, or triacle, agaynst the poyson of Pelagius, lately renued, & styrred up agayn, by the furious secte of the Annabaptistes* (London, 30 January 1551), RSTC 24368; sig. A2^r-A3^v.

oute, is more perillous then the others poyson was... I deuised a
lecture in Thistelworth, agaynst two of the opinions of Pelagius... the
enemie is a spirite, that is, the goste of pelagius, that olde heretike: ones
welle laid, but now of late to the great ieperdie of many raysed up
agayne:[643]

The 'woode spirite' referred to here and elsewhere in the book is almost
certainly an allusion to Henry Harte. In his preface to this work Thomas
Norton – Turner's scribe at the Isleworth lectures – writes:

... in certaigne now of late:
A wood spirited hart: with a wayward wyll:
A stubborne stomache, to nourishe debate:
Blered, yea blynded eyes:[644]

Now Turner's book was actually written in reply to a composition by
another court official, Robert Cooche.[645] He had possibly written in
defence of Harte.[646] However, Turner claimed that Robert Cooche had
come under the influence of Henry Harte – 'Thys is the counsell, not of
the spirite of God: but of the wood sprete, who taught yow your
diuinite'.[647]

Thus, it would appear that William Turner had read Harte's publications
of 1548/9. Disturbed by this sudden and unexpected reappearance of
'Pelagianism', he had lectured against Harte's doctrine at Isleworth.
Whereupon, Harte's disciple Robert Cooche had circulated a written
defence of his instructor. This, Turner partially answered in his *A
Preseruatiue or triacle*, published in January 1551. He promised to
complete his answer to Cooche as soon as his 'Newe Herball' was
finished;[648] he apparently failed to keep this promise.

Turner had little respect for Harte's learning or logic. In the course of a
statement on the proper subject of baptism, Turner comments:

In the one place ye offer remission of synne only unto them that
baptism is to be offered to, that is to the that wil repent: and in the

---

643 *Ibid.*, A3^r-A3^v.

644 *Ibid.*, A7^r.

645 *Ibid.*, A7^v, E7^r; Horst, 116 n.80.

646 Below, 242-3. If this work was printed, then it is not recorded.

647 Turner, M5^r.

648 *Ibid.*, N6^r.

other unto all. Is not here a prety argument? thys is the spirit whiche
ye receiued in the wood, wher as ye tolde me that ye learned w^t out any
doctor your diunite.[649]
Neither does he think much of Harte's usage of Scripture '...ye haue be
like authorite of youre woode spirite to make new textes of scripture, and
to bylde thereupon what ye lyst'.[650] He also criticises Harte's manifest
disregard for theological scholarship and formal learning:
> What wood spret taught you this folish philosophy: that one cause
> shuld bring furth two diuerse and contrary effectes, as ar saluation &
> condemnacio? It is a great maruell, to se such great arrogancie as ye
> haue, to be ioyned wyth so lytle knowledge. But so are thei al, that are
> blasted with the Anabaptistical sprit, as you be.[651]
Finally, Turner concludes with the prayer –
> Almighty God kepe the from al phantasticall and straunge spretes and
> their learnyng also. Amen.[652]
Clearly William Turner had read Harte's writings. He may have known
him personally. For, the fact that Harte's teaching had made such an
impression upon these two court officials suggests that our subject – like
Joan Bocher – was known at court.

Perhaps the establishment of the heresy commission in the spring of
1549 and the subsequent persecution of leading radicals such as Joan
Bocher and John Champneys reduced Harte to a prudent silence. There
is no evidence that he published any more printed treatises. Moreover, it
seems that Harte was not among the Kentish conventiclers who travelled
to Bocking at Christmas 1550. His name does not figure on the lists of
those ordered to appear before the Privy Council on 3 February 1551,
neither did he appear before the heresy commissioners at Canterbury
later that year. In this connection Harte's admonition to his readers in the
Newe short treatyse to be discreet is noteworthy. He writes:
> By your deydes be no longer slouthefull, nether ouer muche afrayed,
> neyther to hastye wythowte measure, wantynge dyscrecyon. But kepe

---

[649] *Ibid.*, K1^r-K1^v.
[650] *Ibid.*, L2^r.
[651] *Ibid.*, L5^r.
[652] *Ibid.*, N6^r.

measure in all youre wayes: and wysely consyder place and time…[653]
There is none of the bravado of Joan Bocher or John Champneys here –
a bravado for which they paid a heavy penalty in 1549/50. Rather, Harte
extols the virtues of prudence – 'Be ye therefor dyscret and sobre', he
advises.[654] Implementation of his own advice may have preserved Harte
from imprisonment by the Edwardine authorities and from death under
the Marian regime. On the other hand, his opponents interpreted this
characteristic prudence as deviousness and calumny.[655]

However, while Henry Harte did not appear in person before the Privy
Council or the heresy commissioners, his name figured prominently
among the depositions of the Kentish witnesses. When examined upon
the tenth and eleventh articles, John Grey testified:
> henry harte aboute bartholomewtide laste saide and affirmed in the
> presence of diuers that ther was no man so chosen but that he mighte
> dampne hime selfe Nether yet anye man soo reprobate but that he
> mighte kepe goddes Comaundements. He saide that Saincte paule
> mighte haue dampnid hime selfe if he listed… harte said that Learned
> men were the cause of grete errors.[656]

Laurence Ramsey deposed concerning the tenth article:
> that henry harte saide and affirmed as it is conteyned in tharticle that is
> that ther is no man so chosen or predestynate but that he maye
> condempne himselfe. Nether is ther anye so reprobate but that he
> maye if he will kepe the commandementes and be saluid… harte saide
> that lernyd men were the cause of grete Errors.[657]

William Forstall agreed with Laurence Ramsay's deposition on the tenth
article. Concerning the eleventh article Forstall stated that:
> henry harte saide the same tyme that his faithe was not growndid upon
> Lernyd men for all errors were broughte in by Lernyd men.[658]

Thus, from this fragmentary record we learn that Henry Harte was
among the leaders of the conventicle that met at the house of Robert Cole
in Faversham in August 1550. At that gathering Harte vehemently

---

[653] Harte, *Newe short treatyse*, A7^r.
[654] *Ibid.*, A8^v.
[655] Bradford, I, 318; II, 131.
[656] Burrage, *loc. cit.*
[657] *Ibid.*
[658] *Ibid.*

denounced the doctrine of predestination and urged man's ability to keep 'goddes Comaundements' and thereby be saved. Furthermore, Harte warned his hearers against the teaching of scholarly clerics and learned writers because formal theological study nurtured 'grete errors'. Similar themes had been enunciated in his writings of 1548/9 and are to be found in his later literary remains.

Nothing further is known about Harte's activities during Edward's reign. In a letter written from his Oxford prison *circa* 19 January 1555 Ridley refers to Harte as:

> a man, so far as I have heard of him (my lord of Canterbury knoweth him best of all us), which hath been often monished, and, I suppose, hath in time past acknowledged certain of his follies, and yet hath not ceased, as I have heard say, to fall in them again.[659]

One of these admonishments may have been administered by the Archbishop during his investigation of heresy at Ashford in 1552/3.[660] Nevertheless, it is clear that Harte was treated very leniently by the Edwardine authorities – more leniently than some of his fellow sectaries.[661]

The next record of him is in connection with the controversy among the prisoners in the King's Bench during the years 1554, 1555 and 1556. The controversy seems to have broken out soon after John Bradford was transferred from the Tower to the King's Bench on 24 March 1554. There he found fellowship with Nicholas Ferrar, Rowland Taylor and John Philpot[662] – fellow members of the former Edwardine establishment, men with a similar social status and educational background. However, Bradford was also brought into close contact, perhaps for the first time, with a number of radical sectarian prisoners from London and south-east England. This conjunction between learned Protestant clerics and lay sectarian radicals soon became explosive.

---

[659] Bradford, II, 173.

[660] Above, 143-5.

[661] M.T.Pearse, 'Free Will, Dissent, and Henry Hart', *Church History* 58 (1989), 452-9 refers to 'Hart's apparent immunity from arrest' (p.455). This seems to have been the case throughout the last twenty years of his life and may have been due to his court connections (Above pp. 185-6, 191).

[662] Foxe, *AM*, VII, 146.

Sometime after the incident which, according to John Trewe, provoked the controversy,[663] Bradford lent a written doctrinal statement to one of these sectarian Free-willers.[664] When his statement was returned, enclosed with it were three letters and a printed tract. One was from 'my brother Simson', another from Henry Harte, and the third from his correspondent.[665] The printed tract may have been one of Henry Harte's publications. With regard to Harte's letter, Bradford comments:

> Concerning the second, which I have not read also, hereafter I trust shortly to answer, and that in such sort that I doubt not to have the hands of all prisoners in England to subscribe to the condemnation of them all of error: I speak it of the prisoners that be of any learning.[666]

Towards the end of this letter Bradford returned to the subject:

> As concerning Henry Hart's errors, which I have now read, that he by blanching [evading] goeth about to defend, if after the doings of some things I have in hand I do not by God's grace evidently make them to appear to such as will not shut their eyes, then suspect me to have slandered him...[667]

Clearly John Bradford had as little regard for Harte's abilities as Harte had for the doctrines of learned men. It is equally evident that Bradford was planning to write a treatise which would serve as a reply both to Harte's letter and to his general teaching on free will and justification.

Sometime later Bradford received a letter from Robert Cole and Nicholas Sheterden on the subject of 'God's election'.[668] Bradford's reply has been preserved. In his conclusion Bradford refers to Harte:

> Thus briefly I have sent you my mind and meaning concerning this matter. Hereafter you shall have, I think, your letter particularly answered by Master Philpot, as also if I have time, and you so require it, I will do after that I have answered my father Hart, the which thing hitherto to do God by sickness hath letted.[669]

---

663   Below, 264.

664   Bradford, II, 128.

665   *Ibid.*, and II, 129 margin.

666   *Ibid.*

667   *Ibid.*, II, 131.

668   Above, 158-9, 173-4.

669   Bradford, II, 134-5.

Evidently the projected treatise was weighing upon his mind. It was important that an adequate reply was made to Harte because, according to Coverdale, he was 'the chiefest maintainer of man's freewill'.[670] However, apart from illness, Bradford was also occupied with pastoral duties and thus far had neglected to write the promised reply.

Then, sometime before 11 October 1554, Bradford received a treatise entitled, 'The enormities proceeding of the opinion, that predestination, calling, and election, is absolute in man as it is in God'.[671] He then wrote a rebuttal entitled, 'Defence of Election', which is dated 11 October 1554.[672] To this Bradford added an answer (Part II) to 'The Enormities'.[673] Within this answer Bradford preserves the text of this latter treatise. In his dedicatory epistle he writes:

...immediately after the true doctrine of election, which I briefly first set forth, and then do particularly answer every part worthy the answering; not leaving out one tittle of every word as he hath put it abroad, so far as the bill that was sent to me from him, I think; for it was subscribed with his name, and the superscription was to me by name as truly written.[674]

It is almost certain that Henry Harte was the author of 'The Enormities'; that having received no reply to his communications he directed it to Bradford in person, who was then provoked to compose his long awaited 'Defence of Election'. In a marginal note Coverdale stated that Harte was the author of a treatise against election which John Bradford had forwarded to Cranmer, Ridley and Latimer at Oxford.[675] Bradford in a letter to Ridley dated *circa* 18 January 1555 writes, 'I have sent you here a writing of Harry Hart's own hand...'.[676] This writing was almost certainly 'The Enormities'.

Harte deduces six 'enormities' or objections to the Reformer's doctrine of election, and in the process reveals greater ability than Bradford is

---

[670] *Ibid.*, II, 170 margin.
[671] *Ibid.*, I, 318.
[672] *Ibid.*, I, 310.
[673] *Ibid.*, I, 305-330.
[674] *Ibid.*, I, 309.
[675] *Ibid.*, II, 174 margin.
[676] *Ibid.*, II, 170.

prepared to admit. He states the objection and then quotes passages from Scripture which apparently support his contention. The first 'enormity' proceeding from this doctrine is, 'that God's justice is general over all men, but his mercy is not so'.[677] The second that, 'the virtue of Christ's blood doth not, neither can, extend to all people'.[678] 'The third is, saith he, that there is no sin in man, for if man have no choice, then the evil man doth that which God would have him to do, as well as the good man'.[679] Harte's fourth objection is, 'that God's power and omnipotence is thereby denied, in that it is said, that he cannot know first, predestinate, and elect all men in Christ Jesu to salvation, and also to give the choice during this life'.[680] Fifthly, he objects that the doctrine of election, 'putteth away the covenant between God and man; yea, partly on God's part, in that Christ is denied to be a general Saviour to all men; but wholly and altogether on man's part; for it taketh all the power and ableness, which God hath before given, from him'.[681] The sixth and final 'enormity' is that, 'it colourably denieth excommunication to be had and used in the congregation of Christ; for such as they call good they say are predestinate, and those that they call evil may ...be called'.[682]

Evidently Harte sent this treatise initially to the Free-willers in the King's Bench. As it circulated among them before reaching its addressee they added two further points –

Other some would be satisfied, how that God's elect people are so 'elected from the beginning' in Christ that they cannot utterly fall away, and yet all men, they say, fell to damnation in Adam; and how that his mercy in saving his, and his justice in condemning his, could be at one instant with God.[683]

The identity of these questioners must remain open to conjecture. It may have been John Trewe and his company of Sussex Free-willers.[684]

---

677 *Ibid.*, I, 319.
678 *Ibid.*
679 *Ibid.*, I, 320.
680 *Ibid.*, I, 321.
681 *Ibid.*, I, 322-3.
682 *Ibid.*, I, 327-8.
683 *Ibid.*, I, 330.
684 Below, 266.

It would appear that the 'Defence of Election' failed to serve as the decisive answer to Harte that Bradford had hoped. Instead, the prisoners in the King's Bench had been aroused to a fervour of debate and dissension by these two treatises. Eventually Bradford and his associates decided to seek the endorsement of the senior Protestant Reformers who were held in prison at Oxford. In particular (according to Coverdale) he sought assistance from his former patron, the learned Bishop Ridley.[685] In a letter which was probably written on 18 January 1555 Bradford asked Cranmer, Ridley and Latimer for their support. He asked for their approval of 'a little treatise which I have made' and enclosed with it 'a writing of Harry Hart's own hand'. Bradford's letter was also signed by Ferrar, Philpot and Taylor, and was conveyed to Oxford by Latimer's Swiss servant, Augustine Berneher.[686] It is evident that they took a serious view of the situation that was developing in the King's Bench. Bradford writes:

> The matter may be thought not so necessary as I seem to make it: but yet if ye knew the great evil that is like hereafter to come to the posterity by these men, as partly this bringer [Berneher] can signify unto you, surely then could ye not but be most willing to put hereto your helping hands.[687]

He continues:

> The effects of salvation they so mingle and confound with the cause, that if it be not seen to more hurt will come by them, than ever came by the papists, inasmuch as their life commendeth them to the world more than the papists... In free-will they are plain papists, yea, Pelagians... They utterly contemn all learning: but hereof shall this bringer show you more, what he hath seen and heard himself.[688]

Bradford concludes with a formal appeal to his ecclesiastical superiors, 'As to the chief captains therefore of Christ's church here, I complain of it unto you...'.[689] Ridley, however, did not regard the issue so seriously. In his letter of welcome to Berneher he briefly touches upon the subject:

---

685 Bradford, II, 174 margin.
686 *Ibid.*, II, 169-71.
687 *Ibid.*, II, 170.
688 *Ibid.*, II, 170-1.
689 *Ibid.*, II, 171.

... but your and his [Bradford's] request I cannot for divers causes satisfy... I will be glad to hear and know what my lord of Canterbury and your master [Latimer] will say; and [I] shall also think of the matter to do the best that shall lie in me. If the matter be not more for other, than for Harry Hart's scribbling, I would think a man might be better occupied otherwise than in confuting of them...[690]

On 20 January 1555 Ridley replied to Bradford, and again he treated the matter lightly. He writes:

...I have seen what he [Berneher] brought from you and shortly surveyed the whole, but in such celerity, that others also might see the same before Austin's return, so that I noted nothing but a confused sum of the matter; and as yet what the rest have done I can tell nothing at all.... To your request and Austin's earnest demand of the same, I have answered him in a brief letter; and yet he hath replied again: but he must go without any further answer of me for this time.[691]

Evidently Ridley shared Bradford's low opinion of Harte's scholarship. Nevertheless, he had taken trouble to write a note to Harte – and received a prompt reply.

Less than two weeks later (31 January 1555) John Bradford was taken from the King's Bench and brought to trial. He was found guilty of heresy, condemned to death, excommunicated and delivered into the custody of the Sheriff of London, who imprisoned him in the Counter.[692] On 4 February (the day that the proto-martyr John Rogers was burned at Smithfield) Bradford was interviewed by Bishop Bonner.[693] Then, on two successive days (February 15th and 16th) Bradford was interrogated by Nicholas Harpsfield.[694] That evening (16 February 1555) Bradford – fully expecting to follow Rogers to the stake – wrote a long farewell to some of his former antagonists.[695] Significantly, Bradford placed Henry Harte at the head of a list of twelve addressees. He also directed his letter to, 'all other that fear the Lord and

---

[690] *Ibid.*, II, 172-3.
[691] *Ibid.*, II, 174.
[692] Foxe, *AM*, VII, 165.
[693] *Ibid.*
[694] *Ibid.*, VII, 168-74.
[695] Bradford, II, 194-8.

love his truth, abiding in Kent, Essex, Sussex and thereabout'.[696] This provides some indication of the areas from which the Free-willers derived their support. As one might expect in such circumstances, this letter is highly eirenic containing moving appeals for unity. Nevertheless, Bradford refused to yield on the central issue. While wishing controversy to cease, he commended his 'Defence of Election' to their careful consideration –

> Although I look hourly for officers to come and have me to execution, yet can I not but attempt to write something unto you, my dearly beloved (as always you have been, howsoever you have taken me), to occasion you the more to weigh the things wherein controversy hath been amongst us, especially the article and doctrine of predestination, whereof I have written a little Treatise... so answering the 'enormities' gathered of some to slander the said necessary and comfortable doctrine. That little piece of work I commend unto you.... I heartily pray you and every of you, for the tender mercies of God in Christ, that you would not be rash to condemn things unknown....[697]

Bradford concludes:

> If this my poor advice be observed, my dear brethren in the Lord, I doubt not but all controversies for predestination, original sin, free-will etc. shall so cease that there shall be no breach of love nor suspicion amongst us... I am persuaded of you, that you fear the Lord; and therefore I love you in him, my dear hearts, though otherwise you have taken it....
> Now I am going before you.... Howbeit I could not but, before I go, signify thus much unto you as I have done, that you might see my love and thereby be occasioned to increase in love, and learn rather to bear than break.[698]

In the event Bradford's foreboding was mistaken. He remained in the Counter for a further four months and more, maintaining a correspondence with the prisoners in the King's Bench. John Bradford was eventually burned at Smithfield on 1 July 1555.

Despite his refusal to entertain a doctrinal compromise with the King's Bench Free-willers, a few of their associates outside the prison appear to have been influenced by Bradford. In particular, Robert Cole – Harte's Kentish associate – replied to Bradford's letter of farewell, and from the

---

696 *Ibid.,* II, 194.
697 *Ibid.,* II, 195.
698 *Ibid.,* II, 197.

content of Bradford's response it would seem that Cole was at least partially persuaded.[699] There were others too like John Lydley, Richard Prowde and William Porrege who subsequently sought and found acceptance within the fellowship of those who adhered to the Edwardine and Elizabethan settlements.[700] Furthermore, there is the record of a certain Skelthrop – a Free-willer imprisoned in the King's Bench – who became persuaded of the truth of the Reformed position about this time.[701]

This evidence for a departure by some former conventiclers from the doctrines of free-will may well provide the context in which a letter preserved by John Strype was written.[702] Strype entitles it, 'A pious letter against complying with idolatrous worship in Queen Mary's days, written by a freewill man'. However this is misleading, for the bulk of the letter consists of an exhortation to separation from the world, obedience to the commandments, and a defence of free-will. The author is anonymous, but Strype suggests that it was written by Henry Harte. He writes:

> Among the rest I find one writ by a 'freewill-man', as they styled them, being an exhortation by one of that persuasion in the country to some friends in London…. In which letter he took occasion, largely to prove men's abilities to keep the laws of God, and the freedom of their wills. The writer of this letter is unnamed, but I suppose him to be Henry Hart, one of the chief of this sort of men, and afterwards a prisoner himself….[703]

Certainly its themes and phraseology are similar to those found in works known to have been written by Henry Harte, and there seems no reason to doubt Strype's identification. Strype ascribes this letter to the year 1555 and states that it was written 'in the country'. This suggests that at that time Harte was living quietly in Kent, perhaps at Pluckley. News of declension among some of those refugee Free-willers who had formerly looked to him for leadership would have provided ample reason for the despatch of such a letter. It was intended to rally the secret congregation

---

[699] *Ibid.*, II, 215-6; 243-4; Above, 173-5.
[700] Above, 165-6, 181-3.
[701] Bradford, II, 242-3; Foxe, *AM.*, VIII, 242.
[702] Strype, *EM.*, III (ii), 321-5.
[703] *Ibid., EM.*, III (i), 413.

of Free-willers in London to those doctrines which gave them a distinctive character *vis à vis* the secret congregation that adhered to the Edwardine Prayer Book and articles of faith. Without such doctrines the congregation had no *raison d être*, and Harte no constituency.

The last extant document attributable to Henry Harte also represents an attempt to 'reclaim' former associates who had passed beyond his influence and who were now in fellowship with the magisterial reformers. Unlike the letter preserved by Strype, the authorship, origin and date of this document can be delineated precisely.

Located among the collection of original letters and transcripts bound together under the title 'Letters of the Martyrs' in the Library of Emmanuel College, Cambridge, is a copy of a letter written by Henry Harte.[704] It consists of a single folded sheet which is headed –

A true coppye of letter w^{cc} Henrye Harte sent to newegate to ye prysoners ther condemndd to dy for ye conffessyone of christes ueryetye Agaynst sertayne Artycles w^{cc} they alowed y^t wer sette furth by sertayn prysoners c in ye Kyngsbench to appiase ye contencyon y^t theyr fellowe prysoners had w^t them if it myght haue ben.[705]

On the reverse side the Newgate prisoners to whom Harte directed this letter signed a brief repudiation of Harte's doctrine. Heading the list of twelve signatories is William Tyms, deprived curate of Hockley in Essex –

be fore god and mane I protest this doctryn of henrye hart to be most blasfemose to chrystes death and passyon by me willyame tyms the xxjst day of apryll in newegate condemned to dye for chrystes uerytye.[706]

William Tyms, together with six other men from Essex, was brought to London, examined by Bishop Gardiner, and sent to the King's Bench on 22 March 1555.[707] There they rejoiced to find fellowship with Ferrar, Philpot, Taylor and John Careless. The latter seems to have

---

[704] Emmanuel College MS. 260, folio 87. See Appendix I.
[705] *Ibid.*, F87^r.
[706] *Ibid.*, F87^v.
[707] Foxe, *AM.*, VIII, 105.

assumed Bradford's mantle as the leading protagonist for predestinarianism in the King's Bench. They also encountered five Sussex laymen, and presumably some of their former Kentish associates – at least three of the Essex men came from Bocking.[708] A year later, they were examined by Bishop Bonner at Fulham Palace (21 March 1556) and again in S. Paul's on 28 March 1556, where they were condemned, excommunicated, committed to the secular authorities and sent to Newgate.[709] Tyms, together with four of his Essex associates, was burned at Smithfield on 24 April 1556, three days after writing this repudiation.[710] Therefore, Harte's letter must have been sent between 28 March 1556 and 21 April 1556, the latter being the date of Tyms' reply on the reverse of the sheet.

Evidently Harte was in close touch with the progress of the controversy in the King's Bench, which suggests that he was in London by the time he wrote this letter. It may well have been a last ditch attempt to win back to their former doctrinal allegiance a group of men with whom Harte had been acquainted for many years – at least since the days of the Bocking conventicle. In the course of this letter Harte exclaims:

frynds I feare ye accept a carles mane to be yor teacher and he hath tawght ye as carles a fayth....[711]

Clearly this is a reference to John Careless and the influence which he had exerted upon the Essex men during their year in the King's Bench.

When John Careless was examined by Dr Martin on 25 April 1556 (the day after the burning of Tyms), Martin embarrassed Careless by producing two opposing sets of articles that had been sent to Newgate.[712] Martin read out a set of articles to which Careless had subscribed, and which Careless had had a hand in drawing up, and which all twelve condemned men from Essex had signed.[713] On the reverse of the sheet Henry Harte had written a reply to these articles.[714] Careless stated that Harte, Kemp and Gybson had attempted to persuade

---

[708] *Ibid.,* VIII, 121.
[709] *Ibid.,* VIII, 109, 112-13.
[710] *Ibid.,* VIII, 105.
[711] Emma. MS. 260, F.87^r.
[712] Foxe, *AM.,* VIII, 164.
[713] *Ibid.*
[714] *Ibid.*

Tyms and his fellow prisoners, but had failed.[715] Apparently Tyms had already sent Careless a copy of Harte's articles.[716] The Emmanuel manuscript appears to be a transcript of the copy that Tyms made, with the Newgate prisoners' reply appended.

John Careless had a very low opinion of Harte. During his first examination Careless claimed that he neither knew nor had heard of Henry Harte. However, in his commentary upon this interrogation, Careless admitted:

But yet I lied falsely; for I knew him indeed, and his qualities too well. And I have heard so much of him, that I daresay it had been good for that man if he had never been born: for many a simple soul hath he shamefully seduced, beguiled and deceived with his foul Pelagian opinion, both in the days of that good King Edward and since his departure, with other things that I will forbear to name for divers considerations. But I would wish all men that be godly-wise, to beware of that man, whose opinions in many points are very noisome and wicked: God convert him, or confound him shortly....[717]

This statement confirms the impression that Harte taught other doctrines, apart from free-will and separatism, which the Protestant Reformers considered heretical. Doubtless John Careless had in mind Harte's rejection of *sola fide*, but there may well have been more. Furthermore, this statement indicates that Harte gathered his constituency from among the less literate and more gullible proletarian sympathisers with religious reform in south-east England.

John Careless did not live to see either the conversion or the confounding of Henry Harte. Less than three months after his examination, on 1 July 1556, he died in the King's Bench.[718] No doubt this explains the preservation of Careless' papers, including Tyms' copy of Henry Harte's letter.

---

[715] *Ibid.*
[716] *Ibid.*
[717] *Ibid.*
[718] *Ibid.*, VIII, 170.

The last record of our subject dates from early 1557 when an informant deposed to Bishop Bonner that Harte was leading a company of Free-willers in Southwark.[719] Evidently Harte was at liberty at the time of this deposition. In fact, notwithstanding Strype's assertion that Harte was a prisoner (followed by Oxley, Horst and Martin),[720] there is no concrete evidence that Harte was ever imprisoned in the King's Bench. In 1555 Harte was living in the country.[721] By 1556 he was probably living in London;[722] yet John Careless writing from the King's Bench in April of that year remarks, 'I would I might come to talk with him face to face'.[723] Harte was living in Southwark, and the King's Bench was situated in Southwark. Doubtless he maintained communication with the Free-willer prisoners there, and he may have visited them, but it is suggested that Harte himself avoided imprisonment. Furthermore, it is suggested that Henry Harte fled to London about the same time as some of the other Kentish conventiclers (Robert Cole, John Lydley, Chidderton's widow, Richard Prowde), that is, between the spring of 1555 and the spring of 1556. In the summer months of those two years the vigorous visitations and investigations of Nicholas Harpsfield wrought havoc among Protestants of every hue in the diocese of Canterbury.

In January or February of the year 1557 the priest, Stephen Morris, submitted a written deposition to Bishop Bonner entitled 'The Principal Teachers of Heretical Doctrine in London'.[724] Among those listed are John Kempe and Henry Harte, concerning whom Morris deposed –
... these two do lie at the bridge-foot, in a cutler's house whose name is Curle; and namely Henry Hart is the principal of all those that are called free-will men: for so they are termed of the Predestinators. And he hath drawn out thirteen articles to be observed amongst his company, and, as far as I do learn, there come none into their

---

[719] *Ibid.*, VIII, 384.
[720] Strype, *EM.*, II (i), 413; Oxley, 192; Horst, 125; Martin, 56.
[721] Above, 200.
[722] Above, 202.
[723] Foxe, *AM.*, VIII, 164; and Below 268-9, 279.
[724] *loc. cit.*

brotherhood except he be sworn. The other is a great traveller abroad into Kent, and what his doctrine is, I am not able to say.[725] From this we learn that Harte was at liberty, that he was the leading exponent of the doctrines of free-will in London, and that he had organised a church which adhered to a confession of faith consisting of thirteen articles. Moreover, this church exercised congregational discipline, maintained strict secrecy, and was in fellowship with like-minded groups or individuals in Kent. Clearly Harte was the minister or elder of the congregation while Kempe acted as its deacon or messenger. Thus, the congregation of Free-willers was organised along similar lines to that of its rival – the 'official' underground congregation of London Protestants led by Rough and Sympson (and subsequently by Thomas Bentham and Robert Cole), which adhered to the Edwardine Prayer Book and Articles.[726] The London congregation of Free-willers may have been on the point of disintegration in 1555/6, but with Harte's arrival the conventiclers were revitalised and reorganised.

Thereafter all is silent concerning the fate of Henry Harte. If our subject is to be identified with the Henry Harte of Pluckley mentioned in the Canterbury Archdeaconry Act Book, then he died at Pluckley on 6 March 1557.[727] Perhaps he had returned to Kent on learning of his detection to Bishop Bonner, and shortly afterwards died there from natural causes. In this connection it may be significant that in 1554 John Bradford referred to him as 'my father Hart'.[728] If Henry Harte was already an elderly man when Edward VI succeeded to the throne, that would account for his seniority and influence among the Free-willer conventicles notwithstanding the presence of more able and better educated men such as Thomas and Robert Cole.

---

[725] *loc. cit.*
[726] Foxe, *AM.*, VIII, 384, 456, 788.
[727] Above, 184-5.
[728] *loc. cit.*

II. His Writings

Horst regrets the paucity of Harte's literary remains.[729] Yet, slender though these may be, they are nevertheless considerably more extensive than the 'few fragments' that Horst supposes. In his capacity as 'the chiefest maintainer of man's free-will' in England in the mid-sixteenth century, Harte no doubt wrote very much more than is now extant. However, most of his writings may never have been printed, nor enjoyed a wide circulation. They probably circulated in manuscript form among small groups of erstwhile Lollards in rural areas of south-east England.

(a) A Consultorie for all Christians

Although this work was published over three months after the publication of his *A Godly Newe short treatyse* it is suggested that this was Harte's first, and most important, manifesto. Not only is it far longer than any other of his extant works (sig. A1^r-H3^v), but also the circumstances in which it was published were unusual. On 6 January 1549 John Oswen received a royal privilege to print service books and religious works in Wales and the Marches, with seven years' rights of publication. On 30 January he published Harte's *Consultorie* at Worcester. It appears to have been the first book that he printed after he left Ipswich. Oswen had moved from Ipswich sometime in the Autumn of 1548, and presumably took the manuscript of Harte's work with him. Perhaps it was the success of *A Godly Newe short treatyse* with its second edition appearing on 1 January 1549 that persuaded him to publish the work of an author whose religious orthodoxy he must have known to be suspect.

Actually, an element of mystery surrounds the printers of Ipswich.[730] Around twenty books are known to have been published in Ipswich by three printers:– John Oswen, John Overton and Anthony Scoloker. However, they were all published between January and August 1548. Clair observes,

> We are confronted with the unlikely situation in which three printers suddenly decide to go to Ipswich for a few months, print a number of controversial books, and then go their separate ways, leaving Ipswich without a printer for the next century or so.[731]

---

[729] Horst, 132.
[730] Colin Clair, *History of Printing in Britain* (London, 1965), 116-118.
[731] *Ibid*, 117.

Clair further notes that Scoloker used type that originated in Antwerp, and suggests that the books that he published were in fact printed in the Low Countries. Here may lie the answer to the mystery. For English printers of radical persuasion living in exile in Antwerp, Ipswich was the gateway to England. What more suitable town in which to settle and test the English political climate and religious market of 1548? If these proved favourable they could move out into the hinterland, if not, they could beat a hasty retreat back to the Continent. Henry Harte would have been able to trust a printer with such a background with his manuscript. As an itinerant Lollard carpenter Harte had close associations with Essex. Doubtless he visited Ipswich in the course of his travels around the conventicles.

There are three extant copies of Harte's *Consultorie* – two in the Cambridge University Library and one in the British Library. The book's full title is, *A Consultorie for all Christians. Most godly and ernestly warnyng al people to beware least they beare the name of christians in vayne.* As the title states, this rambling exhortation is directed to the nominal Christians of England. Its purpose is to provoke them to obey God's revelation of the truth. Harte writes:

> For as moche as I perceyue that the earth maketh haste to bringe fourth her children, and the tyme draweth fast toward the end… my desyre is also to occupie my talente accordynge to ye wyll of the geuer, wherebye I may please my lorde, which is my desire aboue all thynges, & not onely therby to gather tresure for my selfe, but also to prouoke as wel my bretheren and naturall countrymenne of thys realme of England/as al other nations and named Christians to bryng fourth their frutes redyly accordyng to their nature that they may be rype against the day of haruest…. Therefore beloued fathers and brethren, seyng ye haue taken the name of holynes upon you, beying called Christians of Christ, and do in word professe the same, estemynge your selues the trewe churche and espouse of God upon earth, as al that lyue godlye doubtles be, See that ye be dilygente to obey to the word of truth which our heauenly father hath now sente and set abroade by his beloued messengers, as wel within this realme of England, as in all other regions on the earth…. If ye accepte the voyce of the shepherde, then wyll he know you for his owne, and lead you in and oute, where ye shall all wayes fynde riche pasture.[732]

---

[732] Harte, *Consultorie*, sig. A6^v-A7^v.

The international flavour of this statement is noteworthy. It suggests that the author was aware of movements for religious reform beyond England, and was associated with them. Harte's references to the agents of Divine revelation are equally interesting, if only because of their ambiguity. Who were these 'beloued messengers' whom God had called to a world-wide ministry and whose utterances Harte's readers should be 'dilygente to obey'? He was not referring to the new Protestant preachers of the Edwardine establishment because he later exclaims:

> Wo be to those false prophetes whiche under the name of gouernours and teachers doo the deades of false deceyuers, seruyng their owne lustes, and yet saye, do as we byd you, and all is forgeuen.[733]

We have already referred to William Turner's criticism of Harte's use of Scripture.[734] Certainly the *Consultorie* supplies justification for this. The greater part of the work consists of denunciation and exhortation couched in Biblical phraseology, but Harte echoes Biblical terminology rather than quotes the Bible as authoritative. Both in this work and in *A Godly Newe short treatyse* we find an inaccurate paraphrasing of Scripture rather than direct quotation. The author appears to be more intent on conveying spiritual insights as directly as possible to his readers rather than in teaching specific doctrines. The great Pauline passages on grace and faith flow from his pen – sometimes they are identified in the margin, sometimes not, and sometimes incorrectly identified. Rarely are they presented in the kind of context that a trained teacher would provide, and often they are joined to other Biblical texts in new and unlikely combinations. Martin comments:

> For [Harte], [the Bible's] great appeal evidently lay in conveying sudden religious insights, not in providing detailed textual support for specific doctrines to be logically integrated into a theological system.[735]

Furthermore, the author intersperses his own statements within what are supposed to be Biblical texts. This gives his writing an authoritarian tone, yet no distinction is discernible between the authority belonging to the statements of the Biblical writers and that which the author attaches

---

733   *Ibid.*, C5ᵛ-C6ʳ.
734   Above, 190-1.
735   Martin, 61.

to his own words. Thus, Harte's style resembles that of the Continental Spiritualists.

A veritable torrent of words pours forth from the writer's pen. Although his introduction – in which he explains his purpose in producing this manifesto – is adequate,[736] the rest of the work consists of brief denunciations and prophesies set amidst long, tedious and repetitive passages of ethical exhortation. The final pages (sig. F8^r-H2^v) are almost totally repetitive, full of prophetic denunciation and exhortation of nominal Christian society in the language of Scripture. Then the work suddenly tails off without any proper conclusion.

Within this disorganised and shapeless piece of writing only two distinct features appear. Imitating, perhaps, *Habakkuk 2* Harte issues a series of twelve 'woes' in the style of the Old Testament prophets (sig. C5^v-C8^r). They are all anti-clerical and anti-establishment in character. For example, the first 'woe' reads:

Wo be to those proude boastyng spirites which liuing wickedlye, teache their flockes by poure and penaltie, and not rather by ensamples of vertue and godly lyvyng.[737]

And the twelfth reads:

Woo be to those bishops, pastours and lawiers of what name and place souer they be, whiche boast of power and auctoritie to rule and gouerne other and yet haue no respecte to their owne soules... wiche seke holynes only by outward sacramentes and signes, not regardyng what the hert & inwarde consience bee, and also saye in your selfes, tushe we be well inough, for the holy lawes, ceremonies and Sacramentes of god are remaining among us, and thereby we are knowen to be his people.[738]

The second feature within the book is a brief prayer (sig. D2^r-D3^r) that the author suddenly utters in the midst of a long passage of exhortation to repentance and pleas for tolerance directed towards the 'Englysshe nation'. In this prayer Harte beseeches God to extend mercy, forgiveness and deliverance to His 'poore oppressed' people, and he urges his readers to pray likewise.[739]

---

[736] Harte, *Consultorie*, A4^r-A8^r.
[737] *Ibid.*, C5^v.
[738] *Ibid.*, C7^v-C8^r.
[739] *Ibid.*, D2^r.

Although this work contains a rather sophisticated ode to wisdom, which may be described as mystical rather than Biblical since there are no references to Scripture within it (sig. A8^v-B2^v), spiritual regeneration is not emphasised. Instead, throughout the book is to be found Harte's characteristic teaching on free will and works-righteousness,

O thou wilful nation and why wyll ye thus perishe thorow your owne folly? Truly except ye doo repente, and tourn from your euyl waies (what name of holynes so euer ye haue) ye canot be made the sonnes or Children of god... I pray you, cut away your carnall desires and fighte against your fleshly lustes, too subdu them: that ye dwel w^t in ye holy sainctuarye and receiue enheritaunce amonge sonnes and daughtours.[740]

Whether unreformed or reformed, the author is clearly unimpressed by the worship and works of the English Church. He asks:

Thinke ye that god wyl accept [your services], which are not all grounded upon the worde, but partly invented and set up by natural wisedom, and carnall reason, yea altered and chaunged among your selues at youre pleasure.[741]

Harte's concluding paragraph echoes concluding phrases in the Pauline Epistles. His signature, however, is characteristic. It is also found at the conlusion of his *A Godly Newe short treatyse* and *A Godlie exhortation*. This reads:

Geue praise only to god.

yours as charitie byndeth me.

H.H.[742]

The phrase, 'yours as charitie byndeth me' is also found at the conclusion of his letter to the Newgate prisoners, and is particularly significant. J.A. Van Dorsten points out the Familist associations of the word 'charity', especially among printers and publishers. He writes:

Some Familists were helpful enough to follow the example of H.N., who signed his work 'Charitas vincit omnia' or 'Charitas extorsit H.N.'. Plantin's 1556 device 'Christus vera Vitis' was based on a symbolic representation in H.N.'s '*Spiegel der Gerechtigheid*'. More

---

[740] *Ibid.*, D4^v-D5^v.

[741] *Ibid.*, E6^r.

[742] *Ibid.*, H3^r.

straight-forwardly, an English printer in Leiden, Thomas Basson, who was secretly responsible for the dissemination of Familist literature in the North in later years, signed himself 'Love maketh labour light T.B.', and used a 'Charitas' figure....[743]
The similarity between Harte's signature and Niclaes' 'Charitas extorsit H.N.' is remarkable. However, as Van Dorsten subsequently observes, 'The very word "charity" ... was not the exclusive property of the Domus Charitatis'.[744] It was equally central for most Continental Spiritualists from Castellio to Joris. Furthermore, even allowing for Harte's possible Continental connections, 1548 is rather early for a specifically Familist publication to be circulating in England. Nevertheless, here is further evidence that Henry Harte emerged from the same school as Hendrik Niclaes. That is, from the school of Melchior Hofmann and David Joris – from the Spiritualist movements of North Germany and the Netherlands.

(b) A Godly Newe short treatyse
Perhaps it was the failure of Oswen to publish the *Consultorie* immediately that caused Harte to write this treatise in the autumn of 1548. It contains much the same themes and sentiments, but its comparative brevity (sig. A1^r-C1^v) would have made it easier reading than the *Consultorie*. A hint that there had been at least one earlier work from the writer's pen is indicated by the title. Moreover, the 'Newe' treatise is 'short' compared with a previous one. Finally, Harte refers to more than one publication when he states his purpose in writing –
...I thynke it not vayne by these letters to styre upp your remembraunce for trulye it is my dysyre that ye shuld turne from your synnes, and liue.[745]
There are at least six copies of the *Treatyse* extant. Its full title reads:– *A Godly Newe short treatyse instructyng euery parson, howe they shulde trade theyr lyues in ye Imytacyon of Vertu, and ye shewyng of vyce, & declaryng also what benefyte man hath receaued by christ, through the effysyon of hys most precyous bloude.* It was printed in London by

---

[743] J.A.Van Dorsten, *The Radical Arts* (London, 1970), 29-30.
[744] *Ibid.*, 34.
[745] Harte, *short treatyse*, sig. B5^v.

Robert Stoughton, 'dwelling with in Ludgate, at the synge of the Bysshoppes Myter'.
The concluding signature reads:
  Yours as charytye byndeth me,
  Henry harte.
  Geue all the prayse to God, and be alwayes thankfull unto hym.
  Anno. 1548. the 23 October.[746]

Actually, this work is not so much a treatise as an epistle. Harte has deliberately attempted to imitate the Apostle Paul both in the style of his book and in the phraseology he employs. For example, the *Treatyse* ends with the following exhortation–

> Attende therfore to ye thing that ye haue now harde (my deare bretheren) and as deare chylderen labour earnestly by the helpe of the spyryt to kepe your selues unspotted of the worlde, that ye may be saued and be made the parfecte sonnes of God and coheyres wyth our sauyoure Jesus Chryste of hys euerlastyng heauenly kyngdome. Amen.
> The god of all patience and consolatio geue to eueryone of you grace so to labore and trauayle in youre callynge after the example of Chryste that your gyfte maye encrease, least you also be plucked away in the erroure of the wycked, and fall from your stedfastnes.[747]

Once again we find a collage of Biblical phrases; but while the language is Pauline, the doctrine Harte conveys through it is hardly Pauline. The themes of following Christ, obedience to Scripture, nonconformity with the world, and acceptance of suffering are treated in the same unsystematic fashion as in the *Consultorie*. There is the same anti-determinism –

> Some because they Wolde be hydde from God wynde them selfes in a folyshe cloke of myare necessyty, sayng in themselfes y^t it can not otherwyse be: When in dede they stryue not at all to make resystaunce but doo lette the fleshlye mynde runne whether it lusteth. So for lacke of obedyence they fall into wyllfull synne, deceauyng them selfes in their owne ymagynacyos. To do yuell thei haue power because they wyll, but to doo well they haue none at al, for they wyl not.[748]

746 *Ibid.*, C1^v.
747 *Ibid.*, C1^r-C1^v.
748 *Ibid.*, A4^v-A5^r.

and the same anti-intellectualism –

> Truly knowledge is daungerous where loue and obedyence is lackynge, for it tyckelyth the mynde of foles.... But such as seke to encrease in vertu walke surely. Therefore searche not unreuerently the sacred worde of god least ye, stumble in your way... knowledge is a gyfte of the spryte, and in the hand of god.... Therefor, whether ye obtayne at hys hand ether much or lytyll praise him for it, and be content w^t his doying. Search not the gronde of such thinges (sayth the wyse man) as are to myghty for the: But loke what god commaundeth and thynke apon that alwayes: ad be not curyous in many of hys works for he that louethe pereyll shall peryshe therin.[749]

Harte's concern to provoke righteousness of life among nominal Christians may well have arisen from a sincere abhorrence of the pervading antinomianism in London and the south-east of England in 1547/48. The half-digested doctrines of the Reformers were proving destructive and disruptive rather than to the enhancement and edification of English society. Harte comments:

> Many do heare rede & speak the holye scryptures (praysed be God) and many desyre to know muche. But blessed and happye are ye, whych obeye to the truthe... for the kyngdome of God standeth not in words... the wycked synners haue God and hys holy worde many tymes in their mouthes: but they walke styll in ther own corrupt ways.[750]

Thus, the central section of this work contains an exhortation to his readers to follow Christ by taking up the cross of suffering. For, only through self-denial in this life can beatitude be obtained in the next.[751]

The second edition of the *Treatyse* was published on 1 January 1549, under the title – *A Godlie exhortation to all suche as professe the Gospell, wherein they are by the swete promises therof prouoked & styrred up to folowe the same in liuing, and by the terrible threates, feared from the contrary.* It was printed in London by John Day and William Seres, 'dwellyng in Sepulchres parish, at the signe of the Resurrection, a little aboue Holbourne conduite'. Only one copy of this

---

[749] *Ibid.*, A8^r-A8^v.
[750] *Ibid.*, B1^r.
[751] *Ibid.*, B4^r-B5^r.

edition is known to survive, and this is to be found in the Library of Emmanuel College, Cambridge. It is slightly shorter than the *Treatyse* (sig. A1^r-B8^r), and is altogether a superior piece of printing. Despite the fresh title, there are very few emendations to the text. Superfluous words and phrases have been précised, printer's errors corrected, spelling standardised, and punctuation improved. It must remain an open question whether Harte played any part in the production of this second edition.

(c) The Enormities

This document was circulated in manuscript form among the prisoners in the King's Bench in the autumn of 1554. It is only known to us through the eight excerpts recorded by John Bradford in Part II of his *Defence of Election*. An outline of the contents of these excerpts has already been given.[752] Harte's six carefully deduced 'enormities' or objections to the doctrine of predestination are supported by quotations from Scripture, most of which appear to have been succinct and to the point. The exception is the fifth enormity where Bradford quotes a lengthy digression on the subject of accountability.

A favourite description employed by the predestinarians to denote their characteristic teaching seems to have been 'a strong faith'. In the sixth enormity Harte criticises this phrase as illusory, wishful-thinking. He continues with a veiled warning which may have been directed at Bradford,
> ...but, when the inward eyes of them are truly opened, it will appear either here, or in another place, where it will not be so easy to help a very vain and naughty opinion.[753]

The 'other place' where assistance would not be so easily forthcoming was probably the condemned cell at Newgate.

Bradford assures his readers that he has transcribed the text of the 'Enormities', 'word for word after the copy delivered to me'.[754] He criticises Harte's grammatical construction of the sixth enormity –
> These be the words of the last 'enormity', which words are so either ignorantly or untruly written, or both, ... that the sentences hang not

---

752 Above, 195-6.
753 Bradford, I, 327.
754 *Ibid.*, I, 328.

together, or else there wanteth words to make sentences.[755]
This suggests that Harte wrote the manuscript in haste and was then
forced to despatch it without further perusal. Bradford preserves Harte's
conclusion –
> Whether these be good matters to be had, taught, and holden of such
> as think themselves not only true and right Christians, and the very
> 'sons of God', but also to be masters and teachers in the church of
> Christ; I appeal to the judgment of the Spirit of God, and to all men
> that have true judgment.[756]

In the margin beside this quotation Bradford has added the interesting
comment: 'The author writeth anabaptistically in applying to the Spirit
without the scriptures'.[757]

As Harte's manuscript circulated among the King's Bench prisoners
before reaching its addressee, others added two further questions:
> Other some would be satisfied, how that God's elect people are so
> 'elected from the beginning' in Christ that they cannot utterly fall
> away, and yet all men, they say, fell to damnation in Adam; and how
> that his mercy in saving his, and his justice in condemning his, could
> be at one instant with God.[758]

In his reply, Bradford's intellectual pride once again comes to the fore:
> These words first shew curious heads, as you may see by their
> 'hows': secondly they shew ignorant persons as may appear by their
> style and words improperly placed: therefore I stand in a doubt
> whether they understand what they demand.[759]

Nevertheless, this arrogant comment fails to conceal the fact that
Bradford was at a loss for an adequate answer to the questions posed by
these simple men. No wonder he had to appeal to Ridley for assistance.
The identity of these questioners must remain open to conjecture. It may
have been John Trewe and his company of Sussex free-willers.

---

[755] *Ibid.*
[756] *Ibid.*, I, 329.
[757] *Ibid.*, margin.
[758] *Ibid.*, I, 330.
[759] *Ibid.*

(d) The Letter to the London Congregation

It is clear both from this letter and from the one which follows in Strype's collection[760] that there was a distinct congregation of free-willers worshipping in London at this time. This letter is particularly addressed to an unnamed member of that congregation; other members are greeted by name,

> ...I do hertely recommend me unto you, and to my especiall good frind John Smyth the porter, and also to his wife, and also to my mother and yours, and to all my good fellowes, and to my brother Thomas Dodmer, yf he be in London....[761]

It has not proved possible to identify John Smyth the porter or Thomas Dodmer. The reference to 'my mother and yours' is problematic if Henry Harte was born as early as 1490.

This long letter is filled with echoes of, and quotations from, Scripture. Again one notes a certain shapelessness, a lack of organisation of the material as the words flow from the writer's pen. Two primary concerns form the subjects for his exhortations: – separation from the world and the keeping of God's commandments. Harte writes:

> Bere not a straunger's yoke with the unbelevers. For what fellowship hath rightwisnes with unrightwisnes ... this I say therefore, and exorte you in the name of the Lorde, that ye walke no more as the other heathen walke....[762]

Later he exhorts,

> And say no more, We be not able to kepe his commaundments, as many hath sayd, and doth say. But Christe sayeth, He that loveth me, kepeth my commaundments .... But God is not so unresonable, althowgh we have counted hym to be unresonable: for he knoweth what we are able to do and doth nother not commaunde more than we are able to fulfylle, althowgh we be slowthful in fulfilling yt.[763]

The writer concludes the letter on a similar note; thus indicating that Harte's chief concern is not (as Strype suggested) compliance with Roman forms of worship but failure to live righteously. He concludes:

---

[760] Strype, *EM.*, III (ii), 325ff.
[761] *Ibid.*, III (ii), 321.
[762] *Ibid.*
[763] *Ibid.*, III (ii), 322-323.

Wherfore, derely beloved, let us loke ernestly to the commaundments of the Lord; and let us fyrst go abowght to kepe them, before we say that we be not able to kepe them. Let us not play the slowthful servants, but let us be willing, and go about to do them; and then, no dowght, God shall assiste us....[764]

Unfortunately, the manuscript contained no concluding signature – an example, perhaps, of Harte's prudence.

(e) The Letter to Newgate (see Appendix I)

The articles of faith that Harte opposed in his letter to the Newgate prisoners seem to have been six in number. They were probably the mediating articles which Cuthbert Sympson had drawn up *circa* Christmas 1555, and which John Trewe and his company had reluctantly signed at the behest of John Careless.[765] The latter seems to have regarded these articles as a yard-stick of doctrinal orthodoxy. He probably sent a copy of them to Newgate in order to ascertain the faith for which the condemned prisoners were about to die a martyr's death – predestinarian or free-willer. According to the manuscript heading, the Newgate prisoners had 'allowed' these mediating articles. Neverthless, the articles had failed to 'appease' the contention in the King's Bench.[766]

The first article, briefly combatted by Harte, appears to have referred to the nature and constitution of the Godhead. The second article appears to have been a statement on the nature of Jesus Christ, and the third may have dealt with the nature of the Church. Harte – pressed for time and space – gives scant attention to these. However, when he turns to the fourth article we find ourselves in familiar territory:–

In your fourth artycle you saye y^u do belieue all your saluacyon redempcyon and y^r remyssyon of syns comeste unto you holye and solye by ye mercye & fauor of god in chryst purchased unto you through his most p^{r}cyous death & blod shedynge onlye/& in no parte or pece by or through any of your owne meryts workes or deseruyng howe manye or good so euer they be and yet ye saye ye do not denye nor destroy good workes but yu acknowelege & confese y^t all mene are bownde to do them and to knowe and kepe gods comandement but

---

[764] *Ibid.*, III (ii), 324-325.

[765] Below, 272-4.

[766] Emma. MS. 260 f.87 recto.

for all the confessyon of this your stronge fayth yu were best to
follow saynt pall whu thought it no derugacyon to chrystes death nor
passyone to saye/nowe joye I in my sufferynge w^{cc} suffer for you and
fullfyll y^t w^{cc} is behind or lackynge of ye passyons of chryst in my
flesh for his bodyes sake w^{cc} is the congregacyone: for indede frynds
if ye do then ye shall fynd ye workes of christ ar therfore
profyttable/for all things ye alowe good workes in worde yet if ye
declare no benefytte to be towards them w^{cc} do them/ye wer all most
as good to do [wyth owt]/[767]

This retort, and especially Harte's two marginal annotations, indicates
that he was still a strong opponent of *sola fide* doctrine. For him, good
works were essential for man's salvation. To proclaim the necessity to
perform good works and yet to deny that any soteriological benefit can
be accomplished by them, is tantamount to advocating antinomianism.
Harte continues,

put yourselues under ye couenants of god/and do it & se y^t your
hearts at ye least kepe his comandement w^{cc} thinge if you do/you shall
obtayne all ye benefyts of christ promysed w^{cc} ye speake of& at thend
the crowne of glorye but if no/ye shall be sur by gods promysse
though you gaue your selues twyse to be refused & cast out of y^e
kyngedome of god/[768]

This final remark was, in the circumstances, highly insensitive and
contentious. Those to whom it was addressed had been condemned to
death, and were in fact burned within a week of penning their reply.

Harte then explains that since he lacked time he will not reply to the fifth
and sixth articles until he has learned their reaction to what he has
already written. He concludes:

by yor frynd what so euer ye say or judge harrye hart/ as far as
charytie byndeth me as knowest god/[769]

Evidently the Newgate prisoners' response was to copy out Harte's
rebuttal and add their own fervent refutation of his teaching. This was
then sent to John Careless for circulation around the King's Bench. In
view of this negative reaction, it is doubtful whether Henry Harte would
have bothered to refute the fifth and sixth articles – even if William

---

767 *Ibid.*
768 *Ibid.*
769 *Ibid.*, verso.

Tyms and his fellow prisoners had survived longer than a week.

III. His Theology

Although the chief sources for the life and work of Henry Harte only cover a period of approximately ten years, they leave a strong impression of doctrinal consistency. This is particularly apparent in the theme that dominates all his extant writings and all the references to him – the Christian man's ability and obligation to live righteously. In 1548 Harte wrote, '…ye are made able through the spyryte whiche abydeth in you whyche ye haue of God to chose ye good & to leaue ye euyll'.[770] In 1557 Stephen Morris deposed that, 'Henry Harte is the principal of all those that are called free-will men'.[771] Furthermore, this theme is given a consistent practical application. In 1548 Harte asked, 'whye esteme ye so much the vayne pleasures of thys worlde?'[772] In 1556 John Trewe testified that the King's Bench controversy began when the free-willers rebuked their fellow prisoners for their worldliness in preferring gaming to prayer and fasting.[773]

In chapter eleven of his comprehensive work, Williams describes certain unusual doctrines and institutions of the Radical Reformation. Referring to Melchior Hofmann, Caspar Schwenckfeld and Michael Servetus he states:

> Common to certain spokesmen in all three groupings of the Radical Reformation were: (1) a distinctive Christology (the celestial flesh or body of Christ); (2) a corresponding deificatory, as distinguished from a forensic, view of salvation; (3) also in most cases an espousal of the freedom of the will in striving for sanctification made possible by the incarnation or the example of Christ….[774]

We will examine these key areas of doctrine – christology, soteriology and anthropology – together with that more obviously distinctive feature of Anabaptism, ecclesiology, in this final section. What did Henry Harte have to say about these things?

---

[770] Harte, *short treatyse*, sig. A3r.
[771] Foxe, *AM*, VIII, 384.
[772] Harte, *short treatyse*, B2v.
[773] Below, 264.
[774] Williams, *The Radical Reformation*, 325.

(a) Christology

An unorthodox understanding of the nature of Jesus Christ is characteristic of all those religious radicals in the Netherlands who came under the influence of Melchior Hofmann and his disciples. If Continental Spiritualism exerted any influence upon English radicals at this time, then it is reasonable to expect to find evidence of its distinctive christology in the teaching of the leading English radical of the period. John Careless hinted darkly that Harte held other opinions apart from his 'foul Pelagianism' which were 'very noisome and wicked', but he didn't care to name them.[775]

In Harte's extant writings there is very little that could be held to be exceptionable on this subject. However, there are three occasions when his words tend to substantiate Careless' insinuation. Twice in his *Consultorie* Harte describes our Lord as the Son of God and the true pattern and image of his most godly substance.[776] On the latter occasion he writes:

for as a most gentle & louing father hath he set his holy word, ye sone of god, ye very true patrone [*sic.* pattern] & ymage of his most godly substace to deliuer you fro al captiutie & blindnes.

This emphasis upon the physical accuracy of Christ's reflection of the Divine substance does at least suggest sympathy with the doctrine of the celestial flesh. Stronger evidence in this direction is found within Harte's 'Letter to Newgate'. The second of the articles to which John Careless and the twelve condemned men in Newgate had subscribed appears to have been a statement on the nature of Jesus Christ. Harte's reply to it is as follows:

In ye ij artycle ye saye y^t god & mane were joyned to gether in christ into one persone neuer to be deuyded/ and and [*sic.*] in ye fyrst ye saye y^t god was iij persons w^t one begynnynge and ending so y^t ye make qwaternytye in god if ye holde the humanytye w^cc our sauyour christ toke of ye blessed virgyne marye for a person and is not: this is a verylye uncertayne fayth for a mane to gyue his lyfe for when ye hold and affyrme in yor fyrst artycle that god is iij persons and then ye sayd in ye second that he is made one persone for euer/I praye you lett

---

[775] *loc cit.*

[776] Harte, *Consultorie*, D3^r and F5^v.

me knowe w^{cc} of these ye intend to hold for ye truth when ye haue
well wayed ye matters amongst your selues/[777]
Here, Harte clearly denies that our Lord derived any personal humanity
from Mary, the implication being that Christ's humanity was not a
normal humanity. He evidently felt that if Christ was truly an individual
man then that made the Godhead into a 'qwaternytye' rather than a
trinity. Thus, Harte emphasised the personal divinity of Christ as the
second person of the Trinity at the expense of his personal humanity. If
we link this emphasis with his earlier statements about Christ's 'moste
godly substaunce', then there are strong grounds for maintaining that
Henry Harte believed and taught a version of the Melchiorite doctrine of
the celestial flesh of Christ. Certainly he appears to have opposed all
Trinitarian formulae.

Citing Zur Linden, Williams writes:
 Hofmann was quite specific 'that the Eternal Word of God did not
 take our nature and flesh from the Virgin Mary but himself became
 flesh (John 1:14), that is, our Lord Christ has not two but only one
 nature'.[778]
It is granted that, in his letter to the Newgate prisoners, Harte denies
Christ's personal 'humanytye' rather than his human nature or flesh *per
se*. Nevertheless, his earlier use of the words 'godly substaunce' in
connection with our Lord suggests that he associated personal humanity
with physical flesh. Thus, for Harte (as for Joan Bocher) the flesh that
Christ possessed was not human but divine – part of the very Godhead.

(b) Soteriology
It must be stressed at the outset that the concept of salvation as
'deificatory sanctification' which is prominent in the teaching of
Schwenckfeld (who links it with the Lord's Supper) and Servetus (who
links it with Believers' Baptism), is less apparent in the soteriology of
Hofmann.[779] Certainly the forensic views of the magisterial reformers
are not found in Hofmann, but for him the redemptive work of Christ is
still central. At Calvary Christ redeemed mankind from death and
removed the power of sin. Just as all the descendants of Adam and Eve

---

[777] Emma. MS. 260 f.87 recto.
[778] Williams, 330-331.
[779] *Ibid.*, 331, 335.

are cursed, so all the descendants of the Second Adam and the 'spiritual Eve' (the Church) are redeemed. This redemption is appropriated through spiritual regeneration and its associated moral renewal or sanctification.[780]

Similarly, in Harte there is none of the mystical sacramentalism of Schwenckfeld or Servetus, but we do find an emphasis upon the ethical concomitants of spiritual regeneration. Furthermore, like Hofmann, Harte believes in the centrality of the atonement. This is particularly apparent in the list of objections against the doctrine of predestination which he sent to the King's Bench in the autumn of 1554. In two of his six 'enormities' Harte points out that the doctrine of election reduces the efficacy of Christ's work of atonement. By it, 'Christ is denied to be a general Saviour to all men', and again – 'The second [enormity] is that the virtue of Christ's blood doth not, neither can, extend to all people'.[781]

In his *Consultorie* Harte quotes *1 John 3:9* in support of his contention that the spiritually regenerate can, and should, attain moral perfection. He exhorts:
> Obey unto god, and then shall ye receiue a good spirite of hym which (as S. John saith) wyll loose the woorkes of synne, & geue you a will to loue him and to kepe his commaundements: for thei that ar born of hym synne not (saith he) because they haue the sede remaining in them, the earnest of saluacion: I meane the spyrite of truth,…. This is he that losseth the workes of sinne and bringeth a godly desire unto righteousnes, and a longing to fulfyll the wyl of god: & they that haue opteined a mynde to loue god, are begotten & borne of hym, and they are knowen & loued of hym.[782]

It is evident that Harte's thinking is confused and contradictory here. Is spiritual regeneration essential before a man can obey God's commandments, or is obedience a prior requisite before spiritual regeneration? Harte seems to want to have it both ways. Earlier in the *Consultorie* he asks his readers:
> If ye thynke youre selues heyres with Christ and gods chyldren: where is youre loue and readye obedience, towarde his will? Where is the victorie which ye haue gotten against your flesshe, synne and the

---

[780] *Ibid.*
[781] Bradford, I, 322, 319.
[782] Harte, *Consultorie*, G7^r-G7^v.

deuyll: the extreame enemies of vertue and godlynes....
However, on the very next page, he states:

Truly excepte ye doo repente, and tourne from your euyl waies (what name of holynes so euer ye haue) ye canot be made the sonnes or Children of god.[783]

Thus, Harte teaches that sinners are transformed into saints – the 'chyldren of the flesshe' are made the 'chyldren of god' – through repentance and obedience to the will of God as it is revealed in His commandments. The Holy Spirit then indwells the repentant and obedient seeker, working his spiritual regeneration. This ontological transformation not only affects a man's activities but his attitudes, creating within him the desire to live righteously and the ability to live sinlessly. This tautological scheme leaves little room for 'justification by grace through faith alone'. For Harte, works of righteousness are essential for the sinner's salvation –

Wherfore, stryue daily against your lustes, and mortyfie your affections, compell youre fleshe to be ruled and ordered by the rules of Christe, prescrybed in the sacred worde of god, unto you. Then doubtles our heauenlye father wyll not onelye loue us, & take us for hys dear children, but also for Christes sake... beare our imperfection durynge the tyme of this lyfe....[784]

However Harte realises the danger in placing reliance upon the merely mechanical performance of external acts. In a subsequent marginal note he comments:

Deades be accepted for ye mannes sake that doth them, and not ye man for the goodnes of the deades.[785]

Despite this qualification, it is abundantly clear from Harte's last extant work – 'The Letter to Newgate' – that he rejected *sola fide* doctrine. In answer to the prisoners' fourth article he writes:

Though ye confess all y^t chryst hath done & belieued it as an undowted verytie as it is in dede yet if ye leaue y^t undone w^{cc} ye shuld do yet shall ye perysh.[786]

Then, quoting *Colossians 1:24* as his authority, he says bluntly –

---

783 *Ibid.*, D4^r and D5^r.
784 *Ibid.*, B7^v.
785 *Ibid.*, E5^v margin.
786 Emma. MS. 260 f.87 recto. margin.

yu shall fynd some what also for you to do in ye flesh besyde all y^t chryst hast done w^{cc} if ye do not ye shall perysh not w^t standynge all his doings.[787]
Earlier in the controversy John Bradford had accused Harte and his associates of mingling and confounding the effects of salvation with the cause after the manner of the papists.[788] The statements in Harte's 'Letter to Newgate' certainly substantiate this assessment.

Therefore, in his doctrine of salvation Henry Harte acknowledges the centrality of Christ's general atonement for the sins of mankind, he urges the necessity for spiritual regeneration, but above all he emphasises that obedience and good works are indispensable in man's salvation. If it were not for the fact that Harte placed works of righteousness before regeneration and salvation, then his teaching would have been closely akin to that of Menno Simons, Dirk Philips and the Dutch Anabaptists. Writing of their teaching on the necessity for ethical evidences of spiritual regeneration, Keeney states:

> The new creature results from a metaphysical change in the nature of man. Man is not merely given a new status before God, a forensic change. The transformation is dynamic affecting man's activities, resulting in a new spiritual nature but also producing fruits which are manifested concretely in his moral and ethical behaviour. If the transformation cannot be identified by other men, it is not ontological and is therefore meaningless.[789]

However, they denied that any human activities, whether of works, ceremonies or sacraments, were of any value for justification – which was by faith alone, and given by God.[790] Nevertheless, Harte's soteriology has sufficient in common with that of the Mennonites to indicate that it came from the same stable – Melchiorite Spiritualism.

---

[787] *Ibid.*
[788] Bradford, II, 170-171.
[789] Keeney, *op. cit.*, 74.
[790] *Ibid.*, 72.

(c) Anthropology

Williams states that most of the radical reformers espoused 'the freedom of the will in striving for sanctification'.[791] This was certainly true in the case of Melchior Hofmann, one of whose major works was entitled *An Explanation of the Captive and Free Will*. In this he taught that, after regeneration, the will is freed and thereby made responsible for its decisions. Hence, after believer's baptism all sin deliberately committed is against faith – the gift of the Holy Spirit – and is therefore unforgiveable.[792] At the Synod of Strassburg in June 1533 Hofmann maintained that divine illumination could restore to every man the freedom of will once possessed in Paradise, and that believer's baptism testified to this renewed mind and will. After entry into the 'covenant of a renewed will' the Christian life is a great struggle against falling from this second Paradise, the church of the regenerate, for there can be no second restoration.[793]

As we noted at the beginning of this section, Henry Harte was a consistent and fervent advocate of free-will. However, within his extant writings he offers three different and conflicting explanations as to how this freedom was (or can be) achieved. In the *Consultorie* he states that it came about through the Fall –

> ... man is by ye transgression of Adam, set at lybertie in ye knowledge of good and euyll.[794]

In *A Godly Newe short treatyse* he states that it is the regenerate who possess freedom of choice –

> And through hym [Christ] ye haue obtayned not only knowledge and Judgemente to dyscerne and iudge betwyxe the good & ye euyll: but also ye are made able through the spyryte whyche a bydeth in you whyche ye haue of god to chose ye good & to leaue ye euyll.[795]

However, in the 'Letter to the London Congregation', Harte argues forcefully that man was created with freewill, and that it is this attribute which makes him superior to the rest of creation and liable to Divine judgement. He writes,

---

[791] *loc. cit.*
[792] Kawerau, *op. cit.*, 58-60.
[793] Williams, 285.
[794] Harte, *Consultorie*, B6^r.
[795] *Ibid., short treatyse*, A3^r.

Marke well, he biddeth us to 'come to' him… and yet we will say, we have no 'free-will'; we can do nothing of ourselves. Trewth it is, yf God had lefte us uncreated, and had geuen us nether understanding nor reason, then myght we say, that we cold do nothing of ourselves: but God hath made us better than unreasonable beastes, and yet they have power to use themselves according to theyre nature, and yet they are creatures without reason: are we not better than they? No, I thinke we are much worse, except we use reason reasonably, and according to the lawe of God, better than we do… therfore for man is the day of judgment sette, and not for the unreasonable creatures…. Wherfor, derely beloved, let us loke ernestly to the commaundments of the Lord; and let us fyrst go abowght to kepe them, before we say that we be not able to kepe them.[796]

Similar apparent contradictions can be discerned in Harte's statements concerning the extent of sin. In some places he argues that original sin reigns in all men before they are regenerated, preventing them from obeying God's will. For example, in the *Treatyse*, Harte echoes the Apostle Paul when he writes:

In Adam we were all deade, but in Chryste we are al made alyue, as manye as beleue in hys name as perteynyng to the flesh (as S. Paule sayth) we wer all naturally born ye chyldern of wrath, as wel as al other because of orygynall Synne, that reygneth in all fleshe.

Reason was blynd and nature corrupte, therefore coulde it not obeye to the wyll of GOD, but vyolentlye stroue agaynste hym….[797]

However, in many other places he urges man's ability to keep God's commandments despite his sinfulness. For example, among the depositions of 1551 Laurence Ramsay stated:

that henry harte saide and affirmed… that there is no man so chosen or predestynate but that he maye condempne him selfe. Nether is ther anye so reprobate but that he maye if he will kepe the commandementes and be saluid….[798]

Once again Harte wants the best of both worlds. He wants to hold a strong doctrine of original sin and its devastating effects upon mankind,

---

[796] Strype, *EM.*, III (ii), 323-324, 324-325.
[797] Harte, *short treatyse*, A3ᵛ.
[798] *loc. cit.*

yet at the same time to maintain mankind's capacity to obey God's commands.

If Henry Harte recognised the extent of original sin, he also realised the power of regenerating grace. 'Brethern', he writes, 'youre mindes are now lightned by grace, and ye haue now receyued the spyryte of God, whych bryngethe knowledge and a perfecte willinge obedyent mynde to do the wyll of God.'[799] This emphasis upon a renewed mind and will is very similar to that found in the teaching of Melchior Hofmann and his disciples. Twenty years later it was to be found among the English Familists, whose sympathisers were termed the 'good-willing'. The Familist apology of 1575 was entitled *A Brief Rehersal of the Belief of the Good-willing in England*.

Furthermore, for Harte, spiritual regeneration makes moral perfection attainable – at least in theory. In the same important opening section of the *Treatyse* he writes –

Bretheren, yf ye obey & be now ledde by the holy spyrit of God, then trulye are ye made the fre sonnes of God, then shal ye also be made perfet and obteyne vyctory agaynst syn, death and hell, whych is the whole power of Sathan our mortall ennemye.[800]

The Melchiorite Anabaptists were frequently charged by their opponents with claiming perfection after regeneration. While the more orthodox Mennonites never claimed that they were free from sin, such views can be attributed to David Joris and his followers.[801]

As with the Spiritualists, Harte tends to qualify by means of internalisation his claims for the possibilities open to the regenerate individual. While much of his writing is taken up with exhortations to obedience and good works, it is nevertheless apparent that it is the renewed mind that really counts. For Harte, the psychological revolution wrought by regeneration is of paramount importance. Such an evaluation – given a hostile environment – easily develops into a rigid internal/external dichotomy. Even in 1548 Harte could say,

But ye haue not receyued the spyryte of the world... that ye seke God all way outewardely and to serue hym in the letter. But ye haue

---

[799] Harte, *short treatyse*, A4^r.
[800] *Ibid.*, A3^v.
[801] Keeney, 117-118.

receyued the spyryte of God, whyche lowsed in your hartes the woorkes of synne, and opened the inwarde eyes of your mynd that ye shulde nowe haue no more pleasure in them. For ye vayle is take away for [sic] your hartes…. Therfore truly we are called and taughte of God to serue hym in a new conuersacyon, in spyryte and verytye and not in the olde conuersacyon of the letter.[802]

In the *Consultorie* this internalising of the ideal of sinless perfection is more apparent –

O thou Christianitie, brynge forth worthy fruictes of repetaunce… y^t ye may see the perfecte way of lyfe. For except ye utterlye renounce and forsake, *at the least in affection*, all that is in you of flesshe and bloud… ye can not see the glorie of god nether be partakers of his eternall kyngdome.[803]

Finally, in 1556, Harte exhorts the Newgate prisoners to:

put yourselues under ye couenants of god/and do it & se y^t yor hearts at ye least kepe his comandement w^{cc} thinge if you do/you shall obtayne all ye benefyts of christ promysed….[804]

Henry Harte was not alone in experiencing difficulties – both practical and theoretical – with this type of anthropology. While seeking to reconcile the text of Scripture and their own experience of spiritual regeneration with the more harshly mundane realities of Christian living, Menno Simons and Dirk Philips were also guilty of contradiction and equivocation. Keeney comments:

Menno and Dirk were somewhat contradictory when they attempted to recognize the paradox of a fully sovereign God, and man created with sufficient freedom to remain morally and ethically responsible for his behaviour, and, therefore, of his destiny;[805]

and again:

The Dutch Anabaptists also at times tended to telescope the event of justification with the process of sanctification. The failure to distinguish them contributed to their legalism and gave rise to some

---

[802] Harte, *short treatyse*, B7^v.
[803] *Ibid., Consultorie*, F2^v [my italics].
[804] Emma. MS. 260 f.87 recto.
[805] Keeney, 72.

confusion between perfection as a demand resting upon them and perfection as a claim to have arrived at the goal.[806]
Harte was in good company!

(d) Ecclesiology

Here the differences between Harte and the Continental Spiritualists and Anabaptists are most apparent. Unlike them he takes virtually no interest in the ordinances of Baptism and the Lord's Supper. For him, internal regeneration and external amendment of life are far more important than any sacrament. He asks:

> What auayleth then a christen name, or baptising and receiuyng of Sacraments although it be neuer so many, yf there folowe not amendment of life, but that the hert delite in euyll as before. Haue ye not the made your baptisme, which signifieth repentaunce, the new regeneration and amendment of lyfe... of no value?[807]

Claire Cross remarks that, 'neither Harte's book [*i.e.* the *Treatyse*]... nor the reports of his teachings contain any mention of re-baptism or pay any particular attention to baptism at all'.[808] She is quite correct, and her statement is equally applicable to Harte's other extant writings. No doubt Hofmann's two year suspension of believer's baptism after the executions of 1531 and his recantation while in prison in Strassburg in 1539 (in which he admitted the legitimacy of infant baptism) left a strong impression upon his followers.[809] Certainly there is little sign that David Joris ever evinced much interest in either ordinance. Harte continues:

> yf an infidell turne in his hert fro his infidelitie, and do y^t thynge that is equall & right, although he neuer receiue christen name nor outward sacrament, thinke ye that he shal not be saued? It is the circumcision and baptysyng of the hert... that is of value before god.[810]

In this connection it is significant that Harte exhorts his readers to 'put themselves under the covenant of God'. This is reminiscent of the Anabaptists' *bundtsgenossen* – the 'Covenant of the Regenerate' as

---

806 *Ibid.*, 196.
807 Harte, *Consultorie*, E3^v-E4^r.
808 Cross, *op. cit.*, 99.
809 Kawerau, 120; Williams, 309.
810 Harte, *Consultorie*, E4^r-E4^v.

Armour designates it.[811] For Hofmann this was linked mystically with the public covenantal act of baptism, but for Harte entry into the covenant was through acts of obedience. He defines Christian believers as, 'all that beleue in hym [Christ] (y^t is to say) whych wyth a free harte do put them seleues under the couenaunt of God to do hys wyll'.[812]

Unlike Hofmann or his Spiritualist successors Joris and Niclaes, Henry Harte understood the local church to be a concrete and distinct entity. Perhaps it was as a result of pressure from his Reformed opponents as well as from persecution by the Marian authorities that the London underground churches with which Harte was associated drew up a confession of faith, advocated separation from unbelievers, and practised a strict discipline. In this they were more akin to Mennonite conventicles than to the more amorphous and Nicodemite gatherings of Davidists or Familists.[813] Harte exhorts the London congregation of free-willers to, 'Bere not a straunger's yoke with the unbeleuers'.[814] The sixth 'enormity' that Harte deduces from the Reformer's doctrine of election is that, 'it colourably denieth excommunication to be had and used in the congregation of Christ'.[815] That he practised what he preached in these matters is borne out by Stephen Morris' deposition concerning Harte and the congregation that he had gathered at Southwark in 1556/7. Morris stated that Harte had 'drawn out thirteen articles to be observed amongst his company' and that 'there come none into their brotherhood except he be sworn'.[816] The enforcement of strict discipline was a characteristic of the congregations organised by Menno Simons and Dirk Philips, but not the adoption of a detailed confession of faith. Notwithstanding the early appearance of the Schleitheim Confession (1527), Continental Anabaptism was not addicted to confessionalism. The reference to initiation by oath-taking is particularly interesting. The refusal to swear or take an oath was another characteristic of Anabaptist separatism. Only the previous year (1556) Menno Simons had written his *Epistle to Martin Micronius* in which he

---

[811] Armour, *op. cit.*, 99, 138-9.

[812] Harte, *short treatyse*, B1^v.

[813] Keeney, 153-154.

[814] Strype, *EM.*, III (ii), 321.

[815] Bradford, I, 327.

[816] Foxe, *AM.*, VIII, 384.

strictly prohibited all oaths.[817] It is apparent, therefore, that Harte's ecclesiological thinking had developed independently from the Dutch Anabaptists and along somewhat different lines. For him, oath-taking and secrecy had replaced public believers' baptism as the rite of initiation.

Morris' description of Harte's conventicles as a 'brotherhood' also has some significance, especially when it is linked with his subsequent statement that Harte's associate, John Kempe, was – 'a great traveller abroad into Kent'.[818] Early in 1553 Thomas Cole, schoolmaster of Maidstone, had preached a sermon against certain Kentish separatists who denied the doctrines of election and original sin and who called themselves 'Brothers and Systers'.[819]

The London congregation of free-willers against which Stephen Morris deposed, to which Henry Harte had written, and for which he had drawn up a confession of faith, had probably developed in opposition to the 'official' Protestant underground church in London. Nevertheless, the evidence from the Kentish depositions of 1551 and Thomas Cole's Maidstone sermon of 1553 indicates that Henry Harte was not only a consistent free-willer, but a consistent separatist as well. However, by 1557 his ecclesiology had developed even further along the narrow path of exclusivist sectarianism – a path which could have taken him into Familism.

IV. Conclusion

Horst argues that Henry Harte was 'consistent in his spiritualistic anabaptism'. He continues:

> It is quite possible that Hart... was a consistent separatist and later under Mary accepted or turned in the more spiritualistic direction of

---

[817] Keeney, 133-134; Menno Simons, *Works*, 915-43.

[818] Was John Kempe related to Stephen Kempe of Northgate, Canterbury? In *circa* 1539 Stephen Kempe had opposed the preaching of Cranmer's chaplains (*LP.*, IX, 76), but he ended his life as a Protestant martyr. He was burned at Canterbury on 15 January 1557 (Foxe, *AM.*, VIII, 300). The rector of Northgate parish from 1520 was a William Kempe (Hasted, XI, 248). He seems to have been extremely lax, for John Tofts appears to have been allowed to implement reforms and commit iconoclasm in the parish (Strype, *Memorials of Cranmer*, I, 231; Above, pp. 46, 51). According to Clark (*op. cit.*, 130, 179) the Kempe's of Wye were a Henrician Catholic/Recusant family.

[819] Above, 146, 152.

the Family of Love… the religious heir of the Davidjorists.[820]
On the other hand, Martin maintains that the characteristic anabaptist tenets of the celestial flesh of Christ and the impeccability of the regenerate were not held by Harte and the Free-willers. He writes:

Hart, spending his life in the parts of England most exposed to books and immigrants from the continent, can hardly have been unaware of religious developments there, but in any direct and immediate sense the evidence for continental influences on him seems remarkable thin.[821]

Certainly Horst is correct when he uses the word 'consistent' in his assessment of Harte. All the sources indicate that Henry Harte was a consistent Free-willer throughout his career. Consistency is particularly apparent in the theme that dominates all his extant writings and all the references to him – the Christian man's ability and obligation to live righteously.* Furthermore, Harte seems to have been consistent in his dislike for scholarship – particularly Reformed theology – and in his advocacy of separatism.

A man who counsels prudence and who swears his congregation to secrecy cannot be expected to publish his most radical beliefs, or even commit them to writing. Nevertheless, there are signs of what Horst terms 'spiritualistic anabaptism' within Harte's literary remains. The curious formula he uses with his signature and the unorthodox manner in which he cites the scriptures have already been noted.[822] There are other indications of Spiritualist tendencies.

First, as with the Spiritualists, Harte tends to qualify by means of internalisation his estimate of the moral possibilities open to the regenerate individual. 'Brethern', he writes, 'youre mindes are now lightned by grace, and ye haue now receyued the spyryte of God, whych bryngethe knowledge and a perfecte willinge obedyent mynde to do the wyll of God'.[823] In the *Consultorie* internalisation of the ideal of sinless perfection is more apparent:

*see page 236

---

[820] Horst, 154.
[821] Martin, 73-4.
[822] Above, 210-11.
[823] Harte, *Newe short treatyse*, A4^r.

O thou Christianitie, brynge forth worthy fruictes of repetaunce... y^t ye may see the perfecte way of lyfe. For except ye utterlye renounce and forsake, at the least in affection, all that is in you of flesshe and bloud... ye can not see the glorie of god nether be partakers of his eternall kyngdome.[824]

Writing to the Newgate prisoners in 1556 Harte exhorts, 'put yourselues under ye couenants of god/and do it & se y^t yor hearts at ye least kepe his comandement'.[825] This emphasis upon a renewed mind and will[826] is very similar to that found in the teaching of Melchior Hofmann and his disciples.[827] In his *Consultorie* Harte quotes *1 John 3:9*[828] in support of his contention that the spiritually regenerate can, and should, attain moral perfection. He exhorts:

Obey unto god, and then shall ye receiue a good spirite of hym which (as S. John saith) wyll loose the woorkes of synne, & geue you a will to loue him and to kepe his commaundements: for thei that ar born of hym synne not (saith he) because they haue the sede remaining in them.... This is he that losseth the workes of sinne and bringeth a godly desire unto righteousnes, and a longing to fulfyll the wyl of god: & they that haue opteined a mynde to loue god, are begotten & borne of hym, and they are knowen & loued of hym.[829]

Harte's teaching on the psychological effects of spiritual regeneration also bears strong resemblance to the 'Good-willing' of the Familists and to their 'service' or obedience of 'love'.[830]

Secondly, there is a single statement among Harte's extant writings which suggests that he was opposed to the 'orthodox' trinitarian and christological formulae of the Reformers. The first two articles to which

---

[824] *Ibid., Consultorie*, F2^v.

[825] Emma. MS. 260, F.87^r.

[826] Harte, *Newe short treatyse*, B7^v.

[827] Peter Kawerau, *Melchior Hofmann als Religiöser Denker* (Haarlem, 1954), 58-60; Williams, 285.

[828] Joan Bocher quoted the same verse in support of her christology and John Champneys cited it in support of the impeccability of the regenerate (Above, pp. 62-3, 79).

[829] Harte, *Consultorie*, G7^r-G7^v.

[830] The Familists' first English publications (1575) were entitled, *An Apology for the Service of Love and the People that own it, commonly called 'The Family of Love'. (Wing STC. N1122)* and *A Brief Rehersal of the Belief of the Good-willing in England, which are named the 'Family of Love' (Wing STC. B4621).*

John Careless and the twelve condemned men in Newgate subscribed appear to have been statements on the nature of the Godhead and on the person of Christ. Harte's reply is as follows:

In ye ij artycle ye saye y^t god & mane were joyned together in christ into one persone neuer to be deuyded/and and [*sic*.] in ye fyrst ye saye y^t god was iij persons w^t one begynnynge and ending so y^t ye make qwaternytye in god if ye holde the humanytye w^{cc} our sauyour christ toke of ye blessed virgyne marye for a person and is not: this is a verylye uncertayne fayth for a mane to gyue his lyfe for when ye hold and affyrme in yor fyrst artycle that god is iij persons and then ye sayd in ye second that he is made one persone for euer/I praye you lett me knowe w^{cc} of these ye intend to hold for ye truth when ye haue well wayed ye matters amongst your selues/[831]

Here, Harte clearly denies that our Lord derived any personal humanity from Mary, the implication being that Christ's humanity was not a normal humanity. He evidently believed that if Christ was truly an individual human personality then that made the Godhead into a 'qwaternytye' rather than a trinity of persons. Thus, Harte here emphasises the personal divinity of Christ at the expense of his personal humanity. Moreover, the whole tenor of Harte's argument could be interpreted to mean that he was against trinitarian formulae.

Thirdly, evidence of Harte's Davidist/Familist predilections is to be detected in his style of writing and ministry. His manner is authoritarian, his style denunciatory and exhortatory after that of the Melchiorite prophets. Furthermore, in his *Consultorie* there are some interesting references to 'the Prophet David'. For example, echoing *Jeremiah 30:9* and *Micah 5:2-5*, Harte prophesies:

For thus saieth ye lord god... I wyll rayse up unto the one onely shepeheard, euen my seruante David, he shall feede them, and he shalbe their shepeherd, and I the lord wilbe their god and my seruante David shalbe their prynce, euen I the lord haue spoken it.[832]

Finally, there is his admonition to accept the authority of God's 'beloued messengers' –

---

[831] Emma. MS. 260, F.87^r·
[832] Harte, *Consultorie*, F7^r; note also A6^r, F5^r, and compare above, pp. 15-17.

See that ye be dilygente to obey to the word of truth which our heauenly father hath now sente and set abroade by his beloued messengers, as wel within this realme of England, as in all other regions on the earth.... If ye accepte the voyce of the shepherde, then wyll he know you for his owne...[833]

Who were these 'messengers' whom God had called to a world-wide ministry and whose utterances Harte's readers should be 'diligent to obey'? He did not hold the learned Protestant preachers of the Edwardine establishment in such high esteem. Was Harte, in fact, seeking to establish the authority of his own 'prophetic' ministry among the conventiclers through his publications of 1548?

It is possible that Henry Harte had known David Joris personally in the 1530s, if not earlier. Harte was probably too old (and his publications are almost certainly too early) to have been a disciple of Hendrik Niclaes. Nevertheless, William Wilkinson, in a historical introduction to his confutation of the Family of Love included an account of Henry Harte and the Free-willers.[834] This indicates that Wilkinson believed there to be an historical connection between the two groups of sectaries. After Harte's death in *circa* 1557 his remaining followers doubtless provided a fertile recruiting ground for Familist evangelists.

Martin entitles his article on Henry Harte and the Free-willers – 'English Protestant Separatism at its Beginnings'.[835] It is suggested to the contrary that Henry Harte was a product of the combined influence of radical Lollardy and Continental Spiritualism. By no stretch of the imagination could he be designated a Protestant. Furthermore, the conventicles with which he was associated were not a new phenomenon. The beliefs, practices and attitudes enunciated at these gatherings reflect a considerable degree of continuity with later Lollardy but have little connection with Elizabethan Protestant Separatism.[836] Therefore, it is concluded that Horst's assessment is to be preferred to

---

[833] *Ibid., Consultorie*, A6ᵛ-A7ᵛ.

[834] William Wilkinson, *A Confutation of Certaine Articles deliuered unto the Familye of Loue* (London, 1579), RSTC. 25665, A3ʳ -A3ᵛ.

[835] *loc. cit.*

[836] B.R.White, *The English Separatist Tradition* (Oxford, 1971), 162; Martin, 72; Below, 338-40.

that of Martin.[837] If it is necessary to apply a label to Henry Harte's position within the theological spectrum of the mid-sixteenth century, then probably the most appropriate is 'Davidist'.

*Note from page 232:

> In c. 1512 Henry Harte was circulating a 'book' of the Ten Commandments among London Lollards. Bishop Fitzjames' Court Book describes it as 'very old and worn out'(*A&M* IV, 215-6). Harte's choice of scriptural reading material is significant. Forty years and more hence, he would still be contending for works-righteousness based on the commandments.

---

[837] Above, 231-2.

D. ROBERT COOCHE
Introduction

Although Cooche wrote at least three important doctrinal treatises – on infant baptism and original sin, on predestination and election, and on the Lord's Supper – none of these have survived. In fact, only one piece of writing produced by Robert Cooche is extant. This is a brief letter which he wrote from London to Rodolph Gualter in Zurich on 13 August 1573.[838] However, lengthy excerpts from the first and second of these treatises, preserved within the replies of Cooche's opponents, provide some information on his teaching.

Undoubtedly Robert Cooche was the most able of the English religious radicals. Yet, while a writer and controversialist of ability, it is questionable whether he was (as Jordan states) the most important member of the 'Anabaptist communities' to be found in London and Kent during the reign of Elizabeth.[839] Bishop Parkhurst supplies an interesting description:

> Robert Cooche is a very accomplished man, and well skilled in Music. When I was a preacher at the Court of Queen Catherine, he was Steward of the Wine Cellar…. He very frequently troubled Coverdale and myself by controversies… so that we were quite weary of him. He was verbose to an extreme. When Jewel and other learned men came… to visit me, this man instantly began to enter on these subjects with them, nor could he make an end of his loquacity. Now he is even in the Queen's Court –
> > A singer now, he may be seen,
> > In the fine chapel of the Queen.
> Such is his situation….[840]

Further personal references to Cooche were made by William Turner in the course of his reply to the former's views on infant baptism. Criticising Cooche's employment of the argument from silence, Turner comments –

> I make such lyke negatiue argumentes of scripture: whych if they be not sure but false and folishe: then… your negatiue argument is both unsuer false and folishe.

---

[838] *Zurich Letters*, Second Series, ed. Robinson (PS., Cambridge, 1845), 236-7.
[839] Jordan, *Religious Toleration*, 295.
[840] Gorham, *Gleanings*, 481-2.

Christe neuer commanded yow, to were a ryng on your finger, and be
cause it shuld not be smothered under your gloue, to make a wyndow
to let the ayre cum in to it, I dare not say that it myght be seene, nether
comande he yow to syng in his church any pypyng Christe neuer
commaunded prycksong or any besy discant: therfore ye offend to be
a curious musician....
GOD neuer in his worde expressedly commauded his Apostelles to
suffer suche tal men as you bee to lyue syngle: therfore your curate
doth wrong to suffer yow to lyue syngle....[841]

Thus, the picture emerges of a tall, urbane, loquacious, somewhat
foppish, minor courtier whose musical ability gained him preferment at
the courts of the Dowager Queen Katherine Parr and the young Queen
Elizabeth. Evidently well-educated, or at least well-read, it is nevertheless
apparent that Robert Cooche had not received any formal theological
training. Turner states:

...for al the learned men that haue disputed with you in your opinions,
whit whom I haue spoken, iudge you to be so sklender a clerk: y^t they
think y^t ye neuer lerned nether sophistry, nor logike nether anye good
scyence in all your life, sauinge only musyke... it had ben better for
you to haue songe your part agaynste me in tune: the to haue so
unlearnedly, and lyingly written against me, out of ordre, and oute of
tune, from the truth.[842]

The fact remains, however, that Cooche commanded sufficient respect to
justify the attention and response of several of the leading theologians of
the time. He defended his opinions in debates with Miles Coverdale,
John Parkhurst, John Jewel, William Turner, John Knox and Peter
Martyr – the latter wrote a long letter to him from Oxford. He
corresponded with Rodolph Gualter. Both William Turner and John
Knox published careful refutations of his doctrine.

Two reasons for this attention can be deduced. First, Cooche had access
to the Court. Although he only held minor appointments in the royal
household, the Reformers may have adjudged him capable of exerting
influence in high places – especially among the ladies. As Turner
remarked:

---

[841] Turner, *A Preseruatiue or triacle*, K6^r-K6^v.
[842] *Ibid.*, B1^v.

...whether it be yeoperdous for me, and expediente for the rulers of this realm, to haue such nere hand or no the: I reporte me unto all wyse, & godly me.[843]

Second, while Turner and Knox claimed to hold Cooche's powers of logic and scholarship in low esteem, he had still produced a powerfully reasoned, well-organised, easily-understood challenge to the theological system they sought to promote. No reasoned defence of the anabaptist position on infant baptism, no systematic attack on Calvin's 'new' doctrine had previously been published in English. Committed Calvinists could not afford to ignore this challenge. Cooche's views had to be nipped in the bud before they could mature into a non-Roman alternative to the Reformed position.

In 1721 John Strype used Parkhurst's letter to Gualter as the basis for his account of Cooche. 'Robert Cooche', he wrote, 'was a person of a very courteous fair deportment, of some learning, and particularly well skilled in music'.[844] He accounted for Cooche's correspondence with Gualter by supposing that Cooche had become acquainted with Gualter while in exile in Zurich during the reign of Mary Tudor.[845] However, there is no evidence that Cooche was a Marian exile. Moreover, as Whitley pointed out, Gualter (having received Cooche's letter of August 1573) wrote to Parkhurst in 1574 to ask who Cooche was.[846] Certainly John Knox was acquainted with his opponent when he wrote his reply from Geneva, probably in 1558. However, that does not imply that Cooche was a fellow exile in Switzerland for, as Laing observed, Knox had the opportunity of making Cooche's acquaintance while he was a chaplain at the court of Edward VI in the early 1550s.[847]

A parallel exists between the career of Robert Cooche and that of John Champneys. When the latter was ordained presbyter by Bishop Bullingham at Lambeth on 10 March 1559/60, Robert Cooche was also ordained presbyter at the same time.[848] This indicates that Cooche, like

---

[843] *Ibid.*, F1^v.

[844] Strype, *EM.*, II (i), 111-12.

[845] *Ibid.*

[846] W.T.Whitley, 'The Confutation of the Errors of the Careless by Necessity', *Transactions of the Baptist Historical Society*, IV (1914), 90.

[847] *The Works of John Knox*, ed. Laing, (Edinburgh, 1846-64), V, 17. [pagination incorrect].

[848] Above, 97-8.

Champneys, was an Edwardine ordinand. He was clearly not in orders when Turner wrote his *Preseruatiue* in 1550.[849] Therefore, Cooche must have been ordained to the diaconate between 1551 and 1553. Cooche lived in or near London, yet Ridley did not ordain him.[850] Thomas Cranmer was more liberal in his attitude towards 'anabaptists'; Cooche (with his court connections) was probably among the Archbishop's ordinands. Like Champneys, there is no evidence that Robert Cooche was ever collated to a living after 1560. Doubtless his peculiar talents were put to better use in and around the court.

While Bishop Parkhurst's reminiscences concerning his verbal disputes with Robert Cooche date back more than twenty-five years to the time of Queen Katherine Parr,[851] the main evidence for his teaching derives from his three later literary controversies. In 1549-50 Cooche disagreed with Peter Martyr and William Turner over the practice of infant baptism and the doctrine of original sin. In 1556-58 he clashed with John Careless and John Knox on the doctrines of predestination and election, and in 1573-74 he entered into discussion with Rudolph Gualter on the nature of the Lord's Supper.

I Cooche on Baptism
(a) Contra Vermigli
On 1 December 1550 Peter Martyr Vermigli – Regius Professor of Divinity at Oxford since 1548 – wrote to Robert Cooche.[852] He wrote in terms of familiarity and even affection – twice he referred to Cooche as his 'deare friende in the Lorde'. Apparently the latter had written to Martyr some time before on the subject of infant baptism, but Martyr 'distracted continually with great businesse' had neglected to reply. Furthermore, the points which Cooche had raised in his letter were the

---

[849] Turner, K6[v].

[850] Above, 97-8.

[851] Parkhurst was a fellow and tutor of Merton College, Oxford until he went into exile in 1553. He was appointed chaplain to Queen Katherine Parr after the royal visit to Oxford in the summer of 1543. Cooche may have visited him in his rooms at Oxford, as did Jewel, Aylmer and Coverdale. However, Queen Katherine was regent during most of the year 1544, and Parkhurst's meetings with Cooche could have occurred in London during that year – or at any time until June 1547 when the Dowager Queen married Thomas Seymour. She died in September 1548. (*DNB.*, IX– Catherine; XLIII – Parkhurst).

[852] Peter Martyr Vermigli, *The Common Places*, trans. Marten (London, 1583), RSTC. 24669. Ep. 34 in *Divine Epistles*, 113-5.

same as those they had discussed at length in an earlier conversation – presumably at the court of Queen Katherine some two or three years before. Martyr's reply was written out of courtesy rather than from conviction that it would serve any useful purpose:

> ...in the question which you moove, I perceiue you sticke to those arguments wherewithall by speech you delt with me ...I answere therefore rather, least I shoulde seeme to want curtesie than that I thinke you can be remooued from that conceit wherein so stifly you haue setled your minde.[853]

Again at the close of his reply Martyr refers to their previous conversation:

> To write unto you what foundations in the scriptur our faith of childrens baptisme dependeth uppon, I haue thought superfluous: partlie for that I discoursed them unto you at large when you talked with me.[854]

Clearly Cooche had some knowledge of patristics. He had apparently quoted Tertullian on baptism and cited Origen's *Commentary on Romans*. At some point in his argument he questioned whether some of the biblical commentaries attributed to Origen were not in fact the work of Rufinus. He appealed to Vives' commentary on Augustine's *De civitate Dei* and to Erasmus' views on infant baptism. Regarding the opinions of the more recent scholars, Martyr makes the interesting retort:

> Wherefore both Vives and Erasmus might in this matter haue spoken more warily. But where you seeme to denie baptisme to infants, for my part I doe contrariwise by al meanes affirme and beleeue the same.... Now if you admit Originall sinne to be in children, and yet will not permit them to be baptised, you are not of Origens iudgement....[855]

Cooche's letter to Peter Martyr of *circa* 1550 may have been an attempt to test the climate of scholarly opinion before the publication of his book, which included similar arguments and was doubtless well advanced in preparation by that time. Likewise, Cooche's letter to Gualter on the subject of the Lord's Supper was also an attempt to

---

[853] *Ibid.*, 113.
[854] *Ibid.*, 115.
[855] *Ibid.*, 114.

sound out reputable opinion prior to publication of a treatise on the matter.[856] However, the main point here is that, at the time of his communications with Peter Martyr, Robert Cooche was still ready to accept that infants were tainted by original sin. His chief concern was to deny that children under the age of fourteen were proper subjects for baptism. By the time his book was published in 1550-1, Cooche had added to his arguments against the practice of infant baptism a second section in which he denied that there was any original sin in infants.[857] Turner, however, could only spare the time to answer the first of Cooche's arguments against original sin before bringing his book to a sudden conclusion. He adds the promise that he will answer 'the rest of thys mas boke' when he has published his *new Herball* 'yf it shall be thought expedient to the churche to do so'.[858]

Therefore, it is evident – both from his correspondence with Peter Martyr and from the format of his book – that Robert Cooche's primary concern was with the rite of baptism rather than with the doctrine of original sin. It was only under pressure from traditional theological scholarship that he was forced to consider their connection.

(b) Contra Turner

The circumstances under which William Turner wrote his *A Preseruatiue or triacle* have already been suggested.[859] Turner's references to the 'woode sprite' who taught his opponent are almost certainly an allusion to Henry Harte.[860] Cooche's book amounted to a defence of the 'Pelagian' principles proclaimed by his instructor, Harte; and it was this work that Turner partially answered with his *Preseruatiue*.[861] Turner was pressed for time as he admits in the course of his reply.

---

[856] Below, 255.

[857] Turner, M8^r-M8^v.

[858] *Ibid.*, N6^r.

[859] Above, 189-91.

[860] *Ibid.*

[861] Parkhurst was mistaken when he informed Gualter that William Turner had written a book refuting Cooche's opinion on original sin (Gorham *Gleanings*, 481-2). Parkhurst's error was relayed by Strype in his account of Cooche (*EM.*, II (i), 111), and more recently continued by Horst. He states that Turner only dealt with the first of Cooche's opinions, 'that children "do not stand in the corruption of originall or birthe sin". The opinion about infant baptism Turner promised to answer later' (Horst, 116). In fact, it was the other way round.

Nevertheless, beneath the characteristic vigour of his language, Turner was at pains to produce a careful, reasoned defence of infant baptism. Quoting at length from his opponent's work, he systematically answered the points raised by Cooche.

It is evident from Turner's references that Cooche's attack on infant baptism and denial of original sin was published in a printed book or tract.[862] This was circulating 'within a few wekes after' Turner's Isleworth lecture,[863] which suggests that it was written in the latter part of 1550 or early in 1551.[864]

The first part of Turner's reply (sig. B1^v-E7^v) is occupied with an explanation of the illustration with which he had commenced his Isleworth lecture. He accused Cooche of deliberately misapplying his introductory remarks concerning the Oxbridge custom of regularly reading college statutes to scholars and fellows to the baptising of infants. Cooche had seized upon this statement and argued that a similar custom had been the practice of the early Church in its treatment of candidates for baptism. Turner quotes Cooche as follows:

> ...such a lyke costome was once in our moost holye relygyon, as was in colleges and in orders of relygyon, wher as none were admitted, before they had a year of probation. Wher unto ye put this that they that cam to be baptised, demaunded, and desyred to be receiued to the fellow ship of the christias after dewe proofe of unfeyned repentaunce, & thereby were called competentes. Young men, and wymen requyrynge baptysem: and then were taught the principles of the christian faith and were fyrst called Catecumeni. And after those principles learned, were upon certayne solemne dayes, at two tymes of the year approued, therfore baptysed....[865]

The authorities cited by Cooche in support of this statement appear to have been the same as those used earlier in his letter to Peter Martyr.

---

862 Turner, B1^r, C8^r, E6^v, H3^r, I3^v *etc.*
863 *Ibid.*, A3^r.
864 Turner's *Preseruatiue* was published on 30 January 1551/2.
865 Turner, B7^v-B8^r.

It is evident that Robert Cooche believed that there should be a period of probation and instruction before a candidate was baptised, and to this end he advocated the delaying of baptism until a child had passed the age of fourteen.[866] Furthermore, he viewed the rite as a sign of personal commitment to Christian discipleship and as a means of public instruction.[867]   Cooche concludes his comments on Turner's illustration:

> Where men and women of perfyt age are baptised, all the three sortes of scolares take profite of the openynge, and declaryng of baptyme: but when as childer are baptysed, none of them all... when men and wemen are baptised, all receyue admonishmet: by which the good amend theyr lyues, and are saued: the other knowynge, that they stonde bounde styll to amende or to be condemned. Therfore to rede the statutes to infantes is of no exemple nor value, but to them that be growen it is an occasion to get scolers.[868]

One of the more significant of the criticisms that Turner levels at Cooche is his attack on the latter's method and style. Turner demands:

> Answer me wyth scrypture, as I do confute you wyth scrypture: and let your arrogant, I says (whyche ye haue wythin thre leues of the begynnyng of your booke in the stede of scrypture boldly brought in thre tymes) goo shake theyr eares. For thoughe ye haue inchaunted `your wretched scholars, so that they beleue, that it is the gospel, whatsoeuer ye say: yet are ye in no such autoryte, maister doctor with me, y^t I wyll beleue your I say.[869]

According to Turner, Cooche's conclusion here was that baptism (with the gospel of forgiveness) was to be offered to all men, but it was not to be given to all men.[870] For baptism is 'onli dew to the elect churche, chosen in Christe Jesus, before al worldes'.[871] Therefore, baptism should be administered only to those who have repented and by faith received God's salvation in Christ –

> Thys I say ... the remissio of synnes is offered to all: but all receyue it not: the churche sanctifyed by faith in the blood of Christ only

---

866   *Ibid.*, D7^r, H5^v.
867   *Ibid.*, I7^r, L2^v.
868   *Ibid.*, E3^r, E7^r.
869   *Ibid.*, I3^r-I3^v.
870   *Ibid.*, I4^v.
871   *Ibid.*, I6^r.

receiueth it: and unto the only baptime belongeth: therefore none ought
to receiue it but such as haue not only heard the good promises of
God: but haue also thereby receyued a syngular consolation in their
hartes through remission of synne whiche they by fayth haue
receyued.[872]
Since infants and young children are incapable of such a response, they
are not suitable candidates for baptism.[873]

Next, Cooche pointed out that while Christ had commanded his disciples
to preach the 'confortable tydynges' to all mankind, he had never
commanded them to baptise 'other then such as at theyr preachiryng
wold beleue'.[874] Part of Turner's amusing reply to this argument from
the silence of the New Testament has been noted.[875]

Thereafter the debate degenerated into personal taunts and abuse. At one
point the exasperated Turner exclaims:

...ye are so unlearned and so foolyshe in your reasonyng, that ye are
utterly unworthy to be reasoned wythall, so that it hath repented me
ofte sence, that I began to write: y^t I troubled my selfe wyth such a
bungler.[876]

Having repeatedly stated that 'the baptym of chylder is a popish
ordinance',[877] Cooche attempted a double pun – first on Turner's
profession as a physician and then on his earlier anti-Catholic treatise.
He wrote:

It is spoken lyke a phisicion & that maketh yow to lay a plaster of
colde water to the synne of the infantes so tymely, but suerly out of
dew tyme, and other to yearly or to late, for they ar worse afterward
then euer they were before. For I heare of a poxe that is now
begynnyng to spryng up, not of a romysh pok, but of an other
deuelysh pok, as euell as it. 'Medice curate ipsum'. The deuelysh pok
whiche is syn, is not healed but thorow faythe. But your deuelishe pok
is thys to cleare infantes from synn whiche ye call originall. This is the
pok ye take in hande to cure, ether with water or fyer.[878]

---

872 *Ibid.*, K3^r.
873 *Ibid.*, L5^v.
874 *Ibid.*, K5^v.
875 Above, 237-8.
876 Turner, L2^v-L3^r.
877 *Ibid.*, M7^r-M7^v.
878 *Ibid.*, M3^v-M4^r, M8^v, N1^r.

Here is another example of the impact which Reformed theology was making among 'Gospellers'. For some, like Harte and Cooche, this new teaching which was 'begynnyng to spryng up' was a 'deuelysh pok' just as bad as Roman doctrine.

Evidently it was at this point that Cooche passed on from his attack on infant baptism to his assertion that children have no original sin.[879] However, before proceeding to a consideration of Cooche's first argument, Turner takes up his remark about curing sin with fire. Apparently Cooche had added a marginal note to the effect that Turner wished to cure him by means of the fire. Turner comments:

> ...ye wryte in the margen, that I go about to cure yow with fyre. For if I wolde haue gon about that: I knew and know meanes enow to bryng that to pas. For as muche as ye ar an open felon against the Kyngis lawes, and haue committed suche felony, as ye ar excepted out of the pardon, where of theues and robbers ar partakers.[880]

This altercation appears to echo two events of the year 1550 – the burning of Joan Bocher and the proclamation of a general pardon for all criminals excepting anabaptists. Each protagonist had written within a few months of these events, and doubtless they were both very conscious of their implications.

Turner only deals with the first of Cooche's arguments concerning original sin, which he quotes as follows:

> If Christe had counted infantes so defiled with Adames sinne, as ye do: he would neuer haue sent his Apostelles & us unto childer to be defyled of them. But now he sendeth us thyther for clennes, to becum such as they ar; if we wold entre into the Kyngdom of God: wasshed to the unwasshed, Christened to the unchristened, beleuers to unbeleuers. Not to becum pocky or leprose, [but] that we shuld be ful of innocecie & simplicitie. For it is write: except ye conuert & becum as these infantes ye shall not entre in to the Kyngdom of heauenes. Christe, the prynce of physiciones, sendeth his chefe surgeones and physiciones to be cum suche as the babes wer.[881]

---

879 *Ibid.*, M8ʳ.
880 *Ibid.*, N1ᵛ.
881 *Ibid.*, N2ʳ, N4ᵛ-N5ʳ.

In this closing citation there is a hint of that implicit perfectionism present also in the writings of John Champneys and Henry Harte. However, Turner abruptly terminated his reply on the very next folio (sig. N6), and so we have no further knowledge of Robert Cooche's views on this matter.

(c) An Assessment

Robert Cooche lived in London during the 1540s and was influenced by the radical teaching of Henry Harte. He was also well read. In these circumstances it seems highly likely that he had met with the teaching and literature of the refugee anabaptists in London. However, Cooche's arguments against infant baptism include none of the positive arguments for believers' baptism advanced by Melchior Hofmann or Pilgram Marpeck. Neither Hofmann's teaching on the baptismal covenant nor his association of baptism with eschatology are to be found in Turner's citations. Neither Marpeck's emphasis on baptism as a symbol of the inner process of spiritual regeneration, not his careful arguments against infant baptism based on his distinction between the old external covenant and the new covenant of the heart, are to be found in Cooche's teaching.[882] Nevertheless, it is evident that his opinions were a definite advance on the extreme sacramentarianism of later Lollardy. This had caused many Lollards to deny that the baptism of children was necessary; but there is no evidence that any proceeded to embrace a positive doctrine of believers' baptism. Indeed Lollard teaching – apart from its insistence on preaching and the reading of the Scriptures in English – was almost totally negative. No doubt this was the result of their bitter anti-clericalism, but it did militate against the development of a positive view of baptism.[883] However, it is noteworthy that a certain Thomas Watts of Dogmersfield, who was connected with the Berkshire Lollards and who was detected in 1514, possessed an English book which contained a treatise on baptism.[884]

It is suggested, therefore, that the views enunciated in Cooche's book were developed from the low estimate of baptism traditionally held by

---

[882] Armour, *Anabaptist Baptism*, 99-102, 102-7, 118-20, 129-32.
[883] Dickens, *Lollards and Protestants*, 9; Thomson, 244-5; Norman Tanner, *Heresy Trials in the Diocese of Norwich, 1428-31*. (London, 1977), 81-2 *etc.*
[884] Thomson, 88-9.

Lollards. Robert Cooche had imbibed this 'received' view from Henry Harte. However Cooche was more widely read than Harte.[885] The younger man developed and published his more positive views on the subject quite independently. Any Continental anabaptist influence mediated through foreign refugees was minimal. Robert Cooche's simple statements on baptism represent the first known, albeit hesitating, attempt by an Englishman to reach forward towards a mature biblical doctrine of believers' baptism.

Within three years of the publication of William Turner's defence of infant baptism Robert Cooche had been ordained into the ministry of the Church of England. To have been present when the irascible Turner heard the news would doubtless have been a memorable experience.

II Cooche on Predestination
(a) The Book

Robert Cooche is reputed to have been the author of a work entitled, 'The confutation of the errors of the careless by necessitie'. The attribution was first made by David Laing in his edition of *The Works of John Knox*, and was followed by Whitley.[886] As with Cooche's earlier book, this work is no longer extant. However, large portions of the text are preserved within John Knox's reply entitled, *An answer to a great nomber of blasphemous cauillations written by an Anabaptist and aduersarie to Gods eternal Predestination*.[887] In fact, Knox's quotations are so extensive that Whitley made an attempt to reconstruct the original book.[888] Horst, however, points out that 'The confutation', 'cannot with certainty be considered the work of Robert Cooche', and he emphasises his uncertainty by repeatedly referring to the author as 'the anabaptist'.[889] However, as Whitley remarks, 'no other person has ever been suggested, and Cooche seems to meet all the conditions'.[890]

---

885 Martin, 61.
886 Knox, *Works*, V, 16-18; Whitley, *A Baptist Bibliography* (London, 1916-22), I, 2.
887 (Geneva, 1560), STC, 15060.
888 *op. cit.*
889 Horst, 119.
890 Whitley, *The Confutation*, 89.

The only other possible candidate for the authorship is Cooche's former instructor, Henry Harte. Yet the forthright, self-confident style of the writer again suggests Robert Cooche rather than the more prudent Harte. Furthermore, a similar set of circumstances to those that occasioned the publication of Cooche's earlier work on baptism could account for the appearance of 'The confutation'.

John Bradford's successor as the leading exponent of 'Calvinism' in the King's Bench was the Coventry weaver, John Careless. He seems to have had greater success than Bradford in persuading some waverers such as Skelthrop, Thomas Upchard and William Tyms to accept the Reformers' position.[891] In the spring of 1556 Careless drew up a set of (possibly six) articles of faith, a copy of which he sent to William Tyms and his associates in Newgate. On the reverse of this statement Henry Harte added a reply to Careless' articles. However, Harte's reply was strongly repudiated by Tyms and his colleagues.[892] Thus, there was a similar situation to that which had occurred in 1549-50. Then, Harte had been under attack from William Turner over the doctrine of original sin and the practice of infant baptism, and Cooche had written in his defence. Now, in 1556-7 Harte was again on the defensive against the attacks of another fervent predestinarian, John Careless. Once again, Robert Cooche rose to the defence of his friend and mentor by composing a treatise against the doctrine of predestination. In the title he punned the surname of Harte's adversary. Moreover, in stating the 'errors of the careless' before confuting them, the writer appears to be making direct citations from a statement of faith. John Careless died in the King's Bench on 1 July 1556, and this had doubtless given his articles of faith added authority and influence within the underground congregations.

While Knox did not disclose the identity of the author of 'The confutation', several passages within his reply indicate that he knew him personally. Knox states that he had previously rebuked the writer's 'corrupt manners, friendly and secretely'.[893] Later in his answer he writes:

---

[891] Bradford, II, 242-3; Coverdale, 475 ff.; Foxe, *AM.*, VIII, 112-13.
[892] Above, 201-2.
[893] Knox, V, 128.

Thy manifest defection from God and this thy open blasphemie spoken against his eternall trueth, and against such as most constantly did suffer for testimonie of the same, have so broken and desolved all familiaritie which hathe bene betwixt us, that althogh thou were my natural brother, I durst not conceale thy iniquitie in this case.[894]
The two men may well have become acquainted during Knox's period of residence in London as one of King Edward VI's chaplains. Perhaps it was his personal acquaintance with the author which persuaded Scots and English predestinarians to write to Knox in exile in Geneva in 1557 asking him to compose a refutation of this reasoned attack on Calvin's doctrine.[895] Knox's *An Answer to a great nomber of blasphemous cauillations* was published by Jean Crespin at Geneva in 1560 after considerable delay by the censor. Since Knox had left Geneva in January 1559 the work must have been completed during 1558. It proved to be popular among English Puritans. In 1580, when concern over the spread of Familism was at its height, Toby Cooke obtained a licence to reprint it; another edition appeared in London in 1591.

The date of 'The confutation' can be determined with fair accuracy. In the course of his argument Cooche mentions the burning of Cranmer (March 1556); Harte's reply to the articles of John Careless can be ascribed to March/April 1556, and Careless died on 1 July 1556. In this connection it is noteworthy that Cooche refers to 'Careless Men', that is, the followers of John Careless, rather than to Careless himself. Therefore, Robert Cooche probably wrote his confutation of the articles of John Careless during the latter half of 1556.[896]

Laing considered it 'most probable that ['The confutation'] only circulated in manuscript'.[897] At one point Knox remarks, 'The copie which came to my hands was in that place imperfecte, for, after the

---

894 *Ibid.*, V, 222-3.
895 Whitley, *The Confutation*, 89.
896 Robert Cooche's powerful attack on the teaching of John Careless and his associates could have been the reason for Robert Cole, John Lydley and William Punt going to the Continent that year, (Above, pp. 166-7). The exiles asked Knox to compose a reply and sent Bentham to assume leadership of the predestinarian cause (White, 11-12).
897 Knox, V, 15.

former wordes, it had onely written...'.[898] In 1556/7 the English printing presses were firmly under the control of the Marian authorities. Clandestine religious literature either had to be smuggled out of the country to be printed on the Continent and then reimported, or else it had to circulate in manuscript form. In the case of Cooche's work, his Free-willer clientèle would doubtless have been satisfied with the old Lollard propaganda methods.

(b) Its Contents

Cooche's arguments against the doctrine of predestination differ from those of Harte in 'The Enormities'.[899] His criticisms are based on philosophical rather than biblical grounds. Cooche cites three 'errors' or statements – presumably from the articles of John Careless – and writes a lengthy confutation of each of them. Then he adds a description of 'these Careless Libertines' God' constructed from his understanding of the doctrine of predestination. He then compares this parody with the properties of 'the true God'.

The first error cited by Cooche related to reprobation – God had chosen 'a small flock' to salvation, while the rest 'which be innumerable' he had ordained to condemnation.[900] To this he makes a double retort. First Cooche asks what wild animal would bring forth its young to destruction, what man would beget a child to misery, and yet it is said that a good God has pre-determined such a destiny for the majority of those whom He has created in His own image.[901] Secondly, he argues that if all things 'of mere Necessity must come to pass' because they have been pre-determined, then Adam had no freedom of choice in the fall and Christ had no freedom in his obedience.[902]

The second error cited by Cooche was that the elect can never finally perish since, even though they sin grievously, they remain the subjects of God's favour.[903] Cooche replies that such a doctrine only serves to advance the devil's kingdom. It encourages men to 'live a careless and libertine life' because they believe that 'well-doing' will not avail with

---

[898] *Ibid.*, V, 122.
[899] Above, 195-6.
[900] Whitley, *The Confutation*, 91.
[901] *Ibid.*, 91-2.
[902] *Ibid.*, 102.
[903] *Ibid.*, 110.

God if they are among the reprobate and 'evil-doing' will not hinder their salvation if they are among the elect.[904] He maintains that it was this erroneous principle that had enabled the Reformers to persecute those who opposed them. Cooche quotes as an example of this Calvin's treatment of Servetus. Furthermore, he implies that the English Reformers were guilty of similar crimes – but God had now punished them. He writes:

Such disciples, such masters; for your chief Apollos be persecutors, on whom the blood of Servetus crieth a vengeance; so doth the blood of others more, whom I could name. But forasmuch as God hath partly already revenged their blood, and served some of their persecutors with the same measure wherewith they measured to others, I will make no mention of them at this time.[905]

This remark aroused Knox to a fury of vituperation and righteous indignation. He assumed that Cooche was referring to the burning of Joan Bocher in 1550, but since Cooche uses the plural 'others more', he was probably thinking of George van Parris as well. Knox answers:

… I thinke ye meane of your prophetesse Jone of Kent, do crie a vengeance in your eares and heartes. That none other cause do you see of the shedding of the blood of those most constant martyres of Christ Jesus, Thomas Cranmer, Nicholas Ridley, Hugh Latimer, John Hooper, John Rogers, John Bradfurth, and of others mo, but that God hathe partly revenged their blood, that is of your great prophet [Servetus] and your prophetesse, upon their persecutors, and hath served them with the same measure with the which they served others, I appeale to the judgment of all those that fear God.[906]

In fact, Knox felt so strongly about this slanderous statement that he issued a solemn warning to Cooche. He warns:

What is thy judgment of those most valiant soldiars and most happie martyres of Christ Jesus, upon whom, O blasphemous mouth, thou saiest God hath taken vengeance, which is an horrible blasphemie in the eares of all the godlie; I will not now so much labor to confute by the pen, as that my ful purpose is to lay the same to thy charge, if I shal apprehend thee in any commonwelth where justice against

---

[904] *Ibid.*, 110-111.
[905] *Ibid.*, 112.
[906] Knox, V, 221-2.

blasphemers may be ministered, as God's Word requireth. And hereof I give thee warning, lest that after thou shalt complein, that under the cloke of friendship I have deceived thee.[907]
As a result of his own literary indiscretions John Knox was unable to denounce his adversary to the English authorities in 1559. Cooche seems to have resumed his position at court unimpeded. Indeed, in 1560 he was admitted to presbyters' orders in the Church of England while Knox remained *persona non grata*.

The third error cited by Cooche concerned the predestinarians' teaching on the 'secret will' of God.[908] Again, Cooche's answer is two-fold. First he points out that the Bible says nothing about God having two wills, one revealed (concerning salvation) and one secret (concerning reprobation). Secondly he asks – if God has a secret will 'only known to Himself', how is it that you know about it?[909]

The next section of the book was headed 'The Properties of the god of the Careless by Necessity'. Cooche maintains that his description conforms with the predestinarians' doctrine in all points. He writes:
Their god's wrath exceedeth all his works, for he hath reprobated the most part of the world afore the foundation of the world. He is slow unto mercy, and ready unto wrath; for he will not be entreated to save any of them whom he hath reprobated afore, but of necessity, do what they can, they must be damned.... He is worse than the devil, for not only tempteth he to do evil, but compelleth by immutable fore-ordinance and secret will, without which nothing can be done....[910]
Cooche then lists 'The Properties of the True God', whose 'mercy exceedeth all His works'. He 'will be entreated of all' and 'biddeth all men everywhere to repent' and 'offereth faith to all men', willing the salvation of all. The true God, 'hath but one will, which is ever only good, revealed in His Word to them that fear Him and keep His commandments'.[911]

---

[907] *Ibid.*, V, 222.
[908] Whitley, *The Confutation*, 118.
[909] *Ibid.*
[910] *Ibid.*, 122.
[911] *Ibid.*, 122-3.

Finally, Cooche maintains that these two differing concepts of God have repercussions in the contrasting manner of life of their respective adherents. He states:

> The false god begetteth unmerciful, proud, ambitious and envy-ful children, bloody persecutors of others for their conscience sake...
>
> The true God begetteth merciful, humble, lowly and loving children, abhorring from blood, persecuting no man, good speakers, patient, and detesting all contentions, chiding and brawling.... They be always moved with good thoughts and godly revelations, for such grace receive they plenteously of their Father.[912]

To this Knox replies:

And that ye extolle yourselves, that ye are merciful, humble and loving children, abhorring from blood, persecuting no man... because we have a just judge, who shall revele the secretes of all heartes, we will rather susteine to be of you unjustly accused, than become proud braggers of our owne justice, as you be...

Bragge what ye list of your justice, of your mercie, of your godly revelations, and other such, ye are the brethren, mainteiners, and children of those in whom the contrarie was plainely found....[913]

Knox then concludes his answer with a lengthy translation of John Sleidan's account of the Peasants' War in Germany and of the rise and fall of Münster. Cooche's own conclusion had been far more concise –

> And as for you, Careless Men, you ought to take it in good worth, whatsoever I have said. First, because it is truth. Secondly, because ye hold that 'all things be done of mere necessity', then have I written this of necessity.[914]

Thus, we learn from these excerpts from Cooche's treatise that the writer aligned himself firmly with the Free-willers in the current controversy. He marshalled formidable arguments against a doctrine that was cherished by the overwhelming majority of English reformers. It is not surprising that the London predestinarian congregation was disturbed. Even though 'The confutation' only circulated in manuscript form, this aggressive piece of writing demanded an answer – an answer

---

[912] *Ibid.*, 123.
[913] Knox, V, 421-2.
[914] Whitley, *The Confutation*, 123.

far more succinct than the ponderous reply produced by John Knox.

III Coeche on the Lord's Supper

On 13 August 1573 Robert Cooche wrote to Rodolph Gualter at Zurich stating that he had composed a treatise on the nature of the Lord's Supper which he hoped to have printed. However, since 'nothing can be printed here in England without the licence of the bishops', he sought Gualter's written approbation for his opinions.[915] The reason for his choice of Gualter can be detected from a statement within the letter:

> It is your part, who have brought forth into the light and view of mankind so many excellent works; to wipe away, or altogether remove these blemishes of error and superstition. And this you have admirably effected in your explanation of those epistles in which Paul addressed the Corinthians, in which you have chastised the arrogance of the popes, and the thunders of the papists, and the extraordinary excommunication and separation of the Calvinists.[916]

Evidently Cooche had read Gualter's commentary on the Corinthian Epistles and concluded that there was in Zurich a reputable theologian of liberal sympathies, who was opposed to the rigors of Calvinism, and who might be persuaded to sponsor his treatise. Furthermore, unlike the theologians of England, Gualter of Zurich would be unaware of his dubious ecclesiastical activities during the reigns of Edward and Mary.

Cooche raised two points in his letter. The first concerned the manner in which the ordinance was celebrated and the second the day on which the original supper took place. Cooche maintained that the service should include a proper meal. He writes:

> My remarks relate to the last supper of Christ; in the administration of which a mistake is made now-a-days, and ever has been made, almost from the time of St. Paul; since he placed before the Corinthians a supper to be eaten, we only a morsel of bread in mockery of a supper. They used a variety and abundance of meat and drink, so as to depart satisfied; we return home hungry. And as Paul blames too dainty a

---

[915] *Zurich Letters*, II, 237.
[916] *Ibid.* 236.

table, so also does he a too sparing and scanty one. Moderation is best. Neither did our forefathers, who lived before the birth of Christ, practise that abstinence, which is rather a fast than a dinner or a supper; inasmuch as they partook of the [paschal] lamb. It is not to be believed that Christ would take such pains to have a supper prepared in the guest-chamber at Jerusalem, and invite so many guests, and yet place nothing before them but a most minute morsel of bread and three drops of wine.[917]

Secondly, concerning the Last Supper, he states –

I very much dissent from Beza and others as to the day when Christ took supper with his disciples. For they assign the supper to the fourteenth day, I to the thirteenth, in which, according to the law, the old passover was not to be sacrificed. Christ therefore instituted a new passover in remembrance of his death....[918]

Notwithstanding Bishop Parkhurst's derogatory references in reply to Gualter's enquiry, the latter composed a long reply to Cooche. He disagreed with Cooche on the first point, explaining that the term 'bread' was capable of both interpretations. On the second point, Gualter concluded that 'this difficulty is more curious than useful'.[919]

Thus, Cooche advocated the observance of a full evening meal – 'a new passover' – as a commemoration of our Lord's passion. There are certainly Lollard precedents for Cooche's interpretation of the ordinance as a commemoration of Christ's death.[920] However, there are no English precedents on record for the celebration of a full meal. The nearest contemporary groups observing such a rite appear to have been the Waldensians and the Hutterites.[921] Cooche's view of the Lord's Supper was probably an idiosyncrasy and developed quite independently. Horst implies that this development occurred during the reign of Elizabeth – late in Cooche's career as a controversialist.[922] However, it is clear from statements made by both Bishop Parkhurst and William Turner that Cooche had been advocating this unusual view of the Lord's Supper for at least twenty-five years prior to his correspondence with Gualter. Referring   to   his   debates   with   Cooche   at

---

917 *Ibid.*
918 *Ibid.*, 237.
919 *Ibid.*, 237 n.2.
920 Thomson, 246-7; Above, 37.
921 Williams, 525f., 670ff.
922 Horst, 122.

the court of Queen Katherine Parr, Parkhurst recalls:

At that time he held erroneous sentiments on Infant Baptism. He entertained some dreamy, unheard of, notions respecting the Lord's Supper. He very frequently troubled Coverdale and myself by controversies on these matters....[923]

In 1551 Turner, with characteristic robustness, had commented –

Ye axe [ask] me, why is baptym not differred, as wel as the supper of the Lorde? A ma might answer you, y^t they wer lyke to be lurched [discomfited] at your gluttenous supper, yf that they were with you: for ye wolde haue at the supper of the gluttenous catabaptistes (whiche ye call the supper of oure Lord) befe, mutton, vele, capons and such harde meates, as the pore sucking childer can not eat: and therfore it were no wisdom that thei shuld suppe with you, untyl theyr teeth wer growen.[924]

IV Conclusion

In accordance with his premise that 'anabaptists were generally unknown in England at this time' Burrage maintained that Robert Cooche was an isolated individual. He asked:

Are we then justified in believing that his case was isolated, and that he did not belong to a congregation either of English or of foreign Anabaptists? Certainly, for Cooche is nowhere mentioned as a separatist, but as a member of the Church of England....[925]

However, both Turner and Knox knew Robert Cooche personally,[926] and they were of a different opinion. Knox regarded Cooche as a sectarian – 'Impudent lier! which of us hath promised unto thee, or unto any of thy pestilent Sect, that which he hath not perfourmed?'[927] On several occasions Turner referred to Cooche as a sectarian and a gatherer of disciples.[928] Towards the end of his book Turner states:

...ye haue with your importune bablyng bewiched certayn unlearned simple me, that thei beleue to be true what so euer ye say ons unto the:[929]

---

[923] Gorham, 481.
[924] Turner, G7^r-G7^v.
[925] Burrage, I, 60, 64.
[926] Turner, G1^v; Knox, V, 222-3.
[927] Knox, V, 128.
[928] Turner, G6^v, H1^v, I3^v.
[929] *Ibid.*, M7^v.

Elsewhere, Turner's understanding of Cooche's ecclesiological position is summarised in the following accusation:
> ye... separate your selfe both in the supper of our Lorde, and also in baptyme, and in the understandyng of original sin, from us: and make your selfe of an other religion:[930]

Cooche's later correspondence and Parkhurst's remarks to Gualter reveal that our subject was consistent in his doctrine of the Lord's Supper, and there seems no reason to doubt that he also retained his opinions concerning baptism and original sin. Nevertheless, the entry in Parker's *Register* indicates that he was an ordained minister of the Church of England prior to 1553, and that he sought confirmation of his orders in 1560. In this technical sense Burrage was undoubtedly correct.

Horst's emphasis is somewhat different. He concludes:
> Robert Cooche was a representative of the liberal protestantism in Edward's reign which was well in advance of the government and the leading reformers ... he may well have been a member of [*sic*] the aristocratic admirers of Bernardino Ochino.[931]

However, while it is agreed that Cooche was probably the best educated of the English religious radicals and that he had read Erasmus, that does not make him an Erasmian liberal. There are indications that Cooche had come under the influence of Henry Harte, he sympathised with Joan Bocher, and had gathered around himself a group of unlearned, simple disciples. Is there any evidence that the sophisticated liberal humanists of the period ever attempted to gather a following among the poor and illiterate – let alone succeeded in so doing? There is not the slightest evidence to support Horst's suggestion that Cooche was an aristocratic admirer of Bernardino Ochino. He simply occupied a minor position at the court of Queen Katherine Parr where such talents as he possessed would have been admired and rewarded.

On the other hand, Horst correctly observes that 'The denial of the necessity of infant baptism is not an indication that Cooche was an anabaptist; similar views were existent among the Lollards'.[932] It has been suggested that Cooche's views on baptism represented a

---

930 *Ibid.*, F1^r.
931 Horst, 121.
932 *Ibid.*, 117.

development from the Lollard position. Likewise, Cooche's equivocal attitude to the ecclesiastical authorities bears a strong resemblance to earlier Lollard practices and precedents. William Turner provides yet another most interesting item of information. At Easter 1550, Robert Cooche received communion in a manner that would have satisfied any Roman Catholic. Turner remarks:

...we call suche as yow Popysh: whych, at the last ester, right Popishly knelyng, take ye sacrament, geuyng occasyon unto all men to thynke, y^t ye were a sterke ydolater, and beleued, that bread was turned into a God.[933]

Subsequently Turner accuses Cooche of deliberately misrepresenting his remarks at Isleworth after the manner of the Continental anabaptists. He believes Cooche to be among those who, lacking all conscience, claimed that the telling of lies was justifiable against the 'ungodly'.[934] Some twenty years later Cooche made a public recantation of his doctrine in order to retain his situation as a Gentleman of the Queen's Chapel. In his letter of February 1574 Parkhurst writes:

...and this situation he nearly lost a few years ago, in consequence of such [strange] opinions; so the Duke of Norfolk told me in his life-time: but at that time he sang his Palinodia [recantation]; as I heard from the same Duke.[935]

As Strype observes, Cooche had evidently retained his earlier opinions on believers' baptism, original sin, *etc.* [936] Furthermore, notwithstanding his recantation of *circa* 1570, Cooche's letter to Gualter proves that he continued to maintain his distinctive view of the Lord's Supper. All this evidence is reminiscent of both Lollard abjurations and Familist Nicodemism.

Therefore, it is suggested that Robert Cooche was no eccentric individualist, neither was he an aristocrat with Protestant humanist sympathies. Rather, he was a leading member of that final generation of Lollards which maintained the doctrine of free-will and which continued to maintain a tenuous, but distinctive, existence first without, and then within, the established Church of England. Like the Familists, Cooche esteemed the former Lollard, Joan Bocher, to be a martyr for their

---

[933] Turner, D6^v.
[934] *Ibid.*, E8^r-F1^v.
[935] Gorham, 482.
[936] Strype, *EM.*, II (i), 112.

cause.[937] It may well be that by 1570 he had become a member of the Family of Love.[938] Certainly the Familists made a great many converts during the 1570s and became increasingly influential. This provoked the official campaigns against the sect of 1579-80.[939] In these investigations evidence of the presence of Familists within the court of Elizabeth I was found.[940] Some years later Samuel Rutherford stated that, 'Divers of the court of Queen *Elizabeth* and of K. *James,* and some nobles were Familists'.[941] He published an abjuration that had been tendered to several courtiers and nobles, who sympathised with the doctrines of H.N., on 10 October 1580.[942] No names were named, but it seems likely that Cooche was among them. Moreover, at least three Anglican ordinands were discovered to be members of the sect during this period.[943]

In the service of the Tudors, Robert Cooche would have needed to keep his sectarian associations a close secret, otherwise his life as well as his position would have been in jeopardy. Neither Turner nor Knox succeeded in removing him. Indeed, Cooche received preferment in the Church of England. When eventually he was detected the traditional practice of abjuration proved yet again to be an effective expedient.

---

[937] Thomas Rogers, *op. cit.,* 350. Below 331, 384.

[938] Familist evangelism began during the Marian persecution – Cooche could have been a convert before 1560 (Below, pp. 301-4).

[939] Felicity Heal, 'The Family of Love and the Diocese of Ely', *Studies in Church History* IX, ed. Baker (1972), 216-7.

[940] *APC.,* X (1578), 332, 344; XII (1580-1), 231-3.

[941] Samuel Rutherford, *A Survey of the Spiritual Antichrist Opening the Secrets of Familism* (London, 1648), Wing STC. R2394, 347, 349.

[942] *Ibid.,* 353-4.

[943] Robert Sharpe, curate of Strethal in Cambridgeshire (Strype, *Parker,* II, 381-5), John Etchard, vicar of Darsham in Suffolk (Strype, *Annals,* II (i), 562.), David Thickpenny, curate of Brighton in Sussex (*Remains of Archbishop Grindal,* ed. Nicholson, 359-60), also Robert Sterte, curate of Dunsfold in Surrey (*VCH.,* Surrey, ed. Malden, I, 382).

Chapter Three

The English Radicals under Mary Tudor, 1553-58

By the final year of the reign of Edward VI some extremely radical opinions were being propounded in England. In order to show that the associates of Robert Cooche called in question the authority of the scriptures, preferring dreams and revelations to the written word, John Knox recounted an incident that occurred in London during 'the winter before the death of King Edward'.[1] He describes how 'one of your faction', who appears to have been an Englishman, 'required secrete communication of me'. Knox continues,

In the ende, after many wordes [urging 'closeness and fidelitie'] he gave me a booke, written (as he said) by God, even as well as was any of the Evangelists. This his booke he abjured me (as it were) to reade, and required to have my judgement of it.... Alwaies he urged me to reade his booke. And I wondering what mysteries it should conteine... begonne to reade his boke.[2]

Unfortunately, Knox only records the first of the propositions in this book. This he cites as,

God made not the world, neither yet the wicked creatures in the same conteined, but they had their beginning from another, that is, from the Devill, who is called the Prince of the World.[3]

When Knox pointed out that this was contrary to the plain teaching of scripture and began to explain the reason for Satan's title, his companion 'utterly denying either to reason and dispute... commanded me to reade forwarde, and to beleve howbeit I did not understand'. When Knox asked whether any reasonable man could believe things that were contrary to God's revealed truth, his companion was deeply offended.

'Tusch', said he, 'for your written Word, we have as good and as sure a word and veritie that teacheth us this doctrine, as ye have for your opinion'.[4]

Whereupon, Knox sharply rebuked him and said that he deserved to be punished for blasphemy if he preferred any other authority to the scriptures. Knox's account concludes,

---

[1] Knox, *Works*, V, 420ff.
[2] *Ibid.*, 420.
[3] *Ibid.*, 421; see *Original Letters*, II, 560 for a reference to 'Marcionists' among foreign refugees in London.
[4] *Ibid.*

At which wordes he toke pepper in [the] nose, and snatching his boke furth of my hand, departed after he had thus spoken: 'I will goo to the end of the world; but I will have my boke confirmed and subscribed with better learned men then you be'. In me, I confesse, there was greate negligence, that neither did reteine his boke, neither yet did present him to the Magistrate.[5]
Then, addressing Robert Cooche, Knox states – 'your faction is not altogether cleane from the heresie of the Manichies. I could name and point forth others who labour in the same disease; but so long as their venom doth remaine secrete within themselves, I am purposed to spare them'.[6] This incident provides clear evidence that Gnostic teaching was circulating in London in 1552-3. In addition it supplies an example of Spiritualist proselytism – secret instruction of potential converts by means of clandestine heterodox literature. Such literature had been imported from the Continent in the 1530s[7] and the practice was to be resumed in the 1570s – if not earlier.[8]

No doubt the establishment of organised worship for refugee Walloons at Canterbury at this time, also possibly for Dutch refugees at Sandwich, served to inhibit the influence of any Spiritualists, anabaptists or anti-trinitarians among them, as it had among the Strangers in London.[9] Jan Utenhovius and Francois de la Rivière stayed at Cranmer's residence near Canterbury in 1548-9 and eventually founded the refugee congregation in the city.[10] With regard to native English nonconformity and heterodoxy, Bishop Ridley waged an active campaign against heresy in London and Essex, while John Knox had a roving commission to advance the Edwardine reforms. Between July and October 1553 Knox was engaged in an itinerant preaching ministry in Kent and Buckinghamshire. Both these counties had contained

---

5   *Ibid.*
6   *Ibid.*
7   Above, 3-8.
8   Below, 306.
9   J. Southerden Burn, *The History of the Foreign Protestant Refugees settled in England* (London, 1846), 38, 205-6; Above, 115-16. A more recent work on the Strangers' Churches is Andrew Pettegree, *Foreign Protestant Communities in Sixteenth-century London* (Oxford, 1986).
10 *VCH.*, Kent, II, ed. Page (1926), 79.

centres of Lollard nonconformity, and Knox was particularly successful in the latter.[11]

Knox had left London immediately after the death of Edward VI on 6 July 1553. On 19 July 1553 Mary Tudor was proclaimed Queen of England. It was not, however, until November 1554 that parliament took formal steps to proscribe heresy. In that month an act was passed which revived three statutes enacted during the previous century for the repression of Lollardy. This act took effect on 20 January 1554/5.[12] Nevertheless, long before that date Protestants were being arrested on charges of heresy. It was not without justification that Nicholas Sheterden claimed that his arrest on suspicion of heresy *circa* September 1554 was illegal.[13]

On 5 September 1553 Nicholas Ridley had been deprived of the see of London and Edmund Bonner reinstated. A year later (3 September 1554) Bonner commenced a visitation of his diocese. Like those of Ridley, Bishop Bonner's articles reveal a concern over the presence of religious radicals. Article seventy-eight reads,
Whether there be any that is a Sacramentary or Anabaptist or Libertine, either in reiterating baptism again, or in holding any of the opinions of the Anabaptists, especially that a Christian man or woman ought not to swear before a judge, nor one to sue another in the law for his right, and that all things should be common?[14]
The three-fold nomenclature is noteworthy. Presumably a 'Sacramentary' was an orthodox Protestant. An 'Anabaptist' is defined in terms which approximate to the definitions of 1540 and 1550,[15] but what was a 'Libertine'? Veron and Knox also use this term in their respective attacks on Champneys and Cooche. It was probably an all-inclusive epithet covering radical Spiritualists and rationalist anti-trinitarians.

---

11   Thomas M'Crie, *The Life of John Knox* (Edinburgh, 1814), I, 114.
12   *Statutes of the Realm*, IV, 244.
13   Foxe, *AM.*, VII, 308; Above, 160-1.
14   *Visitation Articles*, II, 349.
15   Above, 28-9, 28-9, 114.

A. THE SUSSEX RADICALS

I. The King's Bench Controversy

From the extant sources it would appear that the party which opposed the Predestinarians in the King's Bench was largely composed of Free-willers from Sussex. They were led by John Trewe and Thomas Avington, and from outside the prison they received encouragement from Henry Harte.

According to John Trewe[16] it all began in 1554 when the Free-willers led by Trewe protested to the Predestinarians over their use of pastimes, especially gaming, which the Free-willers claimed were an offence to the weak.[17] However gaming was not the root cause of the controversy. Persecution had thrown together in the prison two disparate groups of Christians each of which claimed the Bible as the sole basis of its doctrine. The contention in the King's Bench was in reality a dispute between those influenced by the old English biblical traditions and those who had embraced the new Reformation movement from the Continent.[18] Trewe adds,

> Moreover, we saw in that they did hold and affirm, that none but great learned men could have the true understanding of the word of God....[19]

Here is the same suspicion of formal theological scholarship and the same vigorous refusal to respect the opinions of trained clerics found in John Champneys and Henry Harte. The greatest disparity between the two parties, however, was in the area of soteriology. Trewe continues, 'Moreover besides all these aforesaid detestable errors... they affirm that Christ hath not died for all men. Whereby they make Christ inferior to Adam and grace to sin'.[20]

---

[16]   John Trewe sent out from the King's Bench an account of the dispute which he entitled – 'John Trewe... signifieth the cause of contention in the King's Bench as concerning sects in religion'. This is dated 30 January 1555-6. It is part of Bodleian MS. 53 and was printed by Richard Laurence in his *Authentic Documents*. See Appendix Document 1.

[17]   Laurence, 37-8.

[18]   See O. T. Hargrave, 'The Predestinarian Offensive of the Marian Exiles at Geneva', *Historical Magazine of the Protestant Episcopal Church* 42 (1973), 111-23.

[19]   Laurence, 44.

[20]   *Ibid.*, 45-6.

As a result of these differences and the intransigence with which the Sussex men advocated their beliefs, notwithstanding the weight of Reformed scholarship pitted against them, the Predestinarians resorted to disciplinary measures. According to Trewe the penalties they inflicted were not only spiritual but physical –

For these aforesaid causes and no other they did evil us, rail on us, and call us heretics, cast dust in our faces, and give sentence of damnation on us, and excommunicated us, and would neither eat nor drink with us, nor yet bid us God speed; and did keep away such money as was given them in common to distribute amongst us, that did lie [in prison] for the truth, and caused us to be locked up that we should speak to nobody by their minds, lest we should warn them of their false and erroneous opinion....[21]

The time when these disciplinary proceedings were instituted can be determined from the correspondence of John Bradford. Letter LX is addressed 'To Certain Free-willers' and is dated 1 January 1555.[22] Coverdale stated that these advocates of man's free-will were then prisoners with Bradford in the King's Bench.[23] Bradford begins,

Hitherto I have oftentimes resorted unto you, my friends as I thought, and by all means sought to do you good, even to mine own charges and hindrance. But now I see it happeneth otherwise; and therefore I am purposed... to absent myself from you.[24]

Bradford proceeds to state succinctly another aspect of the difference between them over soteriology. He writes:

I believe and affirm the salvation of God's children to be so certain, that they shall assuredly enjoy the same. You say it hangeth partly upon our perseverance to the end; and I say, it hangeth only and altogether upon God's grace in Christ, and not upon our perseverance in any point.[25]

He concludes with a solemn warning:

...they take Satan's part, which go about to let or hinder this certainty, in themselves and in others... I cannot but, as I have done often

---

21 *Ibid.*, 47.
22 Bradford, *Works*, II, 164-7.
23 *Ibid.*, 164, n. 5.
24 *Ibid.*, 165.
25 *Ibid.*

before, admonish you of it eftsoons, that your bloods may be on your own heads, if you persevere in your obstinacy.[26]

Since this letter is dated 1 January, the Predestinarians must have agreed to sever communications with the Free-willers during December 1554. This action marked the conclusion of the first stage in the controversy. John Trewe simply records:

They... did both in word and writing most shamefully slander us to be such hypocritish dissentious persons and notorious heretics, that we were not worthy to receive the benevolence that was due unto Christians; for no other cause, but that our consciences grounded on God's word would not suffer us to be of that sect.[27]

Included among the pieces of writing that Trewe had in mind were doubtless Bradford's *Defence of Election* and Philpot's *Apology for Spitting upon an Arian*. It is equally clear that Trewe and his company had been encouraged during 1554 by a treatise which Henry Harte had sent in to them entitled, 'The Enormities Proceeding from the Doctrine of Election'.[28] This had moved Bradford to compose his *Defence of Election*, but equally it had inspired Trewe and his colleagues to compile no less than twenty-three additional 'enormities' arising out of the same doctrine.[29]

At the end of January 1555 Bradford was transferred from the King's Bench to the Counter in Bread Street. At about the same time Robert Cole wrote to Bradford asking him to attempt a reconciliation with the Free-willers by writing to them again. Bradford informed Philpot of this and adds, 'Therefore I purpose to write something to Trew and Abyngton thereabouts'.[30] In fact he must have written to the Sussex men that same day – if Letter LXVIII in the Bradford correspondence was written from the Counter on 30 January 1555. According to Coverdale this letter was addressed to 'Trewe and Abyngton, with other of their company teachers and maintainers of the error of man's free-will'.[31] The circumstances under which this letter was written are poignantly described in the opening paragraph –

---

26   *Ibid.*, 167.
27   Laurence, 48.
28   Above, 195-6.
29   Laurence, 48-54, 361-4.
30   Bradford, *Works*, II, 244.
31   *Ibid.*, 180, 180 n.1.

Yet once more, beloved in the Lord, before pen and ink be utterly by all
means taken from me, as I look it to be this afternoon, I thought good
to write unto you, because I stand in a doubt, whether at any time
hereafter, I shall see or speak with you.[32]
The whole tone of this letter is conciliatory. Bradford continues,
God knoweth I lie not, I never did bear you malice, nor sought the
hindrance of any one of you, but your good both in soul and body....
For mine own conscience can and doth bear witness with me, that I
never defrauded you or any of you ... but have sought, with that which
hath been given, not only in common, but also unto me and to mine
own use, discretion and distribution, to do you good. Therefore
disdain not the good-will of your lover in God; and, in hope that you
will not, I have eftsoons even now sent unto you thirteen shillings, four
pence: if you need as much more, you shall have it, or anything else I
have or can do for you.
Though in some things we agree not, yet let love bear the bell
away; and let us one pray for another...[33]
In his 1564 edition of this correspondence Coverdale remarks,
At this letter these men were so sore offended, because he said he had
hindered himself to further them, as though he had thereby upbraided
them, that in displeasure they sent it to him again.[34]
However, Coverdale appears to have been mistaken because it was in his
letter of withdrawal from the Free-willers that Bradford wrote that he had
hindered himself to further them. One can understand the Sussex men
returning Bradford's letter of excommunication of the first of January to
its author. Furthermore, in his subsequent letter of 30 January Bradford
urges them not to disdain the accompanying tokens of his goodwill.

It may be, therefore, that Bradford's second letter 'To Trewe,
Abyngton & others' which has been allocated to 31 January 1555, was
actually written before Letter LXVIII (of 30 January) and in response to
their rejection of his letter of 1 January.[35] In this brief letter Bradford
argues,
He that seeketh not to hinder himself temporally, that he may further
his brother in more need, the same wanteth true love. I have done, do

---

32 *Ibid.*
33 *Ibid.*
34 Coverdale, 365.
35 Bradford, *Works*, II, 181.

and will (except you refuse it) hinder myself this way, that I may further you…. If I would seek mine own gains temporally, then could I have taken and used many portions of money which have been given me to mine own use. I never minded to upbraid you: but that which I did write of mine own hindrance was, that you might see I loved you, and sought your weal, as I do and will be glad to do it continually – The Lord of mercy hath forgiven us all: wherefore henceforth let us rather bear than break.[36]
It is apparent from John Trewe's subsequent account of the controversy that Bradford's explanation of his stewardship failed to satisfy them. Throughout 1555 the Sussex Free-willers continued to complain that they were not receiving their fair share of the alms donated to the prisoners in the King's Bench.[37]

On 16 February 1555 Bradford sent out a general letter to the Free-willers of Kent, Essex and Sussex.[38] Expecting to follow Rogers to the stake, he wrote this long letter of farewell to Harte, Barre, Ledley, Robert Cole and others. It is highly eirenic. Bradford commended his treatise on election to them, and stated that it contains the faith that he will die for, but he wished all controversy to cease.[39] Surely it is significant that Trewe and Abyngton are not listed among the large number of addressees. It suggests that this letter was not being directed to those Free-willers who were imprisoned in the King's Bench, but to men whom Bradford knew to be at liberty in the south-eastern counties – including Henry Harte.

One further reference to the Sussex radicals occurs in the Bradford correspondence. In a letter addressed to 'John Careless, prisoner in the King's Bench', which must have been written between February and June 1555, Bradford concludes,

Commend me to our good brother Skelthrop, for whom I heartily praise my God, which hath given him to see his truth at the length…. Forget not salutations in Christ, as you shall think good, to Trew and his fellows. The Lord hath his time, I hope, for them also, although we perchance think otherwise….[40]

---

36 *Ibid.*
37 *loc. cit.*
38 Bradford, *Works*, II, 194-8.
39 *Ibid.*, 197.
40 *Ibid.*, 243.

John Careless appears to have assumed Bradford's mantle as the leading advocate of predestinarianism in the King's Bench. Nevertheless, despite his success with Skelthrop and his similar social background, the Coventry weaver failed to win over the obdurate John Trewe.

During 1555 several attempts were made to unite the two parties but they all came to nothing. According to Trewe's version of the dispute it was the Free-willers who took the initiative. He writes:

Our request herein they granted three or four times, but indeed they soon break it... either by slandering of us or sending out writings against us, or maintaining this their folly, by racking the pure and holy word of God in their talk and open lectures.[41]

He provides important information on the reasons behind the failure to reach agreement. Trewe continues,

One time they fell out with us, and reported us to be abominable heretics, because we would not grant to them without approbations of the holy Scriptures, that our children might receive a lawful baptism in the church of Antichrist... and that we should have nothing to do with them, but separate ourselves from them, lest we be partakers of their sins, and so to receive of their plagues.[42]

Thus, the Sussex radicals rejected the Roman Church's sacrament of baptism on the grounds that it was an heretical church. Indeed they advocated total separation from 'the church of Antichrist'. The Reformers – anxious to preserve some continuity – could not accept this radical separatism. However, the really noteworthy feature for this study is that the Sussex radicals did not reject infant baptism *per se*. They were ready to accept the practice provided that the ordinance was administered within a 'true' church. In this they foreshadowed the Independents rather than the Baptists.

At another time we were like to come to an unity also, but then in an open lecture... they taught and affirmed... play and pastimes to be clean to Christians... and after the old custom fell out with us, and would neither eat nor drink with us, nor yet bid us God speed, for

---

[41] Laurence, 54.
[42] *Ibid.*, 54-5.

nought else, but because we would not consent with them, that play at bowls, dice and cards was cleansed by the word and not sin, nor offence to all men.[43]

Here Trewe describes how the Free-willers' stringent attitude towards all forms of entertainment prevented unification. In fact the Predestinarians were so angered by the Free-willers' intransigence in this matter that they threatened to make them suffer for it. The irony in this did not escape John Trewe –

> They that before confessed us to be of the true church and no heretics and upon the same would have received us to the communion... because we would not with them affirm against these Scriptures... that vain play may be used of such as be in bands, and look every day to suffer for the truth, they did not only fall out with us... but also threatened us, that we were like to die for it, if the Gospel should reign again, affirming that the true church might shed blood for believers' sake, of the which we brought to disprove them... but it would not serve.[44]

The rejection of persecution in matters of conscience and advocacy of religious tolerance is typical of most sixteenth-century separatism – Continental as well as English.[45] Equally, the readiness to use physical force to achieve its ends if all else failed was characteristic of Calvinism.

The year 1555 was also almost certainly the year in which John Philpot wrote his *Apology for Spitting upon an Arian*.[46] It must have been composed in the King's Bench in response to these controversies, and in particular as a reply to Henry Harte's 'Enormities'. Later, in April 1556, John Careless admitted that there were two simple men imprisoned with him in the King's Bench who denied the divinity of Christ.[47] In the midst of his vitriolic denunciation Philpot referred to the situation in the prison:

> This have I touched to give you warning, how to behave yourselves with the Arians and other schismatics and heretics, whom all godly order and good learning displeaseth.... If you hear that there is contention between us and them that be in prison, marvel not therefore.... Such they be as break the unity of Christ's church,

---

43 *Ibid.*, 55-7.
44 *Ibid.*
45 Jordan, *Religious Toleration*, 136-41; Horst, 118-9.
46 RSTC 19892; *The Writings of Archdeacon Philpot*, ed. Eden (PS., Cambridge, 1842), 293-318.
47 Foxe, *AM.*, VIII, 169.

neither abide in the same, neither submit their judgment to be tried...
by the godly learned pastors thereof; but arrogantly deprave them, and
take upon themselves to be teachers, before they have learned,
affirming they cannot tell what... and judge themselves best of all
other.[48]

The Free-willers' ardent separatism, their attachment to their own lay
ministers, and their refusal to submit to formal theological scholarship
were all anathema to Calvinist ministers of the Edwardine establishment
like Archdeacon Philpot. He proceeds to give an interesting description
of the prison debates –

These brawling heretics are under a pretence of feigned holiness....
Still they have the scriptures in their mouth, and cry, 'The scripture, the
scripture', but it cometh like a beggar's cloak out of their mouth, full
of patches and all out of fashion; and when they be (by the word
rightly alleged) overthrown... yet will they never be confounded; but
either depart in fury, or else stop their ears... or else fall to scolding....
And if perchance any of them be soberer than other, their answer is 'I
pray you let us alone; our conscience is satisfied; you labour but in
vain to go about to turn us.'[49]

Next, Philpot records the objections that the Free-willers levelled at the
Predestinarians' teaching and practice. In so doing he corroborates John
Trewe's account. Philpot complains,

...they imagine most spitefully and falsely ... blasphemies; spreading
the same abroad... that we make God the author of sin, and that we
say, Let men do what they will, it is not material if they be predestinate;
and that we maintain all carnal liberty, dice, cards, drunkenness, and
other inordinate things.... Only because I hold and affirm (being
manifestly instructed by God's word) that the elect of God cannot
finally perish... and because at another time I did reprove them for
their temerarious and rash judgment for condemning of men using
things indifferent, as shooting, bowling, hawking, with such like,
proving by the scripture that all men in a temperancy might use them
in their due times, and shewing that honest pastime was no sin....[50]

---

48 Philpot, *Works*, 305.
49 *Ibid.*, 306.
50 *Ibid.*, 306-7.

The writer concluded his remarks on the contemporary situation with the suggestion that the Free-willers leave theology to the professionals and return to their secular occupations. Philpot writes,

It had been better for them never to have known the gospel than by their proud free-will knowledge to go about to subvert the same. I would they would be taught by the church of Christ, where they ought to be, and become sincere confessors... and fall to their own occupation, every man according to his own calling... and not to lie in corners like humble dories [drones], eating up the honey of the bees, and do nothing else but murmur and sting at the verity, and at all faithful labourers in the Lord's vineyard.[51]

One further piece of evidence derives from the pen of John Philpot. The letter he addressed to 'my brother John Careless, prisoner in the King's Bench'[52] must have been written after 2 October 1555 – when Philpot was removed from the King's Bench – and before 18 December 1555, when he was martyred at Smithfield. Evidently Careless had written and complained about the opposition he was encountering from the Free-willers. Philpot commiserates, 'I am sorry to hear of thy great trouble which these schismatics do daily put thee to'. He advises, 'Commit the success to God; and cease not with charity to be earnest in the defence of the truth, against these arrogant and self-will blinded scatterers. These sects are necessary, for the trial of our faith'. In the margin of the 1564 edition, Coverdale comments – 'These were certain free-will men, arrogant, froward and unquiet spirits'.[53]

By the autumn of 1555 all communication between the two parties had ceased. However, the burning of John Philpot on 18 December and the release the same day of four of the King's Bench prisoners signalled the beginning of one final attempt at unity. Trewe states,

Wherefore we gave them over, and meddled as little with them as we could, until Simson Upchear and Woodman, with other that were delivered out of prison (for Simson came to us, and desired us to be at unity in the truth).[54]

Cuthbert Simpson, Thomas Upchard and Richard Woodman were released on the express order of Bishop Bonner on 18 December 1555.[55] Simpson seems to have made his approach to the Sussex men

---

[51] *Ibid.*, 308.
[52] *Ibid.*, 247-9.
[53] *Ibid.*, 247.
[54] Laurence, 57.
[55] Foxe, *AM.*, VIII, 333.

before he left the King's Bench a free man. The events that followed upon Simpson's attempt to break the stalemate are described in great detail by John Trewe, and because of this they can be precisely dated to the week before Christmas Day (18-25 December 1555).

Apparently the Sussex men responded positively to Simpson's efforts and, 'the order of the unity was of both the parties put into Simson's, and others that were of that sects' hands, that they with the consent of other Christians should devise such order between us'.[56] This appears to mean that the prisoners left it to members of the two underground congregations in London (Free-willer and Predestinarian) to hammer out the terms of the agreement between them. For two or three days 'love and familiarity' prevailed in the King's Bench. Then, on 23 December, before any formal agreement had been concluded –
    ...certain of them came to us to give us warning that they would have a communion on Christmas day, which was not two days off, demanding of us whether we would receive with them or not.[57]
The Free-willers' response provides a valuable glimpse of separatist eucharistic doctrine. They replied,
    that we would gladly receive with them, but we would have the unity thoroughly established first, lest we did receive it to our damnation; for we take the communion to be (as it is) a thing of great efficacy and bond of peace, perpetual love, and perfection, that men should well examine themselves, whether they were in perfect love, and through God's gift and assistance able to keep the promise they make by receiving thereof.[58]
The Predestinarians said that they were determined to hold the communion service with or without John Trewe and his associates. Nevertheless, the Predestinarians returned the next day (24 December) with a document containing articles of faith which were designed to bridge the doctrinal gap between the parties. It transpires from later evidence that John Careless was the chief influence behind the compilation of these mediating articles, which thus forestalled the

---

[56] Laurence, 57-8.
[57] *Ibid.*
[58] *Ibid.*

negotiations between the two parties outside the prison.[59] John Trewe maintains that, although he was unhappy about aspects of the phraseology, for the sake of unity he and some of his company signed the document.[60] Within a few hours – having had time to compare the articles with Scripture – John Trewe was bitterly regretting his action. Then John Careless, 'the chief of their company', came to him and asked him what was wrong. Trewe recalls,

I told him plainly, that I thought my conscience would have borne with it, but because it is like to come into so many men's hands, it certifieth me.... Therefore I did most heartily desire him, that as he would my salvation the unity might go forth without writing, because we did not agree in doctrine.[61]

Careless was not prepared to grant Trewe's request. Here, again, we can detect a characteristic difference between the two groups. The Free-willers' reluctance to commit their faith to writing is apparent at several points in Trewe's account[62] whereas the Predestinarians were ever anxious to issue an agreed confession of faith. Such an agreed doctrinal statement among confessors in prison awaiting martyrdom would be of far-reaching influence when circulated among the underground congregations.

Doubtless it was for that reason that John Careless then approached Trewe's associates, asking them to go ahead and sign the mediating articles and then share in the communion service without their leader. This they refused to do. Whereupon Careless asked them to draw up their own set of articles, which the Predestinarians would sign if they complied with Scripture. Again the Sussex men said that they would do nothing without the agreement of their leader. 'Notwithstanding he laid importunately on my fellows to make a writing', which some of them were prepared to do, 'being not so much against the word', and so they went to John Trewe and asked him to draw up a confession of faith for them.[63]

Thus, Trewe described the events that led to the production of the Sussex Free-willers' articles of faith in December 1555. He continues,

And so I went about it; and when it was made, my fellows shewed it to him [Careless]. The which when he saw it, he kept it to pick out

---

[59] Foxe, *AM.*, VIII, 164.
[60] Laurence, 59-60.
[61] *Ibid.*, 60-1.
[62] *Ibid.*, 59, 60-1, 63.
[63] *Ibid.*, 61-2.

heresies against us in it, refused to put his hand to it according to his faithful promise, and yet he would not disprove it by the word. Thus he brake off the unity, and reported it to be my doing....[64]

It was under these circumstances, then, that the final attempt at reconciliation among the prisoners in the King's Bench failed. It foundered on the reefs of confessionalism. Henceforward the attitudes of the members of each party hardened around their respective doctrinal statements, and there was no united Christmas communion service.

Trewe's account of the controversy continues –

...we offered and desired to have fellowship with them without writing. The which they refused; and out of these articles have raised up new slanders on us, reporting us that we should deny that Christ was come in the flesh, and that he passed through the blessed Virgin Mary, as saffron doth through a bag; which detestable opinion we hate and utterly abhor....[65]

The vigorous repudiation of 'Melchiorite' christology is of great significance. In this the Sussex Free-willers were at one with their fellow Free-willers, Nicholas Sheterden of Kent and John Barre of Essex. It was to counteract the misrepresentation of John Careless and the Predestinarians that John Trewe wrote his account of the King's Bench controversy in January 1556. In order to disprove the slanders of Careless and shew the orthodoxy of their beliefs John Trewe concluded his account by reproducing his articles 'word for word'.[66] The confession begins,

Here followeth the articles word for word, as they have a copy of them to shew, the which, if they would have set their hands unto according to their promise, as we would have done ours, we had come to an unity.[67]

The first article was a simple expression of orthodox trinitarian belief, and doubtless was intended to refute any charges of Arianism – 'We all consent and constantly confess and believe that there is one, and but one, very true living and everlasting God, which is three in persons, and but one in substance'.[68] Likewise, the second article proved their christological orthodoxy – 'And we confess and believe, that the second

64 *Ibid.*
65 *Ibid.*, 62-3.
66 *Ibid.*, 64-70.
67 *Ibid.*, 64.
68 *Ibid.*, 64-5.

person in trinity, which is Jesus Christ, the very self-same woman's seed, that God promised to Adam... and that he took so much flesh and blood and nourishment of the blessed Virgin Mary, as any child doth of his mother'.[69] The emphasis upon doctrinal orthodoxy is continued in Article Three – 'We confess and believe all the articles of the Christian faith, contained in the symbol commonly called the Apostles' Creed'.[70] Article Four deals with soteriology and, again, no Predestinarian could find fault with the greater part of it –

Also we confess and believe and faithfully acknowledge, that all salvation, justification, redemption, and remission of sins cometh unto us wholly and solely through the mere mercy and free favour of God in Jesus Christ, purchased unto us through his most precious death and bloodshedding, and in no part or piece through any of our own merit, works, or deservings, how many or how good soever they be....[71]

However, the concluding paragraphs contain statements which give some place to human autonomy and good works as well as a categorical denial of reprobation. The fourth article concludes,

...and all, that truly repent, unfeignedly believe with a lively faith, and persevere therein to the end of this mortal life, shall be saved, and that there is no decree of God to the contrary.[72]

The clearest statement of characteristic Free-willer teaching occurs in the fifth article which deals with sanctification –

And also we do acknowledge and confess, that all Christians ought to know and keep God's holy commandments in as ample manner, as our Saviour Christ, and his Apostles have left unto us by example or writing, that is to say, they must continually watch and pray to God, to assist them with his holy Spirit, that they may leave, and utterly forsake all idolatry, whoredoms, murder, theft, extortion... with all vain gaming, slandering, lying, fighting, railing, evil communications, with sects and dissensions; and not to be curious in many of God's works, nor to make too much searching in superfluous things....[73]

The references to curiosity in God's works and 'searching in superfluous things' appear to be aimed at systematic theological

---

[69] *Ibid.*, 65.
[70] *Ibid.*, 66.
[71] *Ibid.*
[72] *Ibid.*
[73] *Ibid.*, 66-7.

investigation; they amount to a rejection of detailed doctrinal statements. They are also in accord with Henry Harte's comment upon the first article in John Careless' statement to the Newgate prisoners –

If ye knowe not whatt god is other wyse than he hath showed him self in his word no more do you or any man elss knowe whether he haue any parts or passyons or not/wherfor as ye owght to boast nothinge w^{cc} ye cannot proue: no more owght you... to search after cecrets w^{cc} ye holy gost for bydeth you least you perysh.[74]

The Free-willers' insistence upon theological simplicity, their repudiation of scholarship, and their dependence upon their own lay teachers are all reminiscent of early Familist emphases. The Familist teachers did not promote individual Bible reading, in fact they encouraged their simple adherents to remain illiterate.[75] For this reason the writings of H. N. were not translated into English until the 1570s.

Article Six is concerned with ecclesiology, and it reveals a surprising degree of respect for the previous religious establishment on the part of John Trewe and his associates. It reads,

Also we do heartily acknowledge, confess, believe, and are most assuredly certeined by God's most holy word, that our Saviour Jesus Christ, his pure religion... was in this realm declared and known in good King Edward the VI th his days; which word of God was then truly preached, and sufficiently taught, and his sacraments duly ministered, and of some followed; therefore we acknowledge them in England Christ's true church visible....[76]

Had the Sussex Free-willers moved away from separatism, or was this article originally intended as a gesture towards the ecclesiology of John Careless and his party?

The seventh, and final, article is eirenic in tone. It enshrines the radicals' advocacy of religious tolerance –

And forasmuch as St Paul saith, that our knowledge is imperfect, there is none of us, but that we be ignorant in some things, therefore ... the Holy Ghost hath moved us to leave contention, and to seek

---

[74] Emma. MS., 260 F. 87^{r}.
[75] Below, 330-1, 380-1.
[76] Laurence, 67-8.

peace and ensue it, and to let things pass, which are not to be concluded on, seeing they may be borne by God's word, rather than still to contend about them to the derogation of God's glory, and hurt of his church.... And if we do miss in any point, we confess, that it is of simplicity, and not of obstinacy.[77]

There were twelve signatories to Trewe's articles and account of the controversy. These were printed as follows:–

John Trewe, Thomas Avington, Richard Harman, John Jackson, Henry Wickham, Cornelius Stevenson, John Guelle, Thomas Arede, John Saxbye, Robert Hitcherst, Matthew Hitcherst, Margery Russell. All we do affirm this to be true.[78]

John Trewe dated the document, 'the 30th of January, Anno Dom. 1555', that is, 1555/56.[79] Therefore, the articles were drawn up at Christmas 1555 and the account of the controversy was written during January 1556.

Articles One to Four bear a striking resemblance to the first four articles in the confession of the thirteen prisoners who were burned at Stratford-le-Bow on 27 June 1556.[80] Trewe's fifth article also has some basis in the fourth of the Stratford martyrs. Were the eight articles of the Stratford martyrs based upon Careless' original articles, a copy of which he had sent to Newgate? John Trewe and his company possessed a copy of the same articles. If Trewe had also used John Careless' mediating articles as a basis for his own confession, that would account for the similarities in phraseology – both Trewe and the Stratford martyrs were dependent on the same source.

All of the Stratford martyrs were apprehended in Essex, but one of them – Harry Adlington – originally came from East Grinstead, and John Careless was in friendly communication with him. At first the Essex prisoners were held in the Lollards' Tower; they were examined by Bonner's chancellor on 6 June 1556, and after their formal condemnation on 14 June they were transferred to Newgate.[81] Although this was two months after William Tyms and his associates had been

---

[77] *Ibid.*, 68-9.
[78] *Ibid.*, 69-70.
[79] *Ibid.*, 37.
[80] Strype, *EM.*, III (ii), 469-71. John Strype discovered this confession among Foxe's manuscripts. Why did John Foxe choose not to publish it?
[81] Foxe, *AM.*, VIII, 151-6.

taken from Newgate to execution, and the original copy of Careless' articles had been seized by the Marian authorities, Tyms may well have made another copy of the articles (as he had of Harte's critique) and circulated it among the other prisoners in Newgate. By this means a copy of Careless' articles could have come into the possession of Adlington and his associates when they arrived in Newgate. Alternately, Careless may have sent them a copy of his articles when they were in the Lollards' Tower.

Of the twelve signatories to John Trewe's document there is further information on six of them.

(a) John Trewe of Hellingly.
The seizure of the copy of the articles that John Careless had sent to William Tyms and his fellow prisoners in Newgate alerted the Marian authorities to the situation in the King's Bench.[82] Doctor Thomas Martin was commissioned by the Privy Council to ascertain, 'what opinions are amongst you in the King's Bench, for the which you do strive amongst yourselves'.[83] Accordingly , on 25 April 1556, Martin interviewed the two leading protagonists in the dispute, and the record of their statements was forwarded to the Council.[84] Had Henry Harte been held in the King's Bench at this time as has been assumed,[85] then surely Doctor Martin would have interviewed him rather than John Trewe. Harte's critique of Careless' articles had fallen into the hands of the authorities, and yet it is Careless and Trewe who were interrogated. Unfortunately the record of John Trewe's examination has not been preserved. However, a verbatim account of Careless' examination was published by Foxe.[86] Trewe was mentioned at several points in the interrogation. Martin asked,
Is there not great contention between thee and one Trew, that was here with me erewhile?... I hear say one of your matters is about predestination.... Trew told me that thou dost affirm that God hath predestinated some to salvation that cannot be damned, live they never so wickedly, and some to damnation that cannot be saved, live they never so godly, well, and virtuously.

---

82   *Ibid.*, VIII, 164.
83   *Ibid.*, VIII, 166.
84   *Ibid.*, VIII, 169.
85   Oxley, 192; Horst, 125; Martin, 56-7, 68.
86   Foxe, *AM.*, VIII, 163-70.

'It is not the first lie that he hath made on me...', Careless replied.[87]
Later the questioning proceeded as follows:–

Martin: I tell thee yet again, that I must also examine thee of such things as be in controversy between thee and thy fellows in the King's Bench, whereof predestination is a part, as thy fellow Trew hath confessed, and thyself dost not deny it.

Careless: I do not deny it. But he that first told you that matter might have found himself much better occupied.[88]

Then Martin asked Careless to define Trewe's doctrine of predestination:

Martin: Now sir, what is Trew's faith of predestination? He believeth that all men be predestinate, and that none shall be damned. Doth he not?

Careless: No forsooth, that he doth not.

Martin: How then?

Careless: Truly I think he doth believe as your mastership and the rest of the clergy do believe of predestination, that we be elected in respect of good works, and so long elected as we do them, and no longer.

Martin: Write that he saith, that his fellow Trew believeth of predestination, as the papists do believe.[89]

Finally, Doctor Martin asked, 'What, have you any other matter? How say you to the two brethren that are in the King's Bench which deny the divinity of Christ? How say you to their opinion?' At this Careless exclaimed, 'O Lord! I perceive your mastership knoweth that which of all other things I wish to have been kept from you: verily he was to blame that told you of that matter'.[90] While it is evident from this record that John Careless was guilty of prevarication,[91] it is equally clear that John Trewe had embarrassed him by making a full confession to Doctor Martin.

The next reference to Trewe occurs in a letter written by John Careless to Harry Adlington who was among the Essex prisoners in the Lollards' Tower.[92] This letter must have been written between 6 June and 12 June 1556.[93] Careless concluded his letter with several items of news, including the following –

---

[87]   *Ibid.*, VIII, 166.
[88]   *Ibid.*, VIII, 168.
[89]   *Ibid.*, VIII, 169.
[90]   *Ibid.*
[91]   *Ibid.*, VIII, 765.
[92]   *Ibid.*, VIII, 187-9; Coverdale, 472-3.
[93]   Foxe, *AM.*, VIII, 151 n.1, 765.

My good brother Harry, you shall understand that bragging John T. hath beguiled his keepers (who trusted him too well), and is run away from them, and hath brought the poor men into great danger by the same. The one of them is cast by the council's commandment into the Gate-house at Westminster, the other is fled forth of the country for fear. Thus you may see the fruits of our free-will men, that made so much boast of their own strength...[94]
This information is corroborated by a note in the record of the meeting of the Privy Council on 29 July 1556. It states that Trewe's gaoler had been captured and committed to the King's Bench.[95] Thus, a month or so after his examination by Doctor Martin, John Trewe succeeded in escaping from the King's Bench.

Earlier in his letter, Careless informed Adlington of the recent confession and martyrdom at Lewes in Sussex of, 'our sweet brethren Thomas Harland and John Oswald'.[96] However, on 6 June 1556 four confessors suffered martyrdom at Lewes: – Harland, Oswald, and 'Thomas Avington of Ardingley, turner; Thomas Read'. Foxe's account concludes, 'These four, after long imprisonment in the King's Bench, were burned together at Lewes in Sussex, in one fire'.[97] It is highly significant that John Careless, while mentioning the cowardice of Trewe, omitted to inform Adlington of the constancy of Trewe's fellow Free-willers, Avington and Read. Such selective reporting on the part of Predestinarians at that time is probably the reason why extant source material on the English radicals is so slender.

Harry Adlington was 'a sawyer, and of Grinstead in the county of Sussex, and of the age of thirty years'. He was apprehended while visiting Stephen Gratwick of Brighton who was being held in Newgate.[98] This suggests that he was a member of the London Predestinarian congregation. Within a month of the composition of the above letter both writer and recipient were dead – Adlington was burned

---

94   *Ibid.*, VIII, 189.
95   *APC.*, V, 316.
96   Foxe, *AM.*, VIII, 188.
97   *Ibid.*, VIII, 151.
98   *Ibid.*, VIII, 153.

at Stratford and Careless died from natural causes in the King's Bench.

Even before John Trewe's defection the Free-willers were losing ground to the Predestinarians.[99] Now one of their leading teachers became utterly discredited in the estimation of most English Protestants. John Trewe had volunteered information to the Catholics that was highly embarrassing to Protestants, he had betrayed the trust of sympathetic warders in the King's Bench, and above all, he had fled from suffering martyrdom at the stake beside his associates Avington and Read. Trewe's faith had been put to the ultimate test and been found wanting.

That John Trewe survived the Marian regime is evident from a letter of complaint that he wrote to local magistrates *circa* 1559. At that time,
John Trewe of Hellingly complained of persecutions endured through the malice of Sir Edward Gage, 'an extreme persecutor of the Gospel', who had unlawfully placed him in the pillory in the market towns of Hailsham and Lewes, and had caused his ears to be barbarously cut.[100]
Foxe provides some additional information on these events. He states,
Likewise in Kent, one Trewe was pursued out of his house by Sir Edward Gage, and at last brought to his house, and ther layd in the dungeon: from thence had to the next market town, was set on the pillery, and lost bothe his eares, for dissuading not to come to the churche.[101]
The reference to Kent was a mistake, but Foxe published this information in 1563 and by that time John Trewe may well have been residing in Kent. It cannot be assumed with certainty that these are references to Trewe's initial arrest by a local Marian magnate and that these sufferings preceded his incarceration in the King's Bench. Was Trewe arrested late in 1553 'for dissuading not to come to the churche' because the Edwardine Prayer Book services in Hellingly parish church had been stopped and the Latin mass reintroduced? Or had Trewe's

---

[99]   Above, 165-6, 174-5, 199-200.
[100]   *VCH.*, Sussex, ed. Page, II, 23.
[101]   Foxe, *AM.*, VIII, Appendix III (1563 ed. p. 1681).

separatist principles been reasserted after the Elizabethan Settlement of 1559 and a local magistrate of Catholic sympathies taken severe action to restrain him? Sir Edward Gage was the eldest son of Sir John Gage of Firle Place, Sussex – the faithful servant of Mary Tudor. Sir Edward did not inherit the title until his father's death in April 1556.[102] This tends to support the later date, as does Trewe's own letter of protest. On the other hand, Foxe states that the Sussex prisoners had been held in the King's Bench a long time,[103] which suggests late 1553 as the time of their arrest. Furthermore, on the title page of his 1556 account of the King's Bench controversy John Trewe described himself as 'John Trewe, the unworthy marked Servant of the Lord being in bands for the testimony of Jesu'.[104] 'Marked Servant' may simply be an echo of the Lollard designation 'known man', but equally Trewe could have been referring to his lack of ears. On the whole, the earlier (1553) dating for his arrest and sufferings at the hand of Sir Edward Gage is to be preferred.

After 1559 nothing further is heard of Trewe for twenty years. Then, his name (or that of someone else with the same name) appears in a very different context. In August 1580 a John Trewe was appointed Surveyor of Works by the Commissioners for Dover Haven. Among the commissioners was the radical Puritan, Sir James Hales of Bonnington.[105] On 11 September 1580 Trewe received the Queen's commission to undertake the repair of Dover Haven, and the following November the commissioners reported to Walsingham that John Trewe was 'an able man'.[106] In January 1582 the Council ordered the discharge of Trewe, but in March 1583 he was still in the employ of the Dover Commissioners, for the order was repeated – 'John Trewe to be discharged and the workmen under him'.[107] There is one final record of this man. In December 1588 John Trewe wrote to the Queen. He prays,

... for her preservation and salvation, and though an old man, desires to be employed in the wars. He has an invention which would do as much service as 5000 men in time of extremity; and also an engine to be driven before men to defend them from the shot of the enemy. [He]

---

[102]   *DNB.*, XX, Below, 286.
[103]   Foxe, *AM.*, VIII, 151.
[104]   Laurence, 37.
[105]   *Calendar of State Papers*, Domestic 1547-1580, 671-2.
[106]   *Ibid.*, 676, 685.
[107]   *Ibid.*, Domestic, 1581-1590, 44, 103.

desires to be appointed to some office or pension.[108]
A single reference in his account of the King's Bench controversy encourages the tentative identification of John Trewe of Sussex with the elderly ex-Surveyor of Works at Dover. In his argument against the Predestinarians' doctrine of reprobation John Trewe employed an interesting illustration. He wrote,

> For it seemed to us that they made him [God] author of all the sin.... For he that maketh a thing only to do evil is the cause of the evil; as for example, we have in Sussex very many iron mills, which in wasting wood do much hurt; and yet the fault is not in the mills but only in the beginners and makers of them; they cannot go without coals, that is made of wood; no more can the reprobate live (as they affirm) without committing of actual sin.[109]

It is evident that this early conservationist was a practical man who took a real interest in the mechanics of iron mills. Moreover, for such socio-economic reasons John Trewe would have had little in common with his fellow Sussex prisoner in the King's Bench, Richard Woodman. The latter was not only a committed Predestinarian and fervent supporter of the Edwardine church – he was also the Warbleton iron master.[110]

(b) Thomas Avington/Abyngton of Ardingley.
It appears from John Bradford's two letters of January 1555 that Avington was deputy leader of the Sussex company of Free-willers. Foxe states that he was a turner from Ardingley and that the four Lewes martyrs had been in the King's Bench for a long time. However, Foxe does not supply any details of their examination or state when they were condemned. Avington was burned at Lewes with Thomas Read, Thomas Harland and John Oswald on 6 June 1556.[111]

(c) Richard Harman of Westhothleigh.
In the Privy Council record he is described as 'a sacramentarie'. On 27 May 1554 he was committed to the King's Bench for 'his leude and

---

108 *Ibid.*, 568.
109 Laurence, 42.
110 Foxe, *AM.*, VIII, 436-40; E. T. Stoneham, *Sussex Martyrs of the Reformation* (Burgess Hill, 1967), 39-47.
111 Foxe, *AM.*, VIII, 151, 430.

sedytious behaviour in Sussex'.[112] Possibly Harman had been indicted because he publicly refused to attend mass that Easter. Evidently he was still alive and in prison in January 1556 but his fate remains unknown.

(d) Thomas Arede/Read/Reed.

He probably came from Ardingley like Avington.[113] He was certainly martyred with Avington at Lewes on 6 June 1556. Foxe provides some additional information on the circumstances surrounding Arede's arrest. He states,

> Thomas Read... before he was in prison determined with himself to go to church. The night following he saw a vision, a company of tall young men in white, very pleasant to behold; to whom he would have joined himself, but it would not be. Then he looked on himself, and he was full of spots: and therewith waked, and took hold, and stood to the truth.[114]

This is reminiscent of the circumstances surrounding John Trewe's arrest – and possibly that of Richard Harman. Residual separatism and a refusal to hear mass said in the local parish church resulted in imprisonment in the King's Bench.

(e) John Jackson.

On 11 March 1556 he was examined by Doctor William Cook and then returned to the King's Bench. From there Jackson sent out an account of his examination – probably to the London underground congregation of Free-willers. Foxe published this account but knew nothing else about him. Cook began,

> 'Master Read [Sir Richard Rede, Knt.] told me, that thou wast the rankest heretic of all them in the King's Bench...'. At this Jackson replied, 'He examined five others, but not me...'.[115]

At one point in the interrogation Jackson exclaimed, 'Sir, I can be content to be tractable, and obedient to the word of God', and later he remarked, 'Yet I did tarry there long, and did talk with him'.[116] Thus, it would appear that John Jackson was as willing to talk with his

---

[112] *APC.*, V, 28.
[113] Stoneham, 31.
[114] Foxe, *AM.*, VIII, 380.
[115] *Ibid.*, VIII, 242.
[116] *Ibid.*, VIII, 243.

interrogator as John Trewe was with Doctor Martin the following month. The account concludes,

Then he said to my keeper, 'Have him to prison again'.

'I am contented with that', quoth I… Therefore, good brothers and sisters, be of good cheer: for I trust in my God, I and my other prison-fellows shall go joyfully before you.[117]

(f) John Saxbye.

Saxbye may possibly have been one of the twenty-eight signatories to the submission and confession on the Lord's Supper which some prisoners produced early in 1557.[118] Most of the signatories are listed as coming from the Colchester district, but not Saxbye. The Sussex martyr, Harry Adlington, had been held prisoner, examined, and burned along with confessors from Essex.

II. Deryck Carver of Brighton

There is no evidence to suggest that Carver was involved in the King's Bench controversy over predestination. He was never held in the King's Bench. Moreover, like John Sympson of Essex, he was martyred before the contention reached its peak. Since his views on infant baptism tended to be radical it would have been interesting to know his opinions on free will and impeccability.

Deryck Carver was a Fleming. He was born at Dilsem near Liége and for the greater part of his life he lived in Flanders.[119] In *circa* 1547 he migrated to England, settled in Brighton, and established a brewing business which rapidly prospered. Carver was about forty years old in June 1555 when he was examined before Bishop Bonner. At the time of his arrest he could not read English, but by the time of his examination some seven months later he could 'read perfectly any printed English'.[120]

On 29 October 1554 sixteen people gathered at Carver's house in Brighton to engage in worship according to the Edwardine liturgy. They were apprehended by Edward Gage, who arrested the ring leaders and sent them to London. The Privy Council committed Deryck Carver,

---

117   *Ibid.*
118   *Ibid.*, VIII, 310.
119   Foxe, *AM.*, VII, 322; VIII, Supplenda et Corrigenda.
120   *Ibid.*, VII, 321-5.

Thomas Iveson and John Launder (both from Godstone in Surrey), and William Vesie to Newgate.[121]

In his subsequent confession before Bishop Bonner, Carver admitted that 'he hath had the Bible and Psalter in English read in his house at Brighthelmstone divers times'. Moreover, 'he had the English procession said in his house, with other English prayers'.[122] It is clear from the evidence preserved by Foxe that Carver was the chief inspiration behind these gatherings, which were usually held at his house, but since he could not read English someone else must have conducted the services. Like John Trewe and the Sussex prisoners held in the King's Bench, Carver and his associates had refused to attend mass in their parish churches.[123] They were accused of doing all in their power 'to have up again the English service, and the communion in all points, as was used in the latter days of King Edward the Sixth'.[124]

On 7 June 1555 the Lord Treasurer wrote to Bishop Bonner. Among other instructions, he pointed out that there were several prisoners from Sussex being held in Newgate who had not yet been examined, and ordered Bonner to examine them without further delay.[125] The very next day the bishop had the four men brought to his residence and questioned them informally. Three days later Carver and his associates were brought before Bonner now sitting in his consistory at S. Paul's. Foxe publishes the articles that were objected against them and supplies a detailed account of Carver's subsequent martyrdom. Evidently Carver and Launder (who may have been the reader at the Brighton conventicle) remained obdurate and were condemned to be burnt for their heresy. Thomas Iveson was examined again in private by the bishop the following month. However, he could not be prevailed upon to recant his opinions and was also condemned.[126] It seems likely that William Vesie was also given a further opportunity to recant and that he availed himself of it. At any rate he was reprieved.[127] Deryck Carver, John Launder and Thomas Iveson suffered on three successive days at different towns in Sussex. Carver was burned at Lewes on 22 July 1555, Launder at Steyning the following day, and Thomas Iveson on 24 July at Chichester.

---

121   *Ibid.*, VII, 323.
122   *Ibid.*
123   *Ibid.*, VII, 325.
124   *Ibid.*, VII, 324.
125   *Ibid.*, VII, 322.
126   *Ibid.*, VII, 327-8.
127   *Ibid.*, VII, 369.

Although Foxe printed both the articles that were objected against Carver and Launder and their individual confessions submitted to Bishop Bonner, yet in Carver's case at least this was an expurgated version. Miles Hogarde, writing exactly a year after their trial, mentions these events. He writes:

> Also about xii monethes past before the reuerende father the bishop of London, there were arrayned in ye cosistorie at Paules for their opinios against the Sacrament of the altar, iiii Sussex men, the one of the^m was a ducheman & dwelled besides Lewes, who being demaunded amonge others, what baptisme was, the one aunsered, it was a sacrament, then he was demaunded whether a man myght be a christian without it: yea doubtles qd he. For it is but an externe signe and worketh litle grace.
>
> For said he, like as a ma^n doth washe his handes in a basen of water, signifying that the handes are cleane euer, so the chylde is washed at baptisme to accomplyshe the exterior figure. Then was obiected unto him the saying of Christe: unles a man be borne agayne with water and the holy ghoste he could not be saued.
>
> Tushe sayth he, the water profiteth nothyng, it is the holy ghost that worketh. Who with the rest moste worthely were condempned and burned in Sussex.[128]

In contrast, Foxe printed Thomas Iveson's answer to the article concerning baptism. Iveson stated that it was 'a sign and token of Christ, as circumcision was, and none otherwise; and he believeth that his sins are not washed away thereby, but his body only washed'.[129] Evidently Foxe considered this to be less objectionable than Carver's low opinion of the ordinance.

It is noteworthy that, like John Trewe and his associates,[130] Deryck Carver considered children to be appropriate subjects for baptism. However, for Carver the rite was 'but an externe signe [which] worketh litle grace'. The really essential factor was the subsequent regenerative

---

[128] Hogarde, *op. cit.* sig. B3ᵛ-B4ʳ.
[129] Foxe, *AM.*, VII, 327.
[130] Above, 269.

work of the Holy Spirit. Here, Carver's doctrine bears a striking resemblance to that of one of Joan Bocher's Lollard associates – William Raylond of Colchester. In 1527 Raylond stated that 'baptism in water was but a token of repentance; and when a man cometh to years of discretion, and keepeth himself clean, after the promise that his godfathers made for him, then he shall receive the baptism of the Holy Ghost.'[131]

Deryck Carver had five children, and the Brighton brewery remained the family business for several generations. His eldest son's grandson was Richard Carver, the Quaker servant of Charles II. After the Restoration, he interceded with the King and secured the release of hundreds of imprisoned Quakers.[132]

Conclusion

The extant evidence indicates that the Sussex radicals were as divided over the doctrine of predestination as their colleagues from Essex and Kent. John Trewe and his company would have encountered opposition, not only from Harry Adlington and Richard Woodman,[133] Thomas Harland and John Oswald,[134] but also from Stephen Gratwick of Brighton.[135] Moreover Deryck Carver, John Launder and Thomas Iveson each clearly identified themselves with John Bradford rather than with John Trewe.[136] Where both Sussex Free-willers and Sussex Predestinarians were in total agreement was in their attitude to the Edwardine reforms. Unlike their Kentish neighbours there is no evidence of incipient separatists in Sussex prior to 1559.

---

[131]   Strype, *EM.*, I, (i), 128.
[132]   Stoneham, 24.
[133]   Foxe, *AM.*, VIII, 333, 358.
[134]   Above 281.
[135]   Stoneham, 57.
[136]   *Ibid.*, 27-8.

B. CHRISTOPHER VITELLS AND THE ADVENT OF FAMILISM

Upon the accession of Mary Tudor all foreign Protestants were commanded to leave England, and the Strangers' Churches in London and elsewhere were dissolved.[137] The last party of refugees left London in February 1554.[138] Spiritualists among the foreigners in London would have found themselves freed from the doctrinal strait-jacket imposed by John à Lasco *et al.* Exchanging the mask of orthodox Protestantism for the less demanding mask of orthodox Romanism, they were now free to disseminate the teaching of their latest prophet – Hendrik Niclaes. Within a few years they were sponsoring a 'full-time evangelist' – Christopher Vitells.

Nicodemite practices appear to have been introduced to religious radicals in the Netherlands by David Joris – although Melchior Hofmann had set a precedent in 1533 when he called a moratorium on believers' baptism. At one point Joris urged his followers to attend the Roman mass if need be, but to 'inwardly' abstain.[139] In *circa* August 1554 John Bradford wrote a treatise entitled *The Hurt of Hearing Mass.*[140] It was probably inspired by the recent suicide of Sir James Hales[141] rather than by any threat from Continental Nicodemites. Nevertheless, there were those in England who asked:

> Whether a man or woman may ... be present at the mass with others in bodily presence, in spirit being absent, and not allowing the mass, but rather detesting it?[142]

Later, Bradford refers sarcastically to Protestants who were 'mass-gospellers' or 'spiritual gospellers'.[143] In such adverse circumstances the doctrines of the Spiritualists were bound to prove attractive to those who were already inclined towards sectarianism.

---

[137] Burn, 188; Lindeboom, 20-3.
[138] Lindeboom, 23.
[139] Menno Simons, *Works*, 1020; Horst, 112.
[140] STC. 3494. Bradford, *Works*, II, 297-351.
[141] *Ibid.*, II, 124-6; Above, 181.
[142] *Ibid.*, II, 301.
[143] *Ibid.*, II, 327, 333.

I. The Sources
(a) John Rogers

The second son of the proto-martyr, John Rogers was a scholar, lawyer, diplomat and linguist. Born and brought up at Wittenburg, he was fluent in both German and Dutch. In fact he not only criticised H.N.'s poor Latin, but also his 'rude stile' in the original Dutch – Niclaes' native language.[144] Evidently Rogers inherited his father's dislike for Anabaptism.[145]

However, while John Rogers must be accounted a hostile witness, his material must also be regarded as reliable evidence. Rogers was personally acquainted with several members of the Family of Love, including Christopher Vitells, and his *Displaying* of the Family was the product of careful research. In a preface to the first edition of this work Rogers states that his original intention in writing about Familism was not to publish it but to send it to a friend who had 'entred into that errour'.[146] Later he states that he had known several Familists for a number of years. He writes:
I have beene familiar with some of them of long time, and have had large discourses and conference with many of them.[147]
Apparently he gained their confidence for he claims – 'I was earnestly solicited by some of the Family to imbrace that way'.[148] It was as 'both an eye witnes, and eare witnesse' of the activities and teaching of the Familist elders that Rogers published his revelations concerning the sect in 1578.[149]

Furthermore, the writer was personally acquainted with 'the oldest Elder of our English Familie' – Christopher Vitells.[150] The London Familist elder 'E. R.', who entered into correspondence with Rogers following publication of *The Displaying,* accused him of seeking to

---

[144] John Rogers, *The Displaying of an horrible secte* (London, 1578) RSTC. 21181, sig. C4ʳ-C4ᵛ.
[145] Above, 56, 117.
[146] Rogers, A2ʳ.
[147] *Ibid.,* A4ᵛ.
[148] *Ibid.,* F4ᵛ.
[149] *Ibid.,* H5ʳ.
[150] *Ibid.,* E4ᵛ, I2ᵛ.

discredit Vitells who was his fellow citizen and neighbour.[151] Rogers claims to have been present at Paul's Cross in 1559 when Vitells made a public recantation – 'I heard you at *Paules Crosse* recant the blasphemies of *Arrius* doctrine'.[152] He concludes the first edition of his *Displaying* with 'An admonition to Christopher Vittell' (sig. I2[r]-I4[r]). Here Rogers issues an appeal to Vitells –

...as thou diddest before recant the errour of *Arrius*, so nowe come forth out of thy denne, and recant the blasphemie of *H. N.* [153]

One of the Familists who subsequently corresponded with Rogers denied that Christopher Vitells had recanted Arian doctrine at Paul's Cross.[154] In his reply Rogers stated that Edmund Grindal did 'participate to mee of *Christopher Vittals* behauiour longe agoe', that is, when Grindal was Bishop of London.[155] Rogers also obtained information on Vitells' activities prior to 1559 from another informant who had had personal dealings with him in his pre-Familist days – Robert Crowley.[156] Finally, John Rogers obtained a copy of the confession which two Familists made before the Surrey magistrate, Sir William More, at Guildford on 28 May 1561. Comparison with the original deposition, which is still extant among the Loseley manuscripts, reveals the accuracy of Rogers' printed version (sig. I4[v]-K3[v]).

Thus, out of this personal knowledge and painstaking research, came John Rogers' *The Displaying of an horrible secte* in 1578. It had not been his intention to publish the work, but Stephen Bateman encouraged him to do so and wrote a preface to the book.[157] Rogers' purpose was to reveal the origin, nature and extent of Familism rather than to provide a theological confutation of its doctrine. Nevertheless, he issued an invitation to 'some zealous pastour' to 'confute their doctrin by the testimonies of holy scripture'.[158] Under the sponsorship of Bishop Cox

---

[151] John Rogers, *The Displaying ... Whereunto is added certeine letters* (London, 1579) RSTC. 21182, sig. L7[v].

[152] *Ibid., Displaying* (first edition), I3[r].

[153] *Ibid.,* I3[v].

[154] *Ibid.,* (1579 edition), I6[v], M5[v].

[155] *Ibid.,* K8[r].

[156] John Rogers, *An answere vnto a wicked & infamous Libel made by Christopher Vitel* (London, 1579), RSTC. 21180, sig. L2[v].

[157] *Ibid., Displaying* (first edition), A7[r]-A8[v].

[158] *Ibid.,* H5[r]-H5[v].

of Ely, this challenge was quickly taken up by William Wilkinson and John Knewstub.[159]

These were not the only repercussions from Rogers' pioneer work. By the end of the year (1578) Rogers was receiving letters from irate Familists who claimed that he had slandered Niclaes and Vitells and misrepresented their teaching. These letters, together with his replies, Rogers added to a second edition of *The Displaying* which was published early in 1579. He also appended 'A briefe Apologie to the displaying of the Familie' (sig. O6^r-O8^v). Soon afterwards Rogers received the long-awaited response from Christopher Vitells. This appears to have been a tract in manuscript form entitled 'Testimonies of Sion'. Rogers printed it in entirety within his reply to Vitells, which was entitled *An Answere vnto a wicked & infamous Libel*. It is significant that Rogers concluded his *Answere* with an appendix on the 'state and condition of a regenerate man'. Here he prints a series of quotations from Scripture and from Familist writings to show the differences and error in H. N.'s doctrine of spiritual regeneration (sig. M7^r-N8^r).

(b) William Wilkinson
A graduate of Queen's College, Cambridge, Wilkinson was commissioned by the Bishop of Ely to produce a systematic refutation of Familist teaching. Before this, Wilkinson appears to have been involved in Andrew Perne's investigation of suspected Familists at Balsham in 1574. Although Wilkinson claims to have had 'the experience and practise of three whole yeares' in dealing with the sect,[160] his *Confutation of Certeine Articles* is not nearly so useful as Rogers' books. Like Knewstub's *Confutation*, Wilkinson's work mainly consists of arid, declamatory, theological refutations of Familist doctrine. Furthermore, despite his independent investigation into the subject, Wilkinson makes considerable use of the second edition of Rogers' *Displaying*, especially the correspondence with individual Familists. One is left with the distinct impression that neither Wilkinson nor Knewstub had direct personal acquaintance with members of the

---

[159] William Wilkinson, *A Confutation of Certaine Articles deliuered unto the Familye of Loue* (London, 1579) RSTC 25665; John Knewstub, *A Confutation of monstrous and horrible heresies, taught by H.N.* (London, 1579) RSTC 15040.

[160] Wilkinson, iii^r-iii^v.

Family of Love. Nevertheless, within his *Confutation* Wilkinson does print and preserve three testimonies from those who had been personally involved with Familism – and two of these depositions are of vital importance.

Wilkinson begins his work with an introductory essay entitled 'A very brief and true description of *the first springing up* of the Heresie termed The Familie of Loue' (sig. A2ᵛ-A5ʳ). Making use of Foxe, he maintains that the sect had its roots in the teaching of Henry Harte and the Free-willers. He then suggests that the doctrine of H. N. 'began to pepe out' and find acceptance among these religious radicals in the same year that the interrogations and death of John Careless recorded by Foxe took place, that is, 1556.[161] To justify this claim, Wilkinson reproduces the written deposition of a certain Henry Crinell of Willingham in Cambridgeshire, who was actually present 'at the brochyng of this doctrine'.[162] Apparently Crinell and a friend from St Ives had sought refuge from the Marian persecution at the King's Head in Colchester. There they found Christopher Vitells, recently arrived from Delft, teaching some new and very strange opinions and praising the life and doctrine of 'a man who liued beyond the seas' – H. N.. It is evident that Crinell made this deposition some years after that encounter. Wilkinson may well have obtained it in the course of his investigations into Familism in Cambridgeshire in the late 1570s.

Later in the *Confutation* Wilkinson cites the confession of ' a *T*. in Cambridgeshyre' (? a tailor) who was a friend of Vitells and with whom Vitells stayed when he was in the area (sig. K2ʳ-K2ᵛ). This man Wilkinson simply identifies as '*W. H.* of *B.*'. Strype suggested that the 'B' stood for Balsham,[163] and he was probably correct for Wilkinson also states that this confession was made in Cambridge 'before men of worshyp' on 24 March 1574. This suggests that the confession was obtained during Andrew Perne's investigation into Familism at Balsham in 1574.[164] It is clear that Wilkinson possessed a copy of the declaration which was made on 13 December 1574 by those of Balsham who were

---

[161]   *Ibid.*, A4ʳ.
[162]   *Ibid.*, A4ʳ-A5ʳ.
[163]   Strype, *Annals*, II (i), 486.
[164]   *Ibid.*, *Parker*, II, 381-5.

'sayd to be welwillers that way'.[165]

Finally, Wilkinson had received a first-hand report by 'a worshipfull freind in *Cambridge*' of the activities in Cambridgeshire of Thomas Allen, weaver, from Wonersh near Guildford in Surrey.[166] Allen was an early convert of Christopher Vitells and an itinerant elder of the Family of Love in the 1560s and 70s.[167]

(c) John Knewstub

A contemporary of Wilkinson at Cambridge, Knewstub was a fellow of St John's College. At Easter 1576 he had preached against the doctrines of the Family at Paul's Cross. However, his *Confutation* is of no value in an investigation into the origins of English Familism. It is in fact a turgid refutation of H. N.'s *Euangelium Regni*. The only item of value in the book is an appendix in which Knewstub prints and preserves Nicholas Carinaeus' 'A Confutation of the Doctrine of *David George and H. N.* the Father of the Familie of Loue' (sig. N1ᵛ-N4ᵛ). Carinaeus had returned to England from Emden in 1560. He was made an elder in the reconstituted Strangers' Church in London, and was involved in the controversy over Adriaan van Haemstede.[168] In exile in East Friesland Carinaeus had become acquainted with those who had known Hendrik Niclaes when he lived openly in Emden. Carinaeus had no doubts concerning the close connections and continuity between the teaching of David Joris and that of H. N.[169]

II. The Career of Christopher Vitells

According to the *DNB* and Horst, Vitells came from Delft in Holland.[170] This may be so, but if the authority for this claim is Wilkinson's statement in his introduction to Henry Crinell's deposition, then Wilkinson was referring to Vitells' re-entry into England in

---

[165] Wilkinson, S1ᵛ.
[166] *Ibid.*
[167] Rogers, *Displaying* (1579 edition), O7ᵛ; *An Answere* K1ᵛ-K2ʳ; Below 322-3, 326-328.
[168] Below, 317-8.
[169] Knewstub, N2ʳ.
[170] *DNB.*, XIV (p.428), LVIII: Horst, 153.

1555.[171] Vitells had been resident in England for many years prior to that date. Nevertheless, he may have been (as Rogers suggested) of Dutch origin; he was certainly bilingual.[172]

> Writing in 1579, John Rogers summarised Vitells' career as follows –
> Touching this Christopher Vitel... he is a ioyner by occupation, a wauering minde, and unconsta^{n}t, delighting in singularitys, & alwayes held hereticall opinions: almost this *36* yeares... who in King Henryes raigne, was unconstant, in King Edwardes raigne, a dissembler, and in Queene Maryes raigne a playne Arryan, and now in our Princes raigne, a chiefe teacher of the Familye of Loue.[173]

This indicates that he had been in England since 1543 at least. Elsewhere Rogers describes Vitells as 'sometime a Joyner of London', and as 'a ioyner, dwelling sometime in Southwarke', he also refers to the testimony of Joan Agar who said that Vitells was 'hyr cosin'.[174] This suggests that Christopher Vitells' family were among the Dutch refugees who fled to England in the late 1530s, many of whom settled in Southwark.[175] After Vitells became an itinerant Familist elder, his wife continued to live in London.[176] As a fellow wood-worker residing in the same city, and having a similar interest in radical sectarianism, Vitells may well have made the acquaintance of Henry Harte.[177]

Both Rogers and Wilkinson imply that Vitells was a very able man. Rogers states that, knowing the capacity of Vitells as he did, he was sure that Vitells was aware of the implications of H. N.'s teaching. Wilkinson states that he was reputed to be a very skilful joiner.[178] Among the Familists themselves Vitells was deeply respected. He had organised their conventicles in the 1560s, he had translated into English and published Niclaes' manifold writings in the 1570s (no less than eight of his books appeared in English in 1574), and it was he who

---

171   Wilkinson, A4^r.
172   Rogers, *An Answere*, E8^v, H8^r, K2^r.
173   *Ibid.*, K3^r.
174   *Ibid.*, A2^v, L3^r; *Displaying* (first edition), B4^r.
175   Above, 25-8, 30, 114-5.
176   Rogers, *Displaying* (first edition), E4^v.
177   Above, 185-6.
178   Rogers, *Displaying* (first edition), I2^v; Wilkinson, N3^v.

produced both *An Apology* for Familism and *A Brief Rehersal* of Familist doctrine in 1575.[179]

Like several of the religious radicals examined in this study Vitells seems to have been an inveterate individualist. Rogers comments,

... in deede, they that haue truely noted your disposition, doe affirme, that you could neuer lyke of any publick doctrine, which was taught: but had alwayes a desire of singularitye:[180]

It is quite clear that both Rogers and Wilkinson believed Vitells to be the sole agent by whom the teaching of H. N. was introduced to England and transmitted to native Englishmen. Rogers states that Vitells was 'the only man which was the occasion that any of *HN* his doctrine became conuersant with our natiue Countrey people'. Later he writes,

... I haue uttered you to be yᵉ onely man, yᵗ hath brought this wicked doctrine of *HN*. which lay hidden in the Dutch tongue, among our simple English people.[181]

Wilkinson introduces Crinell's deposition as an account of 'the brochyng of this doctrine by *Vitels* the Joygner'. Later he refers to Vitells as the Familists' 'Elder and *chief Patriarch*'.[182] There does not appear to be any concrete evidence to support the long-standing supposition that Hendrik Niclaes himself visited England. In fact, Rogers – appealing to English Familists – exclaims, 'Alas, why are you so bewitched... [by] an obscure Authour, whome you neuer sawe nor knewe...?'[183]

According to Rogers, in the early 1540s Vitells was 'unconstant'. Presumably this means that Vitells was not among those fervent sacramentarians of London who publicly defied King Henry's Six Articles and were punished. It may even mean that he had publicly recanted sacramentarian opinions at that time. Rogers further states that Vitells concealed his real beliefs during Edward's reign. This suggests

---

179   Rogers, *An Answere*, preface, sig. iiᵛ, D4ʳ; *Displaying* (first edition), B4ʳ; Wing STC. N1122; Wing STC. B4621.
180   Rogers, *An Answere*, L4ʳ.
181   *Ibid.*, A2ʳ, K2ʳ.
182   Wilkinson, A4ʳ, A5ʳ.
183   Rogers, *Displaying* (first edition), G1ʳ; N. A. Penrhys-Evans, 'The Family of Love in England, 1550-1650' (unpublished Kent M. A. dissertation, 1971), 29-30.

that he was among those Davidist Spiritualists who sympathised with Joan Bocher. If so, he was even more prudent than Henry Harte because his name does not figure in any records of heresy at that time. Nevertheless, it was almost certainly during the reign of Edward VI that Christopher Vitells was confronted with Reformed theology, rejected it, and embraced anti-trinitarianism. At several points in his books Rogers accused Vitells of being a teacher of 'Arianism' before he was converted to H. N.'s doctrine. He asks:

> What was the cause that moued you, first to embrace that wicked sect of Arrius, and many yeares became a leader of many pore soules into that gulfe of mischiefe … show some reason that moued you to forsake that opinion, and imbrace this absurde impietye of *HN*…[184]

Previously in his *Displaying* Rogers had accused him of being a teacher of Arianism for a number of years.[185] Indeed, he states that Vitells was an Arian teacher 'all the dayes of *Queene Marie*'. Vitells in his reply admitted that he 'had in some poyntes bin deceiued, by certayne straungers', and that he confessed this at Paul's Cross in 1559. Rogers responded,

> … you confessed then, you were deceaued by certayne straungers: and haue you not as great cause to suspect your selfe deceaued now, by HN. a straunger in nation, and estraunged from God, and Christ, in his doctrine…[186]

Taken at its face value, Vitells' confession indicates that he had been influenced by anti-trinitarian foreign refugees – possibly members of the Strangers' Church in London – at some point in the reign of King Edward VI.

It is apparent that Rogers obtained his information on Vitells' pre-1559 Arian activities from Robert Crowley. He writes,

> I will put you in minde of the disputations, and conference, that diuers men had with you in Queene Maryes dayes: M. Ro. Crowley a reuerent and godly preacher yet liuing who affirmeth, y^t several times he disputed with you, concerning the blasphemy of Arryus, and you continually denied Christ Jesus to be God, equall with his Father: and

---

[184]   Rogers, *An Answere*, B8^v-C1^r.
[185]   *Ibid.*, *Displaying* (first edition), E4^r, G2^r, I3^r-I3^v.
[186]   *Ibid.*, *An Answere*, L1^v, L3^v.

immoveably you remained all her raigne of that minde: and this M. Crowley is redy to auouch...[187]
However Crowley fled the country during Mary's reign. By the Autumn of 1555 he was in Frankfurt, and he did not return to London until 1559.[188] Therefore, the discussions which Crowley had with Vitells over trinitarian doctrine must have taken place in 1553-4, before he left England. Crowley cannot have known from his own experience that Vitells remained an anti-trinitarian throughout Mary Tudor's reign. He must have obtained this information from someone else. The most likely source is the witness whose testimony Rogers cites immediately after Crowley's affirmation. Rogers continues,

> Also one *Ione Agar*, an olde mayde, which wayted on those in office for the Cittye, as Mayors, and shrieffes, did declare to M. Fulkes the Elder [Christopher Fulkes], and others, that you Christopher Vitell, whome she named to be hyr cosin, had taught her playnely, that Christ was not God: but onely a good man, and a Prophet: and that there were men that shee did know liuing, that were as good, and as holy men, as he was: and further, that Maister Latimer, Maister Ridley, and others (which gaue their lyfe for Christes cause) were starke fooles, and did not well in suffering death:[189]

Evidently this instruction must have been given after the death of Latimer and Ridley, and therefore after Vitells' return to England in the Summer of 1555. Henry Crinell's account of the content of Vitells' teaching at the King's Head in Colchester in August 1555 indicates that, while he had been influenced by Niclaes, he still retained many of his former opinions. He continued to deny the divinity of Christ and to advocate perfectionism.[190]

It is suggested, therefore, that Vitells – like other anti-trinitarians[191] – was opposed to the re-introduction of the Roman Mass at the beginning of Mary's reign, that he fled to the Continent in 1554-5, that there he came under the influence of Niclaes and embraced Nicodemism, and that this outward conformity enabled him to return to England in the summer of 1555 and continue his teaching ministry unmolested.

---

[187]   *Ibid.*, L2ᵛ.
[188]   Garrett, 137-8.
[189]   Rogers, *An Answere*, L2ᵛ-L3ʳ.
[190]   Wilkinson, A4ᵛ.
[191]   Above, 154-8.

In the *Displaying* Rogers commences with a brief account of the career of Hendrik Niclaes. He states that he had obtained his information from members of the Dutch church in London who had lived 'in one citie [Emden] and in one streete' with Niclaes.[192] In his *Answere* Rogers responds to Vitells' criticisms of inaccuracies in Rogers' account of H. N. by stating that he had produced it from the testimony of 'his honest neighboures who knew him better then you, longer then you, and before you knew him'.[193] Rogers goes on to suggest that Vitells was 'not acquainted with H. N. nor his doctrine' at the time that Niclaes fled from Emden.[194] However, although Vitells did not become acquainted with Niclaes until 1554-5, he certainly knew him before he was detected to the authorities and forced to leave Emden. Hendrik Niclaes lived in Emden for twenty years and did not leave the city until 1560.[195] There he had developed a flourishing business as a mercer, which entailed regular commercial ventures to Holland, Flanders and France.[196] Vitells may have first met H. N. in Delft when the latter was engaged on one of these business trips.

In his 'Testimonies of Sion' Vitells gives an account of his conversion to Familism. It is couched in the usual esoteric phraseology of the Spiritualists and is difficult to interpret. Nevertheless, it appears that Vitells underwent some crisis experience involving great mental conflict, and that he found deliverance from this trouble through the teaching of H. N. As a result, Vitells rejected rationalist dogma and confessionalism, and adopted a quietist stance towards religious controversy and a Nicodemite attitude to the authorities. Referring to his subsequent recantation at Paul's Cross, Vitells wrote –

...man will iudge the workes of the Lord with his naturall wisdome, or lernedenes. And hereout, namely, out of the wisdome of the flesh, sprang all Christopher Vitelles errors... for mine own sinnes were greater and horribler in my sight, then all other mennes... but the troble that I was in, whereout the Lord delyuered me, is not to be expressed. And if the Lord of his goodnes had not comforted me with

192 Rogers, *Displaying* (first edition), A4ᵛ.
193 *Ibid., An Answere*, E4ᵛ.
194 *Ibid.*, E7ʳ-E7ᵛ.
195 *DNB.*, XL; *ME.*, III.
196 *Ibid.*

his holy spirite, through his most holy seruice of his loue, broght forth through *HN.* his elected minister, I should haue remained without hope of life.[197]

The trouble to which Vitells refers here may have been the difficulties that he experienced with Bishop Grindal and the High Commission in 1559, but it is more likely to have been his flight from the Marian persecution in 1554-5. This is supported by a previous description of his conversion. Vitells states:

Now when the Lord of his goodnes, had released me out of my blindnes... then saw I, that all people vpon earth which were without the house of Loue, were all wrapped in vnbeliefe: and that there was nothing among them but variaunce, stryfe, and contention... and euery one would haue right, and be the comminaltye of Christ, and condemned all others for heretickes... And I saw that by that occasion there was much murmuring, uprore, rebellion, disobedience to God, and to spirituall and temporall gouernors.[198]

Here he appears to be referring to disputes over trinitarian doctrine and resistance to the re-introduction of the Roman mass, as well as to the King's Bench controversy over free-will. Vitells' reaction against rationalism and rejection of all forms of confessionalism, whether trinitarian or anti-trinitarian, may well have been a gradual process. It started when he met Hendrik Niclaes in the Netherlands in 1554-5 and culminated with his recantation of 'Arianism' (Vitells preferred to interpret it as a recantation of rationalism in general[199]) at Paul's Cross in 1559.

William Wilkinson was utterly convinced that Familist teaching was introduced into England by Christopher Vitells in 1555. He asserts:

Before the dayes of *Queene Mary*, or *An. 1555* at the furthest, this Louely Familie was neuer sene nor heard of, onely the hatchers of this Familie, the Libertines, the *Arrians*, the *Anabaptistes*, the *Free will men*, and *Catharistes* were then extant: but as yet this broode of *Locustes* had not broken out of the bottomlesse pitte neither had it the name of Loue, which it now hath.[200]

---

[197] Rogers, *An Answere*, K4r-K6v.
[198] *Ibid.*, C5v -C7v.
[199] *Ibid.*, L6r.
[200] Wilkinson, D2r.

The heresy was 'brought into England by Christopher Vitels and his complices out of Delph in Dutchland'.[201] Henry Crinell's deposition begins,

About the third yeare of Q. *Maries* raigne. *An. 1555* at Michaelmas or not much after, I *Henry Crinell* of *Willingham* in the County of *Ca^{m}bridge* came to the towne of *Colchester* where I happened into a co^{m}mon Inne.[202]

Crinell had fled from Willingham with William Raven of St. Ives in order to avoid persecution arising from their refusal to attend mass in their local parish churches. The inn where they lodged was almost certainly the King's Head, for there Crinell encountered 'diuers of myne acquaintance... who came thether to conferre concernyng the safetie of their conscience'.[203] Crinell continues:

There we founde at our commyng thether one *Christopher Vitels* a Ioigner, who so farre as I could at that tyme learne held many straunge opinions, and also taught diuers points of doctrine scarce fou^{n}d and to me before unheard of.[204]

Furthermore, Vitells spoke of a man 'who liued as he sayd beyond the seas an holy life and an upright conuersation. This man he praysed very much, and reported many wonderfull thyngs of his Angellike behauiour'. Crinell adds that later he learned that Vitells was referring to 'one *Henry Nicholas* a Mercer of *Delph* in *Holland*'.[205] Actually Niclaes was never a resident of Delft, but after he fled from Emden in 1560 he settled at Kampen in Holland. Evidently Vitells had met Niclaes, perhaps in Delft, and been deeply impressed.

Crinell then lists particular 'pointes of Hereticall doctrine' which Vitells did 'then and there' teach. These were: –

1. Children ought not to be Baptised, untill they come to yeares of discretion.
2. He founde fault with the Letany in the booke of Common prayer set forth in King Edwardes tyme, affirming that it was not the right seruice of God.
   1. Because it was sayd, God the Sonne redeemer of the world: for (sayth he) Christ is not God.

---

[201] *Ibid.*, A4^{r}.
[202] *Ibid.*
[203] *Ibid.*
[204] *Ibid.*
[205] *Ibid.*, A4^{v}.

2. Because it was sayd, Haue mercy upon us miserable sinners, for the godly sinne not (sayth hee) and therefore, neede they not to use that prayer.

3. He affirmed also that the Pope was not Antichrist, but he which doth not that which Gods law commaundeth, neither fulfilleth the requiring therof he is Antichrist, & so are there many Antichristes.[206]

This account of Vitells' teaching at Colchester in 1555 tends to corroborate Joan Agar's testimony concerning his subsequent teaching in London. Again there are indications that at this stage Vitells' doctrine was in transition. Point one was not a specifically Familist tenet, but an attitude towards baptism shared by a number of sectarians who were influenced by Continental radicalism. Niclaes himself tended to spiritualise the rite.[207] Point two serves to confirm Rogers' assertion that Vitells disliked 'publick doctrine'. The latter's first objection to the Litany is that of an anti-trinitarian who denied the divinity of Christ. Vitells' second objection is based on an extreme perfectionism which he may have derived from the doctrine of H.N. Point three was almost certainly a new and important feature of Vitells' teaching, derived from his recent contact with Niclaes.

Evidently Vitells made a considerable impression upon the 'Gospellers' who assembled at the King's Head. Crinell describes how John Barre (probably the leading separatist teacher in the region) was sent 'to reason with the Ioigner about the Diuinitie of Christ'.[208] The confounding of Barre greatly disturbed those who witnessed the debate. In fact Crinell asserts, 'I was fully mynded to go to *Oxford* to aske cousaile of Byshop *Ridley* & M. *Latimer* cocernyng that matter'.[209] In the event he did not make the journey, and Latimer and Ridley were burned a few weeks later (16 October 1555). Crinell continues:

The truth of the report of this conference I referre unto the remembraunce of the sayd *Iohn Barry* himselfe if he be aliue as to others also, who were present at that conflict.[210]

---

[206] *Ibid.*

[207] *Ibid.*, E3ᵛ-E4ʳ ;Rogers, *Displaying* (first edition), H1ᵛ-H2ᵛ; *Displaying* (1579 edition), K1ʳ-K1ᵛ.

[208] Above, 130-1.

[209] Wilkinson, A4ᵛ.

[210] *Ibid.*, A5ʳ.

The deposition concludes with a reference to a subsequent attempt by Vitells to contact Crinell in Willingham after Vitells had become a full-time itinerant elder of the Family. Crinell then signed the deposition 'with myne owne hand' – 'By me Henry Orinell [printer's error] of Willingham'.[211]

The next information on the career of Christopher Vitells concerns his recantation at Paul's Cross in 1559. In his *Displaying* Rogers described Vitells as,

a man that all the dayes of *Queene Marie* was a teacher of these famous heretiques the *Arrians*, and at *Paules Crosse* did solemnly in the first yeare of our souereine Ladie *Queene Elizabeth*, recant the same errours, as by the register of ye bishop of Londo^n doth manifestly apeare.[212]

In the correspondence that arose from the publication of these revelations one of the Familists denied that Vitells had ever made such a recantation. Rogers replied that he had obtained the information during a conversation with Edmund Grindal himself.[213] Vitells' own explanation of this event is highly equivocal. He writes:

Co^{n}cerning Christophers being at Paules Crosse, and the cause why he came there: that can my Lord Byshop, doctor Grindall declare best: For he knoweth, he found me in no error, and so he there sayd: neither had he any law, to compell me to come thether: but he desired me to come & co^{n}fesse that I held no such opinio^n, or error, wherby the false brute might be stayed, which went of me, so I accomplished his request therein, albeit I co^{n}fessed, that I had in some poyntes bin deceiued, by certayne straungers etc.[214]

To this, Rogers retorts –

…there are many yet liuing, that were prese^{n}t & doe verefy what I haue sayd: & touching my L. of Cant. whom you appeale unto: if ye case be so, as you haue affirmed: then is he worthy great blame to desire any ma^n to reca^{n}t, which is in no error, & come to such a famous place, as Paules Crosse is.[215]

Later Rogers adds,

211   *Ibid.*
212   Rogers, *Displaying* (first edition), E4^r.
213   *Ibid., Displaying* (1579 edition), I6^v, K8^r, M5^v..
214   *Ibid., An Answere*, L1^r-L1^v.
215   *Ibid.*, L1^v.

... but the trueth is, that you were prisoner in the counter in woodstret, by commaundement of the Byshop that then was, and there is your name regestred: and your comming was not voluntary, as you untruely affirme: but coacted by the law. Magestrates use not to desire men to come to publick place, to confesse their heresies: but the law it selfe doth urge it, and you, according to the law, for your releasement out of prison, did recant at the Crosse: and named your error, to be Arrianisme: whether you did it from the hart, that the Lord God knoweth.[216]

In his previous book Rogers had stated that he was present at Paul's Cross when Vitells made his recantation. Wilkinson also mentions this event, referring to Vitells' 'open' and 'harty repentaunce'.[217]

There is some difficulty over Rogers' dating of this recantation to 'the first yeare' of Elizabeth I. Bishop Bonner was not deprived of the see of London until 30 May 1559 and Grindal was not consecrated to the bishopric until 21 December 1559 – which was actually the second year of Elizabeth's reign. It may be that Vitells was imprisoned in the Counter by Bishop Bonner, and that he was examined by Grindal after the latter had been nominated to the see of London. The Court of High Commission was established on 19 July 1559, and Grindal was among the commissioners. He may have examined Vitells in his capacity as a Commissioner rather than as prospective Bishop of London. Thus, the recantation seems to have taken place in the Autumn of 1559. It appears from Vitells' explanation that he regarded the event as signifying his final rejection of the 'false brute' of human reason. Others identified this 'brute' as anti-trinitarianism or 'Arianism', but Vitells preferred to label it as unregenerate thinking or 'naturall wisdome'. After making this recantation Vitells was 'receiued into the Churche'.[218] By this means he outwardly identified himself with the established Church of England.

However, Vitells' appearance at Paul's Cross also signified the moment of his total commitment to the Family of Love. After his release from prison Christopher Vitells became a full-time agent of H.N.,

---

[216] *Ibid.*, L2^r.

[217] *Ibid., Displaying* (first edition), I3^r; Wilkinson, A5^r.

[218] Wilkinson, A5^r.

visiting his former radical associates, organising conventicles, and maintaining himself on the collections that were taken at their meetings. Crinell deposed:

> The which Ioigner... beyng as it seemed weary of his occupation, left his craft of Ioigning, and tooke unto him a new trade of lyfe: so that of a simple scholer he became a great and learned Scholemaister of the doctrine.[219]

Rogers accused him of leaving his 'arte and calling to liue meere ydlely, by sowing heresies'.[220] In his *Answere* Rogers asserted that many adherents of the Family had been, 'very disorderly impouerished by your vngodly collections, thorow which maintenaunce, you haue continued too long.' Subsequently he states that Vitells had itinerated 'the most part of this *20* yeares', that is, since 1559.[221] A decade or so later Vitells financed the publication of his translations of the writings of Niclaes by means of special collections. Referring to the Familists' advocacy of poverty and simplicity, Rogers accused Vitells of being responsible for the aptness of the epithet 'poore Family'. He writes:

> ...you are the cause therof, for with your manyfold collections to set out the Authors works, you haue in deede made many an honest & wealthy housholder poore, as I can testifie, and name the parties.[222]

Rogers also maintained that leading English Familists regularly travelled over to Flanders (presumably to Kampen) to consult Hendrik Niclaes.[223]

The translation and dissemination of Niclaes' works in England which began in 1574 attracted public attention to the sect. When the following year Vitells' *Apology for the Service of Love* was presented to Parliament and subsequently published, followed by his *A Brief Rehersal of the Belief of the Good-willing in England*, the ecclesiastical establishment was thoroughly alarmed. Puritan preachers began to denounce the sect, bishops ordered investigations into Familism in their dioceses, and Vitells in particular became a marked man. He seems to

---

219 *Ibid.*, A4^r-A4^v, N3^v.
220 Rogers, *Displaying* (first edition), I3^r.
221 *Ibid., An Answere*, preface, sig.iii^v; I5^v.
222 *Ibid.*, E3^v.
223 *Ibid.*, E2^r; *Displaying* (first edition), B4^v.

have gone into hiding, for in his *Answere* Rogers asks – 'why suffer you your schollers to be troubled and imprysoned? but for your selfe you are safe inough?'[224] Perhaps some well-connected Familist was protecting him. However, on 3 October 1580 a royal proclamation was issued proscribing the Family of Love,[225] and thereafter the sect rapidly disappeared from public view. Vitells probably fled the country after the suppression of 1580. Penrhys-Evans suggests that he sought refuge with the English printer Thomas Basson at Leiden, and that it was Basson who supported the elderly and impoverished Vitells during his last days.[226]

III. The Success of Christopher Vitells
In many respects Christopher Vitells was the ideal agent to represent Hendrik Niclaes in England and transmit his teaching to Englishmen. Vitells was a skilled artisan and possessed a similar social background to that from which most English separatists were drawn. Like Niclaes he was of Dutch extraction, but he had lived in England for many years – possibly since childhood. He was bilingual.[227] Above all, he was very persuasive.[228]

As an anti-trinitarian Vitells already possessed many contacts within English radical sectarianism, and it was from among these extreme radicals that the first English recruits of the Family were drawn. Rogers maintained that English Familism was constructed upon a combination of recalcitrant Free-willers and individual anti-trinitarians. He states:
Nowe if I mighte utter my simple coniecture touching the saide Familie… their beginning was in Englang [*sic.*] about the latter end of Queene *Maries* raigne, when many of our brethren were entred into that gulfe of freewill… and likewise certeine *Arrians*, with *Pellagians* ioyning together, found an author for their purpose, under a newe deuised name of *Familie of Loue*.[229]

---

224   *Ibid., An Answere*, D3ʳ; *Displaying* (first edition), G1ʳ, I3ᵛ. Rogers also asserts that Vitells had not visited his wife in London for two years, that is, since 1576 (*Displaying*, first edition, sig. E4ᵛ).
225   *TRP.*, II, 474-5.
226   Penrhys-Evans, 115-8.
227   Rogers, *An Answere*, H8ʳ.
228   *Ibid., Displaying* (first edition), E5ᵛ, G1ᵛ.
229   *Ibid., Displaying* (1579 edition), O7ᵛ.

In fact, Henry Crinell's deposition reveals that Familism made its initial appearance in England somewhat earlier – at Colchester in the summer of 1555. All the extant evidence suggests that these elements were welded together into conventicles, and the entire Familist movement in England organised, solely by Christopher Vitells. Doubtless, the movement really began to gain momentum with the death of Henry Harte *circa* 1557. Thereafter – despite the presence on the periphery of Robert Cooche and John Champneys – Vitells' authority appears to have gone unchallenged. William Wilkinson agreed with Rogers that Free-willer followers of the late Henry Harte formed the basis of the Family.[230] Items 24-26 in the confession made by two Surrey Familists on 28 May 1561 confirm that at that early date they were still fervent anti-trinitarians.[231]

The members of the Family were for the most part poor, simple, rustics.[232] However, Rogers complains that 'not a few ministers of the simple sort are herwith intangled'.[233] In addition the Familists gained recruits at the court of Queen Elizabeth – 'I wold to God that the chiefest place in this realme were free of these men', exclaims Rogers.[234] Seventy years later, Samuel Rutherford published evidence to show that Elizabethan courtiers had embraced Familism.[235] The elders of the Family were generally itinerant artisans. Wilkinson supplies an interesting, if prejudiced, account of their activities. He writes:

> And so it is with the chief Elders of our Louely Fraternitie, some of them be Weauers, some Basketmakers, some Musitians, some Botlemakers, and such other lyke which by trauailyng from place to place, do get their lyuyng. They whiche amongst them beare the greatest countenaunce, are such as, hauyng by their smoth behauiour... gotten Licences to trade for Corne up & downe the countrey, and using such romyng kynde of Traffique... stay not for the most part any where long together, saue where they hit upon some simple husbandman, whose wealth is greater then his wit, and his wit greater then a care to keepe him selfe up right in God his truth and sincere Religion. His house if it be farre from company, and stand out

---

230 Wilkinson, A3ᵛ.
231 Rogers, *Displaying* (first edition), I8ʳ-I8ᵛ. See Appendix Document IV.
232 *Ibid.*, B4ʳ; *An Answere*, A4ᵛ,I5ᵛ.
233 *Ibid., Displaying* (first edition), F5ᵛ.
234 *Ibid.*
235 Above, 260.

of the common walke of the people, is a fit neast wherin all the byrdes of that fether use to meete together.[236]
Rogers accused Vitells of lodging with wealthy adherents until they could afford to entertain him no longer.[237] One of these patrons was Thomas Chaundler, a clothier from Wonersh in Surrey. By 1561 he was totally disillusioned and made the confession before a local magistrate – Sir William More – which Rogers partially published in his *Displaying*.[238] The first point that Chaundler made in this lengthy deposition was –

First, they be generally all unlearned, saving that some of them can reade English, and that not verie perfectly, and of them that can so reade they have chosen Bishops, Elders, and Deacons.[239]

In the second item Chaundler described a Familist conventicle –

2. Their Bishops, Elders or Deacons, do call those that be of their sect together, by the name of a congregation, into one of their disciples houses, which they call also a *Raab*: where they commonly meet, to the number of thirtie or above, and their Bishop or Deacon doth reade unto the congregation the Scriptures, expounding the same according to his owne fansie.[240]

Items four and five doubtless reflect Chaundler's own bitter experience–

4. At their meeting, either to receiue a new brother, or to reade the scripture, they all have meate, drinke, & lodging at the cost and charges of the owner of the house whome they call a *Raab*: and there they doe remaine as long as he hath good victualles for them, wherby sometimes they doe loose their *Raab*, seeing himselfe so farre overcharged with them.

5. They are called together ever in the night time: and commonly to suche houses as be far from neighbours, one of them doth always warne an other: and when they come to the house of meeting, they knocke at the doore, saying: here is a Brother in Christ, or a Sister in Christ.[241]

Notwithstanding Chaundler's defection, the Familist conventicle at Wonersh flourished under the leadership of Thomas Allen and was still

---

236 Wilkinson, K2^v-K3^r.
237 Rogers, *An Answere*, E3^v.
238 *Ibid., Displaying* (first edition), I4^v-K3^v; Below, 328-34.
239 *Ibid.*, I4^v.
240 *Ibid.*
241 *Ibid.*, I5^r-I5^v.

in existence in 1579.[242] There was a Familist conventicle in London, where Rogers' correspondent E.R. was the elder.[243] Conventicles which were in existence in the early 1560s at Balsham and Wisbech in Cambridgeshire were still active in the late 1570s, under the leadership of Edmund Rule and John Bourne respectively.[244] Doubtless there were several more. The complexity of the Familist system and its steady growth in numbers and influence during the 1560s and 70s can largely be attributed to the energetic and skilful manner in which Christopher Vitells applied the doctrines of Hendrik Niclaes to the English situation.

Undoubtedly the chief attraction of H.N.'s teaching, particularly during the Marian persecution, was his Nicodemism. In his 'Testimonies of Sion' Vitells emphasised their insistence on obedience to all magistrates.[245] Rogers replied:

> You may ioyne wᵗ any Church... for you perswaded many in Queene Maries raigne to go to Masse: your brethren in Flanders which are of your Family do the lyke, you also with us come to Church and ioyne wᵗ us in praier, in geuing thanks in hearing the worde preached etc. Yet haue you priuate conuentickles and meetings forbidden by the law, wherin you shewe (not your obedience to the Maiestrates as you affirme) but your wilfull stubburnes and frowardnes: you ioyne with all, to wyne all: but more iustly you flatter with all, to deceaue all.[246]

Wilkinson confirms Rogers' accusation –

> For hereby in yᵉ tyme of Papistry he [H.N.] had his faultors also whom by the *Suthwarke Ioyner* he licensed to be present at Idolaters seruice, and to keepe their consciences secret unto themselues...[247]

Subsequently, Wilkinson repeats that Vitells had 'infected diuers honest and godly men in the troublesome tyme of Q. Marye by perswading

242   *Ibid., Displaying* (1579 edition), O7ᵛ.

243   *Ibid.*, L2ᵛ-L8ᵛ; Wilkinson, B2ʳ-B2ᵛ, Q4ᵛ.

244   *Ibid., Displaying* (first edition), I7ᵛ; G. L. Blackman, 'The Career and Influence of Bishop Richard Cox, 1547-1581' (unpublished, Cambridge Ph.D. thesis, 1953), 140-53; Penrhys-Evans, 84-6; Felicity Heal, 'The Family of Love and the Diocese of Ely', *Studies in Church History* IX (1972), ed. Baker, 213-222.

245   Rogers, *An Answere*, G2ʳ, C7ᵛ.

246   *Ibid.*, G2ᵛ.

247   Wilkinson, I3ʳ.

them that they might keepe their consciences to themselues, and be preset at the masse'.[248] The testimony of Thomas Chaundler provides a connection between the known initial reaction of Kentish anti-trinitarians to the re-introduction of the Roman Mass in 1553-4[249] and the subsequent teaching of Christopher Vitells in 1555. Item Ten of Chaundler's 1561 deposition reads:

> In the beginning of Queen *Maries* time, they would not come to the Church, thinking it damnable so to do: but within a yere after, they were changed from that opinion, openly declaring unto their brethren, that they were al bound to come unto the church, and to doe outwardly, there, all suche thinges as the Law required then at their handes, upon paine of damnation, although inwardely they did professe the contrarie.[250]

Chaundler's statement also confirms the independent testimony of Joan Agar and Henry Crinell concerning Vitells' teaching on observance of the Roman innovations during the Marian period.[251] Thus, from 1555 onwards Vitells (under the influence of Niclaes) advocated outward conformity to the established religion, and thereby his followers gained immunity from persecution. He told frightened simple separatists what they longed to hear. In such circumstances it was hardly surprising that his teaching made an impact, or that Vitells succeeded in gathering conventicles of admiring disciples.

There remains one further piece of evidence concerning the type of person who supported Vitells, and from among whom the Family of Love derived its recruits. Wilkinson cited the confession of W.H. the (?) tailor of (?) Balsham. He states:

> There is a *T.* in Cambridgeshyre, who was *Vitelles* companion, who was a flat Arrian, as by his owne hand I am able to auouch, and before men of worshyp *Anno. 1574* March *24.* in Cabridge denyed Christ to be God equal with his father. 2. He said that children are not by nature sinfull neither ought to be Baptised tell yeares of discretion. 3. The Regenerate sinne not. 4. S. Paule his Epistles be not to be

---

248 *Ibid.*, S2^r-S2^v.
249 Above, 154-8.
250 Rogers, *Displaying* (first edition), I6^r.
251 *loc. cit.*

more accompted of, then the letters of priuate men.[252]
The first three items correspond with opinions which, according to the
depositions of Henry Crinell and Joan Agar, Vitells held in the Marian
period. They also correspond with items in the 1561 confession of
Thomas Chaundler.[253] Wilkinson continues:

This man beyng then a flat *Arrian*, since once recanted his errour, and
secondly is falne into the same opinion. His name is *W.H.* of *B.*
perhaps unto the Family he is not unknowen, for that *Vitels* had
sometymes lodged in his house, and hee useth to conferre with them
concernyng their opinions: this man would seeme in the company of
simple men to be very learned, and they that haue talked with him
affirme, that he hath many wordes but small wisedome, beyng of a
wealthy occupation but smal in wit...[254]

It is significant that .W.H's confession was made on 24 March 1574.
Among the signatories to the declaration made by those suspected of
Familism at Balsham, dated 13 December 1574, none bore the initials
W.H.[255] Furthermore, Wilkinson does not actually state that W.H. was a
Familist. White Vitells had stayed in his house on several occasions he
had never succeeded in recruiting him into the Family. Although W.H.
was prepared to confer with Familists and discuss their doctrine, he
remained in 1574 a rationalist anti-trinitarian individualist. 'W.H. of B.'
belonged to the old school of extreme religious radicalism found in the
Edwardine and Marian periods. Vitells had once belonged to the same
group, and it was from this constituency that he won his first English
converts to Familism, but he never succeeded in securing the allegiance
of 'W.H. of B.' to the doctrines of Hendrik Niclaes.

Thus, it is suggested that between 1555 and 1558 Familism gained a firm
foothold among separatist conventiclers because of the Marian
persecution. The first members of the Family of Love were individual
rationalists who denied orthodox Christology, advocated anti-
trinitarianism, and vigorously opposed the introduction of Reformed
theology in the Edwardine period. Soon afterwards they were joined by
those fervent Free-willers who were most convinced of the possibility of

---

[252] Wilkinson, K2^v.
[253] Rogers, *Displaying* (first edition), I8^r-I8^v.
[254] *loc cit.*
[255] *loc. cit.*

moral perfection after spiritual regeneration. Other simple 'Gospellers', who all their lives had supported the former Lollard conventicles, may simply have been attracted to the Family by its Nicodemism and the immunity from persecution which this afforded.

Conclusion

With the accession of Mary Tudor in the summer of 1553, the English religious radicals came under more intense physical pressure to conform to the religious establishment. Some of them, like John Champneys, Thomas Cole and Thomas Putto, had already yielded. As refugees from persecution Free-willers and Predestinarians were thrown together in secret 'underground' churches and, of course, in prison. By 1556 the Free-willer movement was in decline as many of its more able sympathisers such as Thomas Upchard, Robert Cole, and possibly John Barre, accepted both a modified version of 'Calvinism' and the Edwardine liturgy. However, in that year the Free-willers experienced something of a revival with the appearance in London of the doyen of the movement, Henry Harte. Shortly afterwards their prestige suffered a severe blow when John Trewe defected, but they were greatly encouraged by the circulation of Robert Cooche's treatise 'The confutation of the errors of the careless by necessitie'. Meanwhile, the new teaching of Christopher Vitells had begun to make an impact among fearful 'Gospellers'. These developments caused much anxiety among the Predestinarian congregations, and so they sought help from their brethren in exile on the Continent. That assistance arrived in 1557. The London Predestinarian congregation was reorganised and disciplined under new leadership, and experienced considerable increase during the closing eighteen months of Mary's reign. By then Henry Harte was dead, and Christopher Vitells had gained pre-eminence among the more radical separatists.

Chapter Four

The English Radicals Under Elizabeth I, 1558-65

Introduction

Included within the first piece of legislation enacted by Queen Elizabeth's first parliament (January-May 1559) was a section repealing the heresy laws that had been revived under the Marian regime.[1] Nevertheless, the first year and more of the new Queen's reign were months of great uncertainty for committed Protestants.[2] The Acts of Supremacy and Uniformity became law in the spring of 1559, but it was not until the autumn of that year that new bishops were nominated to fill the many vacant sees. However, with Parker's consecration to the archdiocese of Canterbury on 17 December 1559 and other consecrations following rapidly thereafter, the English ecclesiastical situation stabilised by the beginning of 1560.[3] During the ensuing months the new bishops conducted many ordination services at which large numbers of men were inducted into the severely depleted ministry of the Church of England.

During this twilight period (November 1558-March 1560) religious radicalism appears to have flourished in London and south-east England. In Jean Veron's *A moste necessary treatise of free wil*, which was based upon lectures that he had given at Paul's Cross in 1560, the writer claimed that there were many advocates of human autonomy and impeccability around. He remarks:

> For there be many in the world, which are such enemies of the free mercy and grace of God.... Ye shall not only find them among the papists, but also among them, that will be counted most perfect christians, and most earnest favourers of the gospel.[4]

Later, he again mentions the strength and enthusiasm of these radicals. Referring to *Deuteronomy* 30:19, *Matthew* 11:28 and *1 John* 5:1, Veron comments:

---

[1] I Eliz. c.1. VI (Luders, IV (i), 351-2).

[2] R.W.Dixon, *History of the Church of England* (London, 1884), V, 4-5, 15-17; White, 20-1.

[3] Dixon, V, 198ff.

[4] Veron, *A moste necessary treatise*, A2^r-A2^v. Clearly Veron's Calvinist preaching aroused some opposition in 1560-1. See *Diary of Henry Machyn*, ed. J.G.Nichols (Camden Society, 42, London, 1847).

For there be many, even among them that be favourers of the gospel, or at least, will seem to be favourers of the gospel, that have always these authorities in their mouths...[5]

In the course of his apology Veron defended his previous writings in the following terms –

I have sought nothing else but to advance and set forth god's glory and to arm his church and faithful congregation against all manner of heresies and abominable errors both of the papists and of the Anabaptists, and of all other sectaries, that do now molest and trouble the Godlie quietness and peace of the church. At which thing the free will men, whose standard bearer Champneys would feign be, do not a little stomach.[6]

It is noteworthy that here Veron distinguishes between three types of heretic, *viz.* the papists, the anabaptists, and 'other sectaries'. Moreover he appears to place John Champneys and the Free-willers in the latter category rather than among the anabaptists. When Champneys circulated his protest against the predestinarian teaching of Jean Veron, Christopher Vitells was probably still imprisoned in the Counter.[7] Perhaps Champneys attempted to disentangle the Free-willers from the anti-trinitarians and rally the former to a more orthodox 'standard'. His ordination to presbyters' orders in the Church of England in March 1560 suggests that this attempt ended in failure.[8] It would be interesting to know whether John Champneys himself eventually embraced Familism.

In 1553-4 the Strangers' Church had been dissolved and its members expelled from the country. With the accession of Elizabeth and the increasing difficulties confronting Protestant exiles in East Friesland, many sought to return to England. In May 1559 Adriaan van Haemstede left Emden on his own initiative and returned to London. He was an able preacher, although clearly not an ardent Calvinist.[9] Immediately he began to gather Dutch residents together and lead house meetings. Eventually they were given the use of a church building.[10] Later in the year the official representatives of the Reformed Church in Emden – Jan Utenhove and Peter Delenus travelled to England *via* Frankfurt. They

---

5   *Ibid.*, II^r.
6   *Ibid., A Fruteful treatise* (second edition), E8^v-Fl^r.
7   Above 304-5.
8   Above, 97-8, 104-5.
9   Lindeboom, 41.
10   Strype, *Annals* I (i), 173.

returned with a letter of commendation from Bullinger and the original 1550 charter of the Strangers' Church.[11] Twice they petitioned the Queen for a restoration of the privileges that they had enjoyed under Edward VI and for the return of the Austin Friars church. On 24 February 1560 their petition was granted. However, the Strangers' Church was no longer to be an independent, model Reformed community. Henceforward the Bishop of London was to be its superintendent.[12] A number of elders were elected by the reconstituted congregation, including Adriaan van Haemstede, Jan Utenhove, Petrus Delenus and Nicolaas Carinaeus.

In September 1560 a proclamation was issued proscribing anabaptists. Shortly before, Bishop Grindal had received a supplication from a group of Dutch anabaptists who sought toleration. Their petition had been drawn up by van Haemstede.[13] These anabaptists denied that Christ took flesh from the Virgin Mary. While van Haemstede did not agree with them, he did not regard this doctrine as a cardinal tenet of the faith, and he urged toleration as the best way to win them over to an orthodox christology.[14] Later it transpired that van Haemstede also believed that children were saved without faith.[15] Van Haemstede was summoned before the Bishop of London and censured, while the Dutch congregation referred the issue to Peter Martyr. The latter wrote giving his judgement against the writings and conduct of van Haemstede.[16] On 17 November 1560 van Haemstede was excommunicated, and news of the sentence was sent to the churches at Emden, Antwerp and Frankfurt. Van Haemstede left England, but made a dramatic and unexpected return to London in July 1561. Bishop Grindal drew up a draft recantation, but

---

[11]   *Ibid.*, I (i), 173-6.
[12]   *Ibid.*, Lindeboom 31. John à Lasco, the former superintendent, had returned to Poland where he died in 1557.
[13]   Grindal, *Remains*, 242-4; Strype, *Grindal*, 62.
[14]   Strype, *Grindal*, 64.
[15]   *Ibid.*
[16]   Grindal, *Remains*, 243n.

van Haemstede refused to subscribe to it.[17] Finally, Adriaan van Haemstede was expelled from England on 21 August 1562.[18]

The van Haemstede affair caused considerable disruption in the Strangers' Church. Haemstede was a popular preacher with a personal following in the congregation.[19] The Dutch anabaptists who solicited and received van Haemstede's support in 1560 were almost certainly the followers of Menno Simons rather than Hendrik Niclaes.[20] Van Haemstede made a careful distinction between the strands of anabaptism. Moreover, Nicodemite Familists would not have needed to petition for toleration. At Easter 1575 a number of Dutch Mennonites were discovered meeting in a house at Aldgate. Many were sent to prison, a few recanted, and two were burned at Smithfield on 22 July 1575.[21] Under the watchful oversight of elders like Utenhove, Delenus and Carinaeus it is to be doubted whether any members of the reconstituted Strangers' Church were able to offer much support for the missionary endeavours of Christopher Vitells.

Nevertheless, the London congregation continued to have problems with individual refugees of heterodox persuasion. In March 1563 Justus Velsius was deported for 'prophesying' that after regeneration a man could be inwardly as perfect as Adam was before his fall.[22] The following year there was a dispute in the church over the validity of infant baptism.[23] However, the enforcement of strict congregational discipline served to prevent Familist penetration – at least during the 1560s and early 70s.[24] Correspondence between the Dutch church in

---

[17] Strype, *Grindal*, 67-9.
[18] Lindeboom, 41-6. The van Haemstede affair is discussed very fully by Collinson who suggests that he might have been a Familist (Patrick Collinson, *Archbishop Grindal 1519-1583, the Struggle for a Reformed Church*; London, 1979, pp.134-40). However, the evidence is by no means conclusive.
[19] *Ibid.*, 44.
[20] *Ibid.*, 42.
[21] Stow, *Annales* (1592 edition), 1160-2; Lindeboom, 57-8; *ME.*, II, 218.
[22] Lindeboom, 39-40.
[23] Strype, *Annals*, I (i), 176.
[24] Lindeboom, 51-4.

London and that at Sandwich in Kent indicates that the provincial refugee congregations were equally on their guard against anabaptist infiltration.[25]

If foreign religious radicals found it almost impossible to obtain membership of the London Strangers' churches in the 1560s, their English counterparts would have found even greater difficulty in gaining an entreé to the embryonic English separatist movement. By 1563 the chief bone of contention between the 'puritan' clergy and their ecclesiastical superiors was the surplice and the outdoor clerical dress prescribed in the royal injunctions of 1559. The vestments controversy, which culminated in the defeat of the twenty or so London ministers who made the Vestiarian Protest of 1566, produced the first tangible evidence of nonconformist separation from the Elizabethan church.[26] Writing under the month of July 1567 Stowe notes:

> About that tyme were many congregations of the Anabaptysts in London, who cawlyd themselvs Puritans or Unspottyd Lambs of the Lord. They kept theyr churche in ye Mynorys with out Algate.[27]

Collinson states that, 'the liberty of the Minories… was the original home of puritanism', and suggests that the term 'Anabaptysts' and the phrase 'Unspottyd Lambs of the Lord' were 'opprobrious labels' that Stowe had attached to these congregations, and not what they called themselves.[28] Nevertheless, as Collinson observes, Stowe's use of the term 'anabaptist' suggests that those who gathered in the Minories were prepared to separate from their parish churches and establish independent congregations.[29] Certainly they gathered for worship on Sundays. Stowe writes:

> On Estar day [1568] at Hogston [they assembled] in my Lord of Londons mans house to ye nombar of 120, and on Lowe Sonday in a carpentars hous in Aldarman bury.[30]

It is also evident that these conventicles enjoyed the sympathy and protection of Bishop Grindal. On Sunday 29 February 1568 they gathered at Mountjoy Place where 'ye byshop, beyng warnyd by the

---

25   Heriot, *op. cit.*, 312, 319-20.
26   Collinson, 74-5, 82-3.
27   John Stow, *Three Fifteenth-Century Chronicles*, ed. Gairdner, Camden Society N.S. 28 (1880), 143.
28   Collinson, 86-8.
29   *Ibid.*, 88.
30   Stow, *Chronicles*, 143-4.

constables, bad let them alone'.[31] The previous year (June 1567) about a hundred of these conventiclers were arrested by the sheriff after hiring Plumber's Hall, ostensibly for a wedding. Doubtless Collinson is correct when he suggests that it was 'essentially the same transient congregation' that is recorded as having gathered at several different venues in London during 1567 and 1568.[32] Stowe concludes:

It is to be noated that suche as were at eny tyme comitted for suche congregatynge were sone delyvered without punishemente.[33]

In contrast with his attitude towards true anabaptists, these separatists of the late 1560s were tolerated by Bishop Grindal. Some of them were in contact with John Knox.[34] The parish of Holy Trinity, Minories was exempt from the bishop's jurisdiction, it appointed its own ministers, and in the 1560s radical puritans such as Crowley, Field and Wilcox preached from its pulpit. The aged Miles Coverdale preached his last sermons in this parish. It appears, therefore, that the separatist conventicles which developed out of the Minories congregation were thoroughly Reformed in character. They derived inspiration from the London Predestinarian congregation which met secretly during the Marian persecution.[35] There would have been no place among such company for committed Free-willers and perfectionists like John Champneys, Robert Cooche or John Trewe. During the Elizabethan era there was no alternative 'home' for anti-Calvinist separatists but the Nicodemite and quietist Family of Love.[36]

---

[31]   *Ibid.*, 143.
[32]   Collinson, 88-9; White, 23-7.
[33]   Stow, *Chronicles*, 144.
[34]   Collinson, 88.
[35]   White, 2-3, 14, 24.
[36]   An excellent illustration of the fundamental differences between Puritan separatists and Anabaptists is to be found in the conversations and correspondence between 'S.B.' and William White in 1575. Both were lay artisans, both vigorously rejected the established Church of England, and yet they were at loggerheads. William White was a member of the Plumber's Hall congregation, while S.B. was worshipping with the Dutch Mennonites who were arrested at Aldgate on 3 April 1575. See A. Peel, 'A Conscientious Objector of 1575', *Transactions of the Baptist Historical Society*, VII, (1920-21), 71-128.

I. The Investigation of the Court of High Commission, 1559-61

This new ecclesiastical court was established on 19 July 1559. It consisted of either the Archbishop of Canterbury or the Bishop of London, together with five other senior ecclesiastics, and thirteen lay officials – knights, serjeants and doctors. Their function was :

> to enquire into the working of the new Acts; into seditious books, heretical opinions, false rumours, or slanderous words; into disturbance of divine service, wilful absence from church; to restore unjustly deprived ministers; to deal such punishments as they deemed expedient, use such means as they thought fit, and receive recognisances from offenders or suspect persons who should be referred to them.[37]

Through this instrument the Queen's commissioners compelled conformity from radicals and recusants alike for the next forty years.[38] Like earlier heresy commissions, the commissioners generally sat in the consistory of S. Paul's.[39]

During the first two years of its existence the Court of High Commission appears to have concerned itself with English radicals – particularly members of the Family of Love. Unfortunately no records of its investigations have survived. However, Rogers made use of depositions given to the commissioners, for at one point he claims – 'I finde it collected by the commissioners who delt specially in that matter'.[40] In his *Answere* to Christopher Vitells, John Rogers remarks:

I suppose you meane the commissioners, who examining your Familye, touching their fayth and doctrine: found them so suttle by your instructions, that in ye end they required the, to declare their knowledge, what they thought of their Author HN ... but you have taught them to say, (we know him not,) and therefore, to commend him, or discommend him, wee may not: such sleightes you deuise ... your Elders are safe, when the poore country people, are brought before the Magistrates: but when will any of you the Elders, come voluntarily, and defend your doctrine, and proue it good by sound argument?[41]

---

[37] Dixon, V, 157.
[38] Cross, 136.
[39] Dixon, V, 158.
[40] Rogers, *An Answere* Fl^v.
[41] *Ibid.*, G6^r-G6^v.

Notwithstanding Rogers' assertion that the Familist elders were immune from prosecution, the extant evidence indicates that at least one of them appeared before the Court of High Commission in 1560. Thomas Allen, weaver, of Wonersh in Surrey, was one of the earliest converts of Christopher Vitells and probably the first English elder in the Family.[42] In *circa* 1577/8 Allen was described as 'an eldere amongst theym theyse xx[tie] yeres paste' – that is, since 1557/8.[43] In the same letter, the writer – the Surrey magistrate Sir William More – identifies Allen as a Familist and asserts,

> He was about xvii yers paste conventyd of dyvers herysyes before my L. of Caunterburye, then busshope of London, and before his L. commysyd of [committed for] the same and thereapon dyd openlye recant theym at Guleford and in his own paryshe churche never the les ever syns viohementlye suspectyd to be a chyef sedusere of dyverse to be of his heretycall opynyons....[44]

Among the depositions made before Sir William More in May 1561 one states that Thomas Allen of Wonersh had been brought before Edmund Grindal, Bishop of London, and 'by him made... to recant'.[45] This indicates that Allen's examination by the commissioners, imprisonment, and subsequent recantations had occurred in the year 1560-1. Among Sir William More's papers is another undated letter concerning Allen. It was addressed:

> to M[r] Crowley and others tochyng 'Allen the anabaptist, who after his committal to prison by the commissioners for ecclesiastical causes has shown himself of sound judgment in religion, and has attributed his said trouble to the writer.[46]

This suggests that Allen had been detected to the High Commission in 1560 at the instigation of his local magistrate – William More of Loseley House. While in prison he had succeeded in persuading Robert Crowley and others of his orthodoxy, and they had contacted More on Allen's behalf. More, however, had no doubt that Allen was an 'anabaptist'.

---

42   *Ibid.*, *Displaying* (1579 edition), O7[v]; Folger MS. L.b.51, cited in J.W.Martin, 'Elizabethan Familists and other Separatists in the Guildford Area', *Bulletin of the Institute of Historical Research*, 51 (1978), 90-3. See above, p.388.

43   Martin, 'Elizabethan Familists', 91.

44   *Ibid.*

45   *Ibid.* See Appendix Document IV.

46   Hist. MSS. Com. Rep. VII, 664a.

Thus, Thomas Allen remained in prison in London until he recanted his heretical opinions before Bishop Grindal. He was then taken back to Surrey where he made a public recantation at Guildford and another in Wonersh parish church before being set free.

The investigation of the Court of High Commission culminated with the issue of a royal proclamation on 22 September 1560 which ordered the deportation of all anabaptists, English and foreign.[47] As in earlier proclamations against anabaptists emphasis is placed upon the part played by foreign refugees in disseminating these doctrines in England. The proclamation commences:

> The Queen's Majesty, understanding that of late time sundry persons being infected with certain dangerous and pernicious opinions... as Anabaptists and such like, are come from sundry parts beyond the seas into this her realm, and specially into the city of London and other maritime towns, under the colour and pretence of fleeing from persecution.[48]

The proclamation then refers to the Court of High Commission which had been established to prevent 'the church of God in this realm' being corrupted. The commissioners had been ordered by the Privy Council to investigate 'the parishes in London and other places herewith suspected... and all persons suspected to be openly tried and examined touching such fanatical and heretical opinions.'[49] Doubtless it was as a result of this order that Thomas Allen was tried and imprisoned.

The Queen then commanded:

> ... all manner of persons, born either in foreign parts or in her majesty's dominions, that have conceived any manner of such heretical opinion as the Anabaptists do hold, and meaneth not by charitable teaching to be reconciled, to depart out of this realm within twenty days after this proclamation.[50]

Evidently the authorities had been made aware through the investigations of the High Commission that it was not only foreigners who held these heretical opinions. Furthermore, the concluding paragraph of the

---

[47] *TRP.*, II, 148-9.
[48] *Ibid.*, II, 148.
[49] *Ibid.*, II, 149.
[50] *Ibid.*

proclamation indicates that they were aware of the undercover, Nicodemite character of anabaptist practice. It reads:

> And her majesty also chargeth and commandeth, upon pain of imprisonment, that no minister nor other person make any conventicles or secret congregations either to read, or to preach, or to minister the sacraments, or to use any manner of divine service; but that they shall resort to open chapels or churches, and there to preach, teach, minister, or pray according to the order of the Church of England....[51]

Clearly this paragraph was aimed at the Family of Love, of which Christopher Vitells was now the full-time English agent and organiser. It also suggests that the authorities had received information that not all of those fervent preachers whom they had so recently ordained to the ministry of the Church of England were what they seemed.

Three days before the proclamation was issued, the Privy Council despatched a warrant to William More (he was knighted in 1576) ordering him to arrest:

> the persons of David Orch and other ringleaders of the divers sectaries who purpose to meet together, and have their conventicles at Kateryn hills faire now at hand.[52]

Perhaps the Council had received this information from the imprisoned Thomas Allen, or possibly from the group of foreign anabaptist refugees in London who were under investigation at this time.[53] The fair at S. Catherine's Hill near Guildford was held annually on 2 October. It was the ideal venue for a conventicle –

> Though the days of the pilgrimage were over, yet this spot where the Pilgrim's Way crossed the road through Guildford to Portsmouth was a natural meeting place where much besides merchandise would be exchanged.[54]

There is no further information on David Orch, and so his opinions and fate must remain matters of conjecture.[55] His name, however, does not sound English. He may have been a Familist agent from the Continent

---

[51] *Ibid.*

[52] Hist. NSS. Com. Rep. VII, 615b-616a. Unfortunately the Privy Council Register for the period May 1559-May 1562 is lost.

[53] Above, 317, 323.

[54] *VCH.*, Surrey I, 382.

[55] But see Appendix Document IV notes (p.390).

who was making contact with the new Familist groups in England. Wonersh was only a few miles from S. Catherine's Hill. The sudden arrival of a foreigner in such a remote village would have aroused the suspicion of the villagers, particularly since the local magistrate already had the Wonersh conventicle under observation. A meeting with religious radicals from the district at the local annual fair had considerably less possibility of detection. Besides, it is likely that Lollards had held their conventicles at the same fair for the past century and more.

The disciplinary measures instituted by the Court of High Commission apparently had the desired effect. By 1562 the authorities' concern over religious radicalism in London and the home counties had evaporated. In that year Parliament passed an Act of General Pardon which became effective from 1 January 1563.[56] Although there were many exceptions to this general pardon, anabaptists and other 'heretics' were not among those excluded.

II The Surrey Radicals
(a) The Wonersh Conventicle
The earliest reference to religious radicalism in the Guildford district occurs in a letter which John Parkhurst wrote to Henry Bullinger on 21 May 1559, shortly before his nomination to the see of Norwich. He writes:

> ... within four days I have to contend in my native place [Guildford], both from the pulpit and in mutual conference, with those horrid monsters of Arianism... Christ lives, he reigns, and will reign, in spite of Arians, Anabaptists, and papists.[57]

This suggests that the Familists had gathered their recruits from local anti-trinitarians who denied the divinity of Christ, also that Thomas Allen had originally been one of Christopher Vitells' rationalist contacts. It is significant that the two places named in the sources as containing inhabitants with radical sympathies – Wonersh and Dunsfold – were both cloth weaving villages. In the depths of rural Surrey there were few

---

56 V Eliz. c.30. (Luders, IV (i), 461-4).
57 *Zurich Letters*, I, 30.

other villages where foreigners, or people with foreign connections, could have established themselves.[58]

According to John Rogers, the Familist conventicle at Wonersh owed its existence to Christopher Vitells. In his *Answere* to Vitells he asserts,
...and in deed they were of your hatching, although for further increase of knowledge, Allin their neare neighbor did more instructe them, and lead them forward into your error.[59]
It has already been suggested that Thomas Allen, weaver of Wonersh, was one of Vitells' earliest converts, that he became an elder of the Family as early as 1557, that he was detected to the High Commission in 1560, that he was imprisoned in London, and that he made three recantations in London and Surrey in 1560-1.[60]

It appears that, like Vitells, Allen was an itinerant elder travelling along the Wonersh – Southwark – Balsham – Wisbech circuit. William Wilkinson mentions that on one occasion Allen was apprehended in Cambridgeshire. A 'worshipfull freind in Cambridge' had informed him that:
one *Allen* a weauer being committed for the opinions of the Fami [*sic.*] and HN. he contrary to his promise made departed and fled away, and being afterwardes mette by a iustice of peace which knew him by sight, asked him his name, as he sayd his name was *Allen*, the iustice demaunded if he had about him no bookes of *HN*. he aunswered, no, the Iustice alighting from his horse searched him, and found diuers bokes about him.[61]
Heal doubts whether this man was the same Allen who was the leader of the Wonersh conventicle.[62] However, the evidence subsequently produced by Martin provides a decisive answer to this uncertainty.[63] Allen's arrest in Cambridgeshire appears to have taken place sometime after 1574 because shortly afterwards he was found to have some of H.N.'s books in his possession. Presumably he fled back to Surrey

---

58   *VCH.*, Surrey, II, 27-8. See J.F.Davis, 'Lollard Survival and the Textile Industry in the South-east of England', *Studies in Church History*, III (1966) ed. Cuming, pp.191-201.
59   Rogers, *An Answere*, K1^v-K2^r.
60   Above, 322-3.
61   Wilkinson, S1^v.
62   Heal, *op. cit.*, 217, 217 n.3.
63   Martin, Elizabethan Familists, 91.

after he broke bail in Cambridgeshire, for the magistrate who recognised and searched him was almost certainly Sir William More.

By September 1578 Thomas Allen was dead.[64] In the subsequent edition of *The Displaying* Rogers supplies further information about his demise. Referring to the two witnesses who made the 1561 deposition, Rogers asserts:

> the parties are liuing and followers of one *Allyne* of *Woneherst*, a great companion of *Christopher Vittells*, which *Allin* died soudenly by the high way, going to *Farnam* to be examined before y[e] bishop of winchester.[65]

Evidently Thomas Allen had been arrested – probably in Surrey – and was being conveyed to Farnham Castle (a residence of the bishops of Winchester) to be interrogated by his diocesan. The incident recounted by Wilkinson may be a description of the circumstances surrounding Allen's final arrest. However, Wilkinson's information does not correlate completely with an account given by Sir William More in a letter dated 26 September (? 1577). More states that the Bishop of Winchester, having been informed that Surrey was 'greatlye infectyd' with the Family of Love, wrote to all the justices of peace in the county. The bishop urged them:

> to use some dyllygence for the deteccon of theim and that apon one daye a generall serch myght be made thorowe the sayd Countye of all theyre howses that were suspectyd to be of that famelye for those bokes of hn had in use amongst theym whereapon I serched the sayd Allen's howse and found there a booke of h.n. prevelye hyden at the verye tyme of my comynge for I sawe his wyf when she dyd secretlie covere hit.[66]

The phraseology of the letter suggests that Allen was still alive at the time it was written, but under arrest. Allen may have been in custody even before Sir William More searched his house. The number of occasions on which Thomas Allen was apprehended remains uncertain.

---

64   Rogers, *Displaying* (first edition), E8[r].
65   *Ibid.*, *Displaying* (1579 edition), O7[v]. Rogers also states that an 'R.W.' confessed before the Bishop of Winchester at Farnham that he was a follower of Hendrik Niclaes (*Displaying*, 1579 edition, K4[r]).
66   Martin, 'Elizabethan Familists', 91.

A more interesting problem is that of Allen's status in the Wonersh conventicle *vis à vis* John Water, joiner of Wonersh. According to his confession he was also an elder of the Family during the period 1566-76.[67] In his *Answere* John Rogers makes a remark which suggests that the conventicle was still in existence in 1579. Referring to the two witnesses who made the 1561 depositions he states, 'but this is certain, one of them is liuing, & knoweth you but to well, and is a welwiller to your Family, and scoller of Allin'.[68] On 10 October 1580 the Privy Council sent a letter to the Bishop of Winchester ordering him to investigate and suppress Familist conventicles in his diocese. In the conduct of this investigation the bishop was to seek the assistance of Sir William More. A further communication on this subject was sent to the bishop on 25 January 1581. In this letter the Council ordered him to make use of the services and experience of John Knewstub to detect members of the Family of Love in his diocese.[69]

(b) The Depositions of May 1561 (Appendix Document IV)
Doctor Heal expresses some doubt over the authenticity of the confession which Rogers printed as an appendix to the first edition of his *Displaying*. She notes that the two witnesses 'failed to mention H.N. and his doctrine' and that members of the Family 'denied that the Surrey men were part of their sect'.[70] Rogers' Familist correspondent E.R. pointed out that Sir William More was not knighted at the time the depositions were supposed to have been given before him. He then asserted that the articles were 'false and forged' and that 'the confessours of them, are, nor neuer were of the Familie of Loue'.[71] Christopher Vitells in his 'Testimonies of Sion' maintained that the two witnesses did not know the teaching of H.N. – 'you affirm [them] to be of the Fam. of loue, what they were, that is that, but of *HN* his doctrine

---

67 *Ibid.*, 92-3. Martin cites Folger MS. L. b.99, printed in T.W.Martin, *Religious Radicals in Tudor England* (London and Ronceverte, 1989), 37-9. This contains a deposition concerning 'Anabaptists at Guildford' which is attributed to Roger Goad who was schoolmaster at Guildford from 1565 to 1575.

68 Rogers, *An Answere*, K1^v.

69 *APC.*, XII, 233, 317-8.

70 Heal, 216.

71 Rogers, *Displaying* (1579 edition), L7^r-L7^v.

at that time they knew not'.[72] Rogers, however, had no doubts as to the authenticity of the depositions or that they were made by genuine Familists.[73]

In a sense Vitells was right; 'at that time' (1561) Niclaes' books were not translated into English and so the two witnesses could not have had any direct knowledge of his doctrine. However this was a typical equivocation. Martin has recently shown that the Surrey conventiclers were Familists and followers of H.N.. Rogers published a deposition consisting of fifty-three articles, which was doubtless the entire contents of the copy he received from Sir William More. However, the original deposition consisted of sixty-six articles. Article sixty-four reads:
Henryke, a Dutchman, the hede of all the Congregacion, he is permanent in no place but still wandreth to vysyte his flock.[74]
Furthermore, the identity of the two witnesses is disclosed in the heading above the original depositions. This reads:
The Deposiciouns of Thomas Chaundeler of Wonersse, clothier, and Roberto Sterte of Dunfold, clarke, made vnto me, William More, esquire, ye 28 May 1561, tochynge theyre knowledge of certain sectaryes and of thayer doctrines, proctices, and Diuylish Deuyces.[75]
Article nineteen in the deposition states:
If any of their secte do die, the wife or husbande that overliveth, must marrie againe with one of their congregation, or else the offence is greate: the marriage is made by the brethren, who bring them together sometime, that dwell above a hundreth myles asunder: as for example, *Thomas Chaundler* of *Wonerse*, in the countie of Surrey, had his wife fetcht out of the Isle of *Ely* by two of the congregation: the man and the woman being utter straungers, before they came together to be married.

---

72   *Ibid.*, K1^r-K1^v.
73   *Ibid., An Answere*, K1^v-K2^r.
74   Folger MS. L. b.98 cited by Martin, 'Elizabethan Familists', 91. A reason for these omissions can perhaps be detected elsewhere among the Loseley manuscripts. Martin states that two songs by Hendrik Niclaes have been altered by More's copyist – 'some of the specifically Familist points' being 'doctrinally bowdlerized by minor changes in wording' (Martin 91). Was the clerk whom Sir William More employed in *circa* 1578 a member of the Family of Love?
75   Hist. MSS. Com. Rep. VII, 616a.

The following article provides additional information on this bizarre affair:

> They doe divorce againe themselves a sunder if they can not agree, before certeine of the congregation: as the saide *Chaundeler*, and his wife did, upon a mislyking, after they had bene one yeare married together.[76]

Thus, one of the witnesses had personal experience of Familist marital practice – experience which could only have been gained as a full member of the Family. As a clothier Thomas Chaundler would doubtless have been accorded the status of 'Raab' by the Wonersh Familists. Their meetings would have been held at his house and he would have been expected to provide hospitality for thirty or more conventiclers.[77] In Article four a witness remarked 'sometimes they doe loose their *Raab*, seeing himselfe so farre overcharged with them'.[78] No doubt that was Thomas Chaundler speaking from bitter personal experience. His disastrous marriage to a member of the Wisbech conventicle was probably the last straw. Shortly afterwards he decided to leave the Family and tell all to the local magistrate. By the time Rogers wrote his *Answere* one of the two witnesses was dead, and the other – probably Robert Sterte – had rejoined the Family.[79] Therefore, it is concluded that the 1561 depositions were authentic statements made by full members of an authentic Familist conventicle which had been in existence at Wonersh since at least 1559.

John Rogers recognised that these articles were descriptions of English Familist doctrine and practice when it was at an early stage of development. In 1578 he commented that they had 'reformed some of these grosse matters since that time'.[80] One aspect which appears to have been modified during the first twenty years was the original three-fold ministry of bishop, elder and deacon (Articles 1 and 2). By the 1570s there seem to have been simply two types of elder – the resident leader of the local conventicle and the itinerant teacher. Since the great majority of conventiclers were illiterate, their chief qualification for office was an ability to read (Article 1). Doctrine was learned through

---

[76] Rogers, *Displaying* (first edition), I7^v.

[77] *Ibid.*, I4^v-I5^v.

[78] *Ibid.*, I5^r.

[79] *Ibid.*, *An Answere*, K1^v.

[80] *Ibid.*, *Displaying* (first edition), I4^v.

personal contact and oral teaching from the Familist hierarchy (Articles 6-8). The publication of H.N.'s works in English in 1574 and 1575 was a major cause of the vigorous persecution which the sect suffered during the next five years. Another area where there may have been later modification was their vigorous denial of the divinity of Christ and anti-trinitarianism (Articles 24-26). They certainly modified their pacifist objection to the bearing of weapons (Article 15).

The conventicle was strictly disciplined, complete obedience to the elders being demanded (Article 9).[81] The elders had complete power over the distribution of property (Articles 49, 50, 53). A community in the consumption of goods seems to have been practised (Article 33). Readiness to participate in this policy over material possessions was a condition of entry into the Family (Article 3) – the 'Elder doth declare unto the new Elected brother, that if he will be content that all his goodes shalbe in common amongst the rest of all his brethren, he shalbe received'.[82] The Family was totally exclusivist. Marriages were arranged between members of the sect by the elders (Articles 19-20). In fact they were so rigid in their exclusivism that only other members of the Family could act as midwives to their women (Article 18). Alms were only to be given to other Familists (Article 31); 'whosoever is not of their sect they accompt him as a beast, that hath no soule' (Article 21). All outsiders and those who had left the Family were reckoned to be 'dead' (Article 36). They maintained secrecy about their beliefs and practices (Article 44). The sect was also pacifist (Article 15) and advocated religious toleration – 'no man should be put to death for his opinion'. They particularly criticised Cranmer and Ridley for 'burning *Ioane* of *Kent*' (Article 45).

Penrhys-Evans notes the differences between the Familists and their Mennonite contemporaries. He writes:
Where the Familists of the Surrey confession part company with more orthodox Anabaptists was in their acceptance of, and participation in, the services of the Established Church. Such English Anabaptists as

---

[81] Penrhys-Evans, 32-3.
[82] Rogers, *Displaying* (first edition), I5ʳ.

there were remained truer to their Lollard antecedents.[83]
Certainly, Familist Nicodemism is deeply enshrined within these
depositions (Articles 10, 17, 23, 35); 'They holde, it is lawfull to doe
what so ever the higher powers commaunde to be done, thoughe it be
against the commandments of God' (Article 23). There were, moreover,
several other beliefs which sharply distinguished these Familists from
Mennonite anabaptists. Their vigorous anti-trinitarianism has already
been mentioned, then there was their doctrine that 'heauen and hel are
present in this worlde amongst us, and that there is none other' (Article
30). Mennonites would not have taught 'that there was a worlde before
Adams time, as there is nowe' (Article 43). Even their peculiar view of
the incarnation was not that of the Mennonites – 'They hold, themselves
to be *Maries*: and say, that Christ is come forth in their fleshe, even as he
came foorth of the virgin Marie' (Article 42). This spiritualising or
allegorising of Biblical events is evident in other articles dealing with
Christ's miracles, angels, Sunday observance, and the creation (Articles
29, 38, 40, 41).

The Surrey Familists employed a set of verbal *shibboleths* that must have
served as passwords or means of recognition (Articles 5, 13, 14, 16).
Like their Lollard predecessors they had developed a 'tortuous
casuistry' (Articles 51-2), and they had institutionalised abjuration –
> If any of them be convented for his opinion, and doeth denie the same
> by open recantation: he taketh that to be a glorie unto him, as though
> he had suffered persecution in this doing: and yet still inwardly
> mainteyning these opinions (Article 47).
Apart from their Nicodemism, anti-trinitarianism and denial of the
divinity of Christ, another link with the earlier teaching of Christopher
Vitells was their violent objection to the prayer 'Lord have mercy upon
us miserable sinners', because 'we doe live perfectly and sinne not'
(Article 12). Perfectionist teaching is evident in several other articles;
mature members of the Family were 'to perfect, to pray unto God ...
having no need to do so' (Article 11), all members of the congregation
were 'either as perfecte as CHRISTE, or els a verie divell' (Article 22).

---

[83] Penrhys-Evans, 59.

However, in relation to this study, perhaps the most important aspect of Familist teaching was that on baptism. Article 27 reads:

> They holde, that no man should be baptised, before he be of the age of xxx yeares. And therefore have divers of them beene baptised at those yeares and upwardes.

Penrhys-Evans is probably correct to link this teaching to the baptism of Jesus, and to interpret it as 'an example of their insistence on a symbolical *imitatio Christi*'.[84] Yet, even more important, is the fact that here is the first (and only) piece of evidence that re-baptism was practised in England in the sixteenth century. Between 1559 and 1561 some English members of the Family of Love over the age of thirty had been re-baptised. In 1549 Robert Cooche had advocated that only those over the age of fourteen should be baptised, but this teaching appears to reflect a different approach to the ordinance rather than simple development from Cooche's position.[85] Furthermore, it is evident from the depositions that the rite was not regarded as the means by which candidates were initiated into the Family. Article 34 reads:

> They holde, that none ought to receiue the sacraments before he receiveth their whole ordinaunces: as first, he must be admitted with a Kisse, then his feete must be washed, then handes laide on him, and so received.

The third article confirms that admission was signified by a kiss, 'all the company both men and women kissing him, one after another'.

It appears that the Familists possessed their own parallel sacramental system, including believers' baptism, which their elders administered alongside those of the established church. Vitells himself admitted that 'for the peaces cause' members of the Family 'may ioyne with any congregation or Church... and obserue their politick ordinances'.[86] In the same way the Family had its own marriage ceremony. However, it is certain that the Familist rite of baptism was not administered in the name of the Trinity. Rather, it was given 'in the name of ye father', and Rogers was certainly not prepared to regard that as true baptism. He

---

84 *Ibid.* See also Article 29.
85 Above, 243-5.
86 Rogers, *Displaying* (1579 edition) G2^r.

comments, 'By baptism he [HN.] meaneth not the sacrament of Baptisme'.[87] Later Rogers explains:

> [Baptism] they take not to be ye sacrament of baptism, but a mysterie exceeding my capacity to utter, of incorporating us into God.[88]

One of Rogers' Familist correspondents confirms that they did interpret the rite of baptism in this spiritualist fashion. He states that 'true baptism' was an allegory of the believer's spiritual pilgrimage signifying true repentance and submission, the true taking up of the cross of Christ against sin, and the true resurrection in which Christ was formed within them.[89] Nevertheless, it is evident that – even if its meaning was spiritualised – anabaptism was practised among Familists in England in 1561. They used the rite to symbolise and recognise the spiritual maturity of members of the Family.

(c) Conclusion

The depositions of Thomas Chaundler and Robert Sterte before William More on 28 May 1561 revealed the existence of a sect with sophisticated doctrines and a complex organisation. Undoubtedly it owed its inspiration to the teaching of the Continental Spiritualist, Hendrik Niclaes. Yet it was the energy and self-sacrifice of Christopher Vitells that had enabled H.N.'s ideas to be successfully transplanted in England during the previous six years. However Vitells did not start from scratch. Within the 1561 depositions there is clear evidence of the Familists' connection with earlier separatist congregations.

Like the Kentish conventiclers described by Thomas Cole in his sermon of 1553, like John Sympson of Essex and John Jackson of Sussex, the Surrey Familists referred to each other as 'Brother' and 'Sister' (Articles 3-5).[90] According to the Kentish depositions of 1551 the same conventiclers were exclusivist, and so was Henry Harte's conventicle in London in 1556-7.[91] Like Henry Harte the Surrey Familists emphasised the doctrine of impeccability. In the fifty-three printed articles there is no

---

87 *Ibid., Displaying* (first edition), H1^v margin.
88 *Ibid.,* H2^v.
89 *Ibid., Displaying* (1579 edition), K1^r-K1^v.
90 Above, 152-3, 128, 285-6, 309.
91 Above, 141, 204-5.

reference to man's ability and obligation to keep the commandments – a feature of the teaching of Henry Harte, and of the Kent and Sussex Free-willers. However, in his 'Testimonies of Sion' Christopher Vitells writes:

> You say moreouer, that we affirme that the lawe of God may be kept, it is true, we doe so affirme, that they whiche loue God, will keepe his commaundementes.[92]

Similarly there is no mention within the 1561 depositions of the Familists' opposition to the doctrine of predestination. However, John Rogers – referring to the two Familist apologies of 1575 – asks:

> As for your confession published ... it is a mockerie.... Why halt you so cunningly?... Do you in your confession impugne the doctrine of predestination... and yet in your letters you shewe your dislyking of such doctrine, terming it licentious?[93]

The Surrey Familists' esteem for an itinerant ministry (Article 37), their advocacy of secrecy and abjuration (Articles 44, 47), their rejection of Sunday observance (Article 40), and their respect for Joan Bocher (Article 45) are all echoes of earlier English sectarianism. Yet the clearest evidence of the connection between the English Familists of the 1560s and 70s and the Free-willers of the 1550s is found, not in the depositions of the Surrey Familists, but in those of their brethren at Balsham. On 13 December 1574 a number of people cleared themselves of charges of Familism by making a declaration of their faith. Subsequent investigation of the Wisbech Familists revealed that those who had been interrogated at Balsham were members of the Family.[94] Among the articles in the declaration by the Balsham Familists was one in which they expressed their dislike of card-playing and rejected all forms of gambling.[95] Both the Kentish Free-willers of 1551 and the company of Sussex Free-willers led by John Trewe abominated gambling as 'synne and the worke of the Flesshe'.[96]

Thus, it is suggested that the Familist conventicles of the 1560s and 70s were based upon the Free-willer conventicles of the 1550s, and that they

---

[92]   Rogers, *Displaying* (1579 edition), G7^r.
[93]   *Ibid.*, N5^r-N5^v.
[94]   Heal, 217-221.
[95]   Strype, *Parker*, II, 381.
[96]   Above, 140-1, 264.

in turn were derived from earlier Lollard congregations.[97] The Wonersh conventicle of 1560-1 bears comparison with the Bocking conventicle of 1550-1 in that both appealed to the same type of clientèle. Both were held in weaving communities and led by independently-minded artisans. Like Henry Harte's company, the conventicles organised by Christopher Vitells largely consisted of poor illiterates. Thirty years earlier the Lollard congregations of southern England were still being maintained, as they had been for the previous century, through the itinerant ministry of travelling craftsmen. Familist conventicles functioned by the same means. Thirty years earlier abjuration was accepted as the customary practice of apprehended Lollards. Familist recantations, equivocation and casuistry would have been quite familiar to elderly adherents. Thirty years earlier Lollards had attended the Roman mass in their local parish churches because this was unavoidable. In 1561 Familists were equally prepared to attend Reformed preaching in the same churches because that too was obligatory.

---

[97] Balsham is only twelve miles north-west of Steeple Bumpstead, and just across the diocesan boundary.

Chapter Five

Conclusion: English Radical Theology, 1535-1565

G.H. Williams concludes his examination of 'radical trends' in England during the Reformation period by observing,

> that England's Anabaptism was exclusively Melchiorite, that its Spiritualism was likewise of Netherlandish origin (Libertinism, Familism), that its anti-Trinitarianism seems to have been proportionately more prominent than in the Netherlands, and that except for the still unclarified relationship with indigenous Lollardy, the radical trends in England appear to have been largely an importation and as such an extension of the radical movements engendered in the Hanseatic zone of Low German speech.[1]

Apart from Williams' over-rigid typology, his proviso concerning the part played by England's indigenous radical movement is seriously understated. The object of this investigation has been to throw a little more light on the 'unclarified relationship' between Lollardy and Continental radicalism.

I. The English Radicals and Lollardy

It is suggested that the sectarians and nonconformists of the period owed as much to the precedents and practices of Lollardy as they did to the impact of the 'new' Continental ideologies.[2] The chronological factor must be kept clearly in view; particular doctrines must not be examined in isolation from their exponents or from the historical context in which they were expounded. An English religious radical who was born in 1500 would have been reared in Lollardy until he was thirty. The formative period of his life would have been spent in Lollard conventicles where the Wycliffite literature was still being read and expounded. All his attitudes and values would have been permanently influenced by the traditions of Lollardy. By 1550 the same person may

---

[1]   Williams, *Radical Reformation*, 790.

[2]   See D.D.Smeeton's review of Anne Hudson, *The Premature Reformation. Wycliffite texts and Lollard history* (Oxford, 1988) in *Sixteenth Century Journal* 20 (1989), 507, where he notes the characteristics of Wycliffism as: the value ascribed to the written word, the stress on exegetical sermons, discussions and lay instruction in the literal Biblical text, the leadership opportunities afforded to both sexes – and, by contrast, its objection to the useless knowledge and arrogance of academics. Smeeton concludes, 'Lollardy held, at least in embryo, almost all of the essential reformation concepts'.

have been termed a 'Free-will man'. If he survived the Marian persecution and reached the age of seventy, he may well have joined the Family of Love. Equally, a former Lollard born in 1500 could have subscribed to the doctrine and practice of the Reformed Church of England during the Edwardine period, survived the Marian persecution, grown disenchanted with the Elizabethan Church, and ended his days in the 1580s as a Brownist.

The evidence preserved in Foxe clearly indicates that Lollardy was thriving in parts of southern England at the dawn of the Henrician reformation. In Buckinghamshire, Essex and London Lollards were being apprehended even as late as 1532 and 1533. Foxe had access to the registers of bishops Smith and Longland of Lincoln and bishops Stokesley and Tunstall of London, and his citations indicate that Lollards were active to within five years of our period.[3] Recent research has shown the wide 'variety of Lollard works, apart from Bible translations, in active use and circulation on the eve of the Reformation'. Furthermore, this popular survival was accompanied in the 1530s and 40s by a revival of interest in Lollard literature among Protestant scholars led by Tyndale and Bale.[4]

The vigorous nonconformity and anti-intellectualism of English religious radicalism in the mid-sixteenth century had its roots in the bitter anti-clericalism and radical sacramentarianism of earlier Lollardy. Likewise, the comprehensive knowledge of the Bible revealed in the writings of John Champneys and Henry Harte and in the statements of John Barre and John Trewe had its origin in Lollard biblicism. These radicals belonged within the same social stratum and pursued the same artisan trades as their Lollard predecessors.[5] In the 1550s those Free-willers who resisted Reformed theology and continued to meet in their own conventicles came from areas that had previously been noted as strongholds of Lollardy – the wealds of Kent and Sussex, London and North Essex.[6] It is significant that the Essex Lollards of 1527-8 also

---

3   Foxe, *AM.*, IV, 217-46, 580-7; V, 26-44.

4   Margaret Aston, 'Lollardy and the Reformation:Survival or Revival?, 162-4; Aston, 'Lollardy and Literacy', *History*, N.S., 62 (1977), 351.

5   A.G.Dickens, 'Heresy and the Origins of English Protestantism', *Britain and the Netherlands*, II, eds. Bromley and Kossmann (Groningen, 1964), 58-9.

6   Davis, 'Lollard Survival and the Textile Industry', 191-3.

referred to each other as 'brother' and 'sister'. Moreover, they appear to have used these appellations in conjunction with, and as substitutes for, the more traditional terms of 'known man' and 'known woman'.[7] Above all, the two best known and most influential figures in English religious radicalism in this period – Joan Bocher and Henry Harte – have been shown to have been former Lollards.[8] This surely is conclusive proof of the decisive rôle played by indigenous radicalism.

It may be objected that the doctrines of free-will and impeccability, and the anti-intellectualism of the Free-willers, do not accord with the predestinarianism and scholarship of John Wyclif. However, according to Lambert, later Lollards 'were not very conscious of Wyclif'.[9] They were led by unbeneficed semi-literate clerks like William Swinderby, and by devout laymen like William Smith. Although the Wycliffite literature continued to be read in their conventicles, this uneducated leadership determined the 'essentially practical and moral character' of later Lollardy.[10] Moreover, from the beginning of the sixteenth century other elements – far more 'heretical' than Wyclif's doctrine – began to surface within the movement.[11] Leff notes that the spirituality of the Lollards differed from that of the mystics:

> There was no inner search for God in the soul or withdrawal from the world in order to reach him... it was rather a moral insistence upon individual responsibility before God. Right living was the sole criterion of righteousness; spiritual probity could only be proved in practice.[12]

The Free-willers' insistence upon man's duty and ability to keep God's commandments, their identification of purity of life with election, their

---

7   Strype, *EM.*, I(i), 126-9.

8   Above, 36-40, 185-6.

9   M.D.Lambert, *Medieval Heresy* (London, 1977), 265. However, Anne Hudson (ed. *Selections from English Wycliffite Writings*, Cambridge, 1978) concludes that the Lollards remained indebted to Wyclif's thought and phraseology (p.9). She maintains that the recent tendency among scholars to minimise Wyclif's direct influence is 'untenable' (pp.8-10).

10   Gordon Leff, *Heresy in the Later Middle Ages* (Manchester, 1967), II, 574-5, 583.

11   Foxe, *AM.*, IV, 237; Lambert, 270-1. In 1507 an English edition of the Gnostic *Gospel of Nicodemus* was circulated (RSTC 18565).

12   Leff, 577.

emphasis upon a literal and active obedience to scripture were all derived from this 'secular theology'.

Lollard attitudes to the secular authorities also find their counterpart in sixteenth century radicalism. Later Lollards had 'inherited from Wyclif the belief that the secular authorities should be the instrument to reform the Church'. Lambert continues,

> Wyclif himself constantly appealed to the State; Swinderby to the justices in parliament. Tracts were written with a eye to influencing the upper classes, and in 1395 a Lollard bill demanding reform was put on the doors of Westminster Hall and St. Paul's when parliament was in session. As late as 1410 a proposal came before parliament to disendow the possessioners.[13]

This erastian attitude is reflected in John Champneys' petition to the Duke of Somerset to intervene and arrange the public confrontation with the clergy that he was seeking. It is also evident in Champneys' expectation that the authorities would purge the church of its 'marked monsters'.[14] This is a characteristic feature of English Lollardy not found among the pre-Reformation movements on the Continent. It helps to explain why the majority of 'Gospellers', although theologically and ecclesiologically more advanced than most English reformers, were prepared to co-operate with the Edwardine Church.

The apocalyptic element in later Lollardy[15] is less apparent among the English radicals of the mid-sixteenth century, although, again, John Champneys' *The Harvest is at Hand* probably provides the clearest evidence of its survival. Of greater interest is the Lollards' predilection for the *Epistle of James*, 'that prosaic book which nourished the practical spirit of Lollardy'.[16] It is significant that the Lollards were 'little troubled by those complexities of *Romans* which beset Luther and his English followers'.[17] Similarly the later English radicals appear to have had little grasp of Pauline forensic righteousness achieved vicariously through the substitutionary   atonement   of   a   sinless   saviour.

---

13   Lambert, 249. Also Hudson, 4-5.
14   Above, 84-5.
15   Leff, 602; Dickens, 'Heresy and the Origins of English Protestantism', 59. Lambert maintains that 'exaggerated eschatological views' were not common in Lollardy (pp.269-70).
16   Dickens, 59.
17   *Ibid.*

Such a soteriology demands both the real divinity and the real humanity of the Saviour, and that in turn leads to Trinitarian doctrine. For these radicals, the Reformation brought – not a discovery of the Pauline writings and theology – but inspiration from the Johannine writings and doctrine. For Joan Bocher, Henry Harte, Robert Cooche *et al.* the *Epistle of James* was replaced by the *Gospel* and *Epistles of John* as the biblical cornerstone of their faith.

Undoubtedly the Continental reform movements did make a profound impact upon the last generation of English Lollards. In fact the 1530s, 40s and 50s witnessed a competition for the allegiance of these 'Gospellers' between the 'Word' and the 'Spirit', between Calvinism and prophetism. Referring to the Marian martyrs, Davis asserts –
> It is unlikely that any were true apostles of Anabaptism... rather some belonged to sectarian congregations which continued the speculation of rationalistic and biblical Lollardy. These eclectic conventicles moved towards the Radical Reformation; others were more loyal to the Edwardine orthodoxy.[18]

Some Lollards were certainly more eclectic than others, and their precedent was maintained by that minority of English radicals who preferred the teaching of the Continental Spiritualists to that of the English Reformers. This culminated in the late 1540s and early 1550s with the radicals' outright rejection of Reformed theology when that too eventually reached England from the Continent. Davis states,
> The evidence indicates that Lollardy bifurcated in the days of Edward; the choice before the remaining conventicles lay between reception of, and conformity to, the Protestant pattern; or a continuing sectarianism, a seed bed for Radical doctrines, and separatism.[19]

Notwithstanding the different social and educational background of its exponents, the majority of former Lollards appear to have accepted the doctrine and practice of the Reformed Church of England during the reign of Edward VI. However, with the notable exception of John Careless, theirs was a moderate Calvinism. Few were happy with the

---

[18] Davis, 'Heresy in south-east England', 429.
[19] *Ibid.*, 396, also 400-01.

doctrines of reprobation and the secret will of God.

Furthermore, 'from the first a minority felt itself out of tune with the Anglican compromise'.[20] After the Elizabethan Settlement their numbers increased. Elizabethan sectarianism was founded upon residual eclectic Lollardy. Rogers notes that many of the converts to Familism had formerly been orthodox Gospellers.[21] Such poor, illiterate folk were happy to revert to the psychological security of an exclusive conventicle conducted by artisans and comprised of their peers. After an interval of little more than twenty years they had reasserted their preference for a version of Christianity that rejected theological scholarship and ecclesiological patronage, that preserved its own identity within the traditional practices of Nicodemism, and that deeply respected the sacrificial ministry of itinerant elders.

II. The English Radicals and Anabaptism

During the period 1535-65 most of the beliefs listed as features of anabaptism in the royal pardons of 1540 and 1550[22] appear in English radicalism. However, they are found as single articles of faith propounded by individual radicals rather than as part of a cohesive body of divinity maintained by a distinct religious sect. Codification and organisation of the Spiritualist wing of 'anabaptism' appears to have been the major contribution of Hendrik Niclaes to that movement. The legacy of extreme sacramentarianism left by Lollardy ensured that every English radical denied that it was necessary to baptise infants. Nevertheless, there is no evidence which suggests that believers' baptism was being administered in England before 1559. It appears that the English Familists did re-baptise members of the Family who were over thirty, but for them the rite had a peculiar significance unconnected with traditional interpretations. Therefore, in this study the term 'radical' has been used in preference to 'anabaptist', particularly since it also comprehends the rationalist, anti-trinitarian element.

Believers' baptism as a rite of initiation was not practised in England in the sixteenth century. Horst argues that the practice of rebaptism 'was

---

[20] Dickens, 'Heresy and the Origins of English Protestantism', 64.
[21] Rogers, *Displaying* (first edition), F8^r, G1^v; *An Answere*, A4^v, K6^v.
[22] Above, 28-9, 114.

related to the situation of separation', and since for historical reasons English anabaptism was nonseparatist, 'rebaptism was not practised'.[23] Following this tautology Horst sets foot upon firmer ground when he suggests that the suspension of rebaptism ordered by Melchior Hofmann in 1531 under stress of persecution had some influence upon the English situation.[24] The anabaptist refugees from the Continent who influenced English radicalism in its infancy were all of the Melchiorite variety. By the late 1530s they were followers of the Spiritualist, David Joris. The followers of the more orthodox Dutch anabaptist, Menno Simons, do not seem to have made an appearance in England before 1559. Therefore, rebaptism is not to be expected in English religious radicalism prior to 1559 because the English radicals followed the lead of the refugees from the Netherlands. They adhered to the ban on re-baptism which was imposed by the leaders of the movement at Bocholt in 1536 under the influence of David Joris.[25] Tracing the development of baptismal theology in the Netherlands, Williams writes –

> Hofmann, converted to Anabaptism in 1530, stressed believers' baptism as the bond which constituted the believers members of the covenantal community of the saints, *bondgenooten*. By 1540, though baptism and bond remained important constitutive elements, the inner discipline of the fellowship based upon the ban was now receiving major attention.[26]

The formation of congregations by covenanting rather than by baptism is more akin to the traditions of English nonconformity, which probably owes much to Lollard precedents. Hofmann's changing emphasis, with the stress increasingly placed upon internal discipline rather than external baptism, also had an impact upon later developments in England. The disciplined congregation led by Henry Harte in London in 1556-7 and the rigorous use of excommunication revealed by the Surrey Familists in their depositions of 1561 reflect corresponding developments in Continental radicalism.[27]

---

23 Horst, 174.
24 *Ibid.*
25 Above, 15, 30-1; Williams, *Radical Reformation*, 309.
26 Williams, 396.
27 Above, 204-5, 331.

Notwithstanding the strong influence which residual Lollardy continued to exert upon the English scene, this investigation has been compelled to recognise the vigorous attempts made by Continental radicals to introduce even more unorthodox doctrines into the conventicles. These 'anabaptist' missionaries were usually Dutch or Flemish refugees from persecution. The dynamic proselytisation that was the cause of their suffering in their homelands was continued on a smaller and more localised scale in this country. However, the language barrier proved difficult to surmount, and therefore imported literature played a prominent part in their propaganda.

At the beginning of the period (*circa* 1534-5) a company of English radicals was detected while engaged in the importation of a printed anabaptist confession, probably from Antwerp. The confession may have been the Schleitheim articles of 1527. Associated with this project were at least two Flemish Melchiorites, one of whom was the leader of the conventicle.[28] Even at this early date there were English conventiclers who maintained an unorthodox christology and rejected all expository preaching.[29] In *circa* 1538 Melchiorite refugees in England published and circulated a book that explained their christology. Peter Tasch was able to report that 'the truth' was growing quietly and spreading steadily among English conventiclers.[30] In 1548 Henry Harte commended the work of 'Godly messengers' who were active both in this country and overseas.[31] John Knox was the subject of such an attempt at proselytisation by means of literature in 1553. On that occasion the book was Gnostic in character and probably originated from 'Marcionite' members of the London Strangers' Church.[32] The incident suggests that they had succeeded in securing the fervent allegiance of at least one Englishman.

During the reign of Edward VI Christopher Vitells appears to have been influenced by members of the foreign community in London. He

---

[28] Above, 3-8.
[29] Compare Articles 24, 25 and 46 of the 1561 confession of the Surrey Familists.
[30] Above, 17-8.
[31] Harte, *Consultorie*, A7^r-A7^v.
[32] Above, 261-2.

claimed that they directed his opinions towards anti-trinitarianism.[33] It may be that foreign radicals spearheaded the rejection of Reformed doctrine in the English conventicles. However, rejection of a determinist theology would have been the instinctive reaction of those who were schooled in later Lollardy. On his return to England from the Netherlands in 1555 Christopher Vitells introduced the doctrines of Hendrik Niclaes to English radicals.[34] Thereafter, English Familists regularly visited the Continent to consult the 'bishop' of their sect. When, in 1574-5, Vitells translated the works of Hendrik Niclaes, had them printed in the Netherlands, imported them into England, and distributed them among English conventiclers, he was only continuing a process of literary proselytisation that had been in operation for forty years and more.

Initially the activities of the Continental radicals were centred in London and Colchester. Until 1555 progress was slow, but after the commencement of the Marian persecution they met with considerable success among the surviving English conventiclers. In fact the underground Predestinarian congregations were forced to seek assistance from overseas to combat the influence of English and foreign Nicodemites.

John Rogers and John Knewstub were convinced that the roots of Hendrik Niclaes's doctrine were grounded in the teaching of David Joris.[35] The anabaptist refugees who entered England in the 1530s were (like Joris) followers of Melchior Hofmann. By the end of that decade they were followers of Joris. It was this Spiritualist or Davidist version of Continental radicalism that had a small following of native English men and women (*pace* Joan Bocher) throughout the period. The spiritual doctrines enunciated by Hofmann, Joris and Niclaes were part of a tradition that reached back beyond the Lutheran Reformation. Penrhys-Evans, following Bainton, maintains that 'the *Theologia Germanica* must have been at least a background to HN's thought'.[36] Samuel Rutherford made the same claim as early as 1648.[37] Rupp refers to 'an anti-Augustinian current... with a stress on Free Will, and on the indwelling of the Spirit' that moved along the left wing of the Reformation.[38] This current had begun to move long before 1517; it was making itself felt in

---

[33] Above, 297-8, 304-5.
[34] Above, 301-3.
[35] Rogers, *Displaying* (first edition), C4^v, H5^v; Knewstub, N2^r.
[36] Penrhys-Evans, 23.
[37] Rutherford, *op.cit.*, 163-4.
[38] E.G.Rupp, 'Word and Spirit in the First Years of the Reformation', *Archiv für Reformation geschichte*, 49 (1958), 18.

the weaving communities of England and the Netherlands long before any religious radical had heard of Martin Luther or Melchior Hofmann. Rupp states,

> The Protestant left was the heir of the medieval underworld, to categories of thought and a vocabulary emerging from late medieval heresies, Waldensianism, the spiritual Franciscans, the German mystics, the modern devotion, the revival of Platonism, a varied vocabulary which pre-existed the Reformation and had its own power and momentum quite apart from Luther and from Wittenberg.[39]

In mid-sixteenth century England it was not only the refugee radicals from the Continent who represented that spiritual tradition. Joan Bocher, Henry Harte, Robert Cooche, Christopher Vitells – and perhaps John Champneys and John Trewe – were its best-known English advocates.

III The English Radicals and Anglicanism

It is perhaps anachronistic to refer to 'Anglicanism' in a study that terminates at 1565. Here the term simply denotes the established Church of England.

The English radicals – whether Lollard sacramentarians, Free-willers, anti-trinitarians, or Familists – were non-separatist because they had no option, if they were to survive in the England of the sixteenth century. Only for a brief period during the Duke of Somerset's liberal protectorate (1547-50) may they have asserted their ecclesiological independence. Before 1547 the traditions of Lollardy and the Six Articles ensured that they maintained a superficial conformity. After 1550 the dominance and intolerance of the advocates of Reformed theology in the Church of England drove the radicals back underground.

Therefore, the English radicals can be identified – not because of their nonconformity – but because of their opposition to Reformed doctrine

---

[39]   *Ibid.*, 14.

and preaching. It was the fierce antagonism with which committed Calvinists reacted to this unexpected opposition from English 'Bible-men' that threw the spotlight on the radical movement. Veron, Turner and Hooper during the Edwardine period, Philpot, Careless and Knox during the Marian regime, Grindal, Foxe and Crowley during the early years of Elizabeth's reign – all abominated the doctrines of Free-will and impeccability as much as Romanism. For these ardent Calvinists anti-trinitarianism was the ultimate heresy – worse even than the abominations of Rome. In comparison with these fierce protagonists, the attitude of Cranmer and Ridley during the Edwardine reformation, of Bradford during the Marian persecution, and of Parker after the Elizabethan Settlement, appears deceptively mild and conciliatory.

It was probably as a direct result of the greater breadth of vision exhibited by Cranmer and Ridley that some of the more able English 'anabaptists' such as Thomas Putto, John Champneys, Robert Cooche and Thomas Cole were ordained to the ministry of the Edwardine Church.[40] Of course Thomas Cole's flirtation with religious radicalism was but brief. It may be no coincidence that, among the nine men who are known to have been involved with the English radical movement and who were subsequently ordained, Thomas Cole was the only one who found complete acceptance and pursued a successful career in the Church of England.

After the Marian persecution – and probably as a direct consequence of it – other former radicals such as Thomas Upcharde, Robert Cole, Richard Prowde, and William Porrege sought and gained ordination to the ministry of the established church. There may well have been other former radical Gospellers whose talents the ecclesiastical authorities were prepared to recognise. They would have been admitted to the

---

40   The celebrated George Eagles may also have been an Edwardine ordinand and licensed preacher. Foxe refers to this former Lollard tailor as one 'whom Christ called' to leave his 'base occupation' and 'apply himself to the profit of Christ's Church'. Foxe continues,
Which man, as before in those most bright and clear days of King Edward the sixth, he had not unfruitfully showed and preached the power and force of the Lord, so afterward...
Eagles' associate, Ralph Allerton of Much Bentley, organised a conventicle during the Marian period which used the Edwardine liturgy. George Eagles regularly preached at these gatherings (Foxe, *AM.*, VIII, 393; Above, 112 n. 280.).

diaconate and licensed to preach in a particular diocese. Henceforth they served in the Church of England as wandering unbeneficed preachers. Thomas Putto, the former tanner, served the Edwardine Church in that capacity in and around Colchester. John Champneys probably did the same in the diocese of Exeter, and – perhaps – returned to his itinerant preaching ministry after 1560.

One most surprising example of a radical who became an itinerant preacher in the Elizabethan Church is John Kemp. In 1556-7 he was the deacon or messenger of the Free-willer congregation which gathered in Southwark under the leadership of Henry Harte.[41] In 1579 William Wilkinson noted, 'This Kemp is now living and is preacher in the Yle of wight'.[42] Commenting upon Stephen Morris' deposition, Wilkinson asserts that Kemp was, 'by this popish priest slaundered... being a very Godly man'.[43] However, while Morris was unable to say what Kemp's doctrine was, John Careless had included Kemp with Harte and Gibson at his interrogation earlier in 1556.[44] Careless evidently believed that John Kemp had identified himself with Henry Harte's 'blasphemous articles' and with Harte's attempt to influence the Newgate prisoners against Careless' predestinarian doctrine. It appears, therefore, that John Kemp had been a close associate of Henry Harte during the 1550s, that he had been a Free-willer and possibly an anti-trinitarian, but nevertheless he had been ordained and licensed to preach in the Elizabethan Church. It is questionable whether William Wilkinson – the Cambridge schoolmaster – really knew what John Kemp was preaching on the Isle of Wight.

In conclusion it is suggested that the last generation of English Lollards was confronted by two great challenges during this period. The first was the establishment of a truly reformed Church of England by the Edwardine authorities. Although these reforms were conducted by men with a very different social background and a far wider education, they satisfied the majority of Gospellers. These former Lollards accepted the *Book of Common Prayer* services and articles of faith of the Church of

---

[41] Above, 202-3, 204-5, 231n.
[42] Wilkinson, A3^V margin.
[43] *Ibid.*
[44] Foxe, *AM.*, VIII, 164, 384.

England, and some even entered its ministry. Later they were to form the constituency from which the radical Puritan clergy drew their support. However, a minority of Lollards – more separatist in their inclinations and more radical in their doctrines – refused to accept the Edwardine Reformation. The second great challenge to former Lollard conventiclers was posed by the Marian persecution. In these adverse circumstances, they were forced to choose between joining the underground predestinarian congregations, and thereby risking martyrdom, or adopting a Nicodemite conformity. The courage and conviction with which many supporters of the Edwardine reforms faced the ultimate test persuaded some of the remaining conventiclers to throw in their lot with the 'Anglican' predestinarians. Other less hardy individuals preferred the Familist compromise. Ultimately, the choice facing the Gospellers was not ecclesiological but ideological. In the 1550s indigenous Lollardy and the Continental Reformation movements finally coalesced. Then the Bible-men had to choose between the Reformed conformity of Calvinism and the Nicodemite conformity of Spiritualism.

———————————————————

This study has gone some way to provide answers to two problems that occur in the history of later English Nonconformity. First, why were Baptists so late in establishing their churches in England? Part of the answer surely lies in the fact that the majority of potential Baptists – the Lollards who for so long had denied that the baptism of infants was necessary – joined the Reformed Church of England during the Edwardine period. Furthermore, many English proto-Baptists (the Free-willers) were discredited by their actions during the Marian persecution. These Free-willers either joined their 'orthodox' brethren in the Predestinarian, paedobaptist, underground congregations or became associated with anti-trinitarianism and degenerated into Familist sectarianism. When English Baptists finally returned to their homeland and established Baptist churches, they too came from the Netherlands. However, they came out from the orthodox Mennonite version of Dutch Anabaptism and not from Davidist Spiritualism.

Second, why did the Family of Love survive for so long in England in comparison with the Family in the Netherlands and France? The answer suggested by this study is that it was established upon a firmer indigenous foundation. Christopher Vitells was able to build upon the structures left by Lollardy, and his movement received considerable impetus from the Marian persecution. The Family of Love in England was heir to the ethos and traditions of the Lollard conventicle.

The Appendix

Orthography
Where a text has already been printed (No.1 and Rogers' section of No.4) the spelling is that of the printed text. Richard Laurence modernised the spelling and punctuation of John Trewe's treatise, and John Rogers revised the original spelling of the 1561 depositions. Where the text has been transcribed directly from an original manuscript (Nos. 2, 3 and the end of No. 4) the original spelling and punctuation have been retained including the standard contractions (*e.g.* wcc=which, wt=what, yt=that, electio=election *etc.*).

Document I
The first document appended is an account of the predestination controversy that raged among prisoners in the King's Bench during the years 1554, 1555 and 1556. It is the only substantial text from the freewiller side of the dispute to survive.

John Trewe was the leader of a group of prisoners from Sussex who had been imprisoned in the King's Bench for refusal to attend mass. His account dated 30th January 1555 (*i.e.* 1556) was smuggled out of the prison but, unlike many of the predestinarians' literary remains, it was never printed. However in c.1560 a transcription was made of this and twelve other letters and treatises from the same period and preserved within Bodleian ms.53. Three treatises by John Bradford and one by John Philpot are included in this collection, and it may be that Trewe's account has survived because it was lodged with their originals.

Two hundred and fifty years later, during the course of the long-running (1770-1830) controversy between high Calvinists and high Churchmen over the extent to which the formularies of the Church of England were Calvinist, Richard Laurence, Professor of Hebrew at Oxford, rediscovered this collection of transcripts. As evidence for the anti-predestinarian cause Laurence published in 1819 two documents from the manuscript (R. Laurence, *Authentic Documents Relative to the Predestinarian Controversy*, (*op.cit.*)). In his introduction, Laurence describes how previous scholars thought this work had been lost, and he provides a full description of each item in the manuscript. He prints Bradford's two-part treatise on predestination entitled 'Defence of Election', which includes his answer to Henry Harte's treatise 'The enormities...' (see 194ff., 215-6), but he omits Bradford's dedicatory epistle to Joyce Hales. Since the whole of Bradford's work has been printed by the Parker Society (and reprinted 1979), it is not necessary to reproduce these documents. Then Trewe's account of the King's Bench controversy is added – but that has never been reprinted.

Since Laurence's work was undertaken so long ago and his book is now so rare as to be virtually unobtainable a reprint should prove useful. His text has been checked against the transcription in Bodleian ms.53 and found to be extremely accurate. Where a word is added to the original, Laurence always puts it in square brackets. The italics are, however, Laurence's own polemical emphases. There are no underlinings in the transcription and only an occasional marginal pointer. A detailed consideration of this text and the circumstances surrounding its production is given on pp. 266ff.

Document II
The second document is taken from Emmanuel College, Cambridge, ms.260. This letter, a single folded sheet, is located among a collection of original letters and transcripts which are bound together under the title 'Letters of the Martyrs'. On folio 87 there is a transcript of a letter that Henry Harte wrote to some prisoners in Newgate who were awaiting execution.

At Christmas 1555 Cuthbert Sympson had drawn up a set of articles which were designed to bring to an end the predestinarian controversy in the King's Bench. As the first document records, John Trewe, the leader of the freewillers, reluctantly assented to them when pressed by the predestinarians' leader, John Careless. Subsequently Careless sent a copy of these articles to their former associates, the condemned Essex men who had been transferred to Newgate. However, in the course of transmission, they came into the hands of Henry Harte who added his own comments on the back of the sheet. The Newgate prisoners responded by assenting to Sympson's mediating articles and then their leader, William Tyms, copied out Harte's rebuttal and each prisoner added their refutation of his teaching. This document was then sent to John Careless for circulation around the King's Bench. Three days later (24 April 1556) the Newgate prisoners were burned at Smithfield. The next day John Careless was brought out of the King's Bench for examination and his interrogator embarrassed him by producing the document containing Cuthbert Sympson's articles with Henry Harte's repudiation on the reverse.

The document preserved in Emmanuel College ms.260 is a transcript of William Tyms' copy of Henry Harte's letter. It is dated April 21 and the original must have been intercepted and then sent on to Newgate between March 28 and 21 April 1556. Harte's comments reveal the strength of his opposition to the predestinarians' doctrine of justification by faith alone. His rejection of trinitarian statements and his exhortation to place themselves within God's covenant are also of considerable theological significance. For a full discussion of these issues refer to the section on Harte, 218ff..

Document III
Among the thirteen pieces of writing preserved in transcript in Bodleian ms.53 are three by Hugh Latimer's Swiss servant, Augustine Berneher. He came to Oxford to study in the autumn of 1548 and soon became Latimer's disciple. When Latimer was imprisoned Berneher remained in Oxford assisting the Reformers. In 1554 he helped Jewell to escape to London, and throughout 1554 and 1555 he liaised between the Oxford and London prisoners. He sided with the predestinarians in the King's Bench controversy, and in January 1555 took Bradford's 'Defence of Election' to Ridley seeking his endorsement and urging the Oxford bishops to answer Henry Harte. Berneher travelled around the underground congregations especially after the martyrdom of Latimer and Ridley on 16 October 1555. In December 1557 he assumed leadership of the London predestinarian congregation until Thomas Bentham returned from exile the following spring.

It was probably during this period when he was temporarily responsible for the London congregation that Berneher composed the three works preserved in Bodleian ms. 53. All three are related to the predestinarian controversy. The first (fols.103 ^{r} - 114 ^{v}) is an answer to four questions posed by Henry Harte and was intended for publication. Since Harte died in the spring of 1557 this is probably the earliest of the three pieces. The second is in two sections (fols. 126 ^{r}- 137 ^{v}). The first section consists of Biblical texts and exposition against the freewiller doctrine of general election to salvation, and the second is entitled 'An answer to certain Scriptures which some men bring in for the maintenance of the same proposition'. The men Berneher refers to are John Laurence and his servant John Barre who came from Barnehall, near Wickford in Essex. They had attempted to assume Henry Harte's role as chief exponent of the freewill position.

The next item in Bodleian ms. 53 is the appended letter (fols. 138 ^{r} - 139 ^{v}). It was written by Laurence and Barre in reply to the preceding text. From statements within the letter it would appear that they had left their collection of proof texts with the London underground congregation of predestinarians in August 1557, but when they revisited the congregation later in the year all Berneher had done was to urge them to agree to the statements in his book answering Henry Harte. Their second visit provoked Berneher to write his second treatise to answer their proof texts. Whereupon Laurence and Barre replied with the letter now preserved in Bodleian ms. 53. This in turn produced a reply from Berneher, which is the third of his writings in the manuscript (fols. 140 ^{r} - 146 ^{r}). Both letters must have been written *c.* January 1558.

Laurence and Barre's letter to Berneher reveals that their main objection was to the predestinarians' belief in divine reprobation with its associated teaching on the secret will of God. Reprobation implied that Christ's work of atonement was limited to the elect and that the reprobate were not responsible for their sins. Further information on John Laurence and John Barre is given on pp.129-34.

Document IV
The fourth document contains a detailed account of the Surrey Familists. It is in the form of depositions made by two former members of the sect before a local magistrate, William More, in May 1561. Each deposition is individually attested by the deponents – Robert Sterte, curate of Dunsfold, with his signature and Thomas Chaundler, clothier of Wonersh, with his mark. The original depositions, now held by The Folger Shakespeare Library in Washington D.C., consisted of sixty-six articles. In 1578 John Rogers published these depositions as an appendix to his book, *The Displaying of an horrible secte* (*op cit.*), but only printed fifty-three articles.

These depositions provide valuable information on the beliefs and practices of the Familist conventicle which had gathered at Wonersh in Surrey since at least 1559. They describe English Familist doctrine and practice when it was at an early stage of development. John Rogers was clearly correct in his assessment of their importance, but the reason for his failure to print some of the articles remains a mystery.

Since Rogers' text is faithful to the original – apart from the occasional omission of a phrase or sentence – fifty-three of the articles are taken directly from his appendix (sig. I4 ᵛ - K3 ᵛ). The remaining thirteen have been transcribed from a photocopy of Folger ms. L. b. 98. The number assigned to each omitted article indicates its position on the original manuscript. The final leaf appears to be in very poor condition because the last two articles are almost impossible to decipher. For further information on these depositions refer to the section dealing with the Surrey radicals (above, 328ff.), my notes following the thirteen transcribed articles, and Jean D. Moss, '*Godded with God': Hendrik Niclaes and his Family of Love* (*op. cit.*).

DOCUMENT I

John Trewe, the marked unworthy Servant of the Lord, being in bands for the testimony of Jesu, signifieth the cause of contention in the King's Bench, as concerning sects in religion, the 30th of January, Anno Dom. 1555.

Hitherto I have suffered much injury, and borne many a slanderous report of such, as were the beginners of this lamentable contention, rather than I would disclose their rash and uncharitable behaviour in writing, thinking ever, that they would have repented and amended it, and have come to an unity in the truth with us: which was like three or four times, but most likest at Christmas last, and yet it brake again by me, as they untruly report. For which cause I am now constrained briefly to write the beginning and continuing of this contention with the breaking of the unity, that now was begun, that it might be seen, who was in the fault thereof, that men might leave speaking evil of that they know not. God that seeth the secrets of all hearts knoweth that I lie not. They did give such occasion of evil and offence to the weak by their using of *gaming*, that we could do no less but gently admonish them to leave it, and to exhort them after the Scriptures to redeem the time, seeing the days are evil, and to leave such vain things, and to mourn with us, that did mourn for the great misery that is fallen on this land, and for the lamentable perplexity that many of our weak brethren (that were not able to bear the cross) were in, and to watch and pray continually, that God might mitigate his wrath, and strengthen us and our brethren in his truth to stand, that our lives and deaths might glorify his holy name.

With the which they were not content, but defended it by the Scriptures, and because we would not given them place, but disproved them by the word they were somewhat displeased with us; insomuch that in process of time they began to pick out matter against us, and because we did use abstinence and prayer, they reported us to be justifiers of ourselves, and such like; to the which *we answered that our justification came by faith in Christ's death and bloodshedding,* but that we did, we did it, that God might make us able to bear his cross, and that he would cease these sharp storms of persecution, the which (through this our sloth) was like to drive many one from God unto the devil, to their utter destruction both of body and soul. After other talk, in conclusion they did affirm, that none of them that God ordained to be saved, could be driven from him by persecution, nor yet by any other occasion or means. For all such as shall be saved (say they) were elect and predestinate thereunto before the foundation of the world was laid, and none of them can be damned, *do what wickedness they can.* And whereas we brought against them the Apostle Paul, which affirmeth that all were damned in Adam and destitute of the glory of God, and that the reward of sin is death, &c. that would not serve; for they most stiffly affirmed without any authority of the holy Scriptures, that *if the Elect did commit never so great offence or sin, they should not finally perish.* Whereby they do not only make St. Paul a liar, but also they destroy the fear of God, which is the beginning and right science of wisdom, and that being frustrate, *there is a great gate set open to carnal liberty*; unto the which we saw, that many did fly to their utter destruction, by the means of the said false doctrine.

Moreover we saw that it did put out of credit and unplace all those pithy places, and sentences in the holy Scriptures, that at these troublesome days doth cause men to forsake evils, and to stand to the truth, as their own words did manifestly declare. For when we asked them what was meant by the sentences written in Joshua xxiv. e. 2 Chron. xv. a. Ezek. xxxiii. e. Matt. x. c. Mark xiii. d. Luke xi. d. xxi. g. Romans xi. c. xiv. d. 1 Cor. iii. d. g. x. d. 2 Cor. vi. a. Gal. iii. a. 1 Tim. iv. a. 2 Tim. ii. Heb. iii. a. iv. a. vi. e. x. e. 2 Pet. ii. a. Apoc. ii. a. and such like, which threatened damnation unto God's Elect if they do wilfully sin against him, some of them compared them to the law, which now (as they said) is in no effect to condemn the Elect, because Christ hath fulfilled it. Therefore these sentences (said they) are written to put the Elect in fear to do evil, that their lives might glorify their Father, which is in heaven, and not to put them in fear of damnation. By this in effect they affirmed those Scriptures to be written in vain, or to put men in fear where no fear is, affirming in effect, *that the words of the Holy Ghost doth no more good, than a man of clouts with a bow in his hand doth in a corn field*, which will keep away the vermin crows awhile, but when they know it what it is, they will fall down beside it, and devour the corn without fear. And other some answered and affirmed, that the threatenings of those Scriptures should be no more certainly performed on the Elect of God, than this common proverb, which is, if the sky fall we shall catch many larks. Indeed Christ hath taken away the curse of the law from all his very Elect that continue in his word, or have a mind to do his will, and groweth forward in good works, although they be not come to that perfection, that is required of them; but such as have tasted of the good word of God, and were partakers of the Holy Ghost, &c. and do fall away as Saul, Asa, and Juda, and such like, and become persecutors of Christ in his members, Christ profiteth them nothing at all, but shall receive according to the saying of the Holy Ghost in the foresaid sentences.

This we saw the holy Scriptures did affirm, but they said it doth not; therefore we could not believe them therein, for we saw it was great derogation to God's glory and hurtful to his church; and yet they held and taught more odious things. All such (say they) that were not predestinate to be the heirs of the kingdom of heaven before the foundation of the world was laid, were ordained and reprobated to do wickedly and to be damned, which saying is untrue. Because they affirm contrary to the holy Scriptures, that there was but a remnant predestinate, (that is to say,) few ordained to be saved, and the whole multitude beside to do all manner of sin and wickedness, and that at the end to be damned. *God made them for this evil purpose, (say they,) and there is no means in them to avoid it*, but that those miserable wretches after their troublesome care here, must most woefully abide the terrible pains of eternal fire. To this loathsome end (saith this sect) they were ordained before there was any motion of evil in them, nor yet cause in their behalf, why they should be ordained to destruction more than the other were ordained to be saved; yet God ordained *them* (say they) to be *damned* and the *other* to be *saved*. These Scriptures and other do approve, that God ordained all men to be saved, Gen. i.d. Psal. cxlv. c. Preacher vii. d. 4 Esdras viii. d. Sapi. i. c. ii. d. Eccl. xv. b. 1 Tim. ii. a. 2 Pet. iii. b. but if God had done as they affirm, as he hath not, we saw not which ways to discharge him of *partiality*. For it seemed to us that they made him author of all the sin and abomination that is done and committed on the earth, clean discharging the devil and man thereof, in that they affirm, he made these sinful and miserable creatures only for that purpose and end. For he that maketh a thing only to do evil is the cause of the evil; as for example, we have in Sussex very many iron mills, which in wasting of wood do much hurt; and yet the fault is not in the mills but only in the beginners and makers of them; they cannot go without coals, that is made of wood; no more can the reprobates live (as they affirm) without committing of actual sin. There is no man can invent and finish a thing only to do evil, and he himself to be clear of all evil, even so in that they lay to God's charge, that he ordained and created those reprobates, and hardened their hearts only to commit sin and wickedness, they with the foul error of the Manichees sect do in effect affirm, that God cannot be pure and clean of all evil; and yet in words they will make much of God, and say he is most pure and clean from all evil and motion thereof, as he is indeed, and they will hold and teach the most detestable opinion, that in effect doth affirm, that there is not only a nature of evil in God, *but that he is also partial and the author of sin.*

Moreover to maintain their error contrary to these Scriptures, Gen. iv. a. Exod. xix. a. Deut. xxx. e. Joshua xxiv. 2 Chron. xv. a. 1 Esdras xii. a. Psalm vii. c. xxxii. c. liv. b. Prov. ii. a. Esay v. a. xlv. b. Jer. xi. xii. d. xviii. b. Ezek. xxxiii. Amos iv. Matt. ix. d. Luke xiii. g. John vi. g. vii. b. Rom. vi. c. vii. d. viii. d. 2 Cor. viii. d. James iv. b. Esd. ix. a. Eccl. xv. b. xvii. a. they hold and affirm, that there is no more wit growing in man unregenerated to desire or wish any thing, that should please God, that his free mercy and grace might extend to him to assist him to salvation, no more than is in a brute beast or dry post; whereby they give men occasion to hide and deny the same good gift, that God gave them in the creation, and not to be thankful to him therefore, but rather to curse him for that he hath ordained them to such a miserable estate, and end, as they untruly affirm he hath. Again we saw, that therein they did give great occasion to the wicked to bide still in their sins and wickedness, and to give their minds to fulfil the lusts and pleasures of the flesh and the world, to the utter destruction both of body and soul, thinking (as they teach) if they be elect, they shall come to their time, if not, they shall not be saved, if they suffer never so much straitness or misery to glorify God their Creator. And we saw that in effect *they made God a mocker, a vain person, and a fool. A mocker,* in that he offereth faith and salvation to such as he knoweth cannot receive it. *A vain person,* in sending his messengers, and in writing of his Scriptures, and long calling of them, whom he knew could not repent, come, nor answer. *A fool,* in that he mourned for man's destruction, and repented that ever he made man, for that they would not amend, but wrought out their own damnation; seeing he knew that there was no spark of wit nor will in them, that when they heard repentance and salvation preached, to desire, groan, or wish, that he would perform it in them.

Moreover we saw in that they did hold and affirm, that none but great learned men could have the true understanding of the word of God; and in that they would not nor could not answer us how they approved their doctrine; and in forbidding us to ask how they could approve that, which they taught; and in the defacing, displacing, and washing away of the holy Scriptures, and such like, they do jointly agree with the Papists, that do the like to maintain their superstition, idolatry and blasphemy, and their wicked beastly living; and that if we should have consented with them, we could never more with any good consciences read the holy Scriptures, because we saw not how to place them, nor what profit it could be unto us, seeing that opinion affirmed, that *our salvation rested all together on our fore ordinance, and no part on God's assistance in our perseverance*; which opinion in our sight was and is so wicked and detestable against the holy Scriptures, that our consciences grounded upon God's most holy word will not suffer us to consent to them, except we should do against God's words and our own consciences, and so to despair and be damned.

Moreover besides all these aforesaid detestable errors, enormities, and odious things laid to God's charge, to establish their false and most wicked opinion, they affirm, that *Christ hath not died for all men.* Whereby *they make Christ inferior to Adam and grace to sin, and doth destroy faith, and the certainty of our election;* and it is enough to drive as many, as believe it, to despair, for lack of knowledge whether Christ died for them or not. For their own authors affirm, that if a man were ten years established in the truth, and live very godly five of them, he might be none of them that Christ died for, how doth this agree with that they so stoutly affirm without the Scriptures, they were so elect in Christ's blood before the foundation of the earth was laid, seeing there is *none of them certain* (if they believe their ancient writers) *before their end, whether Christ died for [them] or not.* Thus we saw they did in effect destroy the thing they in words went about to build most strongly. They accused us of that thing we were free, and they guilty themselves. For we, that do hold and affirm the truth, that *Christ died for all men,* as appeareth Gen. iii. c. xii. a. xxii. d. Psal. lxxxii. b. Psal. cxlv. Esay liii. John i. c. Rom. v. c. 1 Cor. xv. c. 2 Cor. v. c. 1 Tim. ii. a. 1 John ii. a. Heb. ii. c.; we do by the holy Scriptures satisfy every man that doth repent and unfeignedly believe with a lively faith *[that he] is in the state of salvation, and one of God's elect children, and shall certainly be saved, if he do not with malice of heart, utterly forsake God,* and despise his word and ordinance, and become a persecutor of his children: until this time God will use his means with him, now his word, then his rod to raise him up again, if he do through negligence or weakness fall; and as long as he feeleth repentance and hope, and that he hath a will desirous to do God's will, he is under the promise of life made by God the Father in and through his Son Jesus Christ, which hath fulfilled that which was lacking in his part; so that he through God's gift and assistance do continue to the end, he shall be saved, though all men in earth, and devils in hell, say and do what they can to the contrary. *This certainty of our Election is sure, and agreeable to the word, but that which they hold is not.* Therefore we durst not for our lives and souls forsake this undoubted truth, and grant to that, which they by the word cannot approve to be true.

For these aforesaid causes and no other they did evil us, rail on us, and call us heretics, cast dust in our faces, and *give sentence of damnation on us,* and excommunicated us, and would neither eat nor drink with us, nor yet bid us God speed; and did keep away such money as was given them in common to distribute amongst us, that did lie for the truth, and caused us to be locked up that we should speak to nobody by their minds, lest we should warn them of their false and erroneous opinion, that is to[b] bad to the name of Predestination, *for that we hold, and also do affirm the certainty of Election in Christ's blood* in as ample manner as God's word doth teach and affirm. They being therewith not content, but did both in word and writing most shamefully slander us to be such hypocritish dissentious persons and notorious heretics, that we were not worthy to receive the benevolence that was due unto Christians; for no other cause, but that our consciences grounded on God's word would not suffer us to be of that sect. And that we would not keep silence hearing them to deceive the people with their imagined Predestination, or rather Manichees sect, that containeth so many detestable enormities and great absurdities against God, and his people, as is before said, and here ensuing again briefly repeated and numbered, to the end that all men

---

[b] So the MS. Perhaps it should be "too bad to bear the "name of Predestination.'

should the better mark it, and to beware that they fall not into the said most wicked, odious and false opinion, lest after they have begun in the spirit, they end in the flesh, as many have done to the great hindrance of the verity and to their own destruction.

1st Enormity. That this foul and abominable error of the Manichees sect or imagined Predestination containeth, is most odious against God; for in that it affirmeth *God ordained and created reprobates and hardened their hearts only to do evil*, it approveth contrary to the truth, that there is a nature or motion of evil in God, for it is written, as the workman is, such is the work.

2d Enormity. Also in that it affirmeth, that *God ordained some to be saved, the residue to be damned, before any of them had done good or evil*, it maketh God partial.

3d Enormity. Also it maketh *God the author of all the sin and abomination that is done or committed on the earth*, clean discharged the devil and man thereof, in that it affirmeth, that he ordained and created those that commit it for that only purpose, the which they cannot avoid.

4th Enormity. Also in that it affirmeth, that God made reprobates, that are altogether sin and wickedness, *it maketh God a liar*, which hath said, that all things, which he hath made, is exceeding good.

5th Enormity. Also *it approveth the holy Scriptures false*, in that they testify, that God is holy in all his works, and that he made all men just and pure, and to the end that they should do good works and to be saved.

6th Enormity. Also in that it affirmeth that Christ died not for *all* men, it defaceth the dignity, efficacy, and virtue of his passion.

7th Enormity. Also *it maketh Christ inferior to Adam*, in that it affirmeth that *he died not for as many as Adam damned*.

8th Enormity. Also *it maketh grace inferior to sin,* in that it affirmeth, that the grace of God in Christ was not of power to save all them that sin damned.

9th Enormity. Also it causeth the wicked to be unthankful to God for that good gift that he gave them in their creation, in that it affirmeth, that *they have no more, that they can use towards God's will, than a dry post.*

10th Enormity. Also *it causeth the wicked to live still in their wickedness*, in that it affirmeth, there is nothing in them, that they can better occupy; against the which if there were no Scriptures written, experience in man, even when he was most wicked, is enough to confute.

11th Enormity. Also in that it affirmeth, that *the reprobates have no way nor means to escape hell torments*, it is enough to cause all such as believe it, and feel not the work of Election working in them, to despair, and blaspheme God for their creation.

12th Enormity. Also *it causeth many to live at free chance careless*, in that it teacheth them, that they were elected or reprobated before the foundations of the world were laid, and *if they be in, they cannot fall, and if they be out, their weeping cannot help.*

13*th Enormity.* Also in that it affirmeth, that *there is none can be damned that are elect into God's church and favour, do what wickedness they can*, it causeth many such as were elect into the number of God's chosen, and have suffered persecution for his word and name's sake, to take liberty, and by that means fall away from God unto the devil and sin, [and be] damned.

14*th Enormity.* Also in that *it breedeth doubt and causeth contention and licentious carnal living*, and such like, it is a great slander to the truth, and causeth the house and congregation of God to be evil spoken of to God's dishonour, and hurt to the weak and ignorant brethren, and to the encouraging, triumphing, and hardening the heart of the enemies, to the great lamentation of many a Christian heart, and the cause, that God's anger will the sooner fall upon this realm.

15*th Enormity.* Also it destroyeth *the certainty of our Election*, and is enough to drive all such as believe it to despair for lack of knowledge, whether Christ died for them or not; yet in words they will say, the same opinion doth most assuredly establish the certainty of our Election, but in effect and deed it doth deny it, in that it affirmeth, that there is no man certain, whether he be elect or no, until the end.

16*th Enormity.* Also *it doth destroy faith* which is a certainty of things which are not seen, in that it affirmeth, that there is no man certain, whether he were predestinate to be saved or not, *until the end*; and yet they will say, that it doth most strongly build faith, and that every one that believeth that he is predestinate, and feeleth that his sins are forgiven, is predestinate, and may most assuredly ground his faith, that he shall be saved; and yet their own writers and doctrine doth affirm, that if a man do believe that he is predestinate, and believeth and feeleth that his sins are forgiven by the blood and death of Christ, and have walked in the way of life, and afterward fall away, *he was never predestinate nor elect.*

17*th Enormity.* Also *it doth put away and make frustrate the grace of Christ,* and principallest point of the fear of God, in that in effect it affirmeth, that none of those that are predestinate and elect can never more finally perish, do what sin and wickedness they can.

18*th Enormity.* Also *it giveth an occasion to neglect prayer,* and to leave it altogether except it be for corporal food, raiment, and health of body, and such like, and nothing for the soul, in that it affirmeth contrary to the Scriptures, that *all such as were predestinate before the foundation of the world was laid, must of necessity be saved,* therefore they need not to pray for it, and the residue must of necessity be damned, and prayer will not help them.

19*th Enormity.* Also *it maketh God a mocker,* in that it affirmeth that he offereth faith to such, who, he knoweth, cannot receive it.

20th Enormity. Also *it doth unplace and wash away the pithy sentences and sharp threatenings of the holy Scriptures*, that are written to the Elect to cause them to take the more heed, and to cleave to God, and to walk the more circumspectly in his ways, lest they be damned, in that it affirmeth, that they *cannot* be damned.

21st Enormity. Also in effect *it affirmeth, that almost the whole Bible is of none effect*, for the whole content thereof is to exhort the wicked and reprobates to repent and believe, that they might be saved, and the godly and elect, that they give not over their members to be servants of sin, and so to be damned, in that it affirmeth, that the reprobates cannot repent in such wise, that God's mercy and grace unto salvation might extend to them, nor yet the elect committing such sin, that they shall be damned for it.

22d Enormity. Also it doth stablish the error of the Papists, in that it forbiddeth, that any should ask, which ways or how it can be proved.

23d Enormity. Also in racking, and washing away the holy Scriptures, and in affirming, that no simple man without the tongues can truly understand them, it doth not only agree with the Papists, but also it doth cause all such as believe it to neglect reading of the holy Scriptures, and to fall to other vanities and wickedness, because *they* are so manifestly and flat *against that most wicked and false opinion.*

Notwithstanding *this foul error of the Manichees sect; that containeth all these detestable enormities and odious things* against God, and hurtful to man, nor yet their revilings, slanderings, and misusing of us, which is so much to be resisted, we forgave them, and desired them to have their love, and promised to say the best of them, and to shew as much familiar joy and love to them as to our own souls, so that they would not teach it (nor other things, that they did hold) to God's dishonour and hurt of his church. Our request herein they granted three or four times, but indeed they soon brake it. For whereas they had concluded, that they should leave teaching of the false doctrine, which did breed doubt, brawling, and striving more than godly edifying, and none to speak evil by another, yet they ever brake it again, either by slandering of us or sending out writings against us, or maintaining this their folly, by racking the pure and holy word of God in their talk, and open lectures. As one time they fell out with us, and reported us to be abominable heretics, because we would not grant to them without approbations of the holy Scriptures, that our children might receive a lawful baptism in the church of Antichrist, in the which we did not stand against, lest we should therein allow and affirm Antichrist to be God's minister, and that he may do some good thing contrary to the Holy Ghost, which affirmeth, that their prayer is sin, and their blessing cursing; and that they should not take God's word in their mouths; and that we should have nothing to do with them, but separate ourselves from them, lest we be partakers of their sins, and so to receive of their plagues, which is after great misery in this world, to be cast into the lake of fire, that burneth with brimstone for evermore.

At another time we were like to come to an unity also, but then in an open lecture, contrary to all good judgements and their own promise, they taught and affirmed, that the voice of God, that said to Peter, make not common or unclean that which God hath cleansed, did affirm *play and pastimes to be clean to Christians*; of the which because we did gently shew them that these Scriptures were applied contrary to the mind of the Holy Ghost, to maintain sin rather than increase virtue, they were displeased, and stoutly defended it against all holy Scriptures, that did threaten punishment unto all such as did give themselves to fulfil the lust of the flesh in following the desire thereof in notorious sins and vanities, and such like; and after the old custom fell out with us, and would neither eat nor drink with us, nor yet bid us God speed, for nought else, but because we would not consent with them, that *play at bowls, dice and cards* was cleansed by the word and not sin, nor offence to all men; the which if they would have granted it to have been so much offence, as an idle word, and that it ought to be repented and grown from, we had been one with them therein; but they would not grant it to be so much, and yet there can no man use it without many idle words, beside misspending of the time, and giving offence to other, and such like. *They before confessed us to be of the true church and no heretics,* and upon the same would have received us to the communion, but then because we would not with them affirm against these Scriptures, as partly is to be seen by these Scriptures, Psal. ii. a. xxvi. a. Eccles. iii. ix. b. Luke xxi. g. Rom. xiv. d. Exod. xxxii. b. 1 Cor. x. a. Gal. v. d. Ephes. iv. d. v. a. Phil. ii. b. James v. b. that *vain play may be used of such as be in bonds, and look every day to suffer for the truth,* they did not only fall out with us, and *after their accustomed manner call and report us heretics*, cast dust in our faces, and *give judgment of damnation on us,* and otherways ungodly handled us; but also threatened us, that *we were like to die for it, if the Gospel should reign again*, affirming, that the true church might shed blood for believers' sake, of the which we brought to disprove them Ezek. xxx. e. Matt. v. e. xiii. d. xv. b. xviii. c. Luke ix. c. John x. b. 2 Thess. iii. 2 Tim. iv. d. Tit. iii. d. but it would not serve, for they would not suffer the holy Scriptures to have place, but wash them away by comparisons and glosses of their own imaginations, without any good ground or authority of the word, as they did all other most pithy and effectual Scriptures, that we did bring against them to confute their other false opinions.

Wherefore we gave them over, and meddled as little with them as we could, until Simson Upchear and Wodman, with other that were delivered out of prison, (for Simson came to us, and desired us to be at unity in the truth,) we answered, that it was our desire, and said to him, that if they leave teaching of their false doctrine, that hath done so much hurt, we would have love and fellowship with them, although they did hold it, so that it were not of obstinacy, as they confessed they did not. And the order of the unity was of both the parties put into Simson's and others, that were of that sect's, hands, that they with the consent of other Christians should devise such order between us (as concerning the unity) as might most redound to God's glory and the wealth and quietness of his church, and so we to have love and familiarity in the mean season, *as we had for a time*, to our great quietness and receiving of the congregation. But or ever the said order was concluded, certain of them came to us to give us warning that they would have a communion on Christmas day, which was not two days off, demanding of us whether we would receive with them or not. We answered, that we would gladly receive with them, but we would have the unity thoroughly established first, lest we did receive it to our damnation; for we take the communion to be (as it is) a thing of great efficacy and bond of peace, perpetual love, and perfection, that men should well examine themselves, whether they were in perfect love, and through God's gift and assistance able to keep the promise they make by receiving thereof. They said they were determined to receive, if we would receive with them they would receive [with] us; if not they would do it without us.

Then lest they should think, that we counted them not of the church of God, and so the unity, that was begun, should not be accomplished by that means, we thought to go as much with them as God's word and our consciences would give us leave, and asked them whether the communion might be received of heretics or ministered to them. They said, it might not be received of heretics nor ministered to them; and because they had called and reported us heretics, we desired that they would in writing confess us to be of the true church of Christ, and no heretics, and then after order taken how we should keep the unity we promised with the assistance of God to receive with them; and *then the order was taken and agreed on*, saving, that they desired, *that we would confess them in writing to be of the true church of Christ, as they would do us. The which we sticked at, because we had not slandered them, as they had done us.* For the which they denied our like request, yet notwithstanding after that we had reconciled ourselves each to other, they so embraced us, that we desired no writing at their hands: so they departed that night. And on the morrow they came all to us again; and brought certain articles with them, wishing us to put our hands to them, as they would do.

I was so overjoyed with the unity, that although I saw something in them not correspondent to the word, I would not find any fault in it, lest some of my fellows, that liked not the unity, should have found more, and so have broken altogether. I and other of my company put our hands to it, I thinking my conscience would have borne with it. But within a little while after, by the means of better perusing it by the word of God, my conscience accused me, that I had set my hand against God, and fell in despair, and sick withal. And within three or four hours after, *Careless, the chief of their company,* came to me, and demanded to know how I did. I said I was sick. Wherewith he would not be answered, but he desired to know whether my conscience did not burden me with any thing that I had done, as concerning this unity, or not. If I would tell him, he promised me of his honesty to keep it secret, and to do me good therein, and not hurt. Whereupon I told him, that my conscience accused me, that I had done evil in putting my hand to the articles; because some of them were not in all points agreeable to the truth, and told him wherein, that which he could not well deny, but yet he said, that it might well be borne withal, until the time of reformation, the which he would not be against, if it did ever happen to come. I told him plainly, that I thought my conscience would have borne with it, but because it is like to come into so many men's hands, it certifieth me, that if it be not sound, (as it is not) it will redound greatly to God's dishonour, the hurt of his church, and to our shame and utter damnation. Therefore I did most heartily desire him, that as he would my salvation the unity might go forth without writing, because we did not agree in doctrine; (I doubted, that if it were sound in all points, he would not put his hand to it,) the which he would not grant me, but wished me to be contented with that was done, and if my conscience would bear with it, he would make a mean with his company, that my hand should be out, (if I would not be a let to my company in putting to of their hands, the which I promised I would not;) but he said he would keep it to himself till the morrow, hoping, that my mind would be otherwise then.

And so he departed, and demanded of my company, whether they would set their hand to it, and receive with them, if I would not. They denied it also; for they had found fault in it also. Then he desired them to make another, and he and his company would put their hand to it, if it were not repugnant to the word. The which they said they would not do, except I did agree with them therein. So he left them, and on the morrow he came to me again, and asked me, whether it were any better with me in soul or body. I said no, but rather worse, (as it was indeed;) for my conscience accused me, if I did receive the communion, as I promised to do, on the morrow after, I should receive it unworthily to my utter damnation; and so I told him. Then he said, that he would not so burden me, and would keep love with me, although there were no writing made at all, the which greatly eased my heart, body, and soul. Notwithstanding he laid importunately on my fellows, to make a writing, even as they would themselves, being not so much against the word. The which some of them granted; and so they came to me to make it. I told them, that his judgement was so corrupt, that if I did make it, as nigh the truth as God's word and my conscience would bear with it, I doubted, that he would not set his hand to it, but rather pick out matters against us in it. The which they thought they would not.

Whereupon I granted them to do it; and then we went to prayer to God, that he would assist me with his holy Spirit according to his will, and as nigh them as he would we should, lest they should resist it, when it was made. And so I went about it; and when it was made, my fellows shewed it him. The which when he saw it, he kept it to pick out heresies against us in it, refused to put his hand to it according to his faithful promise, and yet he would not disprove it by the word. Thus he brake off the unity, and reported it to be my doing: but the truth is so it was altogether his. For I was determined not to withdraw my hand, nor to say against that I had done therein, do God with me what he would, if he in secret had not given me licence. And yet after our agreement (contrary to his promise) he sent out a book, wherein he had slandered us, whereupon we might have lawfully broken off, yet notwithstanding that, nor the betraying of my secrets and refusing to put to his hand to our sound articles, or all other their misusing of us, or their false opinions, so that they would keep their promise in not teaching of them, nor yet slander us in word nor writing, we offered and desired to have fellowship with them without writing. The which they refused; and out of these articles have raised up new slanders on us, *reporting us that we should deny that Christ was come in the flesh, and that he passed through the blessed Virgin Mary, as saffron doth through a bag; which detestable opinion we hate and utterly abhor*, as in these articles among other things is to be seen.

And because you should be certified of the truth thereof, and other things, that we have been slandered of; and not to damn your own souls in believing lies and false reports, that without any occasions (by us given) goeth on us, I have written these articles here ensuing. Read this, and then without affection judge according to knowledge and right, and not by hearsay; for it was expressed that our Saviour Jesus Christ should not give sentence by hearsay, and all Christians must follow his footsteps. Therefore whosoever so doth, declareth himself not to be Christ's disciple; and the Lord for his mercy in Christ's sake amend all things that are amiss. Here you see a great fault; and it is nothing in comparison of the great unnaturalness, that they have shewed us. I beseech the Lord, that it be not laid to their charge, and that he would send his loving rod among us, that thereby the truth might be known, and agreed upon to our salvation in Christ Jesus, seeing his word will not serve. *The Almighty, dreadful God, whose terrible judgment I cannot escape, doth know, that I have not written this of any hatred that I bear to their persons*, nor that I would have them put to utter shame hereby; *but that the people of God should not so much commend them in their doing, and condemn and hate us without a cause*; and that they should not fall to their *detestable* opinions to the utter destruction of an innumerable multitude of souls. The Lord keep us from all evil. Amen.

Here followeth the articles word for word, as they have a copy of them to shew, the which, if they would have set their hands unto according to their promise, as we would have done ours, we had come to an unity.

1. We all consent and constantly confess and believe, that there is one, and but one, very true living and everlasting God, which is three in persons, and but one in substance, the Father, the Son, and the Holy Ghost, of equal power, majesty, goodness, and eternity, as it is truly taught and believed in the true church of Christ, grounded upon God's word, and ever shall be, of which true church we acknowledge ourselves, and every one another, to be true and lively members.

2. And we confess and believe, that the second person in trinity, which is Jesus Christ, the very self-same woman's seed, that God promised to Adam should tread down the serpent's head, yea the same eternal Son of God, that St. Paul affirmeth, that when the time was fully come, God sent made of a woman, and made bound to the law, to redeem them, which were bound to the law, *that we through Election might receive inheritance,* that belongeth to natural sons; and, *that he took so much flesh and blood and nourishment of the blessed Virgin Mary, as any child doth of his mother,* as St. Paul saith; forasmuch then as children are partakers of their mother's flesh and blood, he also took part with them, and *so became very man in all points, like unto his brethren, sin only excepted,* so that two perfect natures, the Godhead and manhood, were perfectly joined together in one Christ, never to be divided, of whose kingdom there is no end.

3. We confess and believe all the articles of the Christian faith, contained in the symbol commonly called the Apostles' Creed.

4. Also we confess and believe and faithfully acknowledge, that all salvation, justification, redemption, and remission of sins cometh unto us *wholly and solely through the mere mercy and free favour of God in Jesus Christ,* purchased unto us through his most precious death and bloodshedding, and *in no part or piece through any of our own merit, works, or deservings,* how many or how good soever they be; and that his body offered to the death once on the cross for all, and his bloodshedding, is as St. Paul affirmeth, *a sure and perfect sacrifice and sufficient reason for all the sins of Adam, and for all and singular of his posterity's sins,* how great and many soever they be; and *all,* that truly repent, unfeignedly believe with a lively faith, and *persevere* therein to the end of this mortal life, shall be saved, and *that there is no decree of God to the contrary.*

5. And also we do acknowledge and confess, that all Christians ought to know and keep God's holy commandments in as ample manner, as our Saviour Christ, and his Apostles have left unto us by example or writing, that is to say, they must continually watch and pray to God, to assist

them with his holy Spirit, that they may leave, and utterly forsake all idolatry, whoredoms, murder, theft, extortion, covetousness, drunkenness, gluttony, rioting, *with all vain gaming, slandering, lying, fighting, railing, evil communications, with sects and dissensions*; and not to be curious in many of God's works, nor to make too much searching in superfluous things, nor yet follow strange doctrine, neither give heed to fables, and endless geneaologies, that breedeth doubts more than godly edifying. And whereas we have offended in any of these things, or in any other ways against God and his Church, we are heartily sorry for it, and do most earnestly repent, and do through God's gift and assistance promise never hereafter to do any more; *but in ourselves to perform it we find not*, therefore we will continually pray, desiring all faithful Christians to pray with us, that God of his mercy in Christ's sake *would perform it in us*, that both our lives and deaths might glorify his holy name.

6. Also *we do heartily acknowledge, confess, believe, and are most assuredly certained by God's most holy word*, that our Saviour Jesus Christ his pure religion, and *secret will revealed in his word*, sufficient for man's salvation, was *in this realm declared and known in good King Edward the VIth his days; which word of God was then truly preached, and sufficiently taught, and his sacraments duly ministered*, and of some followed; therefore we acknowledge them in England Christ's true church visible, as the faithful, thankful, joyful, and most constant persevering, and suffering of our godly preachers and brethren (for whom we cannot worthily praise God) doth most manifestly declare: yet notwithstanding for them, and for other great and manifest benefits, that we have unworthily received of God we most heartily praise and thank, and do give over ourselves, both body and soul, to worship, honour, and glorify the same almighty, eternal, and most living God, the Father, the Son, and the Holy Ghost, now and for ever.

7. And forasmuch as St. Paul saith, that our knowledge is imperfect, there is none of us, but that we be ignorant in some things, therefore through most earnest prayer and diligent seeking of the holy Scriptures, the Holy Ghost hath moved us to leave contention, and to seek peace and ensue it, and to let things pass, which are not to be concluded on, seeing they may be borne by God's word, rather than still to contend about them to the derogation of God's glory, and hurt of his church, and not one to trouble another's conscience in vain dissenting, and reasoning about that thing, that he seeth can do him no good, so that the truth be not defamed, nor evil spoken of, and the falsehood taught to the hurt of others; the which we have promised not to do in word nor writing, but to keep silence from the truth in such things, as God's word is not utterly against, rather than to offend his brother. As we have taken a godly order in that matter, God continue it to his honour and glory, to open to each other the thing that is needful, that he seeth not; and that we and all other true Christians may all be of one heart and of one mind in the undoubted

verity, that every one of us doth unfeignedly seek to maintain, and set forth. And if we do miss in any point, we confess, that it is of simplicity, and not of obstinacy. Therefore in all things known or unknown, *we do most humbly and lowly submit ourselves, and all our judgments unto the pure word of God, and to the true church of Christ, grounded upon the same,* governed continually by his holy, almighty Spirit; who lead and conduct us into all truth for his glorious name's sake and keep us therein unto the end. Amen.

John Trewe, Thomas Avington, Richard Harman, John Jacksonne, Henry Wickham, Cornelius Stevenson, John Guelle, Thomas Arede, John Saxbye, Robert Hitcherst, Matthew Hitcherst, Margery Russell. All we do affirm this to be true.

DOCUMENT II
The Letter of Henry Harte to the Prisoners in Newgate March/April 1556

Recto:

A true coppye of letter w^{cc} Henrye Harte sent to newegate to ye prysoners ther condemndd to dy for ye conffessyone of christes ueryetye Agaynst sertayne Artycles w^{cc} they alowed y^t wer sette furth by sertayne prysoners c in ye kyngsbench to appiase ye contencyon y^t theyr fellowe prysoners had w^t them if it myght haue ben

If[1] ye knowe not whatt god is other wyse than he hath showed him self in his word no more do you or any man elss knowe whether he haue any parts or passyons or not / wherefor as ye owght to boast nothinge w^{cc} ye cannot proue: no more owght you or any other though they thinke them of ye church or ye church it self to search after cecrets w^{cc} ye holy gost for bydeth you least you perysh

And wher ye saye y^t euerye one of you duly acknowledge other to be true and lyvelye members of your church / if ye mayntayne anye errors / ye beare wyttenes agaynst your selues

In ye ij artycle ye saye y^t god & mane were joyned to gether in christ into one persone neuer to be deuyded[2] / and and [sic] in ye fyrst ye saye y^t god was iij persons w^t one begynnynge and ending so y^t ye make qwaternytye in god if ye holde the humanytye w^{cc} our sauyour christ toke of ye blessed virgyne marye for a person and is not: this is a verylye uncertayne fayth for a mane to gyue his lyfe for when ye hold and affyrme in yor fyrst artycle that god is iij persons and then ye sayd in ye second that he is made one persone for euer / I praye you lett me knowe w^{cc} of these ye intend to hold for ye truth when ye haue well wayed ye matters amongst your selues / In your fourth artycle you saye yo^u do belieue all your saluacyon redempcyon and y^r remyssyon of syns comeste unto you holye and solye by ye mercye & fauor of god in chryst purchased unto you through his most p^rcyous death & blod shedynge onlye / & in no parte or pece by or through any of your owne meryts workes or deseruyng howe manye or good so euer they be and

---

[1] *Margin:* Agaynst ye fyrst artycle. eccl. 3, pro. 25, psalms 131a,

[2] *Margin:* Though ye confess all y^t chryst hath done & belieued it as an undowted verytie as it is in dede yet if ye leaue y^t undone w^{cc} ye shuld do yet shall ye perysh /

yet ye saye ye do not denye nor destroy good workes / but yu
acknowelege & confese y^t all mene are bownde to do them and to knowe
and kepe gods comandement but for all / but for all [sic] the confessyon
of this your stronge fayth yu were best to followe saynt pall whu thought
it no derugacyon to christes death nor passyone to saye / nowe joye I in
my sufferynge w^{cc} suffer for you and fullfyll y^t w^{cc} is behind or
lackynge of ye passyons of chryst in my flesh for his bodyes sake w^{cc} is
the congregacyone:^{3} for indede frynds if ye do then ye shall fynd y^e
workes of christ ar therfore profyttable / for all things ye alowe good
workes in worde yet if ye declare no benefytte to be towards them w^{cc} do
them / ye wer all most as good to do [?wyth owt] / frynds I feare ye
accept a carles mane to be yor teacher and he hath tawght ye as carles a
fayth but yet I saye unto you loke to ye matter for it is wayghtye / put
yourselues under ye couenants of god / and do it & se y^t yor hearts at y^e
least kepe his comandement w^{cc} thinge if you do / you shall obtayne all
ye benefyts of christ promysed w^{cc} ye speake of / & at thend the crowne
of glorye but if no / ye shall be sur by gods promysse though you gaue
your selues twyse to be refused & cast out of ye kyngedome of god / I
spare be cause I want tyme to speake anye thinge more –
Verso:
of yor v & vj artycles least I should loase more laber untyll I may heare
howe this is accepted at yor hands / by yor frynd ~~harrye~~ [sic] what so euer
ye say or judge harrye hart / as far as charytie byndeth me as knowest
god / if yor last artycle wer true / then wolde ye heare one mane as a
nother depend not of men but one ye truth for such as trust in men are
cursed of god
hear folowess y^t w^{cc} the aforsayd prysoners in newgat wrot uppon y^e
backe syd of ye brief
be fore god and mane I protest this doctryn of henrye hart to be most
blasfemose to chrystes death and passyon by me willyame tyms the xxjst
day of apryll in newegate condemned to dye for chrystes verytye –
also I Xopher lister do affyrme the same that our brother tyms hath sayd
ye I saye morouer y^t this doctryne of henrye hart is more to the
derogacyon of gods glorye then euer was heard at anye papyste mowth
fro ye w^{cc} good lord delyuer us and all other per me Xopher lyster – also

---

3   *Margin*: Colosy i. yu shall fynd some what also for you to do in ye flesh
    besyde all y^t chryst hast done w^{cc} if ye do not ye shall perysh not w^t standynge
    all his doinges

I Robart drake earnestlye affyrme the same y^t our brother tyms hath sayd ye I saye further y^t this doctryne of henrye hart is more to ye derogacyone of gods glorye and his passyone then all y^t euer anye papyst tawght frome w^{cc} god delyuer us per me Robert drake and so doth george ambrose affyrme the same y^t is aboue sayd also I thomas spurge affyrme ye same aboue wrytten and so doth Rychard spurge and so does Rychard gratwyke

I Jhon mace doth so wyttnes & protest y^t herin is that I do not [allowe] or holde it w^t Rychard nycoll Jhon spenser Jhon harman

This is to sartyfye you and all men y^t I symone Jon do grant to [?be] the wholl of chrysts teastment / but as for yur false oppynyons & slanderss report of my faythfull bretheren I utterlye denye & defye w^t all my heart /

DOCUMENT III

The Letter of John Laurence and John Barre to Augustine Berneher, leader of the London congregation, c. January 1558.

F.138^r The Lord is with you while you are with him; when ye seek him, he will be found of you:

And again, when you forsake him he will also forsake you and, as David said to Solomon, cast you off for ever.

You made us much to marvel that you were so importunate upon us to receive your writing & yet you so denye to defend it, as we never saw ye like of any people; & in deed we were not verie willing to have it because we thought it was, as indeed it is, that is to say against ye truth. But whereas we looked for 2 things, y^t is for an answer of a writing we left with you, or some of your company at Bartholomewtide; & for ye proof of ye affirmation y^t y^e & others made when we were last with you: (which was) y^t god before ye world, when he did elect or chose to lyffe, he did them also reprobate some to eternal Death. But you have neither answered the one, nor yet proved the other.

But you begin in ye style of your book & say that we hold god hath generally chosen all men to salvation, speaking in ye present [t]ence as though we did hold all ye people (whereof most be ungodly) to be in ye election, which is farre from us. Wherefore ye might have spared your writing, in that Matthew[1] dou hold y^t all those which walk in evil waies be out of election as you know & can bear us wittness. Wherefore you do but beat ye ayer therein. But afterward how-so-ever it happeneth you bring [y]or owne worde in y^e [?pretense] y^t god did generally chose all men in Christ to salvation (we meane before ye world) & yet after y^t ye say againe y^t we affirme all men to be chosen, & so slander us without shame (yor owne mouthe being witness) & so ye effort of your book is against y^t which we hold not.[2] For we hold none to be in ye election but those that be sanctified by ye spirite & believe ye truth as y^t holiest

---

[1] *Margin:* Be first sure of ye Matt 2 & then talk y^e of Isaiah 33.

[2] *Margin:* Yu leve ye matt^r and answer yor owne invention, 2 Thess. 2, 2 Pet. 2. We would [? be both] you could prove y^t we hold free will. [Neither] of [our] selves or our owne works do we wish our salvatio^n or any pte therof.

faythe. And sometyme you say y^t we sett up man's freewill & merit of works (speaking by ye same spirit which useth to slander the truth) which is farre from us, as you & ye rest of yor / company /

f.138^v compane can beare us wittnes, if they will speake the truthe, as one day they shall. For they have our owne hands to testiffie. And yo^u say y^t our affirmation is contrarie to ye opentexte & texte of ye scripture, but ye did well y^t you brought no proof by ye open text of ye scripture against us; in deede it was a wise poynt & well foresene, least you should not onlie be against us & ye truth but also against y^{or} selfs. For afterward yo^u say in respect of gods will revealed, w^{cc} should not come to nought. We thank god for this yor affirmation on our behalf for so we hold, & be yo^u sure y^t we have not, neith^r do we meane to speake but of gods will revealed though you dare speak of his secritt will wherein you [are] yorself unreasonably learned, & be yond ye scriptures: but if I might not offend, I would aske when yo^u sawe gods secret will & what is in it. A [?rhyving] spiritte, come downe. Dare you speake of gods secrett will, wch was never revealed, & are you not ashamed to affirme y^t in respect of gods comandyment it was not gods wyll yf Adam shuld syne but in respect of gods secritt will, god would have Adam to synne. A blassphemy against god,[3] making him ye autor of synne & affirme his worde to be [?unsure] sayeing he did will adam to syn though he did forbade. Who can abide ye hearing herof, but yor spirite is sene also, by answering of this scripture y^t foloweth, god created ma^n to be undestroyed, & you say ma^n be not destroyed, though they be damned & in hell. What is destruction if hell & damnation be not? Thus to mantayne yor opinnion yo^u have not [sic] to putt awaye ye mynd of god in ye scripture & to put in yor owne mynd, neither are ye ashamed to saye not all but some not of late but before ye world was made: be chosen to salvatyon, & ye rest repbated [sic] to set forth ye iudgement of god in eternall paynes, we dare say if yo^u could have brought one open place of scripture, for by prov this matt^r of repbation [sic] before ye world yo^u would have brought it, but we will beare wth yo^u for this tyme bicause yo^u have none to bringe. Another tyme yo^u will bringe one we think if yo^u can fynd y^t / or els/

f.139^r or els, yo^u will make nu [–] yor folly & say it is in ye greek tongue: as yo^u have used the same shifte where in yor book & yo^u co^{n}demne all ye english translations: wch were translated, of as well

---

3   *Margin*:   We desire y^t you would (as St Pall sayeth) learn not to blaspheme. I Cor. 2.

learned me^n as yo^u be, but it is a poore shifte to fyght against god w^t all, & whereas yo^u say that yo^u will so prove, & affirme this yor opynion: y^t all ye devills in hell shall not be able to disanull ye same: wee think so too: for ye devills doth never disanull their owne doctryne. But wheras yo^u say y^t adam & eve were made afte^r ye Image of god (y^t is you sayd) rightuouse, holy, prudent, & bewtiffied with all man^{er} of good gifts we say it is ye truth & thereby yo^u gave as the holighest doth y^t the^n there was no repbation, in Adam nor in any other but came uppon all me^n for syne.^{4} Further more as [?touching] all yor evill speakynge of us in yor book, likyng us to papists & spirites, pelagius & Lucifer, we will omytt that to provoke you to use more love: for we perceive y^t all yor mynd is to speak evill of us & to thrust us downe & to exault yor selfe & yor owne company calling some of them: most godly learned, as though neither ye prophets nor apostles were to be compared with them:^{5} for if they be as yo^u say most godly Learned then there ys none like them: but if they have no bett^r Spiritte tha^n we saw w^{hn} we were wth them: they be not verie [?wholsome] but goe and [?tell] them, We wishe yo^u to consider ye matt^r y^t we shuld conclude uppo^n, & come new to it in few words & prove if yo^u can by the open text of ye scripture y^t god bifore ye worlde, did not elect all, or els y^t he did reprobate some, before ye world, as yo^u know it was their affirmatyon: at o^{ur} last meeting & so yo^u affirme in yor writing, but as they could not prov it no more have yo^u now: therfor if you can not pr^{ve} it, I pray yo^u lett us alone, & spend no more tyme w^t us: for we have to constraine in spending of ye tyme:^{6} thoughe yo^u have none, for y^{ou} care not how long tyme yo^u spend about talking of it, nor how great a book yo^u make of it: & yet will not come near the matt^r , w^{h}fore [?rest] we pray yo^u, & let us alone, for if we be elect we ca^n not finally perish, (though we hold all ye error unde^r ye sune) if yor opinio^n be trew / & again /

f.139^v And agayne if we be repbates, we shall nev^r be spared though we come to yor opinion, yo^u can do us neither good nor harme if yor doctrine were trewe. For yor opinion can not save us though we holdit,^{7} & I know y^t ther is nev^r a promisse of lyffe in ye scriptyre to yor

---

4   *Margin*:   We thank god y^t yor p^{r}ooth is, but we are soory y^t y^u fight agaynst it.

5   *Margin*:   Not many wise me^n after ye fleshe before ye world hath god chosen. 2 Cor.2.

6   *Margin*:   Paule sayth redeme ye tyme for the daies be evill. Ephe.5.

7   *Margin*:   So vayne is yor opynion.

opynion y^t god before ye world did not chose all, or els did repbate some. Therfor keep it to yor self, what shall we do with [it], for it will do us no good, & no marvell, for it did not ma^n good yet, nor nev^r will do / but harme / for many have gotte a carnall mynd therby. Wherfor except yo^u can prove ye matt^r before expressed, or els will deny & leave thes[e] opinyons y^t foloweth (seeing yo^u can not prve them by ye open text of ye scriptures) we will leave yo^u / & have nothing to do with yo^u / That is to saye /

First y^t god did repbate some people befor ye world.

Secondly y^t all did not fall by Adam's syne to damnatyon

Thirdly y^t christ was not given of god to die for all adams posteritie

Fourthly y^t god doth not so effectually by his worde call all me^n y^t by it thorow ye blud of christ they might have eternall lyfe

Fiftely, y^t adam, david, Salomon, mary magdale^n & the chosen being in theyre abhominable synes, were also in Christ & in ye election.

Therefore eith^r leave thes opinions, or els fare ye well / for as yo^u say in ye latt^r end of yor book (so say we) we have no custome to stryve: & as we begayn not w^t yo^u hitherto, so we meane not to do hereaft^{er}, though by love we thought it good this once more to tell yo^u of thes yor falltes & so by love we pray yo^u Frnd go & amend them: for we hate not yo^u as god knoweth but yor opinions we hate / Therfore whatsoever is spoken before / is not spoken but against yor opynions: Leave it for ye lords sake y^t his wrathe come not uppon yo^u /

fare ye well /

By yo^{r}s if by any meanes we could do yo^u good

John Laurence. John barre /

DOCUMENT IV

The Familist Depositions of 1561 as published by John Rogers

A confession made by two of the *Familie of Loue*, before a worthie & worship Iustice of peace, the 28 of Maie, 1561. touching the errors taught amongst them at their assemblies, and also their behaviours. And although they have reformed some of these grosse matters since that time, yet I have thought good to manifest their wavering heads & unconstant minds, that Gods children may beware of their impious dealings.

[Article 1.] First, they be generally all unlearned, saving that some of them can reade English, and that not verie perfectly, and of them that can so reade they have chosen Bishops Elders, and Deacons.

[2] Their Bishops, Elders or Deacons, do call those that be of their sect together, by the name of a congregation, into one of their disciples houses, which they call also a *Raab*: where they commonly meet, to the number of thirtie, or above, and their Bishop or Deacon doth reade unto the congregation the Scriptures, expounding the same according to his owne fansie.

[3] When any person shalbe received into their congregation, they cause all their brethren to assemble, & the Bishop or Elder doth declare unto the new Elected brother, that if he will be content that all his goodes shalbe in common amongst the rest of all his brethren, he shalbe received: whereunto he answering, yea, then he is admitted, with a kisse, vz. All the company both men and women kissing him, one after another.

[4] At their meeting, either to receive a new brother, or to reade the scripture, they all have meate, drinke, & lodging at the cost and charges of the owner of the house whome they call a *Raab*: and there they doe remaine as long as he hath good victualles for them, wherby sometimes they doe loose their *Raab*, seeing himselfe so farre overcharged with them.

[5] They are called together ever in the night time: and commonly to suche houses as be far from neighbours, one of them doth alwayes warne an other: and when they come to the house of meeting, they knocke at the doore, saying: here is a Brother in Christ, or a Sister in Christ.

[6] When they be altogether, before their Bishop or Elder or Deacon wil reade the Scripture unto them, he saith these words. All ye that are but weake, and not come to perfection, withdrawe your selves a while, and pray that you may be made woorthie therof. Whereuppon those weakelings doe repaire in to an other place, and be not partakers of the doctrine that then shalbe taught, but afterwardes, as the Bishop, Elder, or

Deacon seeth them frame themselues, they shall be received to heare the doctrine.

[7] The Elder must not speak, the Bishop being present: nor the Deacon in the presence of either of them.

[8] The Byshopp or Elder doeth alwayes tell his congregation, that he hath more to teache them: so he doeth continually feede them with expectations of newe matters.

[9] Everie one of the congregation is inhibited to speake, or declare any thing that he learneth, untill he be admitted so to doe: and if he doe, he shalbe excommunicated, and, with great repentaunce againe received.

[10] In the beginning of Queene *Maries* time, they would not come to the Church, thinking it damnable so to do: but within a yere after, they were changed from that opinion, openly declaring unto their brethren, that they were al bound to come unto the church, and to doe outwardly, there, all suche thinges as the Lawe required then at their handes, upon paine of damnation, although inwardely they did professe the contrarie.

[11] They cannot abide, any of their secte to pray, but those that bee newe received brethren, whome they call weaklings: thinking it a great fault to the rest, whome they affirme to be perfect, to pray unto God, as though they were importunate troublers, and vexers of him, having no need to do so.

[12] They scorne all those yᵗ say, *Good Lorde have mercie uppon us miserable sinners*; saying, they that so say, declare themselves never to amend, but still to be miserable sinners, whereas we doe live perfectly and sinne not.

[13] They may not say, *God speede God morrow¸* or *God even¸* but to those that be of their secte: and to other, they say, *Speede¸ Morrowe, Deven.*

[14] They may not say, *God save any thing.* For they affirme that all thinges are ruled by nature, and not directed by God.

[15] They did prohibite bearing of weapons, but at the length, perceiving them selves to be noted and marked for the same, they have allowed the bearing of staves.

[16] When a question is demaunded of any of them, they doe of order stay a great while, ere they do answere: and commonly, their worde shalbe *Surely*, or *So*.

[17] They may answere to euerie demaundant (not beeing one of their sect) in suche sorte as they thinke best shall please him. For they say, they are bound to deale truely with no man in word or deed, that is not of their congregation: alledging, that he is no neighbour, and that therefore they may abuse him at their pleasure.

[18] When their wives are to be delivered of childe, they must use the help of none other, but of those, that be of their secte: so that sometime the women are delivered in the fieldes, for that they would eschewe the

comming of others unto them: as one of them was, having no woman with her at her travel.

[19] If any of their secte do die, the wife or husbande that overliveth, must marrie againe with one of their congregation, or else the offence is greate: the marriage is made by the brethren, who bringe them together sometime, that dwell above a hundreth myles asunder: as for example, *Thomas Chaundler* of *Wonerse*, in the countie of Surrey, had his wife fetcht out of the Isle of *Ely* by two of the congregation: the man and the woman being utter straungers, before they came together to be married.

[20] They doe divorce againe themselves a sunder if they can not agree, before certeine of the congregation: as the saide *Chaundeler*, and his wife did, upon a mislyking, after they had beene one yeare married together.

[21] Whosoever is not of their sect they accompt him as a beast, that hath no soule and shal yealde no account for his doing: but as a beast shall dye and not rise againe, in bodie or soule. And to prove it, they allege a place out of Esdras that, *Who so is not of God, shall be as a drop of water that falleth from the house, and commeth to nothing.*

[22] They hold, that he which is one of the congregation, is either as perfecte as CHRISTE, or else a verie divell.

[23] They holde, it is lawfull to doe what so ever the higher powers commaunde to be done, thoughe it be against the commaundements of God: and for that they alledge the wordes of S. Peter. *Submit you selves to the ordinaunces of the higher powers.*

[24] They denie that Christ is equal with God the Father in his Godhead: uppon this place of Scripture, *My Father is greater than I.*

[25] It is odious for them to say, *God the Sonne*: for they denie him to be God as is aforesaide.

[26] They denie the Trinitie, scorning them that say, *God the Father, God the sonne & God the holy Ghost*: as though by saying these wordes, they shoulde affirme to be three Gods.

[27] They holde, that no man should be baptised, before he be of the age of XXX. yeares. And therefore have divers of them beene baptised at those yeares and upwardes.

[28] They holde, that everie man ought first to be in an errour before hee canne come to the knowledge of the trueth.

[29] They say, that as Christ raised the dead, cleansed the lepre, gave sight to the blind, and walked on the waters: so doe they.

[30] They holde, that heaven, and hel, are present in this worlde amongst us, and that there is none other: and for proofe thereof, they alledge the xvij. of Mathewe, of Christes transfiguration: that as the cloude removed, *Peter* did see *Elias*, and *Moses*: so if the clowde were removed away, both heaven & hell should be visible unto us.

[31] They holde, that they are bound to give almes to none other persons, but to those of their sect: and if they do, they give their almes to the divel.

[32] They holde, that they ought not to burie the deade, uppon this place of Scripture: *Let the dead burie the dead.*

[33] They holde, that they should so provide, that if any perish, all should perishe: so that everie one of them should releeve him with his goodes that decayeth.

[34] They holde, that none ought to receive the sacraments before he receiveth their whole ordinaunces: as first, he must be admitted with a kisse, then his feete must be washed, then handes laide on him, and so received.

[35] They holde, the Popes service & this service now used in the Churche to be naught, & yet to be by them used as free in the Lorde, to whome nothing is uncleane.

[36] They hold, that all men that are not of their congregation, or that are revolted from them, to be dead.

[37] They holde, that no Bishop, or Minister should remaine still in one place, but that they ought alwayes to be wandering from country to countris.

[38] They holde, that the Angels *Raphael* & *Gabriel* and others, were borne of a Woman.

[39] They hold, that they ought not to say *Davids* Psalmes as prayers: for they are righteous and without sinne.

[40] They hold, there ought to be no Sabbath day, but that all should be like: and for that they alledge. *The Sonne of man is Lord over the Sabbath day.*

[41] They hold, that as God made heaven and earth by Jesus Christe: vz. the word: so did he it by them.

[42] They hold, themselves to be *Maries*: and say, that Christ is come foorth in their fleshe, even as he came foorth of the virgin Marie.

[43] They holde, that there was a worlde before Adams time, as there is nowe.

[44] They hold yt they ought to kepe scilence amongest them selves that the lybertie they have in the Lorde, may not be espied of others.

[45] They holde, that no man should be put to death for his opinion: & therefore they condemne Maister *Cranmer*, and Maister *Ridley*, for burning *Ioane* of *Kent*.

[46] They can not abide any exposition of Scriptures, but their own, conferring one place of Scripture, with an other, and so to save their mindes of it, without any other bodies exposition.

[47] If any of them be convented for his opinion, and doeth denie the same by open recantation: he taketh that to be a glorie unto him, as though he had suffered persecution in this doing: and yet still inwardly mainteyning these opinions.

[48] They bragge verie muche of their owne sincere lives, iustifying themselves, saying, Marke how purelie we live.

[49] If they have anything to doe, touching the ordering of their temporal thinges, they must do it by advise: as to aske counsell of the Lorde, vz. they must go to one of their Bishops, or Elders, and to aske of him counsell, what he shall do, and he must follow it.

[50] When they give their almes, there is a hat set by the Bishop or Elders uppon a table, and then every one of the congregation doth put under the hat that he is disposed to give: all which money commeth to the Bishops or Elders handes, and so the same is by him of them distributed, as they will: but to whome, none of the congregation knoweth.

[51] They have certaine sleightes amongest them, to answere any questions that shall be demaunded of them, with deceiving the demaundent: as for example: if one of them be demaunded howe he beleeveth in the Trinitie, he will answere, I am to learne of you: & so provoketh the demandant to show his opinion therein: which done, he will say then: I do beleeve so: by the which wordes he meaneth, that he beleeveth the demaundant saith as he thinketh: but not that he thinketh so.

[52] They do decree, all men to be infants that are under the age of thirtie yeres: so that if they be demaunded, whether Infantes ought to be baptised, they answere, yea, meaning thereby, that he is an infant, untill he attaine to those yeres, at which time he ought to be baptised, and not afore.

[53] Their Bishoppes, Elders and Deacons, do increase in riches, and become wealthy, but their disciples become poore and fall to beggerie.

The Depositions which John Rogers did not publish

[6] They lodge bothe men and women in one chamber together at thayre sayde generall tyme of meetynge.

[11] Thay used in theyre assembles to pronounce a generall Curse in Quene Maryes tyme agaynst all those that were prasers of the servyce in the Church then used and dyd excommunycat those of theyre sect as thay [?kounted] faultyr therein who could not agayne be restored w^tout great repentaunce and humble [?face] /

[20] Thay saye thay may be suttle and [–] for the holye ghost was suttle /

[24] The wyffe may goo and usuely dothe for a moneth & more at her playsure w^t one of the congregation from her husband to Lerne and as thaye terme yt to seeke the Lord at those places where the congregation assembles / and her husband all the tyme of her [ab]sence knowyth not where she be [?gone] tyll she doo [?te]ll hym at her [?pleasure] w^c must come of her self w^t out Compulsyon.

[25] The wyf in her owne house wyll myslyke to lye in bedde w^t her husbande yf she have a brother put [?by] wyll have her bedde in one Chambre the one for her brother the other for her self and her husband

to be lodgyde in an other chambre she must putte on her brothers kerch [?ief] on hys hed and be responsable unto hym but very stranglye to use her husband a brother beynge re placed / as for Example the sayd Chaundler & hys wyffe.

[26] Theyre busshopes Elders and Decons dothe teche to thayre dyscyples that thaye owght to doo what soever the spryte moveth thaym [?wherefor] thayre spryte as thay saye now movythe thaym to any evyll.

[59] Thayre busshops and Elders dothe mynyster the sacraments (amongst thaym) & dothe marrye [–].

[The final leaf is in very poor condition and may have become detached from the remainder of the manuscript. Since a note in the margin at the top of the page, written by a different and much later hand, reads '1561. Account of Sectaries in Wonersh etc.' None of the depositions on this folio are to be found in Rogers].

[61] There be of thayre Congregat [on] [in] dyvrs places of the Realme wch Doo assem[ble] [to]gether as in the Isle of Elye, Essex, Barksh[ire], Sussex Surrey, hampshyre, Devon Shyre and L[ond]on /

[62] Davyde Oram joyner Resydes [?Basynge] stoke in hampshyre, a busshope whom they do [?esteem] the aple of gods Eye he was before my Lord the busshope of London that now ys and by hym made to recante hys erronyous opynyons at wonersh and Gulford in Surrey /

[63] Thomas allan of wonersh mercer who in lyke man^r was befor my Lord of [Lon]don and by hym made also to recante / he dyd [?herein] sayeth in that Quens Dayes that Dedes ys [–] [?other] lyke opynyons he ys an Eldere.

[64] henryke a Dutcheman the hede of all that Congregaton he ys permanent in no place but styll wandryth to vysytte his flo[ck].

[65] There ys a Shomaker [?that] followeth the Courte a Dutchman. he ys [d–] a [?horsebreder] a blake man, hys name [?we] knowe not he ys an Eldere and a f[ore]teller of newes unto thaym.

[66] John Gryffyn of Loffwood in the [?pari]sh of Grae [?wd] mercer within the Coun[ty] of [Sus]sex he ys an Elder, and a man [?marrayed] [– –] and keepyng strange women in hys hous [–] comyth from Dyvers places & nowe he [– –] from Elye for fear of Excomm[unication].

NOTES

It seems unlikely that John Rogers deliberately omitted these thirteen articles. Their content does not suggest primitive Familist practice which had been modified by 1578 and which were therefore irrelevant. Moreover Rogers' introductory statement appears to mean that 'although they had reformed some of these grosse matters since that time' (i.e. 1561), he had nevertheless published all the information available to him. On the other hand, comparison with the original manuscript reveals that Rogers did omit an occasional phrase or sentence from the depositions that he published. The answer might lie with the clerk whom Sir William More employed to copy out the depositions for John Rogers. He may have supplied a censored transcription. See above, p. 329 note.

Articles 6, 24, 25 and 66 illustrate the Familists' antinomian attitude towards sexual morality and the lower value they placed upon the marriage bond. In typical sectarian fashion loyalty to the congregation was accorded priority over loyalty to the family. Female members of Familist congregations appear to have enjoyed an unusual degree of liberty and to have held equal status with male initiates.

Articles 6, 24, 61 and 66 indicate that Familists gathered on set occasions in 'general assemblies' as well as irregularly when an itinerant elder visited the district. Presumably these 'general assemblies' were held on public holidays as in the time of the Lollards. On these occasions cases for discipline were examined and excommunications pronounced. From Article 11 it appears that these gatherings were taking place in 1553/4,[1] that is, before the doctrines of HN. had reached England. Here again is evidence that the Familist assemblies were but a continuation of the 'separatist' conventicles held in Kent and Essex (and doubtless elsewhere) during the Edwardine period, and possibly a continuation of earlier Lollard gatherings.

Articles 20 and 26 reveal the lengths to which an extreme Spiritualist pneumatology led them. Article 59 states clearly that the Familists had their own sacramental system which was administered by the hierarchy.[2] In 1574 Robert Sharpe, parson of Strethal in Essex, was accused of 'marrying persons in the fields'.[3]

Article 61 supplies new information on the extension of Familism through southern England – although Kent is again conspicuous by its absence from the list. It was not known hitherto that the movement had extended West of London through Berkshire and Hampshire to Devon before 1561. In December 1564 John Veall of Rease near Reading, Joan Stamphorde of Reading, and Edmond Cowper – parson of Burghfield near Reading – were accused of 'purveying false prophecies'. They were held in the Tower before being sent back to Reading to perform public penance.[4] The Hampshire Familists presumably gathered in or near Basingstoke (Article 62). There were Familists in Exeter in the 1580s.

---

[1] Compare Article 10 in Rogers' version.
[2] Above, 333-4.
[3] Strype, *Parker*, II, 381-5.
[4] *APC.*, VII, 176-8.

Anthony Randall was associated with them in his early days as a Devonshire parson.[5]

David Oram (Article 62) is obviously to be identified with David Orch.[6] Here is yet another itinerant wood-worker who was a leader of the radical movement in England. He is described as 'residing' in Basingstoke and not as being 'of' that town. This may indicate that he was a denizen of foreign origin like Christopher Vitells, being responsible for organising and supervising conventicles to the south and west of London. Evidently David Oram was detected to the High Commission in *circa* 1560 like Christopher Vitells and Thomas Allan.[7] Forty years earlier David Joris had lived and worked in Basingstoke (Above, p. 187).

In Article 63 Thomas Allan is described as a mercer rather than as a weaver. However, he may have been among those itinerant elders who, according to William Wilkinson, had obtained licences to trade for corn.[8] Article 64 reveals that the English congregations regarded Hendrik Niclaes as their 'hede' notwithstanding the key role played by 'native' leaders such as Christopher Vitells, Thomas Allan and David Oram. In 1561 Niclaes had only recently left Emden and may not yet have taken up permanent residence in Kampen.[9]

John Gryffyn (Article 66) may have come from either Loxwood in Sussex or Grayswood in Surrey, but he traded in Sussex. Gryffyn's blatant immorality had apparently brought him under the censure of the Ely Familists.

---

5   Parson of Lydford, Devon. Above, 261n.
6   Above, 324-5.
7   Above, 305-6, 322-3.
8   Wilkinson, *op. cit.*, sig. K2^V.
9   Above, 300, 302.

BIBLIOGRAPHY

A. MANUSCRIPT SOURCES

CAMBRIDGE
1. Corpus Christi College
128, fols. 5-361. Cranmer and the Kentish heretics.
2. Emmanuel College
260, fols. 47-8 *etc.* John Sympson to the dispersed congregation.
260, fol. 87. Henry Harte to the prisoners in Newgate.

LONDON
British Library
Harleian Manuscripts:
416, fols. 123-4. Letter of John Day.
421, fols. 9-36. Wharton's visitation records.
421, fols. 133-4. Depositions against some Kentish men.

MAIDSTONE
Kent County Archives
Little Chart parish registers.

OXFORD
Bodleian Library
53, fols. 126-146. Correspondence between Berneher, Laurence and Barre.

WASHINGTON D.C.
Folger Shakespeare Library
Loseley Manuscripts:
L. b. 51, 98, 99. Familist depositions before Sir William More.

B. PRIMARY PRINTED SOURCES

Arnold, G.,   *Unparteyische Kirchen und Ketzer-Historie.*
Franckfurt am Mayn, 1700.
Bale, J.,   A *mysterye of inyquyte contayned within the heretycall Genealogye of Ponce Pantolabus.*
Geneva, 1545; STC 1303.

Becke, E.,   *A brefe confutacion.* London, 1550; STC 1709.
Blesdikius, N.,   *Historia vitae, doctrinae ac rerum gestarum Davidis Georgii Haeresiarchae.* Deventer, 1642.
Champneys, J.,   *The Harvest is at Hand.* London, 1548; STC 4956.
──────────   *The Copie of an answere made unto a certayne letter.* The Netherlands?, 1563?; STC 5742:10.
Cole, R., and Ledley, J., *Godly meditacions verye necessarie to bee sayd of all Christen men,* ?London, ?1554-8; STC 17776.
Cole, T.,   *A Godly and Frutefull Sermon made at Maydstone.* London, 1553; STC 5539.
──────────   *A Godly and Learned Sermon made... before the Queenes Maiestie.* London, 1564; STC 5540.
Crowley, R.,   *An Answer to Shaxton's recantation,* London, 1548; STC 6083.
──────────   *An apologie or defence...,* London, 1566.
Foxe, J.,   *Rerum in ecclesia.* Basle, 1559-63.
Harte, H.,   *A Godly Newe short treatyse.* London, 1548; STC 12887.
──────────   *A Godlie exhortation.* London, 1549; STC 10626.
H.H. (Henry Harte) *A Consultorie for all Christians.* Worcester, 1549; STC 12564.
Hogarde, M.,   *The Displaying of the Protestantes.* London, 1556; STC 13557.
Hutchinson, R.,   *The image of God, or laie mans booke.* London, 1550; STC 14019.
Knewstub, J.,   *A Confutation of monstrous and horrible heresies.* London, 1579; RSTC 15040.
Latimer, H.,   *The seconde... Sermon of Master Hughe Latimer.* London, 1549; RSTC 15274.
Parsons, R.,   *A temperate Ward-word to the ... Watchword of Sir. F. Hastings.* Antwerp, 1599; RSTC 19415.
──────────   *A Warnword to Syr F. Hastings.* Antwerp, 1602; RSTC 19418.
──────────   *A Treatise of three Conversions of England.* St. Omer, 1603-4; RSTC 19416.
Prynne, W.,   *A Quench-coale...* London, 1637; STC 20474.
Rogers, J.,   *The Displaying of an horrible secte.* London, 1578; RSTC 21181.

———————   *The Displaying ... Whereunto is added certeine letters.* London, 1579; RSTC 21182.
———————   *An Answere vnto a wicked & infamous Libel.* London, 1579; RSTC 21180.
Rutherford, S.,   *A Survey of the Spiritual Antichrist.* London, 1648; Wing STC. R 2394.
Sharpe, R.,   *The Confession and declaration of R. Sharpe, clerke...,* London, 1575; STC 22378.
Standish, J.,   *The triall of the supremacy.* London, 1556; RSTC 23211.
Stow, J.,   *The annales of England.* London, 1605; RSTC 23337.
Strype, J.,   *Ecclesiastical Memorials,* 7 vols. Oxford, 1816.
———————   *Life of Archbishop Grindal.* Oxford, 1821.
———————   *Life of Archbishop Parker,* 3 vols. Oxford, 1821.
———————   *Annals of the Reformation,* 7 vols. Oxford, 1824.
———————   *Memorials of Archbishop Cranmer,* 3 vols. Oxford, 1848-54.
Turner, W.,   *A Preseruatiue, or triacle, agaynst the poyson of Pelagius.* London, 1551; RSTC 24368.
Vermigli, P.M.,   *The Common Places,* trans. A. Marten. London, 1583; RSTC 24669.
Veron, J.,   trans. *A moste necessary & frutefull Dialogue.* Worcester, 1551; STC 4068.
———————   *A Fruteful treatise of Predestination.* London, 1561; RSTC 24681.
———————   *A moste necessary treatise of free wil.* London, 1561; RSTC 24684.
Wilkinson, W.,   *A Confutation of Certaine Articles.* London, 1579; RSTC 25665.

C. PRIMARY PRINTED SOURCES, EDITED

Benham, W.G.,   ed. *The Oath Book of Colchester.* Colchester, 1907.
Bradford, J.,   *Writings,* ed. A. Townsend, 2 vols., Parker Society. Cambridge, 1848, 1853.
Brewer, J.S., and Gairdner, J., arr. *Letters and Papers, Foreign and Domestic, of the Reign of Henry VIII, 1509-1547,* 21 vols. London, 1862-1910.

Burnet, G.,   *The History of the Reformation of the Church of England,* ed. N. Pocock, 6 vols. Oxford, 1865.

Coverdale, M.,   *Godly Letters of the Martyrs,* ed. E. Bickersteth. London, 1837.

Cranmer, T.,   *Works,* ed. J.E.Cox, 2 vols., Parker Society. Cambridge, 1844, 1846.

Dasent, J.R.,   ed. *Acts of the Privy Council of England,* New Series, vols. I-XII. London, 1890-1896.

Edward VI   *The Chronicle and Political Papers of Edward VI,* ed. W.K.Jordan. London, 1966.

Foster, C.W.,   ed. *Lincoln Episcopal Records 1571-1584,* Canterbury and York Society XI. London, 1913.

Foxe, J.,   *The Acts and Monuments of the Martyrs,* eds. G. Townshend and S.R.Cattley, 8 vols. London, 1837-1841.

Franz, G., and others, eds. *Wiedertäuferakten* 1527-1626, Urkundliche Quellen zur hessischen Reformationsgeschichte IV. Marburg, 1951.

Frere, W.H.,   ed. *Registrum Matthei Parker,* Canterbury and York Society XXXIX. Oxford, 1928.

Frere, W.H., and Kennedy, W.P.M., eds. *Visitation Articles and Injunctions of the Period of the Reformation,* Alcuin Club XIV-XVI. London, 1908-1910.

Gorham, G.C.,   ed. *Gleanings of a few Scattered Ears.* London, 1857.

Grindal, E.,   *Remains,* ed. W. Nicholson, Parker Society. Cambridge, 1843.

Heylyn, P.,   *Ecclesia restaurata,* ed., J.C.Robertson, 2 vols. Cambridge, 1849.

Historical Manuscripts Commission, *Seventh Report.* London, 1879 (reprinted 1979).

Hooper. J.,   *Later Writings,* ed. C. Nevinson, Parker Society. Cambridge, 1852.

Hudson, A.,   ed. *Selections from English Wycliffite Writings.* Cambridge, 1978.

Hughes, P.L., and Larkin, J.F., eds. *Tudor Royal Proclamations,* vols. I and II. New Haven and London, 1964, 1969.

Jewel, J.,   *Works,* ed. J. Ayre, 2 vols., Parker Society. Cambridge, 1848, 1850.

Knox, J.,   *Works,* ed. D. Laing, 6 vols. Edinburgh, 1846-1864.

Latimer, H.,   *Sermons*, ed. G.E.Corrie, Parker Society. Cambridge, 1844.

———   *Remains*, ed. G.E.Corrie, Parker Society. Cambridge, 1845.

Laurence, R.,   ed. *Authentic Documents Relative to the Predestinarian Controversy*. Oxford, 1819.

Lemon, R., and Green, M.A.E. eds. *Calendar of State Papers, Domestic Series*, vols. I and II. London, 1856, 1863.

Luders, A., and others. eds. *The Statutes of the Realm*, vols. II-IV. London, 1810-1815.

Nichols, J.G.,   ed. *Chronicle of the Grey Friars of London*, Camden Society, Old Series, LIII. London, 1852.

———   ed. *Narratives of the Reformation*, Camden Society, Old Series, LXXVII. London, 1859.

Parker, M.,   *Correspondence*, ed. J. Bruce, Parker Society. Cambridge, 1853.

Peel, A.,   ed. *Calendar of The Seconde Parte of a Register*, 2 vols., Cambridge, 1915.

Philpot, J.,   *The Examinations and Writings*, ed. R. Eden, Parker Society. Cambridge, 1842.

Ricart, R.,   *The Maire of Bristowe is Kalendar,* ed. L.T.Smith, Camden Society, New Series, V. London, 1872.

Ridley, N.,   *Works*, ed. H.Christmas, Parker Society. Cambridge, 1841.

Robinson, H.,   ed. *Zurich Letters*, 2 vols., Parker Society. Cambridge, 1845, 1852.

———   ed. *Original Letters Relative to the English Reformation*, 2 vols., Parker Society. Cambridge, 1846, 1847.

Rogers, T.,   *The Catholic Doctrine of the Church of England*, ed. J.J.S.Perowne, Parker Society. Cambridge, 1854.

Rymer, T.,   ed. *Foedera*, vol. XV. London, 1745.

Simons, M.,   *Complete Works*, ed. J.C.Wenger. Scottdale, Pennsylvania, 1956.

Stow, J., *Three Fifteenth-Century Chronicles*, ed. J.
Gairdner, Camden Society, New Series, XXVIII.
London, 1880.

Tanner, T., ed. *Bibliotheca Britannico-Hibernica.* London,
1748.

Wenger, J.C., ed. 'The Schleitheim Confession of Faith',
Mennonite Quarterly Review XIX (1945), 243-
253.

Whatmore, L.E., ed. *Archdeacon Harpsfield's Visitation*, 2 vols.,
Catholic Record Society XLV, XLVI. London,
1950, 1951.

Whitley, W.T., ed. 'The Confutation of the Errors of the
Careless by Necessity', *Transactions of the
Baptist Historical Society* IV (1914), 88-123.

Wilkins, D., ed. *Concilia Magnae Britanniae et Hiberniae*,
vols. III and IV. London, 1737.

Williams, G.H., and Mergal, A.M., eds. *Spiritual and Anabaptist
Writers, Documents Illustrative of the Radical
Reformation*, The Library of Christian Classics
XXV. Philadelphia and London, 1957.

Wriothesley, C., *A Chronicle of England During the Reigns of the
Tudors*, ed. W.D.Hamilton, 2 vols., Camden
Society, New Series XI, XX. London, 1875,
1877.

D. SECONDARY WORKS, MONOGRAPHS

Armour, R.S., *Anabaptist Baptism: A Representative Study.*
Scottdale, Pennsylvania, 1966.

Aston, M., *Lollards & Reformers: Images & Literacy in
Late Medieval Religion*, London, 1984.

Bainton, R., *David Joris, Wiedertaüfer und Kämpfer für
Toleranz im 16. Jahrhundert.* Leipzig, 1937.

Bauckham, R., *Tudor Apocalypse.* Appleford, 1978.

Burn, J.S., *The History of the Foreign Protestant Refugees
settled in England.* London, 1846.

Burrage, C., *The Early English Dissenters*, 2 vols.   Cambridge,
1912.

Clair, C., *History of Printing in Britain.* London, 1965.

Clark, P.A., *English Provincial Society from the Reformation
to the Revolution.* Hassocks, 1977.

Collinson, P.,   *The Elizabethan Puritan Movement.* London, 1967.
———   *Archbishop Grindal, 1519-1583, the Struggle for a Reformed Church.* London, 1979.
Cross, C.,   *Church and People, 1450-1660.* Glasgow, 1976.
Davids, T.W.,   *Annals of Evangelical Nonconformity in Essex.* London, 1863.
Davis, J.F.,   *Heresy & Reformation in the South East of England, 1520-1559.* London, 1983.
Dickens, A.G.,   *Lollards and Protestants in the Diocese of York, 1509-1558.* Oxford, 1959.
———   *The English Reformation.* London, 1964.
———   *The English Reformation,* second revised ed., London, 1989.
Dixon, R.W.,   *History of the Church of England from the Abolition of the Roman Jurisdiction,* 6 vols. London, 1878-1902.
Dorsten, J.A. van,   *The Radical Arts.* London, 1970.
Frere, W.H.,   *The Marian Reaction.* London, 1896.
Garrett, C.H.,   *The Marian Exiles.* Cambridge, 1938 (reprinted 1966).
Hamilton, A.,   *The Family of Love.* Cambridge, 1981.
Hoak, D.E.,   *The King's Council in the reign of Edward VI.* Cambridge, 1976.
Horst, I.B.,   *The Radical Brethren – Anabaptism and the English Reformation to 1558.* Nieuwkoop, 1972.
Hudson, A.,   *Lollards and their Books.* London & Ronceverte, 1985.
———   *The Premature Reformation: Wycliffite texts and Lollard history.* Oxford, 1988.
Jones, W.R.D.,   *William Turner. Tudor naturalist, physician and divine.* London, 1988.
Jordan, W.K.,   *The Development of Religious Toleration in England.* London, 1932.
———   *Edward VI: the Threshold of Power.* London, 1970.
Kawerau, P.,   *Melchior Hoffman als Religiöser Denker.* Haarlem, 1954.
Keeney, W.E.,   *The Development of Dutch Anabaptist Thought and Practice from 1539-1564.* Nieuwkoop, 1968.

Lambert, M.D.,   *Medieval Heresy; popular movements from*
                      Bogomil to Hus. London, 1977.
Leff, G.,   *Heresy in the Later Middle Ages*, 2 vols.
                      Manchester, 1967.
Lindeboom, J.,   *Austin Friars: History of the Dutch Reformed*
                      Church in London 1550-1950. The Hague, 1950.
M'Crie, T.,   *The Life of John Knox*, 2 vols. Edinburgh, 1814.
Manning, R.B.,   *Religion and Society in Elizabethan Sussex.*
                      Leicester, 1969.
Martin, J.W.,   *Religious Radicals in Tudor England.* London &
                      Ronceverte, 1989.
Moss, J.D.,   *'Godded with God': Hendrik Niclaes and His*
                      Family of Love. Philadelphia, 1981.
Mozley, J.F.,   *John Foxe and his Book.* London, 1940.
Mullett, M.A.,   *Radical Religious Movements in Early Modern*
                      Europe. London, 1980.
Nuttall, G.F.,   *The Puritan Spirit.* London, 1967.
Oxley, J.E.,   *The Reformation in Essex.* Manchester, 1965.
Pettegree, A.,   *Foreign Protestant Communities in Sixteenth-*
                      century London. Oxford, 1986.
Reeves, M.,   *The Influence of Prophecy in the Later Middle*
                      Ages: A Study in Joachimism. Oxford, 1969.
Ridley, J.G.,   *Nicholas Ridley.* London, 1957.
Rupp, E.G.,   *Studies in the making of the English Protestant*
                      Tradition – mainly in the reign of Henry VIII.
                      Cambridge, 1947.
Schoeps, H.J.,   *Von himmlischen Fleisch Christi, Eine*
                      dogmengeschichtliche Untersuchung. Tübingen,
                      1951.
Stapleton, H.,   *The Model Working Parson.* Published privately
                      by the author at Hoveton Vicarage, Norwich,
                      1976.
Stoneham, E.T.,   *Sussex Martyrs of the Reformation.* Burgess
                      Hill, 1967.
Streatfeild, F.,   *An Account of the Grammar School in Maidstone.*
Oxford, 1915.
Tanner, N.,   *Heresy Trials in the Diocese of Norwich, 1428-31.*
London, 1977.
Thomson, J.A.F.,   *The Later Lollards, 1414-1520.* Oxford, 1965.
Tjernagel, N.,   *Henry VIII and the Lutherans.* Saint Louis,
                      1965.

Watts, M.R.,   *The Dissenters*, vol. I. Oxford, 1978.
White, B.R.,   *The English Separatist Tradition*. Oxford, 1971.
Wilbur, E.M.,   *A History of Unitarianism in Transylvania,
                    England, and America*. Cambridge,
                    Massachusetts, 1952.
Williams, G.H.,   *The Radical Reformation*. Philadelphia, 1962.

E. SECONDARY WORKS, ARTICLES AND REVIEWS

Aston, M.,   'Lollardy and the Reformation: Survival or
                    Revival?', *History*, New Series XLIX (1964),
                    149-170.
———   'Lollardy and Literacy', *History*, New Series
                    LXII (1977), 347-371.
Benham, W.G.,   '12 Colchester Persons indicted for Heresy in
                    1566 [*sic*],' *Essex Review* L (1942), 157-162.
Cremeans, C.D.,   'The Reception of Calvinistic Thought in
                    England', *University of Illinois Bulletin* XXXI
                    (1949), 1-127.
Davis, J.F.,   'Lollard Survival and the Textile Industry in the
                    South-east of England', *Studies in Church
                    History* III, ed. G. Cuming (1966), 191-201.
———   'John Wyclif's Reformation Reputation', *The
                    Churchman*, 83 (1969), 97-102.
———   'Lollardy and the Reformation in England',
                    Archiv. für Reformationsgeschichte, 73 (1982),
                    217-36.
———   'Joan of Kent, Lollardy and the English
                    Reformation', *Journal of Ecclesiastical History*,
                    33 (1982), 225-33.
Dickens, A.G.,   'Heresy and the Origins of English
                    Protestantism', *Britain and the Netherlands* II, eds.
Bromley and Kossmann (Groningen, 1964), 47-66.
Dyck, C.J.,   *Mennonite Quarterly Review* XLVII (July,
                    1973), 248-250.
Elton, G.R.,   *English Historical Review* LXXXVII (October,
                    1973), 853-854.
Grieve, H.E.P.,   'The Deprived Married Clergy of Essex',
                    Transactions of the Royal Historical Society,
                    Fourth Series, XXII, 141-169.

Hargarve, O.T.,   'The Freewillers in the English Reformation',
                         Church History XXXVII (1968), 271-280.
————   'The Predestinarian Offensive of the Marian
                         Exiles at Geneva', *Historical Magazine of the
                         Protestant Episcopal Church', 42 (1973), 111-
                         123.*
Haury, D.A.,   'English Anabaptism and Calvin's "Brieve
                         Instruction"', *Mennonite Quarterly Review,* 57
                         (1983), 145-51.
Heal, F.,   'The Family of Love and the Diocese of Ely',
                         Studies in Church History IX, ed. D. Baker
                         (1972), 213-222.
Heriot, D.B.,   'Anabaptism in England during the 16th and
                         17th Centuries', *Transactions of the
                         Congregational Historical Society* XII (1933-
                         1936), 256-271, 312-320.
Hudson, W.S.,   *American Historical Review* LXXX (June,
                         1975), 636.
Kejr, J.,   *Journal of Ecclesiastical History,* 40 (1989),
                         599-602.
King, J.N.,   'Freedom of the Press, Protestant Propaganda, and
Protector Somerset', *Huntington Library   Quarterly,* 60 (1976).
Kreider, A.,   'An English Episcopal Draft Article Against the
                         Anabaptists, 1536', *Mennonite Quarterly
                         Review* XLIX (1975), 38-42.
Loach, L.,   'Pamphlets and Politics, 1553-8', *Bulletin of the
                         Institute of Historical Research,* 48 (1975), 31- 44.
Loades, D.,   'Anabaptism and English Sectarianism in the
                         Mid-Sixteenth Century', *Studies in Church
                         History,* Subsida 2, ed. Baker (1979), 59-70.
Martin, J.W.,   'English Protestant Separatism at its
                         Beginnings: Henry Harte and the Free-will
                         Men', *Sixteenth Century Journal* VII (1976), 56
                         ff.
————   'Elizabethan Familists and other Separatists in the
                         Guildford Area', *Bulletin of the Institute of
                         Historical Research* LI (1978), 90-93.

————   'Christopher Vitel: an Elizabethan Mechanick Preacher', *Sixteenth Century Journal,* 10 (1979), 15-22.

————   'The Protestant Underground Congregations of Mary's Reign', *Journal of Ecclesiastical History*, 35 (1984), 519-38.

Mout, N.,   'The Family of Love [Huis der Liede] and the Dutch Revolt', *Britain and the Netherlands, 7,* 79-93.

Payne, E.A.,   *Baptist Quarterly* XXV (January, 1973), 44-46.

Pearse, M.T.,   'Free Will, Dissent, and Henry Hart', *Church History*, 58 (1989), 452-9.

Powell, K.G.,   'The Beginnings of Protestantism in Gloucestershire', *Transactions of the Bristol and Gloucestershire Archaeological Society* XC (1971), 140ff.

Rupp, E.G.,   'Word and Spirit in the First Years of the Reformation', *Archiv für Reformationsgeschichte* XLIX (1958), 14-26.

Smeeton, D.D.,   *Sixteenth Century Journal*, 20 (1989), 507.

Snyder, A.,   'The Influence of the Schleitheim Articles on the Anabaptist Movement: An Historical Evaluation', *Mennonite Quarterly Review*, 63 (1989), 323-44.

White, B.R.,   *Journal of Ecclesiastical History* XXIV (July, 1973), 309-311.

F. SECONDARY WORKS, UNPUBLISHED THESES

Blackman, G.L.,   'The Career and Influence of Bishop Richard Cox, 1547-1581'. Cambridge Ph.D., 1953.

Brigden, S.E.,   'The Early Reformation in London, 1520-1547: the conflict in the Parishes'. Cambridge Ph.D., 1979.

Davis J.F.,   'Heresy in South-East England, 1520-59'. Oxford D. Phil., 1968.

Kerr, W.N.,   'Henry Nicholas and the Familists – a study of the influence of continental mysticism on England to 1660'. Edinburgh Ph.D., 1955.

Penrhys-Evans, N.A.,   'The Family of Love in England, 1550-1650'. Kent M.A., 1971.

G. REFERENCE WORKS

Bender, H.S., and others. *The Mennonite Encyclopedia*, 4 vols.
  Scottdale, Pennsylvania, 1955-1959.
Cooper, C.H.,   ed. *Athenae Cantabrigienses*, 2 vols. Cambridge,
           1858. Volume III ed. Gray. Cambridge, 1912.
Doubleday, H.A. and Page, W., and others. *The Victoria History of the
Counties of England*. London, 1900-.
Fines, J.,   *A Biographical Register of Early English
           Protestants, 1525-1558*, Pt.1., Appleford, 1981.
Foster, J.,   ed. *Alumni Oxonienses*, 4 vols. Oxford, 1891.
Gough, H.,   *A General Index to the Publications of the
           Parker Society*. Cambridge, 1855.
Hasted, E.,   *The history and topographical survey of the
           county of Kent*, 12 vols. Facsimile edition,
           Canterbury, 1972.
Laurence, R.F., *A General Index to the Historical and
           Biographical Works of John Strype*, 2 vols.
           Oxford, 1828.
Murray J.A.H., and others. *The Oxford English Dictionary*. Oxford,
           1933.
Pollard, A.W., and Redgrave, G.R., *A Short-Title Catalogue of Books
           Printed in England, Scotland & Ireland, and of
           English Books Printed Abroad, 1475-1640*, 2
           vols. London, 1926, 1976.
Read, C.,   *Bibliography of British History: Tudor Period,
           1485-1603*. Second edition, Oxford, 1959.
Reaney, P.H.,   ed. *The Place Names of Essex*. Cambridge,
           1969.
Sayle, C.E.,   ed. *Early English Printed Books 1475-1640*, 2
           vols. Cambridge, 1900.
Stephen, L., and Lee, S., *Dictionary of National Biography*, 63 vols.
           Oxford and London, 1885-1900.
Venn, J.,   ed. *Alumni Cantabrigienses*, 4 vols. Cambridge,
           1922.
Whitley, W.T.,   ed. *A Baptist Bibliography*, 2 vols. London,
           1916, 1922.
Wing, D.,   ed. *A Short-Title Catalogue of Books Printed in
           England, Scotland, Ireland, Wales, and British*

Wood, A.A.,   *America and of English Books Printed in Other Countries, 1641-1700*, 3 vols. New York, 1945. ed. *Fasti Oxonienses*. London, 1815.

H. WORKS CONSULTED BUT NOT CITED

A Brief Rehersal of the Belief of the Good-willing in England. London, second edition 1656. Wing STC, B 4621.
An Apology for the Service of Love and the People that own it. London, second edition 1656. Wing STC, N 1122.

Bale, J.,   *Scriptorum illustrium majoris Britanniae Catalogus*, vol. I. Basle, 1557. STC 1295.
Bax, E.B.,   *Rise and Fall of the Anabaptists.* London, 1903.
Clebsch, W.A.,   *England's Earliest Protestants, 1520-1535.* New Haven and London, 1964.
Duke, A.,   'The Face of Popular Religious Dissent in the Low Countries, 1520-1530', *Journal of Ecclesiastical History* XXVI (1975), 41-67.
Hillerbrand, H.J.,   'The origins of Sixteenth-Century Anabaptism: Another Look', *Archiv. für Reformationsgeschichte* LIII (1962), 152-180.
Houlbrooke, R.,   *Church Courts and the People During the English Reformation, 1520-1570.* Oxford, 1979.
Jenny, B.,   *Das Schleitheimer Täuferbekenntnis 1527*, Thayngen, 1951.
Jones, R.M.,   *Studies in Mystical Religion.* London, 1908.
──────   *Spiritual Reformers in the 16th & 17th Centuries.* London, 1914.
Kliever, L.D.,   'General Baptist Origins: The Question of Anabaptist Influence', *Mennonite Quarterly Review* XXXVI (1962), 291-321.
Krahn, C.,   *Dutch Anabaptism, Origin, Spread, Life and Thought, 1450-1600.* The Hague, 1968.
Littell, F.H.,   *The Origins of Sectarian Protestantism, A Study of the Anabaptist View of the Church.* New York and London, 1964.
Loades, D.M.,   'The Essex Inquisitions of 1556', *Bulletin of the Institute of Historical Research* XXXV (1962), 87-97.

Martin, L.F., 'The Family of Love in England: Conforming Millenarians', *Sixteenth Century Journal* III (1972), 99-108.

McConica, J.K., *English Humanists and Reformation Politics under Henry VIII and Edward VI.* Oxford, 1965.

McFarlane, K.B., *John Wycliffe and the Beginnings of English Nonconformity.* London, 1952.

Moss, J.D., 'The Family of Love and English Critics', *Sixteenth Century Journal* VI (1975), 35-52.

Nicolls, P., *Here begyneth a godly newe story.* London, 1548. RSTC 18576.

Nippold, F., 'Heinrich Niclaes und das Haus der Liebe', *Zeitschrift für die historische Theologie* XXX (1862), 323-394.

Owen, H.G., 'The Liberty of the Minories: a study in Elizabethan religious radicalism', *East London Papers* VIII (1966), 81-97.

———— 'A Nursery of Elizabethan Nonconformity, 1567-72', *Journal of Ecclesiastical History* XVII (1966), 65-76.

Schickler, F. de, *Les églises du réfuge en Angleterre*, 3 vols. Paris, 1892.

Scouladi, I., 'Alien Immigration into and Alien Communities in London, 1558-1640', *Proceedings of the Huguenot Society of London*, XVI (1937-41), 27-49.

Smithson, R.J., *The Anabaptists, Their Contribution to our Protestant Heritage.* London, 1935.

Stayer, J.M., *Anabaptists and the Sword.* Lawrence, Kansas, 1972.

Summers, W.H., *Lollards of the Chiltern Hills.* London, 1906.

Verheyden, A.L.E., *Anabaptism in Flanders, 1530-1650.* Scottdale, Pennsylvania, 1961.

Williams, R.L., 'Aspects of heresy and reformation in England, 1515-1540', unpublished Ph.D. thesis. Cambridge, 1976.

Zell, M.L., 'The Prebendaries Plot of 1543: a Reconsideration', *Journal of Ecclesiastical History* XXVII (1976), 241-253.

INDEX A
PERSONS

INDEX B
PLACES

INDEX C
GENERAL / DOCTRINAL